DEADLY CENSORSHIP

Lieutenant Governor James H. Tillman shooting newspaperman N. G. Gonzales. *Charlotte Observer,* January 15, 1961, C1. Illustration by Eugene Payne. Courtesy of the *Charlotte Observer.*

DEADLY CENSORSHIP

Murder, Honor & Freedom of the Press

JAMES LOWELL UNDERWOOD

The University of South Carolina Press

Published by the University of South Carolina Press
Columbia, South Carolina 29208

www.sc.edu/uscpress

Manufactured in the United States of America

22 21 20 19 18 17 16 15 14 13 10 9 8 7 6 5 4 3 2 1

LIBRARY OF CONGRESS CATALOGING-IN-PUBLICATION DATA

Underwood, James L.
Deadly censorship : murder, honor, and freedom of the press /
James Lowell Underwood.
pages cm
Includes bibliographical references and index.
ISBN 978-1-61117-299-7 (hardbound : alk. paper)—
ISBN 978-1-61117-300-0 (ebook) 1. Tillman, James H., 1869–1911—
Trials, litigation, etc. 2. Gonzales, Narciso Gener, 1858–1903—
Assasination. 3. Trials (Murder)—South Carolina—History—20th century.
4. South Carolina—Politics and government—1865–1950. I. Title.
KF224.T55U53 2013
345.757'02523—DC23 2013015807

To my wife, Joan, and my daughter, Mary Ann

CONTENTS

ILLUSTRATIONS

PREFACE

The twentieth century produced many trials grandiosely labeled "trial of the century," largely because of the involvement of celebrity defendants and famous lawyers known for dazzling displays of legal pyrotechnics. Such trials usually featured grisly or shocking crimes laid bare in graphic testimony. An early entry in this "trial of the century" pantheon was the case resulting from the 1903 killing of N. G. Gonzales, the respected and highly influential, but acerbic, editor of the *State,* the leading newspaper in the South Carolina capital of Columbia, by Lieutenant Governor James H. Tillman, scion of a powerful political family. This killing initially gained notoriety because it took place in broad daylight in the shadow of the State House, on the busiest street corner of the capital city, and the victim was an unarmed journalist of national reputation. His assailant acted because he thought his rising political star and cherished honor had been shot down and trodden underfoot by a ravening pack of journalists following the Gonzales's take-no-prisoners lead. The murder trial that followed involved a clash of revered values: freedom of the press, the sanctity of human life, and the reputation of the deceased on one side, versus the honor and dignity of the defendant on the other. The trial revealed flashes of political verbal swordplay involving the struggle between "conservatives" and Tillmanite "reformers," demonstrating through witnesses' testimony and judges' rulings, the unreconstructed nature of South Carolina after Reconstruction. The trial took place during a time when journalists were sometimes the target of angry and violent reprisals by those who thought their honor had been sullied by cruel and unfair articles. The killing, the trial, and its verdict attracted nationwide attention. The unusual array of important or rising political figures involved in the case as lawyers, judges, and witnesses—and even a court reporter who later became a United States Supreme Court justice and secretary of state—make the case a unique window into the political struggles of that time and place. N. G. Gonzales trained his searching editorial eye on many of these struggles, but sometimes he relentlessly practiced the personal-attack journalism of the day. Did the shooting render him a fallen hero or a vanquished villain? The most intriguing question in this account of the Gonzales-Tillman affair is how did freedom of the press, not James H. Tillman, become the real, though not the legal, defendant in the case?

ACKNOWLEDGMENTS

Anyone who seeks the solution to the historical puzzle presented by the Gonzales/Tillman affair needs a great deal of help. I owe thanks to the many people who provided it. Librarians and archivists are accustomed to helping wandering authors through a thicket of historical documents and books. The administration and staff of the Coleman Karesh Library of the University of South Carolina School of Law have provided their usual expert and energetic help. Particularly deserving of thanks is Dr. Michael Mounter, historian and archivist, who continues to amaze library patrons, including me, with his remarkable research skills and willingness to be of assistance. Trial participants, lawyers, judges, witnesses, jurors, and parties are not only influenced by facts but also by their personal lives and political views. Dr. Mounter was of invaluable help in ferreting out these sometimes elusive background features. Associate Director Rebekah Maxwell has been helpful in a multitude of ways, including acting as liaison to smooth the way for my visits to distant libraries. Associate Director Pamela Melton continues to impress me with her wise perception of authors' research goals. Director of Access Karen Taylor and her circulation-desk staff, including Joey Plumley, have once again demonstrated their talent and dedication in locating research materials through interlibrary loans. As on past projects, the reference librarians were resourceful and indefatigable. I especially thank Terrye Conroy and David Lehmann for help in the search for an elusive and obscure statute.

The administration of the University of South Carolina School of Law, especially Deans Walter "Jack" Pratt, Jr., and Robert M. Wilcox, provided funds for research assistants and granted vital secretarial services. Several intrepid and skillful members of the Information Processing Center did outstanding work in typing my manuscript and keeping up with a continuous stream of revisions. Deanna Sugrue typed the manuscript from its rough-draft phase to its near maturity—and with her usual graciousness dealt politely with the curmudgeonly author. Upon Deanna's retirement, Kimberly Bradshaw took over the typing with consummate skill. Vanessa Byars, former director of the center, lent her formidable knowledge of word processing to the trouble-shooting of problems with the manuscript and quickly mastered the labyrinthine citation system to help with the endnotes. First Ms. Byars, and then Ms. Alyne E. Hallman, as directors of the center, saw to it that I had the assistance I needed. Inge Lewis excelled in the arduous task of converting citations to the publisher's style.

Professor W. Lewis Burke, coauthor and coeditor with me on several earlier projects, read two drafts and offered perceptive and constructive advice, which I used to improve the book. Dr. Antonio Rafael de la Cova, author of *Cuban Confederate Colonel: The Life of Ambrosio José Gonzales,* gave valuable comments and suggestions based on his deep knowledge of the Gonzales family. His website includes many letters showing N. G. Gonzales's interactions with his family during his formative years. This is the third book on which I have worked with Dr. Alexander Moore of the University of South Carolina Press. He has been a benign and sure guide through the intricacies of the acquisition process.

The South Carolina Department of Archives and History and the South Caroliniana Library of the University of South Carolina are wonderful repositories of documents, letters, diaries, court records, statutory and constitutional material, photographs, and hard-to-find books. The South Caroliniana Library and the Richland County Public Library provided access to historic newspapers. Both these institutions were of inestimable help in furnishing photographs of trial participants and key locations to help long-ago events come alive for modern readers. Attorney William S. Nelson II, great-grandson of leading defense attorney Patrick Henry Nelson, came to the rescue when I had difficulty obtaining a good photograph of his ancestor. The *Charlotte Observer* furnished a vivid drawing of the shooting.

The South Caroliniana Library contains deep veins of useful material to be mined. Its collection of newspaper clippings on the shooting, the trial, and its aftermath has been helpful, as have files on N. G. Gonzales and his family and on his assistant, journalist James Hoyt, Jr. This book's discussion of journalists who dueled with outraged readers benefited greatly from material found there. The Thomas Cooper Library of the University of South Carolina has a large collection of books on southern history, which were of inestimable help.

The historic newspapers database of the Library of Congress was a valuable source for contemporary accounts of historic events. I found other newspaper stories, not yet in such databases, on microfilm from libraries all over the country, as well as from the South Caroliniana Library. The David M. Rubinstein Rare Book and Manuscript Library at Duke University provided access to its wide-ranging collection of American newspapers and to diaries of such figures as journalists William Watts Ball, James Calvin Hemphill, and Francis W. Dawson. The Clemson University Library contains information on the Tillman and Thurmond families, including correspondence between Senator Benjamin Ryan Tillman and defense attorneys for his nephew James H. Tillman. The deep research troves of the Southern Historical Collection at the University of North Carolina at Chapel Hill afforded material on the Gonzales and Elliott families, as well as Francis Butler Simkins's notes on the Gonzales/Tillman affair. The South Carolina Historical Society is an excellent repository of historical material, including the papers of journalist Robert Lathan, who was N. G. Gonzales's assistant at the time of the shooting. Edgefield sources, such as the county historical society and local newspapers on microfilm, had information that helped to create a greater understanding of the impact of the tragic events on Mamie Norris Tillman, the defendant's wife, who was able to carry on with her historic-preservation and church work as a vital force in the community. I also made contact with court officials in Richland, Lexington, Barnwell, and Edgefield Counties, but most of the needed court records were at the South Carolina Department of Archives and History.

A succession of diligent and resourceful student research assistants at the University of South Carolina School of Law not only helped to track down evasive historical material but also allowed an aging author to get the perspective of a younger generation. In chronological order of their participation, they include Nicole Wooten, Kevin McCarrell, Ian Duggan, Jacob Davis, Brandon Steen, Alexandra Huber, Charles Alexander Cable, Bradley Maxwell, Jordan Crapps, Mary Holahan, and John Beck. I would like to thank my wife, Joan, for many things, including accompanying me on out-of-town research trips and keeping me from getting lost on more than one occasion. My sister-in-law, Mary Lynn Musgrove, read substantial portions of the manuscript and offered enthusiastic and helpful advice for which I am grateful.

The people, libraries, and other institutions listed above have been congenial companions on a journey of discovery into a fascinating case and time. I thank them.

1.

AN EDITOR IS CENSORED

On Thursday, January 15, 1903, at 12:40 P.M., Lieutenant Governor James Hammond Tillman adjourned the South Carolina Senate, over which he presided. Just before 2:00, accompanied by two state senators who had no foreboding of what was to come, Tillman walked out of the capitol building and across Gervais Street. As they came abreast of a streetcar transfer station at the northeast corner of Main and Gervais Streets, Tillman encountered Narciso Gener Gonzales, editor of the *State* newspaper, walking toward him on his way to lunch at his home on Henderson Street. Gonzales was turning left (east) from Main into Gervais Street. Around him swirled the frantic activity of the transfer station, with streetcars arriving and departing and passengers scurrying to catch their rides. Across Gervais Street loomed the massive north façade of the State House, guarded by a tall, silent sentinel, a Confederate monument surmounted by the figure of a soldier poised as if he were searching for trouble on Main Street. On the northwest corner of Main and Gervais, across from the transfer station, stood the Columbia Theatre with its twin towers, one containing a "town clock" and both "topped by hemispherical cupolas." This building was a frequent host to traveling performers and also provided space for city offices, which lined the front of the building on Main Street. It was often called the opera house or the city hall. The intersection was the busiest confluence of political and commercial activity in Columbia. It was an odd setting for what was about to happen.

At forty-four Gonzales was a bespectacled, scholarly looking man with thinning hair combed close against his scalp and a luxuriant handlebar mustache, hinting that there were adventurous undercurrents to this mild-appearing man.

Narciso Gener Gonzales. Courtesy of the South Caroliniana Library, University of South Carolina, Columbia, S.C.

Tillman was a much taller man of commanding presence set off by an impressively large head with theatrically chiseled bone structure. Tillman blamed Gonzales and his stinging editorials for costing him the governorship and causing his humiliating fourth-place finish in the first 1902 primary. He thought that in Gonzales's hands freedom of the press had degenerated into a weapon of personal spite. Most of the leading South Carolina newspapers had opposed Tillman in the election, but the unsuccessful candidate focused his ire on Gonzales because his mocking words attacked the very marrow of Tillman's personality.[1]

Gonzales had repeatedly impugned Tillman's honor by questioning his courage, his manliness, his honesty, and his veracity in ways that lowered his prestige and his status as a leader.[2] In Tillman's view a man was expected to defend his honor, not by a war of words, not by hiding behind the legal process in lawsuits, but by a direct, physical encounter. Unless he acted, more humiliation would soon follow. The next day, January 16, Tillman would face a deeply embarrassing situation. He would have to lead the Senate to a joint meeting with the House of Representatives at which the returns for the governor's election would be examined and the winner proclaimed, forcing Tillman to participate in the public reopening of his wounds. In a few days he would have to watch another man, Duncan Clinch Heyward, be sworn in as governor, the office Tillman thought should have been his. Now here was the man responsible for humiliating him walking toward him. As Gonzales met up with Tillman's group alongside the busy transfer station, Tillman pulled out a Luger pistol and shot Gonzales. Whether Tillman had cold-bloodedly attempted to put Gonzales off his guard by wishing him "good morning" just prior to shooting—and had cryptically told Gonzales "I received your message" just afterward—became the focus of intense disputes at Tillman's trial. But one thing was certain: according to many witnesses, Gonzales's dying declaration, and Tillman's self-vindicating confessions, James H. Tillman shot N. G. Gonzales.[3] Tillman fired one shot, but he was ready to fire again if Gonzales attempted to answer in kind. The wounded Gonzales clutched a transfer-station pillar for support, faced Tillman, and, according to his dying declaration, contemptuously said, "shoot again, you coward." But one of Tillman's companions, Senator Thomas Talbird, thought Gonzales said, "Here I am; finish me." Any possible second shot was abandoned when Senator Talbird stepped between Gonzales and Tillman and said, "This thing must stop."

Tillman fled the scene. He "sidestepped" across Main Street, dodging streetcars, stepping over the tracks, and keeping a wary eye on Gonzales. On reaching

View of the corner of Main and Gervais Streets in Columbia in 1905, looking north from the State House. Tillman shot Gonzales in front of the streetcar transfer station on the northeast corner at right. The City Theatre and city hall were in the building at left. Security Federal Collection. Courtesy of the Richland County Public Library.

the northwest corner of Main and Gervais Streets, across from the transfer station and in front of the complex housing the city hall and the Columbia Theatre, Tillman was promptly arrested by policeman George Boland, who took Tillman's weapon. Tillman pleaded that he should be given back his weapon so he could fight off the attack he claimed to expect from Gonzales's supporters. He did not want to be "butchered"; he had heard that the *State*'s office had been turned into an "arsenal," an armed camp from which reprisals could be launched. The request was refused.[4] No such counterattack occurred. No gun was found on Gonzales, but at his trial Tillman testified that he had heard repeated reports in the days just before the shooting that Gonzales was armed and prowling the streets of Columbia looking for him.[5] Witnesses disagreed as to whether Gonzales had made a gesture that could be interpreted as going for a gun, or had at most moved his hands further into his overcoat pockets to warm them against a cold January day, or had made no movement of his right hand at all. Witnesses also differed as to whether Gonzales, on approaching Tillman and his senatorial companions, had swerved to avoid a confrontation or had adopted a course that guaranteed one.[6]

After being shot, Gonzales staggered around the corner of the transfer station on to the Gervais Street side and then back to the Main Street side of the station, still sometimes hugging the building for support. Two bystanders, one on each side, took him in hand and helped him remain upright. Gonzales asked to be taken home to his wife. When no cab could be found, they helped him instead to walk back to the *State* newspaper office, which was in the same block of Main Street as the transfer station, where the shooting had occurred.[7] At the office he was made as comfortable as possible, with a stack of newspapers serving as a pillow. Word of the tragedy spread quickly, a crowd gathered outside the paper's office, and soon a bevy of doctors rallied to the injured editor's side. He was taken to the hospital, where Dr. LeGrand Guerry and others performed an operation to repair the injury the shooting had caused to Gonzales's large bowel. Gonzales lingered for four days. Despite the skilled and attentive treatment of the doctors, a septic infection set in and he died at 1:00 P.M. on January 19 from peritonitis. Prior to his death he made dying declarations (statements by one anticipating imminent death) that later became a focal point of bitter controversies during the trial of his assailant.

While Gonzales lingered near death in the hospital, Tillman lingered in quite a different style in the Richland County jail. A *Charleston News and Courier* reporter who visited Tillman found him "comfortably fixed" in a private room on the second-floor corridor.[8] New furniture was moved in to replace the drab jailhouse decor.[9] The atmosphere was brightened by "bunches of flowers" sent by his friends.[10] An *Atlanta Journal* reporter visited Tillman at the jail and found that his second-floor room had "a bed and several chairs, [and] pictures [were] on the walls."[11] The prisoner's wife, Mamie Norris Tillman, was permitted visits lasting several hours. Tillman was the nephew of United States Senator Benjamin R. Tillman, a powerful practitioner of hardball politics, and the son of Ben's brother, the late congressman George D. Tillman, an influential political figure in his own right. Gossip abounded that Jim Tillman was receiving preferential treatment and was "faring sumptuously" in jail. The sheriff heatedly denied allegations of jailhouse high life. He was particularly incensed with charges that Tillman had unrestricted access to liquor and vowed to fire any jailer who permitted such a party atmosphere.[12] While the sheriff fretted over criticism of Tillman's comfortable incarceration, other officials began to investigate the killing.

The county physician moved swiftly, performing an autopsy at 4:30 P.M. on January 19, only three and a half hours after Gonzales's death. On Thursday, January 22, an inquest jury at a hearing conducted by the county coroner found that "the deceased, N. G. Gonzales came to his death by a gunshot wound inflicted by the hand of James H. Tillman on the 15th day of January A.D. 1903."[13] This first official proceeding on the case attracted considerable interest. A reporter observed that there "were about a hundred citizens in the courtroom."[14] The investigation culminated in an epic trial that forced a choice between the values of freedom of the press and the sanctity of life on one side and on the other a belief that personal honor was such an essential ingredient of manliness that it justified violence to vindicate it.

Interwoven with the first steps of the justice system was the community grieving process. Gonzales's funeral offered a solemn counterpoint to the investigation. In its somber pageantry and community-wide mourning, this event had some of the qualities of a state funeral. The last rites attracted so much attention throughout Columbia that they reinforced the defense attorneys' perceptions that a Richland County jury would be hostile to the defendant and that they should thus seek to change the location of the trial to more friendly environs. The funeral was held at Trinity Church (now Cathedral) on Sumter Street in Columbia, across from the state capitol and near the corner of Main and Gervais Streets, where the killing had taken place. The church's twin towers, each with eight pinnacles, added to the air of solemn dignity. The Tuesday, January 20, 4:00 P.M. service was conducted by Bishop Ellison Capers of the Episcopal Diocese of South Carolina, a former Confederate general and a longtime friend of N. G. Gonzales.[15] He was assisted by the Reverend Doctor Samuel M. Smith of the First Presbyterian Church and the Reverend Churchill Satterlee, rector of the Trinity Church.[16]

Several pallbearers who had worked with Gonzales at the *State* carried a "floral tribute" that was arranged to represent the front page of the *State,* with flowers configured in such a way as to represent the paper's colophon, "the palmetto tree, an emblem dear to the heart of the dead editor." A headline composed of flowers stated, "N. G. Gonzales, Born 1858, Died 1903. The *State* Founded 1891."[17] The *New York World* described the wide variety of flower arrangements at the funeral, noting that "a floral tribute of more than ordinary significance came from the Negro porters of the Metropolitan Club, a proof of the gentle courtesy of Mr. Gonzales which endeared him to all classes of people with whom he came into personal contact."[18] News reports said there were so many "floral tributes" that local florists had to order flowers from out-of-town suppliers after the inventory in Columbia was exhausted.[19] Beginning at 3:45 P.M., businesses closed throughout Columbia, including the textile mills, which rarely closed, even in dire emergencies. After the service at the church, a lengthy funeral procession traveled to the "Elmwood Cemetery as night was falling." At this tranquil setting overlooking the Congaree River, Bishop Capers conducted the closing service as the "choir of Trinity sang 'Jesus Lover of My Soul' and other hymns." In Charleston flags outside the offices of the *News and Courier,* for which Gonzales had been a reporter and Columbia bureau chief before he founded the *State,* stood at half-mast. Gonzales was survived by his wife, Lucy (or Lucie) Barron Gonzales, described as a "charming," "civic minded," "former state librarian," whom he had married in 1901, when he was forty-three. Her mourning must have had added poignancy because their only child, Harriett (or Harriott) Elliott Gonzales, had "died shortly after birth."[20]

The services were well attended even though one account described the day as "black and cold, a misty rain falling and freezing as it fell."[21] The large sanctuary at Trinity Church was completely filled, and an overflow crowd of several hundred gathered outside. One observer concluded that "with the exception of that of General Wade Hampton, it was probably the largest funeral assemblage seen in South Carolina in many years and the most representative." Many state officials, including outgoing governor Miles B. McSweeney, attended. Organizations of which Gonzales had been a member, such as the Metropolitan Club and the Knights of Pythias, marched as a group in the long procession to the interment at the cemetery.

In addition to the local sentiment evidenced by the funeral, the killing was taking on a wider significance. The *New York World* was treating it as a blow against freedom of the press with implications throughout the country. If a crusading newspaper voice could easily be silenced by gun-barrel censorship, editors everywhere could grow timid, and the high officials who might otherwise fear newspaper scrutiny and act with restraint, would grow more arrogant. The *World* published an editorial cartoon titled "A National Crime." It shows an assassin with a smoking pistol fleeing the scene of a shooting, leaving a crumpled body in the street. The hand of the body clutches a newspaper labeled, "*The State,* Columbia, S.C." The killer is escaping around the corner of a building on which is written in large letters: "Liberty and Freedom of the Press." The cartoon was not meant to be a literal depiction of the crime, but a symbolic representation of what the paper thought was a serious blow to free expression.[22] Who were the two men whose confrontation led to a city's mourning, and to fear by journalists that the killing was a serious blow to "Liberty and Freedom of the Press"? What historical precedents made such drastic censorship seem plausible to someone such as Jim Tillman, and what kind of background spawned Gonzales's pugilistic style of journalism, to which Tillman thought violence was the only answer?

Jim Tillman's Heritage of Violence

The history of the Tillman family is interwoven with the history and traditions of the Edgefield area. Richard Maxwell Brown notes that the area was the scene of many violent conflicts: the Cherokee Wars of 1759–61 and 1776, Revolutionary War–era clashes between Whigs and Tories (1760–85), the sometimes-violent disciplining of slaves, and the 1876 Red Shirt campaign, which used "fraud, intimidation, and violence (the so-called 'Edgefield Plan')" to bring about the restoration of white rule in South Carolina in 1877. Orville Vernon Burton has observed that "violence was very much a part of the region's culture." Lacy Ford has noted that—although the reputation of Edgefield as a place where violence was sometimes a preferred way to settle disputes concerning affronts to personal honor or the slavery system has been "exaggerated" to the point of "caricature"—it is true that "Edgefield doubtless shared in the nineteenth-century South's propensity for racial oppression and extralegal violence." Defense of one's honor, in the sense of reputation and prestige, was an activity that could take a violent form. Less physical means, such as court suits, often appeared to be unmanly, a refuge for the coward afraid to take more direct, physical action. Fox Butterfield notes that calling someone a "damned liar" was the "worst offence to honor." James H. Tillman found these attitudes exemplified in his family history.[23]

Stephen Kantrowitz, Senator Tillman's biographer, singled out the senator's father, the first Benjamin Ryan Tillman, as providing a family example of someone who could engage in violent conduct and escape social, if not legal, censure: "The elder Benjamin Tillman, fond of drinking and gambling, was among a group of nine men convicted for 'riot, assault and battery' by an Edgefield jury in 1841." For this offense John Belton O'Neall, one of South Carolina's most renowned judges, imposed a fine of one hundred dollars. This conviction did not prevent Tillman from becoming a member, only two years later, of a successor to the grand jury that had indicted him, and the next year he became chairman of a coroner's jury. According to some sources, the elder Benjamin Tillman killed a man in 1847, but Kantrowitz was unable to confirm this report.[24]

It was James H. Tillman's father who provided the most significant and colorful example. Perhaps James H. Tillman inherited his father's talent for making the best of incarceration. Perhaps he also inherited his father's propensity as a young man to react violently to affronts. George Dionysius Tillman (1826–1901) shot and killed J. H. (Henry) Christian in 1856 in a dispute over a faro game to which Christian was "a mere bystander."[25] Though Christian was an unarmed spectator rather than a player, he was swept into an argument over whether Tillman had correctly stated the amount of his earlier bet. When Christian contradicted Tillman's version, Tillman thought his truthfulness, the essence of his honor, had been questioned. In a fury he called Christian a "goddamned rascal" and shot him. Historian Francis Butler Simkins describes the crime as "unpremeditated." George Tillman fled the state even though he had just announced his bid for reelection to the legislature.[26] Christian's brothers offered a two hundred dollar reward for the apprehension of Tillman, whom they called an "unprincipled wretch" who had "so ruthlessly murdered our brother." After two years of adventurous wandering, Tillman returned home, was tried and convicted of manslaughter, and was sentenced to two years confinement and a two thousand dollar fine.[27] Simkins notes that the Edgefield "jailer treated him more like an honored guest than a felon, allowing comfortable quarters, overnight visits from his brother Ben, the pursuit of a courtship, and the resumption of those phases of his practice [of law] not requiring attendance at court."

But George Tillman was remorseful about the crime he had committed in a quick flare of anger, and he tried to make amends by helping to support the victim's daughter. At the conclusion of his sentence, he was welcomed back into Edgefield society and practice in court.[28] Kantrowitz notes that George Tillman was elected to the South Carolina Senate while still serving his sentence.[29] He received a pardon because of his Confederate service.[30] While his political career was not one of unbroken success, his manslaughter conviction did not prevent him from serving as a delegate to the 1865 and 1895 state constitutional conventions and in Congress, where he was chairman of the Committee on Patents. As a state legislator and constitutional-convention delegate, George Tillman sought, through reapportionment and the creation of new counties, to reduce the political sway of the lowcountry and enhance that of the upcountry.[31]

Despite his quick temper, George Tillman had a benign, even avuncular, side. One recipient of his kindly mentoring was young N. G. Gonzales. While he was in the nation's capital as a reporter for the *Charleston News and Courier,* Gonzales boarded for a while in the same Washington, D.C., rooming house as Congressman Tillman. In 1882 letters to an aunt, Gonzales wrote of the mutual affection developing between the two and the education into the political system George Tillman was giving him. In a January 25 letter, he called Tillman, "a splendid old cuss" who had given him "the run of his books and papers, and better than all, his hard sense and legislative experience, which things are of advantage to me." A few days later Gonzales told his aunt that "old man Tillman is a queer genius and 'cranky' on some subjects, but he is a trump for all that and I don't know anybody of whom I would sooner ask assistance when in trouble." Such signs of friendship between N. G. Gonzales and George Tillman are especially poignant in light of the fatal encounter between Gonzales and Jim Tillman twenty-one years later.[32]

Perhaps the lack of harsh censure of the repentant George Tillman by Edgefield society for killing Henry Christian convinced his son Jim that one could commit a violent act without permanently destroying one's social and political standing. Jim Tillman had before him an even more famous example, one in which the perpetrator not only escaped local censure but earned acclaim. That example was South Carolina congressman Preston Brooks, also from Edgefield. Brooks fought with George Tillman in an encounter between two feisty men with a strong sense of honor and sensitivity to insults.[33]

But it was Brooks's caning of Massachusetts senator Charles Sumner that gained the southerner lasting fame or infamy, depending on one's perspective. On May 19 and 20, 1856, Senator Sumner delivered his notorious "Crime against Kansas" speech as part of the debate over whether new states should be admitted as slave or free states. In the course of that debate, Sumner departed from the Senate tradition of avoiding personal attacks against other senators, describing South Carolina senator Andrew Pickens Butler as being in thrall to the "harlot slavery" and deriding his oratorical style. Butler's speech was marred by an impediment caused by a moderate paralysis, and as a result he sprayed his audience with a "loose expectoration." Sumner further excoriated South Carolina as being enmeshed in "shameful imbecility from slavery." Sumner described Butler as an anachronistic "Don Quixote" and Illinois senator Stephen Douglas as his "Sancho Panza."[34] Even those with views similar to Sumner's on the slavery issue recoiled at the crudeness of Sumner's language. But the direction of their sympathies changed drastically when on May 22, 1856, Preston Brooks, a young relative of Butler, confronted Sumner when he was seated at his Senate-chamber desk, dispatching copies of his speech around the country. Telling Sumner that he had insulted Brooks's state and his elderly kinsman, Brooks said he had come to punish Sumner for his boorish behavior. Brooks then pummeled Sumner with a flurry of blows, which he could not escape or respond to since he was entangled with his desk. When Sumner finally freed himself and fled down the aisle, Brooks pursued him and continued the beating even after Sumner had fallen. Brooks's actions were hailed by many in the South, who felt he had delivered a well-deserved punishment to a crude Yankee, who had impugned the honor of Brooks's kinsman and his state and who did not merit the dignity of a duel since he was obviously not a gentleman. Brooks was showered with gifts of canes to take the place of the one he broke during the beating and was formally presented with a replacement by the governor of South Carolina. The anger produced by the incident in the North hardened the resolve of antislavery forces and attracted more adherents to the Republican Party. Brooks's only punishment was a three hundred dollar court fine. Attempts to expel him from the House of Representatives attracted a majority vote but failed to achieve the necessary two-thirds majority. Brooks surrendered his seat anyway, but he felt vindicated when he was elected to fill the vacancy created by his own resignation. After resuming his seat, Brooks was more moderate than fire breathing. Early in 1857 he was stricken with a severe throat inflammation and died at thirty-seven. Sumner was absent from the Senate for several years during his recovery, but he returned to his seat avidly seeking the abolition of slavery, the defeat of the South during the Civil War, and a harsh Reconstruction during its aftermath.[35] British historian Paul Johnson bluntly calls Brooks's conduct "a cowardly assault on an unarmed, older man."[36] But to James H. Tillman, steeped in Edgefield legend, it may have seemed like an example, along with his father's treatment of Henry Christian, of the way to avenge affronts to personal and family honor with minimal adverse consequences. Here again George Tillman set the example for his son Jim. George's father, the first Benjamin Ryan Tillman, said George was "not of a disposition to submit to imposition or insult."[37] Jim proved equally sensitive to slights. During a January 14, 1895, discussion with Barnard B. Evans over an insurance debt Jim owed Evans, Jim's temper flared when he felt Evans impugned his honor. Both parties quickly produced pistols and opened fire, exchanging eight shots altogether. Tillman and Evans received minor wounds, with Tillman being nicked in the face and Evans suffering a shoulder wound.[38]

James H. Tillman in the uniform of the First South Carolina Regiment, which he commanded during the Spanish-American War. Courtesy of the South Caroliniana Library. University of South Carolina, Columbia, S.C.

Tillman's love of the dramatic, of making the grand gesture, is seen in his lavish 1896 wedding to Mamie Norris, a banker's daughter. A newspaper account of the wedding refers to it as "the most brilliant social event Edgefield has witnessed in a score of years" and describes the bride as "one of Edgefield's most beautiful, accomplished, and fascinating belles, and a recent graduate of the Columbia, South Carolina, College for Women." Historian John Hammond Moore describes the marriage as a "troubled" one that produced "one child, Helen." Throughout her long life, Mrs. Tillman was a leader in historic-preservation, church, civic, and cultural affairs in Edgefield as a talented organizer and musician. According to historian Lewis Pinckney Jones, she exhibited kindness and strength of character when she wrote Mrs. Gonzales shortly after the shooting, regretting the incident and expressing hope for N. G. Gonzales's recovery.[39] The marriage seems to have done little to calm Tillman's combative nature.

Jim Tillman's aggression spilled over into his political rhetoric. His successful 1900 race for lieutenant governor stirred the pot of racial hatred. His political base consisted of the men who served in the regiment he commanded during the Spanish-American War in 1898. They regarded him as the champion who fought for their rights.[40]

Tillman reminded voters that he had fought against the tide of racial integration by ordering his men not to salute black officers and not to accept their salaries from a black paymaster.[41] He adamantly opposed state funding of black schools at all levels, including colleges. He argued that such funding would be an insidious move toward social equality of the races, which would undermine the fabric of society.[42] "Amalgamation" of the races, he warned, would mean "damnation of the white man."[43] These appeals to racial fears were the keystone of his 1900 campaign. He also avowed support for the state-dispensary program, initiated by his uncle Ben as governor, as a means of liquor control. Jim Tillman posed as a friend of the factory worker, a group he later sought to place on the jury when he was tried for the murder of Gonzales.[44]

Tillman's aggressive political rhetoric intensified in the 1902 gubernatorial campaign. But it lacked focus; he had no positive program. His speeches became mired down in his many petty quarrels with prominent people ranging from President Theodore Roosevelt to members of the South Carolina Senate. Rather than outline a constructive program of how he intended to improve the state, Tillman attacked his opponents' characters instead of their stands on issues that concerned the public. He called Duncan Clinch Heyward, a rice planter who went on to win the election, a "water farmer" who indolently lounged in his home while an overseer ran the farm.[45] He told his audience that "it would not do to spoil a good farmer like Heyward by making a poor politician of him."[46] By contrast Heyward refrained from petty attacks and offered a forward-looking program to improve education and attract business to the state, while opposing huge trusts.[47] Heyward's commitment to improving the condition of the people through education and economic progress was not an empty campaign promise. As governor, he bolstered funding for white rural schools, increased the length of the school year, and raised the salaries of white teachers.[48] The contrast between Heyward's constructive program and Tillman's bumptious bickering may have been more the cause for Tillman's loss of the governorship than Gonzales's caustic pen. In his successful race for lieutenant governor two years earlier, Tillman had been buoyed by the support of veterans, especially those who had served under him in the Spanish-American War. But in 1902 he alienated this constituency by contemptuously opposing the establishment of an old-soldiers' home because it reeked too much of the poorhouse.[49]

Tillman's gubernatorial campaign was not as racist as his campaign two years earlier, but he directed an ethnic slur at N. G. Gonzales into at least one speech. While Tillman was defending himself against Gonzales's editorial criticism, a supporter in the audience shouted, "He is a half-breed ain't he?" Tillman gave a mangled reply: "I think he is, but thank God, the best half is, South Carolina never claimed him."[50] A veteran of Tillman's regiment deeply resented Gonzales's biting editorials and wrote a letter to the editor of the *Edgefield Chronicle,* adding his voice to the slurs. In an obvious swipe at Gonzales, the veteran said that "we had the honor, thank God, of serving under the leadership of a full-blooded South Carolinian—one whose bravery cannot be questioned." The remark about "bravery" is especially odd because the writer admitted that Gonzales had "seen more fighting during the Spanish-American War."[51] Gonzales wrote a letter in reply, noting that not only was he a native South Carolinian, but on his mother's side he was descended from eminent historical figures such as Landgrave Smith and John Rutledge; furthermore, while his father was a Cuban transplant, he had served as a Confederate officer in charge of Joseph E. Johnston's artillery.[52] Such remarks from Tillman and his supporters show that, far from being a helpless victim of a vindictive, runaway press, he was capable of venomous remarks himself or through his supporters—and of using the press to spread them.

Ambrosio José Gonzales. Courtesy of the South Caroliniana Library, University of South Carolina, Columbia, S.C.

Gonzales: Son of a Cuban Revolutionary and a Southern Belle

N. G. Gonzales had his own prickly sense of honor and combative nature. But these traits were mixed with genuine courage. In 1880, while a reporter for the *Charleston News and Courier,* Gonzales went to Laurens County to interview several "desperate men suspected of the crime" of murdering two blacks and dumping their bodies in a river.[53] Publication of his report provoked threats that, if he ever returned to Laurens County, he would exit as a corpse.[54] This warning made him all the more determined to return, and he did. In 1898, during the Spanish-American War, Gonzales left his powerful and comfortable niche as editor of the *State* to volunteer as a lieutenant with a Cuban revolutionary general. Although he was under hostile fire for only a short while, he underwent many hardships while on an expedition through rough country.[55] As a crusading editor, he showed courage and determination to get the electorate the information it needed to cast intelligent votes, even when doing so involved attacking powerful political figures such as South Carolina governor and United States senator Benjamin Tillman.[56] N. G. Gonzales's father, Ambrosio José Gonzales, had shown conspicuous courage and dedication as both a Cuban revolutionary general and a Confederate artillery officer. His biographer, Antonio Rafael de la Cova, notes that the journalist's father was wounded during an 1850 expedition that landed at Cárdenas, Cuba, in an unsuccessful attempt to ignite an uprising against Spanish rule. He gained renown in revolutionary circles as "the first native to shed his blood in combat for Cuban independence." As a Confederate officer, he developed an innovative system of highly mobile artillery that made possible the rapid redeployment of weapons to counter enemy attacks.[57]

Exemplars of physical and political courage are found in N. G. Gonzales's mother's family as well. Harriett Rutledge Elliott married Ambrosio José Gonzales in 1856, when he was thirty-seven and she was sixteen. From a distinguished lineage, she was part of the lowcountry plantation aristocracy. When N. G. was eleven, during a time when Ambrosio had taken his family to Cuba to live, Harriett died of yellow fever. Her formidable sisters became major influences in N.G.'s upbringing while his father traveled in pursuit of elusive business opportunities. No doubt his aunts contributed to the formation of N. G.'s resolute nature as did the Elliott lineage. Their grandfather, William Elliott II, was a "patriot soldier in the Revolutionary War." Their father, William Elliott III, was a "political non-conformist" who opposed the nullification doctrine, which held that states could block the application in their territory of federal laws that they considered unconstitutional. He persisted in this view even though it cost him his career as a state legislator. He was a slaveholder, who defended that institution on religious and moral grounds, but he opposed secession. Perhaps N. G. Gonzales inherited not only political courage but also literary talent from his grandfather, whose 1846 book, *Carolina Sports by Land and Water,* became a classic, describing with grace and elegance activities that might have seemed mundane in accounts by others.[58]

N. G.'s education was spotty. While in Cuba he was tutored within the family and briefly attended Cuban schools. Back in the United States, he attended private schools in Beaufort, South Carolina, and Herndon, Virginia, but he made up for his lack of formal education by reading widely in his grandfather's large library.[59] N. G. made his first sally into journalism at sixteen while attending St. Timothy's School in Virginia. In 1874 he proudly wrote his aunt Emily (Emmie) Elliott that he and his fellow students "have organized a newspaper, something in the style of the 'Yellow Jacket,' & the members of St. Timothy's are to contribute to it. We are to edit it by turns."[60]

With the grandson, the family traits of courage and literary talent took a less graceful, more contentious, turn than in his grandfather. N. G. Gonzales's courage and dedication were accompanied by the instincts of a brawler and fierce competitor, sensitivity to slights, and an eagerness to show physical bravery. These characteristics were on frequent display in an era of rough-and-ready journalism, during which a reporter or editor might fight physically as well as with the printed word. In 1881, while serving as the *News and Courier*'s Washington correspondent, Gonzales wrote an article accusing various Republican political figures, including South Carolina's African American congressman Robert Smalls, of corruption. When Smalls came upon Gonzales outside the Willard Hotel and denounced him for spreading lies, the two men came to blows. After a brief but sharp exchange involving punches, eye gouging, and kicking, onlookers separated Gonzales and Smalls. Gonzales gloried in the reputation the encounter gave him. He became known as a newspaperman willing to fortify his words with his fists. The time of the encounter was a tense one for Smalls because he was involved in a lengthy and bitter election dispute with George D. Tillman, which was not resolved in Smalls's favor until the following summer.[61]

Another early example of Gonzales's combative nature is his 1883 quarrel with South Carolina secretary of state James N. Lipscomb. Covering political news in the state capital for the *Charleston News and Courier*, Gonzales criticized Lipscomb's firing of a respected clerk to make way for a political crony. Bridling at being accused of playing the political-spoils game rather than running a merit-based office, Lipscomb bitterly denounced Gonzales in the hearing of the reporter's close friend, gubernatorial aide John P. Thomas. A shouting match between Thomas and Lipscomb led to a fight. Gonzales's report of the confrontation championed Thomas, further infuriating Lipscomb, who made even more extreme verbal assaults on Gonzales's character. The touchy Gonzales went to the State House and confronted Lipscomb face-to-face. To head off the potentially disastrous collision of these two angry men, whom he thought were spoiling for a potentially fatal fight, Governor Hugh S. Thompson first asked an emissary to try to persuade Gonzales to back away from the confrontation. When this failed, the governor executed an affidavit that led to Gonzales's arrest and a hearing before a trial justice, who required Gonzales to give five hundred dollars to keep the peace. At the hearing Gonzales established that he had no plans to use a weapon, but he did intend to tell Lipscomb that he was guilty of telling "an infamous falsehood."[62] It is notable that, in this sequence of events, Gonzales did not commit any violent acts. Perhaps the governor's intervention short-circuited such action. But the significant point is that Governor Thompson viewed both Gonzales and Lipscomb as having a propensity to violence when their tempers were aroused.

Gonzales and the Newspaper Wars

A series of clashes that might be termed "newspaper wars" reveals how Gonzales's sensitivity and competitive spirit made a volatile combination that could sometimes lead to violence. Perhaps the willingness of some journalists at that time to engage in physical, as well as verbal aggressiveness, degraded the status of freedom of the press and made it appear to be just another way of fighting that deserved no special protection. When Gonzales was head of the *Charleston News and Courier*'s capital bureau in Columbia, he formed a fierce rivalry with the *Columbia Register.* The rivalry turned violent on February 2, 1886, when a *Register* reporter, Thomas Jefferson LaMotte, maligned a Gonzales article about the failure of a local business. Gonzales angrily accosted LaMotte at a state-government office in Columbia and immediately began to hit him for denigrating Gonzales's professional honor, continuing to strike him until restrained by an "on-looker." *Register* publisher Charles Calvo, Jr., armed himself with a cowhide whip, tracked down Gonzales, and gave him a tongue lashing for attacking LaMotte. Before Calvo could finish his tirade, Gonzales struck him, prompting Calvo to attack with his whip. Gonzales retaliated by throwing Calvo through the plate-glass window of a drugstore. Gonzales wrote that he thought Calvo intended "a war to the knife," so he was felt compelled to pull out a pistol and "belabor [Calvo] across the forehead with the muzzle." Bystanders stopped the brawl for fear that it would turn deadly. In his article on the encounters, Gonzales admitted striking the first blow in both fights. The Calvos stuck together. The publisher's irate younger brother, William, confronted Gonzales and cursed him for injuring brother Charles. Both parties drew pistols, with Gonzales again using his to club his opponent on the head. Gonzales admitted that if this fight had continued much longer, it might have resulted in the death of one or both parties.

Gonzales and the Calvos were brought before the Columbia Mayor's Court, where N. G. was convicted of two counts of carrying a concealed weapon and fined ten dollars on each count. But he was acquitted of disorderly conduct charges, even though he had struck the first blows, because the mayor believed the Calvos' harsh words had the force of blows and had triggered the fighting. Charles and William Calvo were convicted of disorderly conduct, and William was also fined for carrying a concealed weapon. James H. Tillman's defense lawyers later cited Gonzales's concealed-weapons convictions as evidence that he was a dangerous man and often armed. Thus, the attorneys argued, Tillman had good reason to fear Gonzales and to shoot in self-defense.[63]

Another significant chapter in the newspaper wars might be described as the "showdown at the Grand Central Hotel." The *State* newspaper had begun publication on February 18, 1891, as an organ of the conservative persuasion in opposition to Governor Benjamin R. Tillman and his Farmers' Reform movement, which had succeeded in taking over the governorship on December 4, 1890, when Ben Tillman was inaugurated before a large crowd. He proclaimed himself the "leader of the revolution" but one who would govern in a "plain straightforward fashion" for the people.[64] N. G. Gonzales was editor of the new Columbia paper while his brother Ambrose traveled throughout South Carolina as general agent seeking subscribers and advertisers.[65] The fierce competitive spirit of the Gonzales brothers prompted them to vie for state printing contracts, which were awarded to the paper with the largest circulation in the capital city of Columbia.[66] Claiming that it had the largest circulation in the capital city, the *Columbia Register,* then a staunch Tillman supporter, won a major contract in late 1891 for printing legislative materials. The Gonzales brothers brooded over losing the contract, which they attributed to inflated *Register* circulation figures and the connivance of *Register* cronies in state government. On November 24, 1891, Ambrose Gonzales confronted J. Walter Gray, clerk of the South Carolina House of Representatives, one of the officials who had awarded the contract, in the lobby of the Grand Central Hotel in Columbia. Gonzales accused Gray of conspiring to commit fraud with W. M. Rogers, his circulation consultant and a former *Register* employee, and Dr. Sampson Pope—a former editor of the *Register*—as well as a medical doctor, lawyer, and politician—who was at that time Senate clerk, an official involved in the contract award.[67] Ambrose Gonzales and Gray each accused the other of lying.

Ambrose was soon joined by brother N. G., and Gray was joined by Dr. Sampson Pope. Allies of each side began to gather. Gray drew a pistol, which prompted Ambrose to call him a coward and taunt him to put away his pistol and fight like a man. Dr. Pope made menacing gestures at N. G. Gonzales with his walking stick and charged him with being a liar for accusing him of fraud. N. G. Gonzales struck Pope with his left hand. They wrestled and fell to the floor, where they continued to claw at one another. When the *Register* and the *State* both carried stories about the tussle the next day, each paper bragged that the participant most closely identified with it was the victor.[68] Neither paper said it was inappropriate that such distinguished men should engage in what was no better than a schoolyard brawl. In his account of the fight, Lewis Pinckney Jones says the struggle expanded to include the printing-room staff from the *State,* who showed up at the Grand Central Hotel armed with various printing tools as weapons.[69]

Aftershocks of the fight continued the next day, when Ambrose Gonzales and Mathew F. Tighe of the *News and Courier* had a "bloody battle" over Tighe's allegations that Ambrose "did not fight fairly in the battle of the Grand Central."[70] The Mayor's Court hearing in the imbroglio resulted in the dismissal of charges against N. G. Gonzales and a finding of guilty on a carrying-a-concealed-weapon charge against Gray. Although he expressed some sympathy for Gray in light of the charge made against him in the hotel lobby, the mayor chastised him because carrying a concealed weapon was especially unsavory conduct for a high official. Gray became incensed when the mayor told him he should have put his gun away and fought like a man. This remark seemed to condone public fighting so long as it was done in a fair and aboveboard manner.[71] The *State* was ultimately vindicated in its charges that *Register* circulation figures had been inflated and that the *State* had the largest circulation in the capital city.[72] N. G. Gonzales's role in the Grand Central Hotel melee was not that of the aggressor but of one who came to his brother's aid in the face of Gray's drawn pistol and Pope's menacing walking stick. What is striking about the incident is that the elite of the community readily resorted to violence as a means of dealing with a dispute. Again we see the explosive reaction to the charge of lying, which directly cast aspersions on an individual's honor. The public setting of the insults probably made the affront to honor more deeply disturbing to the combatants.[73] We also see from these events that journalists of that time were fighters. Sometimes they fought with words, and sometimes they fought physically. Sometimes these forms of expression melded together, making it more difficult to defend their actions as those of a free press. This may have created the impression among the targets of their barbs that they could respond with violence as well as words.

Gonzales's Editorials: Informative, Progressive, and Vitriolic

That N. G. Gonzales was capable of occasional acts of violence—particularly when his integrity, or that of a family member, was called into question—should not dominate our view of his character. Most of his battles were in print and in pursuit of civic improvements. But he did favor an aggressive, crusading editorial stance for South Carolina papers. When asked by J. C. Hemphill in 1889, shortly before Hemphill assumed the leadership of the *News and Courier,* what editorial posture a paper should take, Gonzales advised that "'a policy of peace' is to be commended, but care should be taken that the paper is not so lamblike as to be inane. Fair, hard blows, on occasion will quicken public respect. The paper cannot succeed as an admittedly money making machine. It must hold opinions and express them boldly or it will lose its moral force."[74] Gonzales took his own advice and expressed his opinions boldly. But the line between boldness and viciousness is often difficult to discern. Hemphill's predecessor as *News and Courier* editor and as Gonzales's boss, Francis Warrington Dawson, had taken Gonzales to task in a long 1885 letter for his penchant for crossing that line and compromising the paper's dignity. Dawson advised Gonzales that, although the *News and Courier* "has no objection to the condemnation of any evil of any sort, no matter how sharp that condemnation may be, and no criticism of yours on any subject has been objected to because of its severity. The objection, which is a continuing one, is to the style of your criticism, which, without being intended to be so, of course, is what I should style bad-tempered or querulous." Dawson thought such a style should be avoided because it "makes enemies unnecessarily" and would harm rather than advance the paper's efforts to achieve government reforms.[75] Dawson told Gonzales that he was free to criticize "persons, as well as things" but that he should do so in a "good-natured and dignified way." Despite this cautionary advice, Gonzales sometimes practiced what newspaper historian James Melvin Lee called "picric journalism," named for the acid known for both its toxic and explosive qualities.[76] But many of Gonzales's editorials were not characterized by personal attacks; they focused on issues of public importance.

In her analysis of his editorial positions, Linda McCarter Matthews found Gonzales to be an ardent advocate of progressive causes and a bold opponent of practices he considered brutish or venal. He attacked the harsh convict-lease system, under which state prisoners were leased to private parties, who often subjected them to cruel treatment, oppressive working conditions, and insufficient food.[77] As a *News and Courier* columnist in Columbia in the 1880s, Gonzales was an energetic booster of civic improvement and economic development in his adopted city, urging the completion of the Columbia Canal and the paving of streets.[78] Matthews found that, as editor of the *State* in the 1890s and turn-of-the-century 1900s, Gonzales championed progressive causes such as legislation imposing humane limitations on the use of child labor.[79] The editorial launching the *State*'s advocacy of legislation curbing the abuse of child laborers was devoid of harsh personal attacks and focused squarely on the plight of the children, the duty of the state to rectify the exploitation, and how this could be done without jeopardizing the competitive position of South Carolina's cotton mills.[80] Gonzales was an ardent advocate of women's suffrage. His editorials on the subject show a sophisticated understanding of the progress of the movement not only throughout the United States but also around the world.[81]

Gonzales's dominant trait as an editor was his dedication to rooting out the misbehavior or poor performance of public officials and exposing it to the voting public. If this public service motive was sometimes mixed with less-admirable personal resentments, it still led to relentless searching for misconduct or questionable decision making by public officials or candidates. Benjamin Tillman and later James H. Tillman were among Gonzales's favorite, but not his exclusive, targets. He was not intimidated by those in power even if his paper lost access to news because of his stands. Early in Ben Tillman's governorship, Gonzales was banned from the governor's mansion.[82] In an 1891 editorial, he bluntly charged that Tillman was "budding into a dictator," that "he is as promising a tyrant as was ever bred by a free republic," and that he was "a usurper" who gained office by "bitter and unjust assaults upon the men who administered the state government."[83]

Ironically some of the *State*'s loudest cries of government abuse during the administration of Governor Tillman were reserved for the dispensary system, which could be viewed as a relatively enlightened attempt to reach a practical compromise between the forces of prohibition and the proponents of open saloons on the liquor-control issue.[84] The Dispensary Act of 1892 created a state monopoly on liquor sales through local dispensaries.[85] The idea was to take liquor sales out of the corrupting atmosphere of saloons by creating a system of dispensary sales to customers who had to consume the product elsewhere, preferably in the more respectable atmosphere of the home under the restraining influence of the family. Proponents hoped that liquor consumption and liquor-fueled rowdy behavior would be diminished and that the revenue produced by dispensary sales would permit the lowering of taxes.[86] Stephen Kantrowitz points out that this system also had an important political byproduct: it gave the governor power to appoint, or influence the appointment of, local enforcement officials throughout the state. Kantrowitz also contends that execution of the law was politicized: "enforcement of the law was mainly intended to demonstrate Tillman's authority over white, urban opponents."[87]

Enforcement of the law was bitterly resented in urban areas when private homes were entered by constables, who were viewed as "spies" by outraged residents, who resented the heavy-handed search for unauthorized liquor.[88] An urban versus rural dimension was added to the conflict when urban militia members balked at such enforcement tactics, but rural elements, the bedrock of Tillman support, were willing to undertake enforcement. Such enforcement difficulties created fertile opportunities for Gonzales and the *State* to rail against abuses of power. Soon after the system's adoption, the *State* began predicting that it would mean flush times for Tillman cronies, uneven and discriminatory enforcement, and "inconveniences for the public at large."[89] The newspaper delighted in accusing the dispensary constables, who should have been paragons of probity and sobriety, of drunken, thuggish behavior during searches of residences. The paper also delighted in claiming that the law had failed, that inebriation was on the rise, and that corruption was rampant.[90]

When rioting broke out in Darlington in late March and early April of 1894, Governor Tillman seized the telegraph offices, believing news reports would further inflame the combustible situation their relentless criticism of dispensary policies had helped to create.[91] Tillman exhumed a seldom-used Reconstruction Era statute, which authorized the governor, when he determined that the public safety required it, to take possession of telegraph facilities and railroads, place them under military control, and set rules declaring who could use them and under what conditions they could be used.[92] The ingenuity of the Gonzales brothers met this challenge to freedom of the press. Both Ambrose and N.G. had worked as telegraphers in their younger days. Ambrose tapped the lines near Darlington and sent reports to N. G. in the *State*'s Columbia office. In a headline the *State* bragged that it had run "the Blockade."[93] Years later Ambrose Gonzales reminisced to journalist W. W. Ball about his inventiveness in keeping one step ahead of the censor. He cut into the telegraph line atop the Enterprise Hotel in Darlington and then sent messages from Florence, first via a "railroad key." When the railroad management put a stop to that, he sent messages from

Senator Benjamin Ryan Tillman.
Courtesy of the Library of Congress.

Florence to Atlanta, where they were rerouted to Winnsboro, near Columbia, where the operator gave the messages to a train conductor, who carried them to Columbia for insertion in the paper.[94] These maneuvers outfoxed the censors, but the contents of the articles were criticized as hyperbolic and incendiary. Noted historian David Duncan Wallace contended that the state's leading newspapers acted irresponsibly, virtually inciting defiance of the lawful authorities by exacerbating public hostility toward enforcement of the dispensary laws.[95]

Although Gonzales and the *State* agreed with Ben Tillman on the goal of white supremacy in politics, they disagreed on the means of achieving it. The *State* advocated an honestly administered literacy requirement that would allow qualified black men to vote but, because of the low literacy rate then prevailing for African Americans as compared to white people, would result in a substantial white majority.[96] To use fraud and intimidation would corrupt those who used such tools. The method preferred by the *State* would disenfranchise some white men who could not pass the literacy test, but so be it; an ignorant electorate would be avoided.[97] By contrast Ben Tillman openly embraced the use of deception and discriminatory enforcement as justifiable means in sustaining white political supremacy. Tillman, by then a United States senator and a delegate to the state constitutional convention of 1895, engineered the convention's passing of article II, section 4(c) and (d), which contrived to register illiterate white voters for a time while excluding black men through discriminatory enforcement. This provision provided for the registration up to January 1, 1898, of any male who could read a provision of the constitution submitted to him, "or understand and explain it when read to" him. Discriminatory enforcement of the "understand and explain" clause meant registrars could read simple provisions to a white man and be easily satisfied by the white applicant's explanation, but they could read complex provisions to a black man and be dissatisfied with his explanation no matter how good. The "understand and explain" alternative route to registration would expire on January 1, 1898, when it would be replaced by another alternative to the literacy standard: an applicant could be registered even if he could not "both read and write any Section of this Constitution submitted to him," if he could prove that he owned and had paid taxes on property in the state valued at "$300 or more."[98] This provision also favored the more affluent white race.[99] The key figures in this scheme were the county registrars, who were to be appointed by the governor with the advice and consent of the South Carolina Senate.[100]

The *State* warned early in the revision process that any plan giving manipulative powers to registrars—and lodging the power to appoint registrars with the governor—would warp the machinery for administering elections to serve partisan purposes; the reputation of the state and the confidence of the people in democracy would be undermined.[101] The *State* argued that placing such broad discretionary power in officials would lead inevitably to fraud.[102] Such well-reasoned editorials were not journalistic bomb throwing. They were the kind of scrutiny government needs in a democracy.

But the clash between Gonzales and his paper and the Tillman forces during the 1895 constitutional convention did sometimes seem like a bare-knuckle fight. While the convention was considering the creation of the new county that became Saluda, a bitter controversy raged over whether that name should be used or if it should be named after former U.S. senator Matthew Calbraith Butler, whom Ben Tillman had deposed from his Senate seat. Ironically George Tillman, Ben's older brother and the driving force behind creation of the new county, favored the name "Butler," which greatly angered Ben Tillman, who personalized the conflict by assuming that a vote for the name "Butler" would mean that the convention thought a mistake had been made in electing him over Butler. The convention voted on a motion to take a recess so that pro-Butler forces could rally their supporters. The next day, September 17, 1895, the *State* published an editorial stating that the convention president, Tillman collaborator and governor John Gary Evans, had "openly and defiantly misstated the returns of the tellers, subtracting two announced votes from [John] Irby's (pro-Butler) side in order that he might show a majority of one against postponement."[103] This provoked a flurry of proposals to censure the *State* and even bar it from access to the convention. Because it would have set a precedent for treating other papers similarly, this denial of access would have been a major blow to the ability of a free press to do its job in evaluating the performance of public officials. The measure that finally passed did not impose the ban but labeled "the editorial in question an abuse of the privilege granted the Press in admitting its members to the floor of this Convention."[104] Gonzales remained unshaken by this public rebuke and kept relentlessly on Tillman's trail. Lewis Pinckney Jones notes that the editor immediately replied in an article titled "The King Can Do No Wrong," which states that "we are invulnerable to compulsory or perfunctory resolutions."[105] Later, during James H. Tillman's trial, it became clear that such intrepid scrutiny of his uncle Ben's every political move, as well as his own rough treatment by Gonzales, contributed to Jim Tillman's bitterness toward the editor.

The 1895 constitutional convention's condemnation of the *State*'s editorial could have resulted in a major blow to press access to important government activities of great interest. It ultimately fizzled down to a sharp but relatively safe exchange of insults between the convention and the paper. Speech countered speech. But nineteenth-century history furnishes other examples of more drastic and damaging acts that were taken to intimidate or silence the press. An examination of several of these as precursors to Jim Tillman's killing of N. G. Gonzales will aid our understanding of the toxic resentment of the press that boiled over in that tragedy and cast its shadow over the trial that followed.

The Past and Oppression of the Press

The shooting of N. G. Gonzales was an extreme form of censorship by a public official acting in a private capacity but with the aura of an important and powerful political family about him. Although coercion or intimidation of the press was not pervasive, there were enough examples in nineteenth-century South Carolina history that Gonzales should have been alert to the possibility of additional abuses. In the century preceding Gonzales's killing, such abuses were most likely to occur when publications were opposing strongly entrenched social or political beliefs or movements. Especially lethal dangers for freedom of the press could occur when it was seen as encroaching on a volatile mixture of deeply felt political beliefs and matters of personal honor. Publications perceived as threatening the slave-labor system that was an integral part of the economy could provoke a severe reaction. John James Negrin was an editor, printer, and Swiss immigrant who did not realize the explosive nature of any publication that described a slave revolt. In 1804 he published in Charleston a pamphlet titled *A Declaration of Independence of the French Colony of Santo Domingo by [Jean-Jacque] Dessalines.* This incendiary pamphlet had originally been published by a revolutionary leader and former slave. Negrin was arrested and charged with trying "to excite domestic insurrection and disturbing the peace of the community." In 1805 Negrin printed a statement in the *City Gazette and Daily Advertiser* in which he appeared contrite and repentant as he tried to curry public favor and restart his printing business. He complained that his business had been destroyed, and his livelihood with it, as a result of his arrest. Not only had he "lost eight months of his time [by confinement] but [also] all the little property he had in his possession," including his "printing implements with which he earned his subsistence."[106] His printing tools had been seized and sold by his creditors.

In a petition to the South Carolina Senate, seeking "some little pecuniary aid or other Legislative relief" that he desperately needed because the punitive action taken against him had left him "destitute," Negrin pleaded that he meant no harm by the publication. He had not sought to incite an insurrection but only to make a profit by publishing a pamphlet on a topic of interest. He claimed that the hostile reaction to the publication caught him by surprise because the same document had been published in other states without causing such alarm. The petition, despite its tone of abject supplication, apparently fell on deaf ears.[107]

The ever-looming fear of slave revolt prompted passage of an 1805 statute that provided for punishing anyone who wrote, published, or delivered "any inflammatory" writing or speech "tending to alienate the affection or seduce the fidelity of any slave."[108] Progressively more comprehensive and restrictive statutes followed.

Anxiety that a slave rebellion might erupt with deadly consequences was greatly heightened by reports in 1822 of the abortive Denmark Vesey plot. Vesey, a former slave who had purchased his freedom and lived in Charleston, was said to have organized a scheme in which slaves in the city were to slay their masters and escape to freedom. The plot was discovered, and those believed to have been involved were arrested and tried. Thirty-five, including Vesey, were hanged. Although a controversy exists as to whether the plot actually existed or was a contrivance invented by masters to justify more repressive control of slaves, the reports alarmed whites. These events—together with the Nat Turner revolt in Virginia in 1831 and increased activity by northern abolitionists—spurred growing concern about incendiary publications.[109]

In the summer of 1835, the American Anti-Slavery Society began a campaign of mailing 175,000 abolitionist tracts. The campaign was nationwide, but it focused most intensely on southerners. Although the recipients were often persons thought by the society to be susceptible to conversion to the antislavery cause, the tracts were usually not solicited by them. Many recipients objected strenuously to getting them, and many slave owners were fearful that the tracts would fall into the hands of literate slaves or of free blacks who would incite slaves to revolt. On the night of July 29, 1835, an audacious group of prominent Charlestonians descended on the local post office and seized abolitionist literature. It was burned the next night before a crowd of two thousand.[110]

The Charleston protest against abolitionist literature took on a quasi-official character on August 4, 1835, when a meeting presided over by the intendant (mayor) resulted in the appointment of a committee whose members were directed to meet incoming mail when it arrived in the city and to escort it to the post office, where they were to halt distribution of incendiary publications.[111] United States Postmaster General Amos Kendall could not officially sanction the withholding of abolitionist literature from the mail by local postmasters, but he gave them discretion to follow the "Higher Law" of local community standards, which—in areas where slavery was an integral ingredient of the economy—meant protecting slavery from attack.[112] The Massachusetts Anti-Slavery Society reacted to the Charleston conflagration by condemning it but rejoicing that, like so many efforts at censorship, it perversely had the effect of publicizing the abolitionist arguments the protestors sought to suppress.[113]

Fear of a servile revolt inspired repressive legislation designed to halt press criticism of slavery. An 1859 South Carolina law was remarkable in the thoroughness with which it attacked every conceivable mode of expressing abolitionist sentiments, if such statements were made with "evil intent" and were "calculated to disaffect any slave or slaves in the state or [tended] to incite any insurrection or disturbance among the same."[114] The law reached letters, books, essays, pamphlets, newspapers, and pictures if they were produced by persons within the state with evil intent. It prohibited distribution of incendiary material within the state even if it had been written or published outside the state. It banned spoken words calculated to stir up the slave population. Subscribing to or receiving abolitionist newspapers, books, periodicals, or pamphlets, whether produced in or out of the state, was also prohibited. Violators were subject to fine or imprisonment. Postmasters were required to notify a magistrate if their office received abolitionist material, and the magistrate was directed to have it burned in his presence.[115]

Freedom of the press in antebellum South Carolina was threatened not only by government action but also by readers whose personal honor had been affronted by stinging newspaper language that they thought attacked their reputations for honesty, veracity, and integrity and who thought the injury could be redressed only by fighting duels with the offending party, often an editor. A historian who has examined this ritualized form of violence, fought according to a socially enforced code of honor, observed that "at least six South Carolina editors fought duels during the antebellum years. Two of these were killed, and a third was seriously wounded."[116] The best known of these was the September 29, 1856, duel fought at Washington Race Course, near Charleston, between Edward Magrath and William R. Taber, Jr., editor of the *Charleston Mercury.* Magrath thought that the good character of his brother, federal judge Andrew Gordon Magrath, then a candidate for Congress, had been impugned by three sharply worded but anonymous letters signed "A Nullifier," which had been printed in the *Mercury.* This dispute occurred during a revival of the nullification controversy in which the nullifiers argued that states had the power to declare federal laws unconstitutional and inoperative within their borders. The doctrine was used to attack the federal tariffs of 1828 and 1832 and to fight federal actions that threatened slavery. The nullification crisis continued until 1834, but the seeds for its resurrection had been planted. As the slavery controversy grew ever more bitter in the late 1850s, the nullification doctrine fueled renewed attacks on federal measures suspected of advancing the abolitionists' cause. The Magrath-Taber duel was part of this larger mosaic and involved issues of both personal honor and freedom of the press. The author of the letters accused Judge Magrath of betraying the state by abandoning his earlier nullificationist principles and compromising with the abolitionists.

Edward Magrath challenged the *Mercury*'s editors to a duel, even though they had not written the letters. He considered the editors responsible because they had printed the attacks and made editorial comments that appeared to endorse them. Both editors, William R. Taber and John Heart, accepted the challenge. In his reply to the challenge, Taber declared that he was participating as a champion of freedom of the press so that "truth shall not be muzzled" and so that "liberty of the press shall be maintained." Taber also noted that vituperative language in the challenge had accused him of acting cowardly by printing an article attacking a judge, who because of his position, could not fight back. This charge of cowardice affronted his personal honor. Thus he would not be a mere defender of freedom of the press but also one seeking satisfaction from Edward Magrath for himself and the *Mercury.* Edmund Rhett, Jr., stepped forward and identified himself as author of the "Nullifier" letters, and argued that the proper duel was not between the judge's brother and the editors, but between the judge and himself. Editor Taber argued that as a conductor of a "public press," a forum for readers to express a variety of opinions, he should not be held responsible for all the opinions aired in the paper. But somebody had to defend freedom of the press, and he was willing to do it. Judge Magrath belatedly heard of the plans for the duel and tried to stop it, but events moved too fast and the duel proceeded. The twenty-eight-year-old Taber was killed in the encounter, and editor Heart stepped forward to fight another round. But Edward Magrath said the demands of honor had been satisfied, and no further jousting was required.

Although the encounter fell short of pristine adherence to the *code duello,* as modified in former governor John Lyde Wilson's *Code of Honor* (1838, 1858), an effort was made to meet its standards. These emphasized the need for a formal, written challenge and response, the use of seconds, friends who would attempt a peaceful reconciliation, and failing that, set the details of the duel such as time, place, identity of witnesses, and physicians, and, most important, ensuring that no one fired prematurely. Even though the Magrath-Taber duel, like Tillman's attack on Gonzales, involved issues of honor and freedom of the press, duels fought according to the code of honor, though it was imperfectly followed, bore little resemblance to Tillman's assault without warning on an unarmed man. The code required advance notice and encouraged the seconds to seek a peaceful resolution. Such attempts by the seconds in the Magrath-Taber duel failed when Taber's second rejected a proposed agreement because it seemed to demand a retraction by the paper, a demand that would undermine the free-press principle for which Taber was fighting.[117]

An earlier skirmish in the nullification dispute involved a lethal 1832 contest between two editors who met on "the field of honor," this time an island in the Tugaloo River in northwestern South Carolina, where the lines demarcating South Carolina and Georgia jurisdictions are conveniently vague. Involved in this clash were Benjamin F. Perry, the hard-charging editor of a unionist paper, the *Greenville Mountaineer,* who became provisional governor in 1865, and Turner Bynum, editor of a rival upcountry paper, the nullificationist *Southern Sentinel.* Perry believed that he had tried to keep their ideological differences on a polite, professional basis, but Bynum had subjected him to relentless, personal attacks. Perry finally concluded that Bynum had been sent to the upcountry by the nullifiers to edit the *Sentinel* in such an abusive manner that it would provoke a duel with him. When the personal attacks continued, Perry felt that he had no choice but to challenge his rival editor. Bynum, a promising and talented young man, was killed in the encounter. Perry deeply regretted Bynum's death all his life, but he recognized that having fought the duel gave him a certain standing as a man of courage who would defend his principles.

An 1812 antidueling statute—despite its imposing heavy penalties of fine, imprisonment, and disqualification to hold office—did little to discourage the well-entrenched practice of dueling. Amendments added in 1823 and 1834, aimed at encouraging witnesses to testify by offering them protection against self-incrimination and by ameliorating the harshness of the penalties, did not improve the effectiveness of the laws. The ever-looming possibility of being challenged to duels by individuals who thought their personal honor had been maligned by a sharply worded article encouraged some antebellum editors to curb the "ardor" of their language. Others continued to launch verbal assaults but kept their dueling skills well honed.[118]

In the midst of all the antebellum dueling by editors, one journalist, Dr. Robert W. Gibbes, a physician, scientist, art collector, and historian, as well as owner of the *South Carolinian,* used the less perilous route of going to court to vindicate freedom of the press. In an 1855 meeting of the Columbia City Council, Mayor E. J. Arthur, an adherent of the so-called Know-Nothing (American) Party, ordered the chief of police to eject Gibbes forcibly from the proceedings because he feared that Gibbes, a critic of his party, would publish a less favorable account of the meeting than that of the paper published by the official city printer. Gibbes sued the mayor and chief of police for assault and battery in civil court in 1857. Even though the jury awarded him only modest damages and the judge recognized the dangers of a malicious press, the court's charge to the jury strongly vindicated the right of orderly city "corporators" and citizens, including journalists, to attend the meetings of public deliberative bodies and publish an account, even a critical one, of the proceedings. During the Civil War, as president of the Press Association of the Confederate States of America, Gibbes was a strong advocate of maintaining press access to war news and a vigorous opponent of drafting journalists into the army because it would compromise the independence of the newspapers.

In wartime there is inevitable tension between the desire of the civilian press to keep the public informed about the progress of military operations and the need of the commanders to keep army movements secret from the enemy. The Civil War was no exception. In her history of the South Carolina press, Patricia G. McNeely concluded that, while "no South Carolina newspaper was ever suspended by either the Congress or Confederate army," the generals "continued to enforce strict censorship." The *Charleston Mercury* was particularly vociferous in complaining about lack of access to information about the preparations for bombarding Fort Sumter, which ultimately occurred on April 12, 1861. The *Mercury* kept a wary eye on Confederate commanders throughout the South for violations of freedom of the press that might serve as precedents for similar affronts in South Carolina. In July 1862 General Earl Van Dorn issued a harsh martial-law order applying to portions of Louisiana and Mississippi, ordering that newspaper editors who published material "calculated to impair confidence in any of the commanding officers" would be subject to fine, imprisonment, and having the publication of their papers suspended. General Braxton Bragg's order that a correspondent for the *Montgomery Advertiser* be arrested for disclosing troop movements to the enemy prompted the *Mercury* to editorialize that it understood the need to safeguard military secrets from the enemy, but Confederate commanders sometimes used that need as a "pretext" for punishing correspondents who were guilty of no more than focusing a "beneficial light on events as they transpire[d]." The paper argued that military officers "have no right to claim exemption from criticism." Perhaps because of the intensity of editorial reactions, Van Dorn rescinded his threatening order, and Bragg released the reporter. But often officials and generals, such as Van Dorn and Bragg, seemed to view the proper role of the press as cheerleaders for the Confederate cause rather than vigilant critics rooting out poor performance. They kept a sharp eye on the conduct of the newspapers, but, when newspapers painted an unrealistically optimistic view of the war, they lost the confidence of their readers.

One of the most drastic intrusions on freedom of the press came from Union rather than Confederate forces when, on the fall of Charleston in February 1865, Union troops took control of the *Courier's* offices to publish what their commanding general called "a loyal Union newspaper." George Whittemore, the northern editor appointed by the general, ran the paper until November 20, 1865, when—as the paper's historian, Herbert Ravenel Sass, put it: "A. S. Willington and Co. were permitted by the U. S. military authorities to resume charge of their property and the *Courier* became once more an independent newspaper (or as independent as it could be under the military restrictions)."[119]

Later, during the last days of Reconstruction, deeply entrenched racial attitudes again spurred action to silence critical press commentary. These actions were aimed at newspaper accounts of the conduct of white rifle-club members in the Hamburg Massacre. This event was a pivotal moment in the campaign of 1876, in which intimidation and violence were used to suppress voting by African Americans and white Republican sympathizers. As a result white Democrats returned to power, and Wade Hampton was elected governor. On July 4, 1876, a confrontation occurred on the streets of Hamburg, South Carolina, between a black militia unit and two well-connected young white men over who should give way to whom in using the streets. On July 8, 1876, attorney Matthew Calbraith Butler, a former Confederate general and Civil War hero, went to Hamburg to pursue a suit against the militia for blocking a public passage and to defend a countersuit by the black militia members claiming the young white men had interfered with their drill. Butler claimed that the militia posed a threat to the white people of the surrounding area and demanded that the militia disarm and turn their weapons over to him. White rifle-club members began to gather in town to support Butler's demand. The militia members sensed that they were in danger and took up defensive positions in a nearby warehouse. The militia members and the rifle club exchanged fire. Who fired the first shot is a matter of controversy. Both sides sustained injuries but the first fatality was a young white man. This angered the rifle-club forces laying siege to the warehouse and spurred them to import an ancient cannon from nearby Augusta, Georgia. After several cannon rounds were fired at their defensive position, several African Americans fled the building. At least one was killed. The remaining African Americans, who had taken refuge in the building, surrendered. Six of the prisoners were executed. The rest were disarmed and released. Some reporters said the prisoners had been fired on as they left.[120]

Francis Warrington Dawson, editor and co-owner of the *Charleston News and Courier,* was an influential figure in Democratic Party circles and initially supported a fusion ticket in the 1876 election.[121] Such a ticket would have included both Democratic and Republican candidates. A faction of the Democratic Party, calling themselves "straightouts," preferred a ticket made up solely of Democrats, which would accomplish a more complete return to white rule and repudiation of the political forces that prevailed during Reconstruction. The straightouts deeply resented Dawson's position and accused him of failing a loyalty test. Dawson's initial commentary on the conduct of the white rifle-club members at Hamburg was sharply critical. This further infuriated the straightouts, some of whom considered the Hamburg incident a major step forward in their effort to regain white rule by a campaign of fear and intimidation, which would paralyze African American voters and their white sympathizers.

In an article and an editorial published in the July 10, 1876, *News and Courier,* Dawson said: "The killing of the prisoners was barbarous in the extreme. We have no words strong enough to express our condemnation of such a crime."[122] In a July 11 editorial, the paper said that, if the "published accounts" of the incident were correct, "there was little if any excuse, for the conflict itself, and absolutely none for the cowardly killing of the Negro prisoners who were shot down like dogs long after they had surrendered."[123] By calling the acts of the white rifle-club members "cowardly," the paper deeply offended their "honor." Even though the paper carefully said it did not think General Butler had authorized the slaughter, it did say that, since he was in overall charge of the operation, he was the one to whom the public would look for an explanation. The *News and Courier* editorials continued in this vein. A July 12 editorial, "The Hamburg Massacre," said that "it was a horrible and revolting deed, and, as we have before said, cowardly in the extreme."[124] But the paper acknowledged that, while it had been careful not to accuse General Butler of precipitating the event, he had called the paper's account "entirely false" and made it clear that he considered the paper's coverage to be an assault on his character.[125] It had turned into a matter of personal honor as well as a political dispute.

Pressure began to be applied to Dawson and the *News and Courier.* Readers and advertisers who were offended by the coverage began to boycott the paper and support a recently founded rival. General Butler called on Dawson and personally delivered a challenge to a duel issued by another former Confederate general, Martin W. Gary, who was a major architect of the plan to regain white control of the state through a campaign of intimidation, threats, and violence.

Since Dawson had long been "a principled opponent of dueling," he rejected the challenge.[126] He began to soften the harsh tone he had used in describing the role of the white rifle-club members in the Hamburg Massacre. By the time an August 14 editorial was published, Dawson had taken a position almost completely opposite to the one he had taken earlier.[127] This editorial placed the onus for causing the incident almost entirely on the black militia, saying the group had been "organized to threaten and intimidate, if not to kill, the whites," calling its officers and members insolent and riotous, and asserting that they "bullied the whole neighborhood." The editorial concluded that "no one in South Carolina justifies the killing of the Negro prisoners," but "the public must admit that the whites were acting in self-defense, in determining to disarm the negroes," and "they were forced to take such steps as were necessary for the protection of themselves and their families." Dawson also dropped his opposition to the "straightout" ticket. One explanation of this sharp change in position is that Dawson was caving in to the pressure placed on him and his paper by the boycott, the challenge to duel, and other powerful Democrats seeking white solidarity in the election.[128] But Dawson was generally considered a courageous man who resolutely defied anyone who tried to intimidate him. An alternate explanation is that given in the August 14, 1876, editorial itself: evidence given at an August 10 hearing in Aiken cast the events in a different light.[129]

Dawson was not the only newspaperman who was threatened as a result of the Hamburg incident. Louis Schiller, a Jewish resident of Hamburg, was a printer who helped to operate the *Augusta Times,* a paper whose Republican editorial policy offended the Democrats who sought to regain white power. Schiller was also suspected of having supplied the black militia members with ammunition and having advocated African American resistance to the return of white rule. For four days following the shooting of the African American prisoners, Schiller was chased through the swamps near Hamburg by dogs owned by a former slave hunter, whose son had been involved in the controversy with the black militia that precipitated the killings. Schiller's printing office was destroyed and his house ransacked. He covertly boarded a train to Columbia and escaped.[130] But Schiller was not a magnet for trouble while Dawson proved to be one again and again.

Dawson's hard-hitting and vilifying editorials drew fire from both sides in the white Democrats' struggle to wrest control of the state government from the Radical Republicans. Dawson revived old charges that Charleston sheriff and former congressman Christopher Columbus Bowen—a Radical Republican who was powerful in Charleston but hated by many as a scalawag—had instigated a murder when he was a Confederate officer. Dawson charged that Bowen had sought revenge against a superior Confederate officer who had caused him to be court-martialed. Bowen had allegedly persuaded an enlisted man to ambush and murder that officer. Bowen instigated criminal libel charges against Dawson and fellow *News and Courier* owner and executive Bartholomew R. Riordan.[131] The grand jury returned indictments against Riordan and Dawson on February 3, 1875, and a seven-day trial began on April 19, 1875. The burden of defending the case was great. Dawson diverted his time and energy from the paper while he pursued evidence to fortify his arguments that his allegations against Bowen were true and lacked malicious intent. He tracked down the assassin who allegedly had been hired by Bowen, negotiated his extradition from Georgia with the governors of that state and South Carolina, and arranged for the South Carolina governor to promise executive clemency so that the killer could testify without fear of incrimination. This remarkable display of ingenuity and political guile kept Dawson from his editorial duties for a considerable time. The trial resulted in a hung jury, and Bowen and the prosecutors never revived the case.[132]

Although he did not achieve an acquittal, Dawson thought he had won a personal victory and a victory for freedom of the press. A significant development in the case was that Circuit Judge Jacob Pinckney Reed's charge to the jury noted that the South Carolina Constitution of 1868 had recognized a broad right in the press to criticize public officials and candidates so long as the right was not abused.[133] The judge instructed the jury that in prosecutions for criminal libel for publications "investigating the official conduct of officers or men in public capacity, or when the matter published is proper for public information, the truth thereof may be given in evidence."[134] To Judge Reed proof of the truth of the statements was a complete defense since the new constitution changed the old rule that the truth of the article increased its harmful nature and did not furnish a defense. Even if the statements were false, if the defendants made them believing in good faith that they were true and based those beliefs on reasonable evidence, a complete defense was achieved if the statements were made to aid the electorate to be informed on public issues. Publications made to discharge the press's duty to keep the public informed were not prompted by malice, an essential element in proving criminal libel.[135] Still, even with such protections, criminal libel cases could cause considerable damage to freedom of the press. The susceptibility of editors to such criminal charges and the expense and embarrassment that accompanied them, could have exercised a strong chilling effect on the vigor with which editors criticized powerful officials.[136]

Dawson survived the tense times surrounding his newspaper's coverage of the Hamburg tragedy and the criminal libel case, but he died a violent and dramatic death on March 12, 1889, when he went to the home of Dr. Thomas McDow, a prominent Charleston physician and neighbor, and accused him of making improper advances to the attractive Swiss governess who instructed Dawson's children. McDow shot and killed Dawson but was acquitted of murder charges. In his trial McDow claimed he acted in self-defense after Dawson attacked him with his cane. The Dawson killing rivals that of Gonzales in notoriety, but unlike the Gonzales-Tillman affair, it arose from a personal dispute rather than resentment over attacks by a newspaper.[137]

Antipress sentiments were by no means monopolized by those opposed to Reconstruction. In a July 12, 1865, editorial, James T. Bacon of the *Edgefield Advertiser* excoriated the Reverend Dr. Mansfield French, an abolitionist and Freedmen's Bureau representative, for a speech in Edgefield that Bacon considered to be "unchristian, malicious, and indecent." Bacon said French's speech was likely to "inflame the minds of the lately freed negroes" and bluntly warned French that "he should always be careful while making these speeches to keep a General at his side and soldiers at his back, for on Friday last, nothing upon earth but the fear of being bayoneted or thrown into prison, kept us from hurling a stone at his head. Perhaps on some future occasion, the indignation of some outraged Southern man will cause him to forget both bayonet and prison." This language must have impressed the authorities as an unvarnished attempt to intimidate abolitionist speakers with a threat of violence. The reaction of the federal forces was swift. Bacon was visited by an army captain who "politely, yet firmly" explained to the editor the "mischievous tendency" of his article. This admonition from the captain resulted in an article in which Bacon expressed regret that some of his language had been "unwise and mischievous" and "violent and unnecessary." He said his greatest regret was that he had "inadvertently conveyed the impression that the soldiers present on the occasion [of Dr. French's speech] were armed" when they were not. He sought to assure the paper's readers and the federal authorities that his paper was not "a fomenter of discord, and an assassin sheet." But he stuck by his warning to Dr. French that, if he continued to make the kind of speeches he had in Edgefield, it would "blot and mar his present labors." This partial recanting was not enough. Bacon was taken to Charleston, where he was placed under confinement and released two weeks later.[138] In this incident, neither side was willing to recognize vigorous freedom of expression rights in the other. The result was that discussion of festering social problems was lost amid the ensuing exchange of verbal and penal grapeshot. Hobbling the press does not always take such heavy-handed forms as imprisonment. It may take the form of exclusion from a news source.

Members of the 1868 South Carolina constitutional convention bitterly resented the savage caricatures of that conclave by the Robert Barnwell Rhett family's fire-eating *Charleston Mercury,* which called the meeting a "Ring-Streaked and Striped Negro Convention."[139] Attempts made early in the convention to exclude the *Mercury*'s reporters from the floor were deflected on the grounds that the delegates should rise above such crude attacks and focus on crafting a new constitution rather than hobbling the press. But when the *Mercury*'s attacks continued and fights broke out between *Mercury* reporters and delegates on the convention floor, a resolution was adopted on the motion of future Republican governor Daniel Henry Chamberlain that the representatives of that paper be barred from the floor.[140] Chamberlain and supporters of his motion—such as Jonathan Jasper Wright, who later became the first African American justice of the Supreme Court of South Carolina—argued that, although they were reluctant to place any curbs on the press, the physical danger presented to both the delegates and reporters by the journalists' continued presence and the delegates' belief that the presence of newspaper representatives on the floor was a privilege rather than a right, led them to seek exclusion of the *Mercury* reporters.[141]

Another move to exclude a reporter from the deliberations of a legislative body also occurred during the Radical Reconstruction period. On January 15, 1869, the House of Representatives voted that "the present reporter of the Charleston Courier be expelled from the floor of this House and be denied entrance to this Hall." The *Courier* charged that this attempt to "muzzle the press" showed the legislators' "incapacity for legislation, and serv[ed] only to render them ridiculous in the eyes of enlightened civilization." The paper further contended that the resolution was retaliation for the reporter's exposure of legislator William J. Whipper's attempt to destroy the University of South Carolina by denying it funding because it had refused to furnish lodgings for Whipper and his family during legislative sessions.[142] Exclusion of reporters, although a serious matter, was not as heavy-handed as prior restraint of a publication or imprisonment for unpopular views. But such punishment was content based; only the *Mercury* and *Courier* representatives were barred, while reporters for papers with less offensive views of the delegates remained.

A bizarre incident occurred when Republican legislators turned on the editor of an organ of their own party, who had the temerity to criticize their actions with belittling language. The *Columbia Union-Herald* was a Republican paper during Reconstruction, but editor James G. Thompson used its columns to denounce what he considered corrupt legislation misusing public funds. On March 18, 1875, he published an editorial praising a gubernatorial veto of a spending measure and castigating members of the House of Representatives as "plunderers" and "animals," saying that "no pack of jackals scenting the carcass ever made night so hideous." The same day a furious House of Representatives rushed through a vote holding Thompson in contempt. He was arrested under a warrant issued by the speaker and brought before the bar of the house, where the charges were read to him and he was asked to respond. This encounter was interrupted by the demands of other business. Thompson was brought before the house again the next day, but he was soon discharged from arrest. Other newspapers chastised the House for a proceeding that was remarkable for its "ludicrousness and stupidity," a clumsy attempt to "muzzle free speech" that was as oppressive as the old English "Star Chamber" proceedings.[143]

Such earlier episodes of hobbling the press were harbingers of what awaited Gonzales. Gonzales faced attempts to intimidate him into silence or a change of views before he experienced the ultimate censorship, murder. In addition to the Gonzales brothers' tapping into telegraph lines so they could report on the Darlington riots in the dispensary controversy, another incident with comic-opera overtones occurred when N. G. Gonzales was accused of criminal libel in late 1892. On December 8, 1892, the *State* carried a story reporting that a court in Barnwell had ordered attorney G. W. M. Williams to pay money he had withheld from a client or go to jail.[144] Williams obtained a criminal-libel warrant for N. G. Gonzales signed by a Bamberg trial justice. In obtaining the warrant, Williams alleged that the article in the *State*, "Pay Up or Go To Jail," libeled him and tended "to incite him [Williams] to a breach of the peace, blacken his name and character and injure him in his profession as a lawyer and an officer of the court." A constable named Moody traveled to Columbia to arrest Gonzales, and, if bond were not posted, to take him to jail in Barnwell. While Gonzales's lawyers sought to find out the amount of the bond, Moody arrested Gonzales but allowed him freedom of movement, accompanying him on his daily rounds, including a convivial visit to Gonzales's Columbia club. Bond was posted, and

Gonzales was freed from the constant companionship of his friendly constable. The final comic turn in the incident occurred when Constable Moody discovered that Williams had not advanced money for his return to Barnwell, and he had to borrow the money from Gonzales.[145]

Gonzales expressed regret that he had been denied the drama of writing editorials from jail.[146] He hinted darkly that the real reason behind the warrant was not Williams's concern for his reputation but his "embracing Tillmanism."[147] In a final editorial on the incident, Gonzales quoted the *Varnville Enterprise* and the *Orangeburg Enterprise,* which characterized the criminal libel case as an "effort to suppress the liberty of the press" that would produce a "sad day for the country" if successful.[148] Gonzales alleged that the case was Williams's attempt to curry favor with the administration of Governor Ben Tillman by attacking Gonzales, who had been a staunch critic of the Tillman regime, and thus get it to drop fraud charges against Williams. Gonzales argued that reporting on public court proceedings, such as that producing the order against Williams; was a core function of the press; if the press were intimidated into silence, the public would be the loser. Gonzales made it clear that he would not succumb to intimidation. He expressed confidence that the case against him would never come to trial, and court records show that the action probably disintegrated because the grand jury failed to return an indictment.[149] But Jim Tillman's anger and retaliation did not disappear so easily as Williams's clumsy attempts at revenge.

These historical examples show a practice of using social pressure, intimidation by threats of violence or criminal prosecution, or destruction of offending material, as means of silencing those critical of the existing social, economic, or political order, rather than simply fighting critical speech with responsive arguments, a mode of reply often considered ineffective or even unmanly. Although such events are not frequent enough to amount to a pattern or custom, they show a serious breakdown in protection of the freedom of the press. Jim Tillman's killing of Gonzales was an extreme example. The pretrial maneuvers in the Tillman case show the beginnings of the defense lawyers' strategy of placing the press in general—and Gonzales and the *State* in particular—on trial and casting the nominal defendant as the victim. In the hands of the defense, a free and vigorous press was painted as an ogre preying on worthy men and destroying the careers of dedicated public servants, rather than as a constructive force providing vital information to voters. This gambit began in the hearings on the applications for bail and for change of venue to a location friendlier to the defense.

2.

PRETRIAL MANEUVERS

Despite the relative comfort in which he was incarcerated, at the jail but amid his own furniture and fresh-cut flowers, Jim Tillman wanted out. His attorneys decided to apply for bail. The South Carolina Constitution at that time provided: "All persons shall, before conviction, be bailable by sufficient sureties, except for capital offenses when the proof is evident or the presumption great."[1] Chief Justice Young John Pope received an application for a writ of habeas corpus and held two hearings to determine whether Tillman should remain in jail or be released on bail.[2]

Bail Denied, Press Scolded

On February 19, 1903, Chief Justice Pope determined that bail should be denied in the case. He observed that "the law is that the taking of human life with malice premeditated constitutes murder," a capital offense.[3] The focus of inquiry in the hearing was whether "malice premeditated" was present.[4] Many affidavits of eyewitnesses, law-enforcement officers, and physicians had been submitted by the prosecution through Solicitor J. William Thurmond and prosecutor G. Duncan Bellinger, and by defense attorneys Congressman George W. Croft and Patrick H. Nelson. Several defense witnesses said that on the fatal day, Gonzales was believed to have been armed and searching for Tillman with intent to do him harm, and when Gonzales and Tillman encountered each other on the street, Gonzales changed direction to confront Tillman directly and thrust his hand into his overcoat pocket as if he were drawing a weapon. This action, they said, made Tillman think he had to fire in self-defense.[5] A self-defense motive might negate the presence of malice in the defendant. Nevertheless the chief justice, with palpable reluctance, found that malice was evident under the constitutional standard for denying bail in capital cases.[6] He observed that "the defendant had been the object of newspaper attacks for 11 years perhaps without a parallel in this state. The liberty of the press does not permit the license of the press. Dr. Franklin said that liberty of the press would often be followed by liberty of the cudgel. In this case no cudgel though was used but a deadly weapon. One could hardly believe that a man could bear the long continued ordeal of the abuse that the defendant underwent without having malice in the heart."[7] The chief justice's distress in denying the application for bail is seen in his concluding remarks that "painful as it is, under my oath of office, so recently fresh on my lips, I must do my duty and decline the application."[8] The brief formal order stated:

> State of South Carolina, County of Richland
>
> This was an application for bail, and after hearing the affidavits both of the State and the petitioner and after argument pro and con it is ordered that bail is hereby refused, however without prejudice to the petitioner to apply to some other judge if he should be so advised.
>
> Y. J. Pope
> Chief Justice
> At Chambers
> 19 February, 1903

The *New York World,* which had followed the case closely from the start, was heartened by Pope's decision. In an editorial titled "South Carolina's Brave Chief-Justice," the newspaper said that Chief Justice Pope showed "courage in holding the politically influential criminal to the strict letter of the law. . . . It encouraged the hope that South Carolina justice will be equal to the task of fully upholding the freedom of the press against the terrors of assassination."[9] The *World*'s optimism was misplaced. Although the result of the hearing was a denial of bail, the opinion accompanying the decision amounted to a scolding of the press for having been so abusive that it went beyond the freedom allowed it. The cryptic opinion seemed to imply that, although the press had the right to criticize those who thrust themselves into the political arena, it should not do so with such relentless intensity or for too long a time.

Showing sympathy for James H. Tillman as one he considered a victim of press vitriol, Pope nonetheless acted as an impartial judge and denied bail. This must have been a difficult decision to make. Pope had been allied with Ben Tillman's Farmers' Reform movement, successfully running for attorney general on its ticket. As an associate justice in 1894, Pope had voted to uphold the constitutionality of Governor Tillman's dispensary system. Pope dissented in the case in which the South Carolina Supreme court struck down the first version of the dispensary law as an invalid state monopoly that intruded on the right of individuals to pursue business opportunities. Then in a case sustaining the validity of a new version of the dispensary system, he formed a majority with a newly selected Tillmanite justice, Eugene B. Gary, to hold that the dispensary was a valid exercise of the state's police power to protect the health, safety, and morals of the public.[10] Pope pursued a policy of judicial restraint under which courts would recognize that broad legislative power had been given to the General Assembly by the South Carolina Constitution. This meant that courts should strike down laws as unconstitutional only when they violated a specific provision of the Constitution, or a principle necessarily implied by such a concrete provision.[11] A byproduct of this cautious approach was Tillman programs that had been enacted into law were less likely to be jettisoned by court interference.

Perhaps in the belief that the evidentiary picture of the Tillman case could change as more evidence developed or out of a desire to share some of the burden of the decision, the chief justice made the bail denial order "without prejudice," thus allowing the prisoner to apply to another judge for bail. No evidence of such further application has been found, and Tillman remained in jail. There were frequent newspaper references to Tillman's incarceration throughout the pretrial period. In early March, Patrick H. Nelson, one of Tillman's lead attorneys, denied rumors that the defense would make another attempt to get bail, this time from a circuit judge.[12] On April 7, 1903, when the Richland County grand jury issued a true bill indicting Tillman for murder, a newspaper account referred to Tillman as still in jail.[13] The defense applied for and was granted a continuance on April 8, delaying the trial until July because of the unavailability of key defense witnesses if the trial were held sooner. Veteran courthouse observers expected this delay would prompt defense counsel to renew the application for bail, but this did not occur. Commentators were surprised with how well Tillman looked despite his imprisonment since the day of the killing. One article noted that "to all appearances the nearly three months in the county jail has had no physical effect on the prisoner, who, but for a little sallowness, looks as usual."[14] The defense used continued jailing of the defendant as a point in favor of their motion to delay the trial: the state would not be injured by the postponement since the defendant would be in jail and pose no threat to the public peace. At a June 24, 1903, hearing on the defense motion to change the venue of the trial from Richland County, where the defense claimed anti-Tillman prejudice permeated the pool of potential jurors, prosecutor G. Duncan Bellinger remarked that Tillman had been in jail five months, and the Richland sheriff had not perceived so much hostility toward the defendant as to require extraordinary security measures.[15]

No anti-Tillman lynch mob had appeared at the jail-house door. No extra guards had been posted. But the sensitive antennae of the defense attorneys still detected virulent bitterness toward Tillman, and perhaps fear of harsh treatment if he were released discouraged them from making another attempt to obtain bail and encouraged them to ask for a change of venue for the trial.[16] The defense attorneys looked around them and thought they saw in Richland County attempts to deify Gonzales and demonize Tillman. Especially galling to them was the marked success of a fund drive to raise money to erect a monument to Gonzales in Columbia, and the community-wide mourning and elaborate solemnity of his funeral. But observers noted that since the fund drive was meeting with success throughout the state, the drive was not evidence of Richland County's being uniquely pro-Gonzales or anti-Tillman.[17]

Moving the Trial: Escape to Tillman Country

A motion for change of venue at that time was based on several constitutional and statutory provisions. The South Carolina Constitution of 1895 guaranteed an accused the "right to a speedy and public trial by an impartial jury."[18] If the jury pool in the place where the trial was originally set, usually the location of the crime, had been tainted by prejudice so that a "fair and impartial trial" could not be had, then a motion for a change of venue could be made.[19] Absent such a showing of prejudice, the trial would normally be held in the county where the crime was committed. Usually this was the location where there was greatest access to the evidence, and the community had the greatest stake in the outcome.[20] The transfer had to be to another county in the same circuit.[21] Such motions had to be supported by sworn affidavits.[22] The Tillman motion produced an avalanche of approximately 750 affidavits, about 450 from the prosecution and the remainder from the defense. Several potential witnesses for the defense were hard to persuade to give affidavits in this controversial exercise of calling their fellow citizens biased against the defendant.[23] Defense attorney George W. Croft enlisted the aid of Senator Ben Tillman in convincing the reluctant witnesses.[24] In support of its contention that Tillman could not get a fair and impartial trial in Richland County, the defense argued that not only had the fund drive for the Gonzales monument kept the killing constantly in the public eye in a way that favored the deceased, but the local newspapers, especially the *State,* had created a climate of fear and intimidation in which a jury would not dare acquit Tillman. The defense claimed that even ministers of the gospel were helping poison the Columbia atmosphere. They contended that local ministers had denounced Tillman from the pulpit and made him appear to be the very devil incarnate.[25]

To counter allegations of coverage hostile to Tillman in local newspapers, the prosecution presented affidavits by officials of the *State* newspaper, including thirty-six-year-old William Elliott Gonzales, N. G.'s younger brother, who had assumed the editorship after N. G.'s death; older brother forty-five-year-old Ambrose E. Gonzales, president of the company; James A. Hoyt, Jr., assistant editor of the *State;* and Paul M. Brice of the *Columbia Evening Record.*[26] They asserted that they had consistently pursued a policy of restrained coverage. Harsh criticism of Tillman had been excised from letters to the editor. Articles on the case published in the *State* had been for the most part written by journalists who were supposedly impartial writers brought in from the outside. Hoyt admitted that, shortly after the killing, he had written an article severely denouncing Tillman and that a commentary by the Reverend William E. Evans, D.D., had called the killing an assassination, but thereafter articles published by the *State* had taken a temperate approach.[27] These affidavits contended that the severe criticism of Tillman came from papers published in other parts of South Carolina and around the country, not Richland County. They responded to defense criticism that the *State* had stirred up hostility to homicide case defendants in general and Tillman in particular in its campaign against murder and violence by contending that it was the legitimate role of a free press to advocate law and order in its community and that such comments were of a general nature and not tailored to the Tillman case.[28] The barrage of affidavits accusing the press of stirring up hatred of Jim Tillman among potential jurors initiated the defense strategy of turning the case into a trial of the conduct of the press instead of the nominal defendant. In the venue-change hearing, they focused on the allegedly abusive articles published after the shooting. In the trial they trained their guns on the excesses of N. G. Gonzales's editorials about Jim Tillman, who was cast as the real victim.

The prosecution produced affidavits from the leading ministers in town as well as from parishioners who had heard their sermons. The Reverend Samuel M. Smith, D.D., of the First Presbyterian Church and Dr. Mark L. Carlisle, pastor of the Washington Street Methodist Church, testified that they had not made, nor had they heard of other ministers or journalists making, appeals "through the local press and pulpit to the prejudice and passion of the people."[29] William H. Lyles avowed that he was a member of the First Baptist Church in Columbia, that he had not heard any pastor or official of the church say anything "calculated to prejudice the defendant in obtaining a fair and impartial trial," and that he had seen no evidence that local newspapers were manipulating the public to hostility toward James H. Tillman.[30]

Defense attorney Patrick H. Nelson tried to refute these affidavits by reading excerpts from newspaper articles describing sermons that he thought made the kind of appeal to anti-Tillman prejudice that the ministers had denied making.[31] The examples he gave were prayers made on Sunday, January 18, while N. G. Gonzales lingered, still alive but with his condition becoming increasingly grave. In refutation of Dr. Samuel M. Smith's denial of having uttered words hostile to Tillman, he quoted the following prayer by Smith:

> We pray thee oh Father bless those who mourn. As wide as is the brotherhood of sorrow, wider is the fatherhood of God. Bless all the sick and suffering; bless all the physicians and nurses. We especially lift up our hearts, oh God for that one for whom many souls today are in great grief and desperate suspense. Grant that this Sabbath Day bring a message of peace to them, and spare him we do beseech Thee, but if in thy mercy it is not to be that he should be spared; do Thy work of Grace in his heart so that whether he lives he may live unto the Lord or whether he dies, he may die unto the Lord.

Nelson read a prayer offered that same Sunday by Dr. Mark L. Carlisle, who had also executed an affidavit used by the prosecution to deny that there had been pulpit utterances prejudicial to Tillman. Dr. Carlisle prayed "that all things may work for the complete healing and recovery of thy servant who has accomplished so much for this city and state. And we pray that it be thy Divine will to spare him, a man who out of sincere heart expressed clearly and fearlessly his judgment."

At Trinity Episcopal Church, a ritual of "public sorrow" was conducted. At the Southside Baptist Church, prayers asked God to comfort the Gonzales family and friends. At St. Peters Catholic Church, the scholarly thirty-two-year-old Father Bernard W. Fleming asked the worshippers to pray for the injured editor. He gave three reasons why the congregation should pray for the "stricken man": "that a valuable citizen might be spared," "that the blood of a fellow man might not be on the second highest officer in the state," and "that the grand old state of South Carolina might not be humiliated by seeing her sons guilty of each other's blood."

Most of the defense's examples of clergy polluting the air with anti-Tillman fulminations were simply appeals to God that Gonzales recover and his family be comforted. Surely it is a heavy price for freedom of worship to bear if a community is stripped of its role in the criminal justice system with regard to acts committed within its boundaries because it engages in prayers for the injured victim's recovery. Other comments, such as Dr. Carlisle's observation that Gonzales "accomplished so much for this city and state," seem to be fair commentary and accurate concerning a man of Gonzales's distinction. Since they do not refer to the facts of the case, they are hardly prejudicial. It is not whipping up gross emotions to say that lives are valuable and should not be taken. However, when Dr. Carlisle went on to praise Gonzales as one who "expressed clearly and fearlessly his judgments," it is easy to see why the defense is so disgruntled. The statement goes directly contrary to the defense's main line of attack: that Tillman was hounded by Gonzales's judgments, expressed in newspaper columns that relentlessly pursued him beyond the point of human endurance. This refers to the main issue in the emotional background of the case, if not the more staid legal foreground: was Gonzales's commentary the sort of intense scrutiny that those who offered themselves for high office could have been expected to weather, or was it a personal vendetta that was beyond the pale? Some of Father Fleming's remarks, well-reasoned and perceptive though they were, probably caused equal alarm in the defense. But did they amount to anything more than the sensible hope that the state be spared a reputation as a haven for violence?

Several prosecution affidavits emphasized the growing calm and detachment in Richland County regarding the killing. The testimony of state senator John Quitman Marshall noted that as an elected representative of the area in the

Senate, it was his responsibility to take the temperature of the voters continually with regard to various public issues. He said the mood of the community had changed drastically between the January 15 date of the shooting and the current change of venue hearings on June 23–24, 1903. He observed that "there was a very strong feeling in Richland County against James H. Tillman at the time he killed N. G. Gonzales but I believe not more so than in other counties in the state."[32] Over time this hostility toward Tillman "has in a great measure subsided and passed away" so that Tillman could receive a "fair and impartial trial in Richland County."[33] There was apparently some residual good will toward Tillman left over from his days as a popular politician. Marshall noted that "it is a known fact that at the time of the homicide James H. Tillman was more popular and had a larger following in Richland County than N. G. Gonzales. In the last primary election for Governor James H. Tillman received the next to highest vote for Governor cast in the county, the vote he received being nearly a third of the entire vote cast in Richland and not withstanding the opposition of N. G. Gonzales and his paper."[34] But the defense probably viewed Marshall's testimony with deep suspicion since he had been allied with the *State,* serving at one time as president of the State Publishing Co. and engineering in the Senate the passage of the child-labor legislation long advocated by N. G. Gonzales. The defense tried to discredit him as a legislator who was so out of touch with his constituents that he could not know their attitudes toward the case.[35]

James H. Tillman, the defendant, executed an affidavit in which he pointed to what he considered a fatal flaw in the Richland County jury system. It was impossible to get a trial by a fair cross section of the community because the registered voters list, from which the jury would be drawn, was jaundiced because of the abysmally low proportion of those eligible to vote who were registered.[36] Tillman's brother-in-law and law mentor, former judge Osmund W. Buchanan, was a member of the defense team. In his affidavit he expressed outrage that a group of pious and socially prominent ladies had made Tillman anathema in Columbia by conspicuously praying for his conviction.[37] Tillman's lead defense attorneys, George W. Croft and Patrick H. Nelson, also executed affidavits. Croft was Tillman's law partner and had recently been elected to the United States Congress.[38] Croft asserted that it had become commonplace in Richland County to refer to N. G. Gonzales as a "martyr." As evidence, he pointed to a resolution passed by the students at South Carolina College saying that Gonzales "was truly a martyr to his love for South Carolina."[39] A community with such veneration for the deceased would turn a deaf ear to even the strongest defense.

The other lead defense attorney, Patrick H. Nelson of Columbia, had served as a solicitor and had wide experience at reading the entrails of jury lists.[40] He contended that an unhealthy atmosphere prevailed in Richland County as far as a fair and impartial trial for Tillman was concerned. The newspapers had created such a climate of fear that anyone who took a stand favorable to the defendant, whether in executing a venue-hearing affidavit for the defense, or serving on a jury that acquitted Tillman, could lose his job and be ostracized in the community.[41]

When presentation of the evidence was concluded, counsel for the defendant made arguments in favor of a change of venue on the grounds of inability to get a fair and impartial trial in Richland County. In addition to arguing that anti-Tillman prejudice tainted the pool of potential jurors, Nelson introduced a new element: prejudice existed not only among the potential jurors but also among the officials who compiled the list from which the jurors would be picked. County auditor W. H. Gibbes normally participated in compiling the jury lists along with the county treasurer and clerk of court. Gibbes had told defense attorney Osmund W. Buchanan when the defense attempt to get Tillman released on bail failed that he hoped Tillman would be convicted. But the prosecution contended that the simpler solution was to remove any biased officials from the jury compilation process rather than moving the trial to another county.[42] Prosecutor G. Duncan Bellinger argued against a change of venue by noting that while the state constitution did guarantee a fair and impartial trial,[43] and it was sometimes necessary to change the location of the trial to obtain an impartial jury, such changes should not be casually granted since the constitution also provided that normally the defendant should be "tried in the County where the offense was committed."[44] Not only is such a venue often convenient for the defendant, a trial at the location of the offense vindicates the interest of the citizens of the community in seeing law and order and justice maintained where they live. These provisions were worded so as to vindicate rights of the defendant, but apparently Bellinger also saw in them a wider community interest that must be considered alongside those of the defendant. Bellinger spoke with considerable personal authority. Not only had he recently completed four years' service as state attorney general, but at the 1895 constitutional convention, he was chair of the committee on jurisprudence, where he was the sole author of article VI, including section 2, containing the change of venue provisions.[45]

Opposing the motion to change venue, former judge Andrew Crawford argued that the burden on the defendant to justify the change in trial location was heavy because he must establish that local prejudice made a fair and impartial trial impossible.[46] Crawford invoked an old case from 1823 that held that the evidence in support of the change must be "very strong."[47] When the county was a populous one, like Richland, so that a large number of jurors could be called to select from, and when the defendant could "challenge twenty peremptorily, and for cause an indefinite number," the burden on the one seeking to relocate the trial was especially heavy.[48]

The role of the newspapers in creating anti-Tillman prejudice, and in fostering an atmosphere of fear and intimidation for potential jurors who might rule for him, was a persistent theme of defense lawyers in the closing arguments at the change of venue hearing. None was more vociferous on this subject than former judge Osmund W. Buchanan, James H. Tillman's brother-in-law and the mentor under whom Tillman had studied for the bar.[49] Buchanan had served as a Tillmanite state attorney general and circuit judge. He took great pride in tracing his ancestry to a signer of the Ordinance of Secession of December 20, 1860, as well as to Revolutionary War soldiers. He was married to Jim Tillman's sister Sophia.[50] Buchanan was the defense team's master of bombast. He played on the public's emotions like a master organist upon his instrument. His remarks seemed to have been aimed as much at the potential jurors as at the judge who would rule on the attempt to move the trial to friendlier territory.

Buchanan berated the American press as having lost the respect of the people because "it was allied with the great force of money."[51] It was the "sweeping wave of the war" that brought about this crass "commercialism." Of course the particular target of his tirade was the *State.* The *News and Courier* observed that "Judge Buchanan bitterly denounced the *State* as a paper which lashed, slashed and beat men to fury." He complained that many people had been "forced" to sign affidavits for the prosecution for these hearings under the threat that their families would suffer economic reprisals if they did not. Both the affluent and the humble were under the tyrannical thumb of the newspapers. He contended that "every businessman in the state is under the domination of the mighty newspapers." Even the men of God had been forced to march in lockstep by the newspapers. He alleged that "ministers of the Gospel" had been "lashed by this fiend [newspapers], and the poor fellows have been made to come here and swear that there is no prejudice in Richland against the accused." We are now in an age of trial by newspaper, he believed: "the newspapers are asserting so much power that they are now leading the fountain of justice. A man is tried these days by the newspaper and is either acquitted or condemned before the case comes to trial." His language became so melodramatic that one can picture his incarnation of the newspaper as an old-fashioned theatrical villain twirling his mustache and giving vent to a sinister laugh as he ties the prostrate public, like a helpless maiden, to the railroad tracks. This populist tapping into the economic resentment of the "have nots" was a favorite Tillmanite theme.[52]

Buchanan's contempt for the press was not a facade created to dramatize his arguments. It revealed a bone-deep hatred of the press as a source of danger. Where did these emotions come from? One source may be an 1894 editorial in the *State* that named Buchanan and other Tillmanite stalwarts, such as Judge Daniel A. Townsend, who later presided at Jim Tillman's venue-transfer hearing, as being beneficiaries of a "Military Promotion" system by which favored lawyers were so rapidly elevated from legislator or assistant attorney general, to attorney general, and then to various levels of judgeships that they had little time to become familiar with their jobs and perform any genuine public service.[53] The implication was that the promotions were based on political expediency rather than accomplishments. Buchanan probably resented seeing his achievements belittled and likely considered the editorial unfair. But the evidence shows that political goals did loom large in the selection of judges during the governorship of Ben Tillman. Historian George C. Rogers, Jr., points to a long list of Tillmanite judges elected during 1893–94, presumably to guard against judicial hostility to the governor's program. Buchanan is listed as one of those judges, as was Townsend, who was elected a circuit judge in December 1893. Townsend was serving as attorney general at that time with Buchanan as an assistant.[54] Retired chief justice Richard Cannon Watts noted in his *Memoirs* that he, as well as Buchanan and Townsend, was elected circuit judge during that time of reshaping of the judiciary, and he declared without embarrassment that "there was a determination to elect for circuit judges, Tillmanites."[55] Buchanan's service as attorney general during the late March and early April 1894 "Dispensary War" in Darlington may have furnished another reason for his bitterness toward the press. David Duncan Wallace concluded that hyperbolic coverage of the Darlington disturbances by the Columbia and Charleston papers had made an already tense situation worse by encouraging defiance of the law. One article in the *State* not only questioned the courage of the governor and his ally John Gary Evans because they did not go to the scene of the riots but also mocked Buchanan for going to Darlington under orders from Tillman and then whining that he should not have had to go because he had "narrowly escaped with his life."[56]

Patrick Nelson made Buchanan's broad antipress fulminations more concrete by giving a specific and recent example of an editorial in the *State,* charging that it was designed to turn public opinion against Jim Tillman. Nelson noted that, while a defendant has a right to seek a change of venue if he thinks it is necessary to get a fair trial, the *State* mocked the defendant's attempt to move the trial location in a commentary titled "Only Criminals Fear a Fair Trial."[57] Nelson argued that New York courts had been particularly vigilant in protecting a defendant's right to a fair and impartial trial by moving the trial when local newspapers had poisoned the atmosphere. He contended that South Carolina should adopt the New York cases as examples. It is difficult to determine which New York cases Nelson was referring to. Several New York cases available at that time dealt with newspaper-created prejudice, but these cases showed that New York courts were very cautious about granting such changes of venue. They usually required not just a showing of published articles denouncing the defendant but also evidence that they had had an adverse impact on the impartiality of the jury pool. When the original trial venue was a large city with a big supply of jurors to choose from, the defendant seeking a change faced a particularly strong burden.[58] An Iowa case of that era that is more favorable to the defense's position is *State v. Crafton,*[59] which held that the trial judge erred in refusing a murder case defendant's request for a change in venue when local newspapers accused him of many other crimes and misdeeds besides the one with which he was charged. But the Tillman defense offered no evidence of such promiscuous accusations by the Columbia papers.

The defense claimed that the newspaper-generated prejudice in Tillman's case was similar to that in an 1899 case that did force a transfer of venue. In that case, *State of South Carolina v. W. R. Crawford,* a dispensary agent was accused of murdering a woman while participating in a raid on a house suspected of harboring an illegal saloon. Tillman's attorneys argued that in the *Crawford* case Circuit Judge Richard Cannon Watts determined that antidispensary prejudice created by the *State* and other Columbia papers made it impossible for the defendant to receive a fair and impartial trial in Richland County, where the killing had occurred, thus necessitating a transfer to Kershaw County. The Tillman prosecutors replied that the current case bore little resemblance to the highly charged atmosphere in *Crawford,* which featured a lynch-prone mob that surrounded the magistrate's office during a preliminary hearing. No such threat faced Tillman, who resided peacefully and comfortably in the Richland

County jail. Furthermore the Crawford case was a mere trial-court decision, not included in official reports, and thus it was of little value as a precedent.[60]

After complimenting the attorneys for both sides on their "able" arguments, Judge Townsend granted the change of venue on June 24, 1903, without explaining the reasons for his decision.[61] The Tillman case seemed to lack the compelling demonstration of pervasive, community-wide prejudice that would prompt the South Carolina Supreme Court in later early-twentieth-century cases to order a change of venue. One case spoke of "the inflamed state of the public mind" as necessitating a transfer to obtain an impartial jury; another described a "spirit of mob law" infecting the town; and still another opinion focused on the "strong sentiment against the defendant" arising from what his attorneys alleged was "intense excitement" generated by the case.[62] The Tillman case by contrast was characterized by Columbia newspaper accounts giving dramatic but relatively factual accounts of the attack that did not amount to a drumbeat for conviction. Sermons, college resolutions expressing hope for the victim's recovery, and admiration for his contributions to his state and city did not amount to an "inflamed state of public mind" or a "spirit of mob law." The ladies who prayed for Tillman's conviction were not part of the pool of potential jurors and did not create a public spectacle. The sharper analytical tools—insisting on finding media-generated prejudice so intense and pervasive that it could be presumed the defendant could not obtain a fair and impartial trial in the original location, or on conducting probing, in-person questioning of potential jurors to determine whether or not an unbiased jury could be found in the current venue—had not become customary by the time of the Tillman case in 1903 as they were later.[63]

The three-day hearing was not a dry, technical exercise. It had been tense and often emotional. The *New York World* noted that several of the lawyers had been armed out of real or feigned fear that those who resented their participation would attack them.[64] The hearing had sometimes gone beyond the factual contours of the case to include a dash of class warfare. Buchanan for the defense had accused the *State* of mobilizing the moneyed interests against the defendant, and Andrew Crawford for the prosecution had accused the defense of overreliance on affidavits from "a migratory class," mill workers, instead of the stable population more likely to serve on the jury.[65]

The fight was not over. The real purpose of the maneuver had not been accomplished yet. That purpose was obtaining a location, and thus a jury pool, likely to favor the defendant. What would the new trial location be? By law the new location had to be in the same circuit as Richland.[66] The possible choices were Edgefield, Saluda, Lexington, and Kershaw Counties. The defense sought a location that was Tillman country politically and in the hometown sense, as well as a location where the influence of the city papers was diluted. From this perspective Edgefield, the fountainhead of the Tillman movement and Jim Tillman's hometown, was the optimum location. Not far behind it was Saluda County, carved out of Edgefield County. The people of Saluda revered Jim's father, George D. Tillman, as its creator. He had advocated the formation of smaller more manageable political units in the 1895 constitutional convention. More small counties meant more legislators from the old Edgefield area, an area that he thought had been underrepresented in the political counsels of the state.[67]

Defense attorney Nelson noted that the accused was entitled not only to an "impartial jury" but also to a "speedy and public trial."[68] The only counties that could satisfy the right to a speedy trial were Edgefield and Saluda because they were scheduled to have court terms sooner than the others. Of course the real reason these counties were the most desirable was that they were closely identified with the Tillmans and beyond the areas most influenced by the *State* newspaper.[69] Prosecutor Bellinger shot back that the defense had waived any right to make a speedy-trial argument because they had asked for and got a delay in the trial until a time when certain key witnesses would be available.[70] Solicitor Thurmond contended that any speedy trial advantage Saluda would have would be outweighed by its inconvenience. It would pose hardships to both sides. The distance of the courthouse from the nearest railroad was too great, making it difficult to transport the approximately two hundred witnesses who were expected to be called, and once they arrived in Saluda, they would find insufficient hotel rooms to house them. Prosecutors Crawford and Bellinger urged the judge not to choose Saluda because of the high esteem in which the defendant's father was held in that county.[71] They contended that the state also was entitled to an impartial jury, and it would not get it in Saluda or Edgefield. Thurmond, the chief prosecutor, had deep ties with Edgefield himself, having been born, raised, and a successful lawyer there, but he preferred Kershaw or Lexington County as the new venue.[72] Lexington County was no metropolis, but it was connected by rail with nearby Columbia. It was solid Tillman country too, but at least it was not the defendant's hometown and that of his father and uncle, the powerful Senator Benjamin R. Tillman. As someone who had been closely allied politically with Ben Tillman, but who also conscientiously represented the state, Thurmond had vigorously opposed the transfer from Richland and opposed both Saluda and Edgefield as the new trial venue.[73] Lexington probably seemed about as good a place as possible given the rule requiring transfer to a county within the same circuit as the original location.

Judge Daniel A. Townsend picked Lexington County as the new venue. His June 25, 1903, order simply stated that "it appearing to the court that a fair and impartial trial of this case cannot be had in Richland County, it is ordered that the case be transferred to the county of Lexington."[74] All records in the case were transferred from Richland to Lexington County, and the Richland County sheriff was ordered to "deliver to the Sheriff of the said Lexington County the person of the defendant by the second Monday of September."

The transfer came at a price, especially for Richland County. It no longer had the burden of hosting the trial, but it retained the burden of paying for it and the price had just gone up. A *News and Courier* survey concluded that the trial would have cost Richland County about $3,500 if it had been held in Columbia. The cost almost doubled to about $6,000, because of the transfer to Lexington. Richland now had to pay much more for witnesses' travel and housing expenses. If the move had been to out-of-the-way Saluda, the cost would have gone up still more, to about $7,000.[75]

After the excitement of the venue-transfer controversy died down, Jim Tillman grew bored. Despite the comfort of having his personal furniture in the Richland County jail, he wanted a change. Although Judge Daniel A. Townsend's order did not require his transfer to the Lexington County jail until the second Monday in September, he requested an early move. There is no indication of whether he was permitted to take his furniture with him or to continue getting fresh flower deliveries. The court gave permission for the transfer, and Sheriff William Henry Coleman of Richland turned Tillman over to Sheriff Thomas H. Caughman of Lexington on July 13, 1903.[76] Now that there was a new venue, the defense needed to create an atmosphere there that was both understanding of, and receptive to, their case.

To Senator Ben Tillman, the press was obnoxious but had its uses. As the trial approached and interest in the attitude of potential jurors grew, he tried to get an article with a viewpoint favorable to the defense into the *Augusta Chronicle,* a paper that circulated in the Lexington area and would influence possible jurors. On July 24, 1903, using his Senate stationery, he wrote to Colonel E. B. Hook, who was associated with the paper, that since he had always "expressed so much of interest and friendship for me that I take the liberty of asking a favor of you, and that is, to insert in The Chronicle the interview I send you with a suppostitious [supposititious] citizen of South Carolina."[77] In other words Tillman was asking the paper to publish a phony interview with a fictional person presenting Jim Tillman's side of the case as if the interview sprang spontaneously from the public. Colonel Hook referred the matter to editor Thomas W. Loyless, who flatly rejected the request. The editor described the senator's request as asking that the *Chronicle* publish "a fictitious interview with reference to the Jim Tillman case."[78] Loyless expressed regret that the paper could not "aid you in this matter in the way suggested" since "it would be entirely improper and unprofessional for a newspaper to publish in its columns a matter of this nature that is admittedly unfounded and for which the newspaper itself has no tangible authority." The editor noted that, while he was refusing to publish a "fake interview," the paper could print a statement representing Tillman's point of view if it were properly identified as coming from Senator Tillman or some other real and responsible person.[79] Apparently Tillman did not find this more open alternative attractive. The episode showed that Tillman valued the press as a docile propaganda outlet rather than as a critic of government that helped maintain an informed electorate. But other means were available for influencing public opinion. George W. Croft, a leader of the defense team, wrote Senator Tillman on September 24, 1903, only five days before the trial, noting that representatives of the defense had "already commenced in Lexington to speak in very positive terms about the result" of the trial, predicting that "Jim Tillman will never be convicted so as to create the impression that it would be best that the trial should be ended at once by acquittal."[80]

"Cousin Frank" Presides

The pretrial maneuvers to determine who would be the key decision makers in the case continued. The transfer to Lexington to get a friendlier jury was only the first round. Who would be the judge? This would normally have been determined by a stately rotation system set well in advance of any trial. But things began to happen, whether by design or a combination of circumstances, that derailed this orderly progression. Under the normal rotation, Circuit Judge George William Gage was set to preside in Lexington in September. However, because of "physical infirmities" he suffered, Chief Justice Young John Pope issued an order on September 1 replacing Gage with Circuit Judge Daniel A.

Townsend. Judge Townsend appeared to have been a logical choice since he had presided over the venue-transfer hearing and was already familiar with the case. Judge Townsend was appointed to try not only the Tillman case but all common pleas (civil) and general sessions (criminal) cases in the September term. Complications soon arose. The chief justice had overlooked the fact that Judge Townsend had already been appointed to preside in Fairfield County at that same time.[81] The prosecution expressed concern about this confusion over who was the proper presiding judge for the Tillman case. Solicitor Thurmond was worried that, if Judge Townsend was performing a special assignment in Lexington the same day that he was scheduled under regular rotation to preside in Fairfield County (Winnsboro), any verdict obtained against the defendant could be attacked on the ground that the trial had been conducted illegally by a judge without jurisdiction. Knowledgeable court watchers believed that the dilemma could be solved by assigning Judge William Christie (W. C.) Benet, who was presiding at Camden, also in the circuit, earlier in the summer, to continue on to Lexington. Chief Justice Pope decided that a hearing was required, and he held one in Spartanburg. Oddly enough defense attorneys did not attend the hearing, perhaps hoping to avoid any appearance of manipulating the choice. At the hearing Solicitor Thurmond stated that the prosecution had no objection to Judge Townsend personally; he was merely seeking to protect any guilty verdict he might obtain from attacks on the ground that the judge had no jurisdiction. In light of these reasonable arguments, it was expected that Townsend would be replaced as presiding judge of the Tillman trial so that he could continue with his regular assignment in Fairfield. The guessing was that Judge Benet would be assigned to move to the Lexington trial after completing work in Camden. This additional assignment of a regular judge already in the circuit seems logical. Instead the chief justice announced the appointment of a practicing lawyer, Frank B. Gary, as a special judge.[82]

Defense attorney Patrick Nelson got news of this appointment in a telegram from Chief Justice Young John Pope on September 17, 1903. Announcing that Pope had revoked the order appointing Townsend to preside in Lexington, the telegram added that "on the recommendation of the Lexington Bar I have appointed the Hon. Frank B. Gary to hold court for Lexington county."[83] The wording of the telegram might have raised some eyebrows. When a regularly rotating judge was not expected to arrive for some time, it was common practice for a bar with an overcrowded docket to request the appointment of a special judge to reduce the overload. But was it wise for the Lexington Bar to name the judge they wanted specifically when they would try cases before him? This situation could create the appearance, if not the actuality, of partiality, especially if the person named was not chosen by the entire bar. The temporary appointment of "men learned in the law" as special judges is made by the governor on the suggestion of the chief justice.[84] Chief Justice Pope followed this procedure by sending a September 17, 1903, request to Governor Heyward asking that he commission Frank B. Gary as special judge to preside over civil and criminal cases in Lexington beginning September 21, 1903.[85]

The *State* treated Gary's appointment as a hijacking of the judicial-assignment process by the defense and as a blow to the independence of the judiciary. Its outrage was expressed in an editorial titled "Juggling with the Courts."[86] The juggling to which the *State* objected was the manner in which the Lexington Bar participated. Under the statute providing for the appointment of a special judge, "the majority of the members of the bar of any county" could certify that the docket of civil cases was so heavy that an extra term of the court of common pleas needed to be held and that a special judge should be appointed by the governor on the suggestion of the chief justice.[87] A majority of the Lexington Bar did request the appointment of a special judge, but there were several characteristics of this bar involvement that went beyond the terms of the statute and raised questions about their impartiality. No special judge was necessary; a regular circuit judge (Benet) would be available after he finished his work in Camden. The paper claimed that the bar's recommendation went beyond requesting a special judge and named a particular person to be that judge. The *State* contended that a majority of the Lexington Bar had been hired by the Tillman defense, which was essentially naming the judge. The *State* further raised its editorial eyebrows at the appointment by noting that Frank B. Gary was known to be closely allied with the Tillman family both in friendship and political persuasion. It revealed that the Tillmans referred to Gary as "Cousin Frank," a relationship of friendship rather than blood.[88] The *State* praised Gary as an able public servant who could normally be expected to do a good job at any task assigned to him. But the closeness of his relation to the Tillmans and the unusual bar involvement in his appointment, made the paper uneasy. The Lexington Bar members associated with the defense had been too involved in Gary's appointment. To the paper the defendant would now have a trial in Tillman country (Lexington) before a Tillman judge (Gary) picked by Tillman lawyers.

The defense attorneys did maneuver to influence the appointment of a new judge who would be sympathetic to the defendant's cause. In a September 16 letter to Senator Tillman, George W. Croft said that the chief goal of their manipulations was to block Judge Benet, who was viewed as hostile to the defense, from presiding. Croft told the senator, "None of the [defense] lawyers want Judge Benet. They are afraid of him, so from the petition to Judge Pope, and the letter, we feel that it makes it very certain that Judge Benet will not preside."[89] The letter confirms that the petition of the Lexington Bar, several members of which had been hired by the defense, was made at the request of Jim Tillman's lawyers. Croft stated that "while we were in Lexington we also got the members of the bar to send Judge Pope a petition asking him, if possible, to appoint a regular circuit judge, and if not then we mentioned several other gentlemen, members of the bar whom the Lexington lawyers suggested as special judges."[90] Oddly enough, Frank Gary, was not mentioned in the letter as a possible special judge, but his brother, Judge Ernest Gary, was mentioned as "the only Circuit Judge that has no engagements now in the regular Court elsewhere."[91] The day after Croft wrote the senator, Frank Gary's appointment was announced.

Who was Frank Gary? He was indeed a "man learned in the law" as the statute specified. In the course of the trial, it became clear his knowledge and understanding of criminal law and the rules of evidence were impressive. At the time of his appointment, Gary was forty-three years old. He was born in Cokesbury, in the Abbeville District of South Carolina, on March 9, 1860. After attending Union College in Schenectady, New York, he practiced law in Abbeville, South Carolina. He was elected to the South Carolina House of Representatives as part of Ben Tillman's reform movement in 1890 and served as speaker from 1896 to 1900. He was a delegate to the constitutional convention of 1895, which produced a state constitution sharply curbing black voting rights.[92] Thus he came to the presiding judge's chair in the Tillman trial carrying the prestige of a former speaker of the South Carolina House of Representatives. His career after the Tillman trial continued to bring him distinction. He served from March 6, 1908, until March 3, 1909, as a United States senator, filling a vacancy caused by the death of Asbury C. Latimer. In 1912 he was elected a state circuit judge and served until his death in 1922.[93]

Judge Gary came from a well-known and well-connected political family. His uncle, former Confederate general Martin W. Gary, known as the "Bald Eagle of Edgefield," was prominent among those called "redeemers," who restored white rule after Reconstruction. General Gary did not recoil from the use of violence and intimidation to squelch black voting.[94] The influence of the Gary family in legal circles was unique. Ultimately three Gary brothers were members of the state judiciary at the same time: Frank as circuit judge, his brother Eugene as Supreme Court chief justice, and his brother Ernest as circuit judge. On one occasion the three sat together with other Supreme Court and circuit judges in a rare combined bench to hear a case.[95] Eugene B. Gary had been elected to the Supreme Court in December 1893 by Governor Ben Tillman's followers in the General Assembly with the expectation that he would help save from constitutional perdition the governor's pet project, the state dispensary created to monopolize liquor sales. When Gary replaced a justice who was hostile to the dispensary, he wrote a majority opinion upholding the constitutionality of the new 1893 Dispensary Act as a valid exercise of the state's police powers to protect the public health, safety, and morality. This ruling reversed an earlier case that struck down an 1892 version of the state liquor monopoly as an undue infringement on the right of private persons to pursue business opportunities.[96] The Tillmans held Frank Gary in the same high esteem in which they held his brothers.

In many ways Frank Gary had a sophisticated and supple mind. In other ways he exhibited the deeply ingrained prejudices of the time and place in which he lived. These prejudices were on proud display in a speech he made when he was a senator on February 19, 1909, advocating an immigration policy that would maintain the purity and dominance of the white race. He argued that it was impossible for two races to occupy the same territory on an equal basis. One must dominate the other. He thought that the white race must be the dominant one because it had superior ability and traditions allowing it to understand the meaning of liberty fully. He argued that these principles had guided the South in its long struggle to provide for white ascendency and that similar principles had to guide the nation in crafting its immigration policy. He was alarmed by the rising tide of immigration from Eastern European and Mediterranean countries, such as Hungary, Poland, Greece, Turkey, Syria, Arabia, and South Russia. In his view these countries did not understand the traditions of western democracy, and a glut of settlers from them would undermine our government institutions. Despite his Union College education, he appeared to have never heard of, or had chosen to forget, the ancient traditions of Athenian democracy.[97] Gary's views on race relations are relevant to his performance in the Tillman trial because they influenced one of his important rulings in the case: he permitted a witness to be impeached because he backed a candidate who sought black as well as white political support. But Gary's views on race certainly did not detract from his command of the courtroom.

Gary's appearance and demeanor inspired respect in courtrooms. A *News and Courier* report describe him at the trial: "In his aquiline features one catches a possible explanation of the sobriquet of a famous uncle [Martin W. Gary] 'The Bald Eagle of Edgefield.' He has stature enough to be commanding. His manner is marked by a generous dignity that impresses. Dark eyes look steadfastly from beneath heavy brows. The jaw is square enough to inspire confidence. Close-cropped dark hair is thinning at the crown and whitening at the temples. The nose comes down and the chin goes up, a guardian each to a thin, vise-clamped mouth. Patient, grave, handsome, Judge Gary adorns the gown he has for the moment donned."[98]

The chain of events leading to Gary's appointment might be catnip to conspiracy theorists. It began with the prosecutor, Thurmond, objecting to the legality of Judge Townsend's appointment and ended with the appointment of a special temporary judge called "Cousin Frank" by members of the defendant's family. Could Thurmond, a Ben Tillman political ally, have initiated the process with a view to getting Gary, a judge perceived as friendly to the defense, appointed? It is possible but unlikely. Thurmond had a legitimate reason to object to Townsend's appointment. It is a prosecutor's duty to protect any guilty verdict he obtains from attack, on grounds such as the judge's lack of authority, by preventing the basis of such attacks from ever taking place. Second, it is unlikely that Thurmond could have foreseen elements in the chain of events, such as Judge Gage's illness, which led to Gary's selection.

Defense Reconnaissance of Potential Jurors

Gary's appointment did not end the pretrial maneuvering to get decision makers favorable to the defense. The case had been moved to Lexington County, an area generally known as Tillman country.[99] Lewis Pinckney Jones has noted that Lexington County "had always shown a larger proportionate vote in support of Ben Tillman than any other county in the state."[100] The broad array of potential jurors was likely to be inclined toward the defense. But what about the particular jury that would decide James H. Tillman's guilt or innocence? Would it be a friendly one? To make sure this question was answered favorably to the accused, the defense team needed knowledge about the individual jurors who would be in the jury pool for Tillman's trial. Senator Ben Tillman closely followed the maneuvers to shape who would decide his nephew's guilt or innocence. Congressman George W. Croft, who was one of Jim Tillman's lead defense attorneys as well as his law partner, wrote Ben Tillman on September 16, 1903, about what was being done to determine which potential jurors were likely to be hostile and which were likely to be friendly to the defendant. Croft informed the senator that "we canvassed thoroughly the jurors of both weeks and many of the jurors had been sounded."[101] Rumor had it that one way the jurors were "sounded" was by hiring Edgefield photographer Ben Covar to call on potential jurors under the pretense that he was offering his services. He displayed pictures of N. G. Gonzales and James H. Tillman as examples of his work and used the photographs to coax comments from a potential juror as to what he thought of the victim and the accused. As intriguing as the rumor is, it has never been confirmed; yet Croft's comment that the jurors had been "sounded" indicates that some kind of personal approach was made.[102]

Efforts to obtain the most favorable jury also influenced the timing of the case. Should it be tried the first or the second week of the September term? A different group of jurors was called for each week. Apparently the defense "sounding" of the jurors caused Tillman's attorneys to like the potential jurors called for the second week better than those called for the first, and they focused efforts accordingly. Croft explained this strategy to Senator Tillman: "We found the second week's jury decidedly more favorable to us, so much so that we have determined if possible to postpone the case so as it will be tried the second week."[103] The argument was over whether local cases would be tried before the import from Richland County that had been thrust on Lexington by the change of venue motion. The argument had broader implications than just the Tillman case, and the debate involved county officials and the grand jury. The grand jury asked that local cases be tried first so that witnesses in those cases would not have to linger in town at county expense while the Tillman case dragged on.[104] County fiscal officers wanted cases that would affect their tax collections tried first.

Two of Tillman's Lexington attorneys, Cyprian Melanchthon (C. M.) Efird and Senator William Henry Sharpe, Jr., argued that the local cases should be tried first and the Tillman case bumped into the second week, but as they did so, they purported to speak as members of the local bar seeking to get a glut of cases disposed of rather than as Tillman counsel angling for a friendly jury. The county, they argued, suffered from a large backlog that should be attended to

"Tillman's Friends Camping at Lexington, S.C., Waiting for His Trial for the Murder of N. G. Gonzales," *New York World,* October 9, 1903, 3. Illustration by W. H. Loomis. Courtesy of the American Newspaper Repository Collection, 1856–2004. David M. Rubenstein Rare Books and Manuscript Library, Duke University.

before it had to do the work of other counties. Thus the Tillman local counsel worked to protect the county's needs from derailment by outside interlopers while they were working with the same outsiders who had engineered the shift of the Tillman case to Lexington. Judge Gary, in his first major ruling in the case, decided to try the local cases first and the Tillman case in the second week. This gave the defense the jury panel that, according to rumor, they preferred. But Gary's decision was based on the seemingly logical ground that the long-standing traffic jam of local cases was in dire need of immediate attention.[105]

As the time of the trial approached, the area outside the Lexington County courthouse took on the aspect of a western encampment. A varied menagerie of Tillman supporters had arrived by covered wagons, which were not only their means of transportation but were also their homes during the course of the trial. A picture by *New York World* artist W. H. Loomis shows a woman in an old-fashioned sun bonnet, long dress, and apron, carrying a bucket of water while another woman hovers over a big black kettle on an open fire and stirs a pungent stew. A man with a broad-brimmed hat and an outfit of coarse material sits in front of a tent while another man stands and stares abstractedly into the distance as a large dog sniffs his leg. Horses are tethered by the tents and wagons.[106]

Pictures drawn or photographed at the time of the trial, revealed the following scene: The Lexington County courthouse is a two-story building with a small balcony over the front entrance.[107] A court crier stands on this balcony and discharges his ancient office by calling the names of the cases and those persons who are needed to attend. Another Loomis drawing shows Senator Ben Tillman entering the courthouse; he wears a large broad-brimmed hat that keeps his bad left eye in a shadow while his good right eye stares balefully, cyclopslike, at all in his path. After his wife was injured in a carriage accident, Senator Tillman went to her side and missed most of the trial. But he was there at the beginning, signaling his intense interest in the case. His supporters and enemies alike were put on notice. In Loomis's drawing the senator appears heavyset, dressed in a dark suit, vest, wing collar, and long thin tie. He carries himself with authority. He expected to be obeyed.[108]

As another Loomis drawing reveals, in the courtroom bailiffs with long thick poles, presumably for keeping order, were on either side of the prisoner's dock.[109] Spectator seating was on "long uncomfortable benches." *News and Courier* color commentator John Marshall gave a vivid description of the setting: "The courtroom itself is high-ceiled and spacious. It is Gothic in simple dignity save for a cheap and gaudy partition that stands immediately behind the judge's seat. The structure is of plank and serves as a shield to the retiring room of his Honor. Its panels are ornamented by roughly executed reproductions of the Roman emblems of justice, done in gaudy colors. Many long narrow windows break the white monotony of the walls."[110]

The Arraignment

On Monday September 21, 1903, James H. Tillman was brought into court for arraignment, conducted into the courtroom by the Lexington County sheriff and a deputy. The charges were to be read and his plea entered. He was seated in an area reserved for attorneys with his uncle, Senator Ben Tillman, beside him. *News and Courier* reporter August Kohn, who later testified in the case as a witness to N. G. Gonzales's dying declaration, described Jim Tillman on that occasion: "The prisoner looked decidedly pale, but as stout and fleshy as ever, and but for his decided paleness, no decided change has occurred in his appearance

James H. Tillman (center) in the prisoner's dock with defense attorneys George W. Croft (left) and Patrick H. Nelson (right) on either side. The other figures are people artist W. H. Loomis considered typical onlookers. *New York World,* October 3, 1903, 3. Courtesy of the American Newspaper Repository Collection, 1856–2004. David M. Rubenstein Rare Books and Manuscript Library, Duke University.

during the eight months imprisonment. He was well dressed in black, was well barbered and wore two badges of secret orders on the lapel of his coat. During the entire hearing today he seemed quite serious and consulted with his counsel during arguments and made suggestions."[111]

A *New York World* photograph of the defendant gives a somewhat different impression of him than Kohn's description of him as "stout and fleshy." His massive head was composed of all angles and planes. He had chiseled features, full curly hair, and a jutting chin. A well-formed straight nose was proportional to the rest of his face and gave him a theatrical appearance. Perhaps the eight months in jail had blurred these features somewhat.[112] The arraignment was not completed on September 21 and was continued on September 28. While being arraigned, Tillman stood in "the dock, a box-like affair, built of pine boards, in which all prisoners in South Carolina [were] compelled to stand while being arraigned."[113] His lead attorneys, George W. Croft and Patrick H. Nelson, stood with him, one on each side of the prisoner's dock as if they were forming a defensive line against attack. Then occurred a venerable ritual that would have been familiar to Tillman as an attorney. The clerk said: "James H. Tillman, prisoner at the bar, if you answer to that name hold up your right hand."[114]

The *New York World* report said: "Instantly the right hand of the prisoner shot far above his head. Without a tremor, he held it there until commanded by the clerk to lower it." While the indictment charging Tillman with murder and carrying a concealed weapon was read, James Tillman listened "attentively" and "stood erect." The clerk asked, "Are you guilty or not guilty?" "'Not guilty' answered Tillman in a clear voice." In a "sing-song voice," the clerk asked, "how will you be tried?" "By God and my country," Tillman replied. This ritualistic language had the flavor of a church litany. "God send you a good deliverance," continued the clerk. "Are you ready to come to trial?" "I am," said Tillman in a resolute manner.[115]

3.

THE FIRST ROUND OF THE TRIAL

Jury selection went faster than expected, taking only two hours. A jury pool, called a *venire,* of thirty-six men had been summoned. These names were written on individual pieces of paper placed in a broad-brimmed hat owned by Sheriff Thomas Caughman. A cloth covered the hat. The custom was to have a small boy who could neither read nor write draw the names. In this odd manner, a child was allowed to participate in the justice system and impartiality was supposedly insured.[1] Jurors whose names were called were questioned by Judge Gary under a process called, *voir dire,* a term from law French, meaning "to speak the truth."[2] The judge sought to eliminate biased jurors by inquiring of each candidate whether he was "related by blood or marriage to either the deceased or the prisoner at the bar," whether he had "formed or expressed any opinion as to the guilt or innocence of the accused," whether he had "any bias or prejudice for or against the prisoner," and finally whether there was "any reason why" he could not "make an impartial juror in this case."[3] If the answers to these questions revealed bias, the juror was eliminated. Four members of the panel were eliminated in this manner.[4] In addition the defense was given ten and the prosecution five peremptory challenges, opportunities to eliminate a potential juror without giving a reason. The defense used nine of its ten peremptory challenges, and the prosecution used all five of those allotted to it.[5] The only dispute was over Murray Parnell. The prosecution sought to have him dismissed because he was not listed in the voter-registration book and thus did not meet the requirement that jurors be qualified electors. The defense wanted him to serve. Even though Parnell did not have a registration card with him, he convinced the judge that he had been issued one, and Judge Gary ruled that Parnell was qualified because the original registration books had been lost and the replacement was incomplete.[6] Since he could not prove a cause for Parnell's automatic exclusion, Solicitor Thurmond was forced to use one of the prosecution's meager hoard of five peremptory challenges to be rid of him.[7] The battle over whether Parnell would be a juror was vigorously fought. Thurmond apparently thought Parnell was dangerously biased for the defense, although his reasons for thinking so do not appear on the record. The fight over Parnell was so intense that one might speculate that the prosecution feared he would not only cast a defense vote but would lead other jurors to do so as well. The skillful and energetic way in which Thurmond conducted his side of the debate indicates that, despite his political alliance with Ben Tillman, the solicitor was not pulling any punches in prosecuting his ally's nephew.

The Jury

The jury as finally selected was made up of these men:

George H. Koon, former county supervisor and farmer (elected foreman by his fellow jurors)[8]
Jacob E. Saylor, merchant and farmer
George F. Leitsey (or Leitzsey), farmer
Irvin Risinger, farmer
Martin L. Lybrand, cotton-mill operative at Lexington Mills
Milton Sharpe, farmer
Jonas Corley, cotton-mill operative at Dutch Mill
Marshall Shealey, farmer
J. B. Jumper, farmer
Willie L. Hicks, cotton-mill operative and police officer
James E. Price, farmer
Homer Woods, operative and weaving-room foreman at Red Bank Cotton Mills[9]

The jury for the Tillman murder trial. Courtesy of the South Caroliniana Library. University of South Carolina, Columbia, S.C.

The political nature of the trial was underscored by the selection of George Hilliard Koon as foreman. As county supervisor, an elective office, he had played a key role in the construction and repair of public works, such as roads and bridges. Koon was later elected supervisor again, but he became entangled in a dispute over whether a bridge-building contract he had awarded in 1908 involved an excessive price and kickbacks. Though he was then defeated for reelection, he held public office again as a member of the county dispensary board, which controlled liquor sales.[10]

This jury of farmers and mill workers must have warmed the hearts of Jim Tillman and his defense counsel. It was among people with such backgrounds that the defendant's Uncle Ben Tillman had found support for his reform movement, which shifted power from the more aristocratic and conservative Bourbon element to the scrappy new class of politicians Tillman led.[11] Such a jury could be expected to give the maximum amount of credence to the defense's grand strategy, which was to demonstrate that Jim Tillman was not just defending himself from the bodily harm he expected from Gonzales but also defending himself and society against forces, supposedly represented by Gonzales, such as out-of-control corporations, including powerful newspapers that had been bullying both Jim Tillman and the little men of society, including the farmers and mill workers on the jury. Such a strategy was designed to reverse roles. Gonzales, the *State,* newspapers in general, and powerful economic forces became the defendants, and Jim Tillman became a victim rather than an aggressor, not an assassin but a hero fighting for liberty.

This antinewspaper, anti-*State* defense had already been implemented. On the opening day, before final jury selection, but in the presence of the pool from which the jury was to be selected, defense attorney George Tillman Graham waved a copy of the *State* in the air and asked for permission to make remarks critical of the editorial titled "Juggling with the Courts," which implied that members of the Lexington Bar had engineered Frank Gary's appointment as special judge to help the defense rather than to reduce the backlog of cases clogging the local court system.[12] Judge Gary was at first inclined to allow the comment since it purported to be a statement on behalf of the Lexington Bar. But Edward Lee Asbill, a Lexington lawyer retained by the prosecution, said the statement did not come from the entire bar, implying it came just from those allied with the defense. Solicitor Thurmond objected to allowing Graham's fulmination against the *State* because it was irrelevant to the case. Ultimately Judge Gary agreed and excluded the statement.[13] Perhaps he also wanted to avoid opening the door to an inquiry into the circumstances of his appointment.

After final jury selection but before the evidence began, another assault on the *State* was made. Judge Gary had decided to sequester the jury. This meant keeping the jury together rather than allowing them to return home after each day's session and meant cutting off all their communications with the outside world. Two constables were assigned to assure that these rules were observed. This action was appropriate as a means to ensure that the jury focused on the evidence presented in court rather than on outside sources such as community gossip. Lead defense counsel Patrick Nelson asked that this sequestration include denial of access to the *State,* presumably because of fears that its trial coverage might prejudice the jury against the defendant. Although this request was an attack on the *State,* it was also reasonable, a logical extension of the attempt to keep the jury focused on the evidence as presented in court. Judge Gary granted the request.[14] However, since this argument seems to have been conducted in front of the jury as finally selected and no other papers were so explicitly mentioned, it could also have served to reinforce the belief that the *State* was a sinister force.

A Swarm of Lawyers and Politicians

Both sides had assembled an illustrious array of counsel with the defense outnumbering the prosecution. The defense team was led by Patrick H. Nelson of Columbia and George W. Croft of Aiken. They were assisted by George Johnstone of Newberry, Osmund W. Buchanan of Winnsboro, George R. Rembert of Columbia, C. M. Efird (or Effird), Franklin Dreher, George Tillman Graham, and William Henry (W. H.) Sharpe of Lexington. Coleman L. Blease was initially a defense attorney but dropped out when it became apparent that he would be a witness. The prosecution was led by circuit solicitor J. William Thurmond and former state attorney general G. Duncan Bellinger of Columbia. They were assisted by Andrew Crawford of Columbia, Gonzales relative William Elliott, Jr., of Columbia, Edward Lee Asbill of Lexington, and twenty-five-year-old Tyrone C. Sturkie of Lexington.[15]

The lead defense attorneys were wise to hire several Lexington lawyers as cocounsel. C. M. Efird and State Senator W. H. Sharpe added local legal folk wisdom and political influence to the defense team.[16] Efird and Sharpe's extensive local contacts afforded the two attorneys insight into the likely attitudes of potential jurors, and the lawyers' high standing in the Lexington community gave the defense a patina of local respectability. Efird had been a state senator and was a pillar of the Lutheran Church, serving as a trustee of Newberry College and the Lutheran Seminary. He had also been reporter of decisions for the state supreme court. Sharpe was still a state senator in an era when the county's senator was typically the most influential local political figure, having administrative as well as legislative powers. Both Efird and Sharpe were loyal members of Ben Tillman's reform movement, which was influential among area farmers, a likely source of jurors. Neither Efird nor Sharpe played a major role in the evidentiary phase of the trial, but they were probably active in the preliminary maneuvers to obtain favorable timing of the case in order to gain the best jury panel for the defense.[17] Asbill, also a Lexington attorney and former legislator, joined the prosecution.[18] A Lexington attorney named J. A. Muller, who had been retained by the prosecution, died prior to the trial. This meant that the defense had a greater showing of familiar local faces than the prosecution, possibly giving them an edge not only in jury selection but also in gaining rapport with the jury.

One of the most interesting features of the cast of attorneys is the intertwining relationship of counsel on the two sides. Perhaps the most striking example of this is the network of connections of head prosecutor John William Thurmond, father of future United States senator J. Strom Thurmond. The most remarkable fact about Jim Tillman's prosecutor is that in 1897, when he was already solicitor, Thurmond was tried and acquitted on a murder charge. His defense counsel in that case were George W. Croft, one of the lead defense attorneys in the current case, and his partner, James H. Tillman, the defendant. As in this case, the killing in the Thurmond case grew from a political quarrel in which the name Tillman played a prominent part and, again as in the Tillman-Gonzales case, the defense was based in part on a claim that the deceased had threatened the accused and made a motion toward his hip pocket as if he were drawing a gun. The victim, W. G. Harris, had confronted Thurmond in an Edgefield store and accused him of foiling the reappointment of Harris's father as magistrate. Harris also accused Thurmond of being the tool of Ben Tillman, who had ordered Thurmond's election as solicitor. Thurmond replied that he had been elected by a bipartisan vote. Then he left the store hoping to avoid provoking the already angry Harris to violence. According to some accounts, Harris bragged about being armed with a pistol, and during the encounter at the store, he had flourished a knife in Thurmond's face. After Thurmond had returned to his office, Harris stood in front of it and resumed his stream of vituperation, including calling Thurmond a "dog," a "scoundrel," and a "dirty Tillmanite." Thurmond said that he pulled his gun and shot Harris when he saw Harris lunge toward him and reach for his hip pocket as if he were drawing a gun. No gun was found on Harris, but a knife was, and Thurmond claimed that Harris had brandished it again at his office. Testimony conflicted as to whether Harris had a gun. The case was prosecuted by State Attorney General W. A. Barber and former Confederate general Matthew Calbraith Butler, who had been hired by the victim's family. Ironically Butler was the former U.S. senator whom Thurmond, while a state legislator, had helped to defeat when he nominated Ben Tillman for the position.[19] Despite this high-powered team of prosecutors, it took only thirty minutes of deliberations for the jury to acquit Thurmond.[20] Commentary in the *State,* written or approved by editor N. G. Gonzales, reeked with eerily prophetic sarcasm about what effect being tried for murder and acquitted on the basis of a controversial self-defense argument would have on Thurmond's credibility as a prosecutor in future murder trials. The *State* observed, "Solicitor Thurmond can now return to his official duties in the prosecution of murderers with a spirit purified for the task and a reputation so enhanced by his experience as to make doubly effective his appeals to jurors to vindicate the law against murder."[21]

The close relationship between prosecutor Thurmond and Senator Ben Tillman was well established before Jim Tillman's murder trial and continued long afterward. In 1915 Senator Tillman persuaded President Woodrow Wilson to appoint Thurmond United States Attorney in South Carolina, despite Wilson's reluctance to appoint a man who had killed someone as chief federal law-enforcement official in the state, even if that man had been acquitted. Wilson preferred Francis Weston, the candidate pushed by the other South Carolina senator, Ellison D. "Cotton Ed" Smith. Tillman solved this dilemma by arranging for the district to be split in two so that both candidates could be appointed.[22] Strom Thurmond was fond of recalling that in 1908, when he was six, his father took him to meet Ben Tillman, and the gruff senator taught him how to give a firm handshake. The elder Thurmond was then serving as a political factotum for Ben Tillman in Edgefield. The story has the air of a laying-on-of-hands ceremony.[23]

Like many lawyers of that era, J. William Thurmond did not attend law school but prepared for the bar by reading law under the guidance of an attorney. His mentor was former governor John C. Sheppard. When Thurmond passed the bar examination, the state Supreme Court complimented him and several others on the high quality of their papers.[24] At the time of the Tillman trial, Thurmond was forty-one years old, and son Strom was less than a year old.[25] Thurmond's correspondence near the trial time indicates careful preparation for his cases. In addition to his work as Fifth Circuit solicitor, he had a private practice including cases involving the structure of railroad companies.[26] In 1930 Thurmond published *Thurmond's Key Cases,* a practitioner's manual of case citations arranged alphabetically by topic with one-sentence explanations appended to each.[27] A photograph published a year before the Tillman trial shows a vigorous man in early middle age with thinning hair on top compensated for by a full but neat coat-hanger-shaped mustache.[28] Earlier Thurmond had been a successful candidate in legislative and solicitors elections, but in a 1902 race for Congress he finished last in a field of three though he won in his home county of Edgefield.[29] The winning candidate was George W. Croft, now

J. William Thurmond in 1920. Courtesy of the South Caroliniana Library, University of South Carolina, Columbia, S.C.

a leading defense counsel for Jim Tillman—and along with law partner Jim Tillman, Thurmond's defense counsel in his 1897 murder trial.[30]

George Duncan Bellinger was the other lead prosecutor alongside Solicitor Thurmond. Thurmond took the lead in presenting the case against Tillman, and Bellinger took the lead in attacking the defense case. Hired by the Gonzales family to assist Thurmond,[31] Bellinger was a superbly qualified prosecutor. He had just concluded his term as state attorney general in 1902. He had served as a circuit solicitor, earning a reputation as a scourge of lynchers when he prosecuted the Broxton Bridge cases in 1896 in Walterboro and Aiken. In those cases prominent citizens, including a physician, formed a vigilante group that captured a young African American man, who—along with his elderly mother and his wife—was suspected of stealing a Bible and pulpit furniture from a church. The vigilantes tied the man to a buggy and dragged him to a site near the Broxton Bridge in Colleton County. Other vigilantes captured the man's mother and wife and brought them to the same site. The man and his mother were beaten to death, and his wife was severely injured. Although many wanted Bellinger to mount only a token prosecution leading to a certain acquittal, he put on a strong, convincing case in the face of threats of physical and political retaliation. The defense blamed the press—such as the *State,* which strongly condemned the beatings—for provoking this fierce prosecution effort. The defendants were acquitted in both the Walterboro and Aiken trials amid rumors that the real reason for the lynching was an earlier attempted rape of a white woman by the young man. Bellinger's courage and dedication impressed William Elliott Gonzales, who was one of the reporters covering the case for the *State,* and this probably led to the family's retaining Bellinger to assist Solicitor Thurmond.[32]

As a delegate to the 1895 constitutional convention, Bellinger was chairman of the jurisprudence committee and drafted most of article VI, which contained forward-looking provisions for settling disputes by arbitration, the collecting of laws into a systematic code, and a watered-down antilynching provision.[33] He was a supporter of Ben Tillman, and the *New York World* speculated that one reason he was retained as a prosecutor was the hope that his presence would defuse claims that the prosecution was directed at Ben through the guise of going after his nephew.[34] Despite his progressive positions in crafting the jurisprudence article, Bellinger's work in the 1895 convention showed that he shared the Tillmanite objective of depriving African Americans of the right to vote. In the convention he introduced amendments broadening the criminal convictions that would disqualify one from voting, adding several offenses that black people were considered, under stereotypical thinking, as likely to commit.[35]

It would be a mistake to assume that, because of his Tillmanite views, Bellinger would not be an effective prosecutor of James H. Tillman. His cross-examinations of defense witnesses were ferocious and unrelenting. Witnesses smarting from his attacks challenged him to meet them outside, where the battle would be more even. But his personal eminence and distinguished ancestry, stretching back to an early colonial landgrave, may have created an aura of pomposity that made Bellinger a favorite object of defense gibes in the trial. Bellinger was forty-seven at the time of the trial. A picture of him published five years later shows an august-looking personage with a well-tended beard and handlebar mustache and a bald scalp camouflaged by combed-over side hairs. He looks like a man who took care of his appearance but also like a determined man.[36] Because of his prosecution of public corruption and lynching cases, he was described by a noted attorney appraising lawyers he had known in more than fifty years of practice as, "a brilliant and courageous lawyer."[37]

These portraits of South Carolina attorneys general include Chief Justice Y. J. Pope, who denied bail to Tillman; D. A. Townsend, the judge who granted the change of venue motion for Tillman's trial; defense attorney O. W. Buchanan; and prosecutor G. Duncan Bellinger. Courtesy of the South Caroliniana Library, University of South Carolina, Columbia, S.C.

In the course of the Tillman trial an intense and sometimes rancorous rivalry developed between prosecutor Bellinger and lead defense attorneys Nelson and Croft. Nelson was already a distinguished lawyer by the time of the Tillman case and became even more so later. He had gained extensive experience in criminal cases during his nine years as Fifth Circuit solicitor, the position now held by Thurmond.[38] Nelson was lauded in a history of the Richland County Bar as "one of the best advocates who has ever practiced in Columbia."[39] His jury-trial technique was described as "simple, straightforward and earnest, without show or effort at oratory, and was very effective. From the beginning of the trial he followed the line of the famous [lawyer and U.S. senator Rufus] Choate—wooed the jury and sought by gaining their friendship to aid in winning the verdict for his client."[40]

In 1911 Nelson served as president of the South Carolina Bar Association. George C. Rogers, Jr., described Nelson's presidency as one focused on raising the educational level of the bar.[41] A picture published at that time shows a man with well-defined aquiline features, clean shaven with a full head of hair parted down the middle. He has a strong chin and a nose that is prominent and sharp but not out of proportion to the rest of his face. His eyes are alert, making a careful appraisal of what is before him. The *New York World* artist, W. H. Loomis, pictured Nelson at the trial as still wearing a full mustache. At that time he was forty-seven. Although he served in the legislature, on the governor's staff, and as solicitor, he was better known for his extensive private practice than for his accomplishments as an official.[42]

Defense counsel Croft perhaps held a psychological advantage over opponents Thurmond and Bellinger. Croft had defeated them both in the 1902 congressional election.[43] Having served with his current client as Thurmond's defense counsel in his 1897 murder trial, Croft was well aware of Thurmond's awkward position in prosecuting a defense attorney who had succeeded in getting him acquitted of a similar charge. The *Edgefield Advertiser* had praised the closing arguments made by Croft and another defense attorney, John C. Sheppard, in Thurmond's case as "magnificent."[44] At the time of the Tillman trial, Croft was at his professional peak. In 1901 he had been president of the South Carolina Bar Association.[45] Before his successful run for Congress, he had served in the South Carolina House of Representatives and Senate.[46] He had the kind of staunch, son-of-the-south credentials that appealed to South Carolina juries. As a student at the South Carolina Military Academy (the Citadel) during the closing days of the Civil War, he was mustered into the Confederate service

Leading defense counsel Patrick Henry Nelson. Courtesy of William S. Nelson II and the Nelson family.

along with other cadets. One hagiographic biographical entry hints with dark romanticism of his participation as captain of a paramilitary group during nocturnal raids in Aiken County as the white population fought to regain control during Reconstruction.[47] Vestiges of such irregular warfare found their way into his courtroom technique. In the course of the Tillman trial, he used a slash-and-burn, take-no-prisoners style in his cross-examinations. Under his leadership the defense often used ad hominem attacks on opposing counsel and hostile witnesses. Such blows assault a witness's character and personality more than the facts they present.

At the time of the trial, Croft was fifty-seven years old. Though he died only six months later, his actions during the trial were vigorous and aggressive. A photograph published at the time of his bar presidency in 1901 shows a man well into middle-age with gray hair parted down the middle and a large handlebar mustache swooping and curving around his cheeks. A drawing made by Loomis during the trial shows Croft wearing reading glasses, which have crept down to the end of his nose and give him the appearance of a stern owl. He is wearing a long frock coat of a type that seems more old-fashioned than attire worn by some other attorneys in the pictures.[48]

These are the leading players. Others will be described as they enter the stage.

Congressman George W. Croft, leading defense counsel. Courtesy of the South Caroliniana Library, University of South Carolina, Columbia, S.C.

4.

THE PROSECUTION CASE

Even before the first witness was called, there were strong signals that the focus of the case would not be on the details of the shooting but on challenges to the fairness of the *State*'s editorials attacking James H. Tillman and on whether they drove him to kill as the only way to stop them. Tillman's argument that he acted to defend his person became overshadowed by the claim that he acted to defend his honor against newspaper vilification. This was not a legally recognized justification for a killing.[1] The defense-of-his-person argument was a transparent pretext for the real justification, which was killing to redeem his honor. The defense had issued a subpoena ordering the victim's elder brother, Ambrose Gonzales, president of the State Company, to appear in court and bring with him the *State* articles and editorials referring to James H. Tillman from April 15, 1902, to September 30, 1902. These publications supposedly contained the attacks on Tillman that cost him the gubernatorial nomination in the 1902 Democratic primary, which would have guaranteed his election to the governorship, and they allegedly intruded into his personal life. Ambrose Gonzales was present and had the files with him. After some argument, they were turned over to the defense.[2]

The taking of testimony began in midafternoon on Monday, September 28. In most jurisdictions, the prosecution would have given an opening statement providing the jury with a framework for the state's evidence, which would have made each witness's testimony understandable by showing how it related to the overall case. This was not done in the Tillman case. Professor W. Lewis Burke has found that the opening statement, after having been inherited from

England in colonial times, was used through the antebellum period but began to fade after the Civil War and disappeared from South Carolina practice by 1890. Rather than an opening statement, the prosecution introduced the case to the jury by simply reading the indictment. The abandonment of the opening statement was supposed to modernize and streamline the trial process.[3] Instead it often denied the jury useful information regarding the relevancy of evidence to the overall shape of the case.[4] In the absence of an opening statement at the Tillman trial, it would have been helpful for the first witnesses to have been people with comprehensive views of the killing, who could have given the jury a good idea of what happened. This also did not occur.

Law-Enforcement Witnesses

The first witness called by the prosecution was the arresting officer, George Boland, a forty-eight-year-old veteran policeman. Jury selection went faster than expected, and it was probably easiest to obtain the law-enforcement witnesses on short notice.

Under questioning by Solicitor Thurmond, Boland testified that he did not witness the shooting but was nearby in the doorway of the city auditor's office, which was across the street from the corner of Main and Gervais where the shooting occurred.[5] His view was apparently blocked by streetcars surrounding the transfer station on that corner. But he heard the shot and saw a lady running from the scene. This prompted him to investigate. He saw James H. Tillman coming around one of the streetcars with a gun in his hand and going south toward the State House. Boland opened his coat to display his badge, addressed Tillman as "governor," and told him he would have to arrest him. Tillman said "all right sir," and cryptically added that he had "received Gonzales's message." Boland asked Tillman if he had shot Gonzales, and Tillman replied that he had shot and hit him.

When Boland reached for the pistol, Tillman "pulled back a little" and said he needed to keep the pistol to protect himself. Boland explained that he would protect him and would have to take the pistol as a necessary part of the arrest. As they were walking west down the Gervais Street hill toward the jail, nearby in the same block, former judge Osmund W. Buchanan, Tillman's brother-in-law, who later became one of his attorneys, came running up. Boland did not know Buchanan and thought he might be there to attack Tillman or himself. He stepped between Buchanan and Tillman, but when Tillman explained that

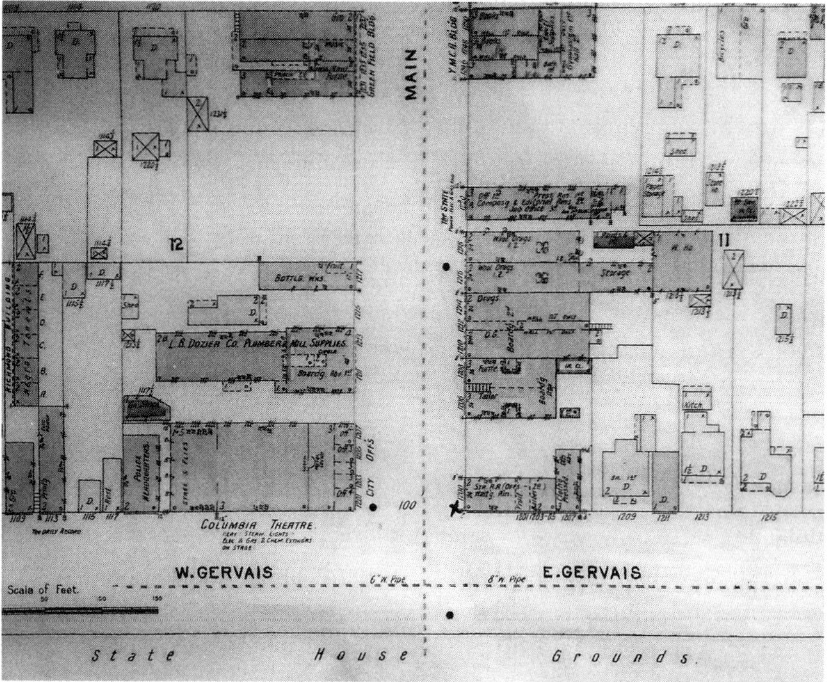

Detail from a 1904 insurance map of downtown Columbia, showing the locations of buildings at the time of the shooting. The "x" marks the spot where Gonzales was shot. Courtesy of the South Caroliniana Library, University of South Carolina, Columbia, S.C.

Buchanan was his brother-in-law, the three walked together to the jail. At the jail Tillman was searched. In addition to the pistol that Boland had taken from him, another was found in Tillman's hip pocket. Tillman was obviously not viewed as a threat at the station. He was escorted not to a cell but to an upstairs room and not by a policeman, but by the housekeeper much as if he were a guest in a private home.

When he was pressed for information about Gonzales, Boland said he saw two men helping the injured editor to walk northward back to the *State* office, which was nearby in the same block of Main Street. Under cross-examination by Patrick Nelson, Boland admitted that Tillman was cooperative, did not resist arrest, and put the pistol on safety as he handed it over to the officer. Nelson asked if Tillman did not at first want to keep the pistol because he was afraid of being "butchered." Boland agreed that Tillman wanted to keep the pistol for his protection but did not remember use of the word "butchered." The cross-examination did not elicit any evidence that Tillman was in fact in danger of being "butchered." Redirect examination by Thurmond brought out that Tillman did not volunteer the information that he had the second pistol that was discovered during the search at the jail. Boland's testimony was important. It contained Tillman's confession to having shot Gonzales and placed an armed Tillman near the scene of the shooting immediately after it occurred.

Thurmond continued to concentrate on the law-enforcement witnesses. He next called the Richland County sheriff, fifty-year-old William Henry Coleman.[6] The sheriff attempted to identify two pistols shown him as those taken from Tillman—and a bullet as the one used in the shooting—but Nelson was able to cast sufficient doubt on the chain of custody for the weapons and bullet

Prosecutors demonstrating the bullet hole in N. G. Gonzales's coat while it was worn by James Hoyt, Jr. Illustration by W. H. Loomis. *New York World,* September 27, 1903, 2. Courtesy of the American Newspaper Respository Collection, 1856–2004. David M. Rubenstein Rare Book and Manuscript Library, Duke University.

to make the identification ineffective. Why this evidence was offered to begin with is puzzling. In light of the witnesses who saw Tillman commit the killing and his confession to having committed it, introduction of these items was not necessary to link Tillman with the shooting. All Coleman's evidence accomplished was presenting the jury a picture of the prosecution trying to prove something and failing.[7]

The next round of prosecution evidence was also ineffective. A series of witnesses was offered to identify entry and exit holes made by the fatal bullet in the clothing Gonzales had worn at the time of the shooting. Here again, Nelson's cross-examination was able to point out gaps or confusion about the chain of custody, leaving open the possibility that someone had tampered with the holes during the time the evidence was not accounted for. The relevance of this evidence was not made clear at the time these witnesses were on the stand. However, it later appeared that it was believed relevant to a dispute over the angle of the shot, which was in turn germane to the question of whether Gonzales was shot while walking directly at Tillman in a confrontational manner, as claimed by the defense, or while he was turning aside to avoid Tillman, as claimed by the prosecution. However, it seems as though the more dispositive evidence on the question would be the location and nature of the wounds on the victim's body.[8]

The state had an unusually strong case because of the eyewitnesses to the shooting and Tillman's confession to Boland. Yet the prosecution led with some of the weakest evidence, and the defense was successful in creating doubts regarding it, some of which was of questionable pertinence.

Medical Witnesses

The highlight of the morning of that second day of the trial was the testimony of several doctors who had attended or operated on N. G. Gonzales. Their testimony indicated the nature of the victim's wounds, precluded the possibility that medical treatment had contributed to his death, and established that when Gonzales made his dying declaration describing the shooting from his vantage point, he believed he was dying. This fact gave his version credibility and made it admissible into evidence even though it was presented in a secondhand fashion by those who heard it. The first medical witness was Dr. Legrand Guerry, one of the first doctors to reach Gonzales as he lay upon a pile of newspapers in the *State* office, where he had been taken after the shooting. Later Dr. Guerry operated on Gonzales at the hospital. Several doctors with offices nearby arrived at the *State* offices shortly after Gonzales was taken there.

Before coming to Columbia, where he specialized in surgery and conducted many operations, Dr. Guerry had been head of the anatomy department at the Medical College of Georgia in Augusta. When he first saw Gonzales at the *State* office, he was "lying on the floor and apparently in a very desperate condition; he seemed to be in a condition of profound shock."[9] It looked as though "he would die right there"; he was "almost pulseless." Soon "every physician in the City of Columbia" was clustered around Gonzales. After a quick consultation, the doctors decided to have Gonzales transported to the Columbia Hospital, where Dr. Guerry operated on Gonzales at about 4:30 P.M. Guerry was assisted by doctors James H. McIntosh, Joseph J. Watson, Lindsay Peters, and James Woods Babcock. Dr. D. Strother Pope administered the anesthetic, and sixty-eight-year-old Dr. Benjamin Walter Taylor—dean of Columbia physicians and an expert on gunshot wounds from his days of Confederate service—was there to give advice and direction. The doctors found that the bullet had entered "two inches from the middle of the line and several inches below the left nipple. . . . It went over the seventh rib and came out in the flank here, about nine inches from the middle line and about eight inches from the nipple, about nine inches from the middle of the body."

The incision was made "in the median line, from about the tip of the breast bone . . . to below his navel." During the operation the doctors attempted to repair serious damage to Gonzales's stomach. Dr. Guerry assured the court that their methods met the highest standards of the medical profession. Gonzales lived from the time of the injury on January 15 until about 1:00 P.M. on the nineteenth. When asked what caused Gonzales's death, Dr. Guerry explained that "the wound upon the stomach, which at the time of the operation had not gone into the stomach, had sloughed out and it was open and the contents of the stomach were discharging itself into the peritoneal cavity, and that is what poisoned him." Then Thurmond wrapped up the cause of death in simpler terms understandable to the jury:

Q. So that produced his death.
A. He died from blood poisoning.
Q. Poison from what?
A. By the injury inflicted by the bullet.[10]

Gonzales's Dying Declarations: A Silenced Voice Speaks

Much of the defense's cross-examination of the medical witnesses was designed to block admission of the victim's dying declaration into evidence. Testimony about Gonzales's dying statement giving his version of the shooting is hearsay because the witness describing Gonzales's statement was not the person who originally made the statement; instead he was someone else repeating what Gonzales said, someone who did not see the shooting and gave a secondhand version of it. Hearsay usually cannot be considered in a trial, but there are exceptions that permit its use when circumstances exist to ensure its reliability.[11] At the time of the Tillman case, the principle was well established that, when a dying person who fully realized that he faced "impending" death made a statement, he did so under circumstances in which the motive to lie was removed and the motive to tell the truth was strongest.[12] The belief was that a person at the threshold of death and soon to be judged by his maker would not dare to lie.[13] A less religious person might still have been struck by the seriousness of impending death to the point that the desire to lie was erased. In an 1892 case that would have been influential at the time of the Tillman trial, the United States Supreme Court explained the basis for admitting dying declarations: "the certain expectation of almost immediate death will remove all temptation to falsehood." This guaranty of truth supposedly justified relaxation of the rule against using hearsay. In most cases the charge being tried had to be the declarant's death, and the focus of the dying declaration had to be "the circumstances of the declarant's death." But the rule was sometimes relaxed to permit the use of a dying declaration from someone other than the deceased whose death was the focus of the prosecution, if the dying statement was made by one whose demise arose from the same events.[14] The declarant must have based the statement on personal knowledge, and he must have been unavailable, through death or otherwise, to testify at the trial.

Gonzales made several dying declarations about the shooting, the most comprehensive of which was at the hospital just before the operation. To use these statements telling Gonzales's version of the shooting, the prosecution had to show that the statements were "made in extremity, when the party [was] at the point of death, and when every hope of this world [was] gone; when every motive to falsehood [was] silenced, and the mind [was] induced by the most powerful considerations to speak the truth."[15] The mental capabilities of a dying man at the time he gave the declaration had to be such that he was competent to give a reliable statement.[16] The doctors in the Tillman case were asked if Gonzales was aware of his impending death when he made the declarations; if he had truly abandoned hope of recovery when he consented to an operation that presumably the doctors and the patient did not consider a pointless exercise; and if he was lucid enough to give a reliable statement even though he had on several occasions been given morphine to ease his pain?

In his response to these queries, Dr. Guerry said that, at the time he first examined his patient, Gonzales thought he was near death. Guerry never heard Gonzales express any hope of recovery.[17] On cross-examination Nelson kept hammering away at this point: why perform an operation if you did not think it had a chance of leading to the patient's recovery? Dr. Guerry answered: "Simply in an effort to do something for him." There was no downside to such an operation Guerry pointed out. It did not add to the patient's pain or cause deterioration in his condition. Nelson also pressed Dr. Guerry with regard to the administration of morphine. The doctor admitted that it was common in cases of such gunshot wounds to use morphine to relieve pain. Given in excessive amounts, morphine could lead to the loss of consciousness, but Guerry did not use such amounts. His practice was to use the smallest dose that could achieve the relief of pain.

Continuing with his attempt to show that a morphine-dazed Gonzales was incapable of giving a lucid dying declaration, Nelson questioned Dr. Pope, who had told Thurmond on direct examination that Gonzales was already giving his declaration when Pope entered the room to administer the anesthetic for the operation. Gonzales was under the influence of morphine, but in Pope's words, the patient's mind was "fairly clear."[18] On the question of whether Gonzales and his doctors had abandoned all hope of recovery by the time Gonzales made his dying declaration, Pope's opinion was somewhat different from Guerry's. Under Nelson's persistent cross-examination, Pope admitted that he would not have participated in the operation unless it offered some hope. Nelson asked: "You would not carve a man up for pleasure unless you had some hope from it?" Pope replied: "Unless we had some hope of favorable results." The implication was that, if one of the doctors entertained hope, then perhaps the patient in agreeing to the operation entertained hope. But later Pope added to the confusion by contradicting himself. Under questioning by the solicitor, Pope testified that, when he saw Gonzales at the hospital just before giving him the anesthetic, he thought death was imminent: "I thought he was going to die on the table. I dreaded to give him the anesthetic." Pope added, "I had no hope of his recovery." Viewed in this light, the operation was a desperate measure, performed without hope but in a conscientious attempt to do everything possible. Gonzales's state of mind when he made the declaration was the crucial one. But presumably it would be influenced by the attitude of his doctors. When he was lying on the floor at the *State* office, prior to being taken to the hospital, Gonzales answered a question from Dr. Pope by saying "I am killed."[19] Part of the controversy was whether this lack of hope for recovery continued at the time Gonzales made his declaration, or had he become more optimistic because of the approaching operation. Another dimension of the controversy was whether death could truly be said to be "impending" when the hospital statement was made nearly four days before death.

Dr. Lewis Allen (L. A.) Griffith was also questioned on the second day of the trial. He gave evidence of Gonzales's condition shortly after the shooting. The first doctor to arrive at the *State* office, Griffith found Gonzales lying on the floor and located the entrance and exit wounds made by the bullet. Gonzales, Griffith said, was "in a state of profound collapse" and "suffering intensely."[20] He gave Gonzales strychnine, nitroglycerine, and whiskey and "morphine hypodermically." The patient revived somewhat after this treatment, without which, Griffith said, he would have died then. A later medical witness, Dr. Benjamin Walter Taylor, explained the purpose of such treatment. The strychnine was given "to stimulate the nerves and to stimulate the heart's action, and the breathing, etc."[21] The whiskey was also a stimulant. The nitroglycerine was given to open up the smaller blood vessels, which became constricted by shock, and to stimulate the heart. Despite the morphine, Dr. Griffith believed Gonzales's mind was clear.[22] Dr. Taylor testified that the morphine was used to alleviate the pain and "remedy in part the shock, it is a stimulant."[23] On direct examination by prosecutor Andrew Crawford, Taylor was asked a question relevant to the admissibility of the dying declaration: "Then, what effect would morphine have on his thinking power? A. It would improve it. Q. Clarify it? A. Yes Sir."

Dr. James H. McIntosh was the chief assistant to Dr. Guerry in treating Gonzales. He arrived at the *State* office at about 2:45 P.M. on January 15, about an hour after the shooting. The patient was suffering from intense shock and internal hemorrhage. McIntosh rode with Gonzales in the ambulance on the way to the hospital. Although the precise time is not known, the ambulance trip must have occurred shortly before Gonzales made his dying declaration in the hospital. Thus Gonzales's state of mind and condition at that time were highly relevant to the admissibility of the hospital declaration. During the trip

Gonzales asked McIntosh, "'Doctor I want you to tell me frankly whether I am mortally wounded or not.' [McIntosh replied] Yes, Mr. Gonzales, I am afraid you are mortally wounded, and he simply said 'yes, I think the fellow got me' and with that he covered up his face."[24] These comments by Gonzales, together with his earlier remark to Dr. Pope that "I am killed," furnish strong evidence that not long before his dying declaration in the hospital, Gonzales had begun to expect imminent death and had given up hope of recovery.

Dr. McIntosh's testimony was also relevant to whether morphine had rendered Gonzales incapable of making a clear statement. McIntosh described Gonzales's mental state as "perfectly calm and cool and clear—I never saw a man more so in his extremely grave condition and his mind was perfectly clear." Death came on Monday afternoon, January 19, as a result of "septic poisoning" "from the bullet wounds in the stomach." In addition to consulting several local physicians, Guerry and McIntosh called in Dr. Walker Gill Wylie, a leading specialist in abdominal surgery from New York, who had been raised in South Carolina and who came to Columbia for a hurried visit.[25]

Dr. Clarendon Witherspoon (C. W.) Barron was Gonzales's brother-in-law. The editor had married Barron's only sister, Lucy (or Lucie). Barron was called to the hospital by another relative, William Elliott, an attorney who later assisted in the Tillman prosecution. Having arrived at the hospital before the anesthetic was administered and before Gonzales made his dying declaration, Barron gave testimony that nailed down Gonzales's state of mind just before he made his statement. Barron asked, "Do you understand N. G. that you will probably die? A. He says, 'I do.'"[26] Gonzales expressed no hope of recovery. Barron testified that present with him in Gonzales's room at the time he made his dying declaration were Dr. James W. Babcock, *News and Courier* correspondent August Kohn, and *State* staff members James Hoyt, Jr., and Robert Lathan. Lathan and Babcock recorded the statement. At the conclusion of the declaration, someone in the room, Barron did not remember who, asked Gonzales "if he made this as his death statement. His answer was, 'I do.'"[27]

Judge Gary admitted two dying declarations into evidence as part of the prosecution's case.[28] Both were taken on January 15, 1903. The first was given to twenty-six-year-old Hoyt at the *State* office about half an hour after the shooting. The second was the declaration Gonzales made in the hospital just before he was given the anesthetic for the operation. Judge Gary defined the requirements for admitting a dying declaration into evidence: "First, the party must be in extremis ['near the point of death']: second, he must believe he is in extremis, and be absolutely without hope of recovery: the subject of the charge must be the death of the defendant, and the subject of the declaration must be the circumstances attending the killing."[29] The judge ruled that death did not have to occur immediately after the declaration.[30] That is, the fact that Gonzales lived for nearly four days after making his declaration did not render it inadmissible if he feared imminent death when he gave the statement.

Hoyt said that the declaration made to him was given by Gonzales while the editor was lying on the office floor. Hoyt did not recall whether anyone else was present,[31] and he did not take the statement down in writing. Gonzales told Hoyt that he had left the *State* office on his way to dinner. He was walking along Main Street toward the capitol and had nearly reached the streetcar transfer station when he saw Jim Tillman, who was accompanied by two men Gonzales did not recognize. There were several people on the corner of Gervais and Main Streets, and Gonzales saw that, if he continued to walk along the edge of the pavement, he would "brush against" Tillman's group; "to avoid them he cut diagonally across the pavement towards the corner of the transfer station, and as he was going across he saw Tillman pull a big pistol and shoot. He said that he turned and faced him and exclaimed, 'shoot again, you coward. You have killed me.'" Tillman held the gun on him but did not shoot again. Gonzales recalled that "just as he shot—just about the time Tillman shot—that he, Tillman, exclaimed, 'I have done what you said,' or 'I have taken you at your word' or something like that."[32] Gonzales said two gentlemen helped him back to his office. On cross-examination Hoyt was questioned about the accuracy of his or Gonzales's memory in saying that Gonzales did not recognize the men with Tillman. They were state senators Thomas Talbird and George W. Brown, prominent politicians who would probably have been well known to Gonzales.

Dr. Babcock heard most of the declaration Gonzales made in his hospital room and took detailed but not verbatim notes.[33] In his testimony Babcock was allowed to refer to his notes, and both his oral testimony and the written notes were introduced into evidence. As reported by Babcock, the dying declaration Gonzales gave in the hospital is similar to that he gave to Hoyt in the *State* office, but the two differ in some respects. Though Gonzales had told Hoyt that he did not recognize either of the men with Tillman, in the hospital version, Gonzales said he recognized Senator Talbird, a close friend of Tillman. According to Babcock, rather than saying he was going to dinner, Gonzales said, "I started for the State House as usual." He again said that as he approached the Tillman group, "I cut diagonally to the left, intending to turn the corner into

Gervais street, which I could have done without touching the inside man." This move, which Gonzales took to avoid a confrontation with Tillman, was later used by the prosecution to undercut defense claims that Gonzales approached Tillman so aggressively that he had to shoot in self-defense. As Babcock continued recounting the dying declaration, he noted how Gonzales said that, when he "got on the turn two or three feet from the exact corner," Tillman pulled a pistol and shot him. In this second statement Gonzales described the impact of the shot, which he had not described in the first declaration: "the shock threw me around against the pillar on Main Street." Gonzales then faced Tillman and called him a coward. Tillman replied, "I have taken you at the word." Gonzales did not know what this meant but thought it might refer to something he had said in an editorial during the campaign. He had not sent Tillman a message. Tillman made his statements after he fired, and Gonzales said he had not expected to meet Tillman. The last time Gonzales had seen Tillman was two days earlier in the State House lobby. According to Gonzales, "The thing was finished as far as I was concerned."[34]

These last statements were important to the prosecution, which could use them to counter defense insinuations that Gonzales was continuing his feud with Tillman, that he had sent threatening messages to Tillman, and that he roamed the streets looking for Tillman, ready to fight him on sight, thus making it necessary for Tillman to shoot in self-defense. The discrepancies between the declarations given to Hoyt and Babcock were slight, but they did cast some doubt on the accuracy of Gonzales's memory in the aftermath of such severe trauma. However, the two declarations agreed on the essential points: Tillman had shot Gonzales, who had tried to avoid the confrontation by turning away.

Later the defense scored points during closing arguments by pointing out that a superior version of the hospital declaration, the verbatim stenographic record taken by Lathan, had not been introduced by the prosecution. Instead it had used the version taken down by Dr. Babcock, who recorded the essence of the statement but did not record it word for word. The defense intimated that the superior Lathan version had been suppressed by the prosecution because it probably contained material damaging to the prosecution's case, such as statements by Gonzales showing Tillman had good reason to fear him and act in self-defense.[35] The prosecution explained that it used Dr. Babcock's version because of his great reputation in the community and his lack of favoritism toward Gonzales, whereas it feared that Mr. Lathan's version would be dismissed as a biased document produced by Gonzales's secretary.

Lathan was at the beginning of a distinguished journalistic career. He won a 1925 Pulitzer Prize for his editorial "The Plight of the South," written while he was editor of the *Charleston News and Courier.* In his history of that newspaper, Herbert Ravenel Sass said of Lathan that "all who worked with him felt and respected his strength and high integrity which seemed to be actually visible upon him." But in 1903 Lathan was a twenty-two-year-old secretary, who had worked directly under Gonzales and would be expected to take the side of his late employer.[36] Lathan's transcribed stenographic version of Gonzales's hospital statement was submitted as part of his affidavit in the bail proceeding. It was printed in the *State,* and its contents were widely known.[37] Lathan's version did not contradict Babcock's. It did not contain any material exculpatory of Tillman or supporting his claims of self-defense. If anything, Lathan's version demonstrated even more emphatically Gonzales's attempt to turn aside to avoid the confrontation and his adamant denial of having sent any threat or other message to Tillman.[38]

In addition to giving testimony with regard to the nature of the victim's wounds, his treatment, his cause of death, and his mental state relevant to the dying declaration, medical witnesses were asked questions involving forensic science that were beyond their expertise. Perhaps because of the aura of scientific authority they projected, they were viewed as universal experts. Dr. James Woods Babcock was a Harvard-educated physician, but as head of the state mental institution, his practice did not involve gunshot wounds. Nonetheless he was asked questions that fell more in the domain of the forensic scientist. One hypothetical question described the entrance and exit holes made in a victim's body, and asked him to deduce from that the relative positions of the assailant firing the gun and the victim. The paucity of information provided in the hypothetical meant that even a forensic expert's answer would have been pure conjecture. But Dr. Babcock was allowed to answer, probably because his knowledge of forensic medicine, while not extensive, was far superior to that of the jurors, and his testimony might assist them in reaching an accurate verdict. Babcock concluded that Gonzales was in the act of "turning" when he was struck, thus supporting the prosecution's contention that Gonzales was not charging aggressively toward Tillman but was moving aside to avoid a confrontation.[39]

Somewhat more useful, and also serving the prosecution's efforts to prove that Gonzales was shot from the side while turning away from Tillman, was the testimony of Dr. Benjamin Walter Taylor. First the prosecution sought to show he was qualified to give the answer by eliciting from him the statement that he had vast experience with gunshot wounds and the behavior of firearms because he had served as medical director of the cavalry in the Army of Northern Virginia during the Civil War. Solicitor Thurmond asked hypothetically:

> Q. If a man be shot and the bullet strikes him two inches to the right of the medial line, and some inches below the nipple, about six inches below the nipple, and ranging downward and backward, making the exit about here (indicating), in your opinion what was the position of the object or the agency that produced that injury?
> A. . . . the pistol must have been about the side and rather inclined so as to throw the ball more outward down here, inclined that way (illustrating).
> Q. From the side?
> A. Yes sir.
> Q. Well then an injury of that kind I have described to you in your opinion which way was the shot from?
> A. Must necessarily have been from the side.
> Q. Could it have been shot in front?
> A. Impossible.[40]

The last remarks refuted in advance Tillman's later testimony that Gonzales was charging directly toward him when he shot him.[41]

One medical witness was cross-examined by the defense on a matter having no relation to his actions or knowledge as a physician. On cross-examination for the defense, Nelson asked Dr. Barron, whether or not he had threatened to kill James H. Tillman if Tillman were acquitted? Barron emphatically denied that he had. Nelson tried again. Had not Barron boasted in a Columbia club that he would kill Tillman if he were released on bail? Barron again denied the allegation.[42] Despite these denials, the mere asking of the question helped paint a picture of Tillman, not as an assailant, but as a victim still struggling to stay alive.

Attacking a Witness as a Religious Outsider

Like Dr. Babcock, Dr. Barron and several other medical witnesses, August Kohn was present in Gonzales's hospital room when he gave his dying declaration, but Kohn arrived a little late, after Gonzales had begun stating his version of the shooting. Kohn was not a passive observer; he asked Gonzales questions. Manager of the *News and Courier*'s Columbia bureau and a longtime friend of

Gonzales's,[43] Kohn was in the unique position of being both a witness in and a reporter of the trial for his newspaper. Gonzales had helped launch Kohn's career in 1889, when Gonzales was manager of the *News and Courier*'s Columbia bureau. When Gonzales was stricken with typhoid fever and was unable to run the bureau, he appointed Kohn, a recent graduate of South Carolina College, to act in his stead. Kohn became known for the accuracy of his coverage of political and business news. He had clashed with Governor Ben Tillman during the April 1894 Darlington "rebellion" over the governor's heavy-handed enforcement of the dispensary laws. When the governor issued orders to militia officers to deny Kohn access to the telegraph lines, Kohn had been able to continue his candid reports by arranging for his own private instruments.[44] In an affectionate memoir of her father, Kohn's daughter described his circumvention of the military control of the telegraph facilities: "he told about driving a fast horse to Florence under cover of darkness, and of how a 'blind tiger' [unlicensed] telegraph was manipulated for him by some friends. [Kohn said] 'General Richburg took my first blind tiger instrument as a souvenir.'" Consequently Kohn had to go to an unguarded telegraph office in a nearby town to send his stories to his paper.[45] N. G. and Ambrose Gonzales, who were covering the Darlington riots for the *State,* had resorted to their own ingenious methods to get their coverage into print.[46] The Tillmans never forgave Kohn for outsmarting the governor in the Darlington episode, and when he appeared as a prosecution witness in Jim Tillman's murder trial, they were eager to take revenge. The most important fruits of Kohn's direct examination by the prosecution resulted from questions he put to N. G. Gonzales in his hospital room about whether or not he had sent a bellicose message to Tillman in the days immediately before the shooting.[47] Kohn's account of Gonzales's answers refuted defense claims that Gonzales had sent a threat to Tillman that made him interpret a hand movement by Gonzales as going for a gun. This blow to their case angered defense counsel, who were eager to cross-examine Kohn. But before cross-examination, counsel for the prosecution and defense agreed to interrupt Kohn's testimony so that he could observe the Jewish holiday of Yom Kippur, for which he was fasting.[48] This postponement for the religious holiday does not appear to have been controversial and was handled as a routine matter out of respect for the Jewish religion. This gesture of religious tolerance is what makes the events that transpired during the cross-examination so surprising.

During cross-examination defense attorney Croft tried to get Kohn to say he knew that N. G. Gonzales hated Jim Tillman and that he had often expressed

August Kohn, the *Charleston News and Courier* reporter who witnessed Gonzales's dying declaration. Courtesy of the South Caroliniana Library, University of South Carolina, Columbia, S.C.

that hatred in wounding language. Kohn admitted that he had read the Gonzales editorials that were highly critical of Jim Tillman as a candidate and public official, but Kohn insisted he did not know what Gonzales's personal opinion of Tillman was. He said that, while he remembered the generally negative nature of the editorials, he did not recall specific language, such as whether or not the editorials called Jim Tillman a liar, drunkard, and gambler.[49]

Croft continued trying to get Kohn to say he knew that Gonzales hated Jim Tillman. The defense believed such a statement would convince the jury that the defendant had reason to fear harm from Gonzales. When Kohn refused to give the desired answer, Croft went on the attack, accusing Kohn of being evasive, of not being manly because his answers were not frank. Croft's tactics quickly turned ugly. He attempted to browbeat Kohn by accusing him of comporting himself in a slippery, weaseling manner. He told Kohn, "you shan't wiggle out of it." He told him: "Take your hands off your knees and sit up straight like a man." He repeatedly ordered him to "answer like a man." These were not questions; they were abusive personal assaults. The cross-examination reached its nadir in the following exchange between Croft and Kohn, when Kohn again said he had no personal knowledge that Gonzales hated Jim Tillman:

Q. Do you swear that before God and the Living Christ?
A. Before God I do.
Q. Do you swear before Christ?
A. I have the right to swear as I please.
The Court: He has the right to respect his religious beliefs.
Mr. Bellinger [a prosecutor]: Mr. Croft knows he is of the Jewish faith and should not ask him that.
The Court: I do not think that proper.
Mr. Croft: Then I won't press it.

Kohn had been sworn like every other witness without his hat.

A. I have a right to swear without my hat. It is not orthodox to wear the hat all the time.
Q. Let's leave the hat alone.
A. You brought it up

Mr. Croft: I will drop it.

Q. (By Mr. Croft) Answer like a man; don't put any ifs in it.

John Marshall, the *News and Courier*'s other reporter at the trial, was sharply critical of Croft's tactics.[50] One of the headlines accompanying his story said: "Amazing Effort of a Lawyer to Browbeat a Gentleman on the Stand." Another headline labeled Croft's cross-examination "A Shameful Performance." Marshall said that Croft raised "his voice to a high pitch" and "shouted his queries to the witness." Concluding that "it will scarcely be denied by the dispassionate observer that Col. Croft went too far," Marshall charitably observed that perhaps Croft had just momentarily lost his sense of propriety because of the partisan nature of the trial and the heavy responsibility of providing Tillman with a vigorous defense as he was "fighting for his client's life." However, viewed in the context of the rest of the trial, Croft's treatment of Kohn appears to have been more a part of deliberate strategy than a momentary emotional outburst. Nearly two weeks after Croft's cross-examination of Kohn, both Croft and Patrick Nelson in their closing arguments stood by Croft's tactics as being justified by Kohn's alleged evasiveness.[51] Croft never apologized for his battering-ram style, and Nelson said such an apology would not be warranted in view of Kohn's recalcitrance. Croft did attempt to soften the anti-Semitic nature of his asking Kohn to swear by "the Living Christ" by using a portion of his closing argument to express his support for freedom of religion and his respect for Jewish cultural contributions.[52]

However, it can still be argued that Croft called attention to Kohn's Jewishness as a signal to the jury that the witness was not a Christian and thus not worthy of belief. This "not one of us" strategy made several appearances later in the trial. Jim Tillman referred to N. G. Gonzales as a "wily Spaniard," a hot bloodied Latin who was not a true son of the Old South. A prosecution witness was impeached for his Republican political affiliation, which meant that he was not a true white man and therefore not one of us and not worthy of belief. A key female witness for the prosecution was stereotyped before the all-male jury as a hysterical woman incapable of remembering the scene immediately before the shooting. Under the defense's antipress strategy, Kohn's outsider status was made even more obvious by his being a newspaperman.

Despite his rough treatment, Kohn fared well on the witness stand. Despite Croft's shouting and hostile posturing, Kohn did not cower under cross-examination. He conceded no points; he left the witness stand with his reputation for accuracy intact. Even though he was a relatively young man, thirty-five at the time of the trial, he was already a veteran reporter who had long ago received his baptism of fire in the no-holds-barred world of South Carolina politics.[53]

Evidence of Premeditation

Early in the trial the prosecution presented several witnesses whose testimony helped show that the shooting was a premeditated one, committed with malice aforethought. This was an attempt to demonstrate that the killing was planned rather than a defensive reaction to a threat at the moment it arose. But sometimes the evidence could be seen in two ways. What may look like malicious planning to kill to one person, may look like prudent defensive planning against a continuing threat to another.

Mr. William F. Stieglitz testified that he was a gunsmith with a store on Main Street in Columbia. When he was shown the magazine pistol taken from Tillman, the one that had been used in the shooting, Stieglitz said that he had seen that pistol, or one like it, a day earlier, when Mr. Fred Dominick brought it into his store. A twenty-six-year-old Newberry lawyer and former legislator, Dominick was a close political ally of James H. Tillman and Cole Blease, whose law partner and campaign manager Dominick later became. Dominick went on to serve in Congress from 1917 to 1933. On the day he visited Stieglitz's shop, Dominick was seeing that his friend Jim Tillman's gun was in good working order. He brought the gun in between five and six o'clock in the afternoon and tried to buy a new magazine because the old one was not working. Stieglitz told Dominick he did not have a new one, but he could repair the old one. He did so, and testified that Dominick picked up the repaired magazine between nine and ten on the morning of the shooting.[54]

Dr. Samuel Theron Dejarnette (S. T. D.) Lancaster, a member of the legislature representing Spartanburg County, testified that on the day before the shooting, shortly after the House adjourned at about one or two o'clock, he saw Tillman standing and talking to someone in front of the State House across from the transfer station at the corner of Main and Gervais Streets. Lancaster said he saw a pistol sticking out of Tillman's coat pocket. On cross-examination Patrick Nelson tried to get Lancaster to admit that he could have seen something other than a pistol, such as a ruler or a bottle, in Tillman's pocket, but Lancaster would not budge from his statement that it was a pistol.[55] The cumulative picture is of Tillman being armed that first week of the legislative session.

Another member of the legislature, Walker Byron (W. B.) Gause of Florence, said that on the first day of the legislative session, a few days before the shooting, he, Tillman, and other legislators were walking down Main Street near the skyscraper, and everyone was talking about what hotel they were staying in during the session. Tillman grimly joked that he told his wife before he left for Columbia, that he had just stuffed a bunch of editorials from the *State* in his pocket and that he guessed he might be stopping at the "penitentiary." The prosecution's implication was that Tillman was planning a criminal act against the author of the editorials, one that might result in Tillman's imprisonment. The defense read a different meaning into it: the paper was calling him a thief and if it had its way, he would be stopping at the penitentiary.[56]

R. G. Arthur claimed to have overheard Tillman plotting revenge against Gonzales, whose editorials Tillman blamed for his loss of the 1902 governor's race. Arthur testified that while he was in Grice's Livery Stable in Edgefield not long after the election, probably in October 1902, he heard Tillman vowing to Major Dick Anderson and others that "if there was any way he could get at him [Gonzales]," he would. Nelson's cross-examination, however, seriously undercut the effectiveness of Arthur's testimony by forcing Arthur to admit that he just heard fragments of the conversation when walking past the group. Further doubt was cast on Arthur's assertions by another witness, R. M. Broadwater, who contradicted Arthur's claim that Major Anderson was in the group listening to Tillman.[57]

But Arthur was not the only witness to hear Tillman, months prior to the killing, plotting to get Gonzales. One witness had Tillman brooding bitterly in the summer of 1902 over the possibility that he must kill Gonzales. The witness was Charles J. Terrell, editor of the *Johnston Monitor,* who had been walking down the street in Edgefield with Tillman not long before the start of the 1902 gubernatorial campaign. Tillman said that "he was going to run for governor and was going to be elected, and if that—referring to Mr. Gonzales with several pretty severe oaths—attacked him like he had been doing that he was going down there and kill him like a dog."[58] Terrell said he argued with Tillman, telling him that it was "wrong in principle and wrong in every way" to kill and that instead he should "go down there and tackle him man and man." In other words it was all right to fight but not to kill. But Tillman said "he was going down there and give him no more show that [*sic*] he would a mad dog."

But Terrell was not through. He recounted a second incident in which he heard Tillman boast of plans to kill Gonzales. Some months later after the election, while Terrell and Tillman were on a train going to Columbia, Terrell was talking to railroad flagman O. D. Black. Tillman joined them, and the conversation turned to Gonzales. Tillman spoke to Black about a previous conversation they had had about what he called "the Gonzales matter." In describing the conversation, Terrell was careful to point out that he was recounting its substance and not giving a verbatim version. He recalled Tillman saying to the flagman, "Black old boy, I am going to do what I said about that old fellow. I am going to put an end to his way of abusing me, slandering me, etc. like that." Terrell still was not done. He told of a third incident, this one in Columbia. Terrell was standing in front of the attorney general's office talking to Attorney General Ulysses X. Gunter, Jr., Secretary of State Jesse T. Gantt, and Ebbie J. Watson, a reporter and city editor of the *State.* When Tillman joined the group, he told Watson his boss was a "scoundrel—with some oaths before it—in that building yonder, [that he] had attacked him," and been "unjust" to him, and "he had had as much of it as he was going to have and he made some demonstrative threat." Tillman made it clear that he wanted Watson to pass the threats along to Gonzales, but Watson refused. On cross-examination defense attorney Croft attacked Terrell as not worthy of belief because he too had committed the cardinal sin of opposing Tillman in his editorial columns and had been at loggerheads with him in a legal dispute over an insurance claim. Croft also tried to get Terrell to recast his description of Tillman's threats against Gonzales as defensive in nature, action he would take only if Gonzales forced him to take it. Terrell did not take the bait. That was not the way he remembered it.[59]

Testimony that had Tillman forming plans to kill Gonzales months before the shooting—and not because Gonzales was posing a physical danger to Tillman but because Gonzales had been "slandering" Tillman in his editorials—struck at the heart of Tillman's self-defense claims. When the defense put on its case, it had to launch a major effort to discredit such testimony.

Not all the damaging testimony depicting Tillman's plans for killing Gonzales came from those the defense could characterize as Tillman's enemies. Dr. Edward Clarkson ("Ned") Adams, a twenty-seven-year-old physician, had been a warm friend and political follower of Jim Tillman. Journalist William Watts (W. W.) Ball described Adams as "an athletic appearing young man" who had served under Tillman when he had been lieutenant colonel and then colonel of the First South Carolina Regiment in 1898, during Spanish-American War.[60] Adams had several conversations with Tillman and other supporters in hotel rooms in August 1902 during the closing days of the gubernatorial campaign. Adams and other Tillman followers were deeply concerned about "some articles written by Mr. Gonzales" that were considered so venomous that they could not be ignored.[61] Adams testified that "I told him that if he wished to be governor of South Carolina he would have to fight Mr. Gonzales; that the men who were supporting him expected him to defend himself." Since this was in the context of a discussion of critical newspaper articles, it was a suggestion that Tillman defend himself against their words. There was no mention of a physical threat from Gonzales, but Tillman was told to defend himself by fighting Gonzales. The suggestion was for a fair fight, not a killing. Tillman's response was bizarre. He said fighting Gonzales "won't do, because I am Lieutenant Governor and will be impeached; but you boys need not worry, for by God, I will snuff his light out with this (indicating)." When he made the "'snuff his light out with this" remark, Tillman was "taking his pistol from his grip [travelling bag]." Adams testified that after displaying the weapon, Tillman said, "I have walked the streets every time I have been here [in Columbia] in the hope of meeting Mr. Gonzales." This evidence of stalking severely undermined Tillman's self-defense strategy. Adams recalled that in one of the hotel-room strategy caucuses, someone read an editorial from the *State,* "which spoke of him [Tillman] as a blackguard and a liar, and I don't know what else, and another speaking of him challenging or fighting—I think Mr. Gonzales [for accusing him of engaging in] 'mock theatricals.'" To which Tillman replied, "He can call it mock theatricals if he wishes to, but I will make it the God damndest tragedy that ever happened in South Carolina."[62] Perhaps this was part of Tillman's motivation—an emotional need to create a tragic spectacle of historic dimensions in which he would play the leading role.

Perhaps the strangest statement Tillman made in the hotel-room sessions was his comment that he could not fight Gonzales because that would lead to his impeachment, but he would kill Gonzales ("snuff his light out") instead. These words seem to indicate that Tillman did not anticipate any punishment for murder from a jury of his legal peers but did fear punishment by impeachment by the legislature, which could lead to his removal from office for fighting. Oddly enough, Tillman must not have considered murder an impeachable offense.

It is an odd set of laws that makes a perpetrator fear sanctions for a lesser crime more than those for murder. Tillman was no doubt aware that the state constitution provided for removal from office and ineligibility to hold further offices if an officer engaged in a duel. In fact the constitution required an incoming officer to take an oath that he had not engaged in a duel during a specified period of time.[63] Tillman must have thought that even a fistfight with Gonzales might have been viewed as a duel requiring his removal by impeachment from his office of lieutenant governor and that such a fight would also render him ineligible to assume the governorship. He must have assumed that a murder as a unilateral act would not trigger the antidueling provisions. If this was indeed his view, as his remarks seem to indicate, it is tortuous logic designed to validate his already formed intent to kill rather than fight Gonzales. Surely murder would justify impeachment of an office holder, but the grounds for impeachment were vague in the 1895 Constitution.[64]

Later the defense called Coleman (Cole) L. Blease, who had been present at the same hotel-room strategy sessions as Adams during the closing days of the 1902 gubernatorial campaign.[65] Blease had known Jim Tillman since they were at Georgetown University together. Thirty-five at the time of the trial, Blease later became an important and controversial figure in South Carolina politics, serving as governor and United States senator. His core constituency was mill workers, to whom he appealed by playing on their economic resentment against the middle and upper classes and their racial resentment against black people for their potential economic competition. Yet he opposed regulatory legislation that might improve the plight of such workers on the grounds that such laws would interfere with their freedom to bargain for employment conditions without government interference. By the time of the Tillman trial, Blease had served in the State House of Representatives and unsuccessfully sought higher office, including a run for lieutenant governor in 1900, which pitted him against his friend Jim Tillman. Blease also justified lynching as sometimes necessary to protect the sanctity of white women. A biographer has attributed Blease's attractiveness to mill workers to "his flamboyant style and his unmatched stump-speaking ability."[66] A photograph of Blease as a young man shows a fierce, rakish appearance, characterized by a full flamboyant mustache.[67] Most photographs show him with a menacing scowl and penetrating eyes, as if he were trying to stare down an opponent.[68] These combative attributes found their way into his testimony in the Tillman trial.

Blease had his own grievances against N. G. Gonzales and the *State* newspaper. In 1892, early in Blease's political career, the *State* accused him of being so completely lacking in principles that he would "reverse his position on any question when proper inducements are held out." Blease replied that "the *State* circulated lies as false as the hinges that swung on the gates of hell." The *State*'s slashing reply insinuated that Blease may have plagiarized his reference to "the gates of hell" since an earlier act of plagiarism had created a scandal that forced him to drop out of the University of South Carolina. After such clashes, Blease could be expected to see the Gonzales-Tillman dispute from his friend's point of view. Throughout his political career, especially his governorship (1911–15), Blease fought the press with unquenchable anger and sought to curb its power. This attitude undoubtedly influenced his testimony.[69]

Under questioning by Patrick Nelson, Blease confirmed Adams's testimony about the topics of conversation in the August 1902 hotel-room caucus but turned their import upside down.[70] Referring to his memorandum book to refresh his memory, Blease testified that there had been hotel-room strategy sessions on August 20 and 21, 1902, in Columbia while the candidates were in town for speeches at the opera house. Blease also confirmed that Tillman had said he would "snuff" Gonzales's "light out" with "this," indicating the pistol he had just taken out of his grip. But the context was entirely different from that described in Adams's statement. According to Blease, Tillman had made such actions contingent on an attack by Gonzales, saying that "you boys needn't be uneasy about this, *if* he undertakes to attack me I will snuff his light out with this [the pistol]."[71] Like Adams, Blease stated that a collection of *State* editorials insulting Tillman had been read aloud to the group. One accused Tillman of engaging in "mock-theatricals" by challenging Gonzales to a duel. Here again, Blease put a conditional, self-defense spin on Tillman's reply, contrasting Adams's description, which had Tillman sounding more aggressive. According to Blease, Tillman said, "*If* he attempts to carry out one of his threats I will make it the God damndest tragedy that has ever happened in South Carolina."[72] Blease also recast in a more favorable light the aggressive posture in which Adams had pictured Tillman, describing him as an armed predator stalking the streets of Columbia searching for Gonzales. According to Blease, Tillman had merely stated that he was not afraid to walk the streets of Columbia minding his own business. He had said nothing about prowling the streets hoping for a confrontation with Gonzales. On cross-examination, prosecutor

G. Duncan Bellinger asked Blease about the pistol Tillman had flourished when he was boasting about "snuffing" Gonzales's "light out." Blease denied that Tillman carried a pistol with him on the campaign trail. Bellinger pounced on this and asked how the pistol got into Tillman's hotel room in his grip? Blease evaded answering by claiming his rights under the state constitution. Judge Gary interpreted this as invoking his right against self-incrimination and ruled that Blease did not have to answer.[73] But Blease was more forthcoming in the following line of questions:

Q. You don't know whose pistol it was you say?
A. I have a pretty good idea.
Q. Whose was it?
A. I have an idea it was mine.
Q. And that was the pistol he was going to snuff Gonzales' light out with as he stated?
A. Under the conditions which I have stated.[74]

This surprising revelation cast further light on why Blease removed himself from Tillman's team of attorneys. It brought him perilously close to being a participant in the alleged crime, and the jury's knowledge of that could have undermined his effectiveness as counsel.

On redirect examination, lead defense attorney Patrick Nelson strived to integrate the presence of the pistol into his self-defense strategy. He got Blease to say that Tillman was carrying the pistol that day because they expected Gonzales to come to Tillman's speech at the opera house and attack him because of hard-hitting answers Tillman would give to Gonzales's insulting editorials. Perhaps Tillman was afraid that the opera house's ornate boxes, high above the stage, would afford favorable firing points for snipers. But on recross-examination by Bellinger, Blease admitted that Gonzales did not attend the meeting at the opera house and that no trouble occurred.[75]

Despite the defense attempt to neutralize Adams's damaging testimony, it is significant that both accounts give a central role in the hotel-room strategy sessions to the reading of editorials from the *State,* and picture anger at their contents as the overriding emotion knitting the meeting's participants together. One is still left with the overall impression that Tillman was planning revenge for the contents of the editorials rather defense of his person.

Eyewitnesses

A pivotal part of the prosecution case was eyewitness testimony by those present at the shooting. No eyewitnesses were more important than the two state senators who were walking with Tillman when he shot Gonzales: George Washington Brown of Darlington County and Thomas Talbird of Beaufort County. They were not complicit in Tillman's plans in any way, and no one was more surprised than they when what they thought was a convivial walk back to their hotels suddenly turned into a lethal encounter.

A forty-six-year-old lawyer and Democrat whose early political career had been temporarily derailed by his opposition to Ben Tillman's rise to power,[76] Brown gave a vivid account of the shock and confusion that ended what he had expected to be a pleasant excursion down Main Street. Senator Brown testified that the Senate had adjourned at about 1:00 P.M. on the afternoon of Thursday, January 15, 1903, but he remained at the State House for a judiciary committee meeting.[77] He, Talbird, and Tillman came together by a chance meeting in the corridor as they were leaving and walked out of the State House together. As they approached the corner of Main and Gervais Streets, Brown was on the right, Talbird in the middle, and Tillman on the left (outside), nearest the Main Street pavement. This positioning became a controversial and crucial point in the dispute over whether Gonzales was turning aside to avoid Tillman, or was walking directly toward him in a confrontational manner. Just as they reached the transfer station at the corner, Brown's attention was diverted from his group when he spotted Mrs. Emma Melton, a friend since childhood, behind them, and he turned to speak to her. He had not seen Gonzales coming toward his group. As he started to speak to Mrs. Melton, he heard an explosion that he described as a "reverberating sound" coming from a location that was difficult to pinpoint. Mrs. Melton began screaming and ran toward the middle of the street. He did not turn to see the origin of the explosion but focused for the moment on calming and safeguarding Mrs. Melton by escorting her to the opposite corner of Main and Gervais in front of the opera house. When Brown turned back, he saw two gentlemen helping Gonzales, one on either side of him and saw Tillman moving sideways across Main Street. He had a gun in one hand, which was hanging by his side. It was the first time Brown had seen Tillman with a pistol on that or any other day. On cross-examination by Nelson, Brown said

Mrs. Melton was walking in the same direction as his group but about three to ten feet behind them. He did not remember what caused him to turn and notice her. When Nelson asked Senator Brown whether Tillman had treated him fairly as presiding officer of the Senate, the prosecution objected to the relevancy of that line of questions, and it was abandoned.

Before becoming a state senator, Thomas Talbird, a Democrat running on a fusion-party ticket composed of black and white Democrats and Republicans, had been declared the winner in a bitterly disputed 1888 probate-judge election, defeating the incumbent, the Radical Republican William J. Whipper, who charged that the election was rigged when officials did not count ballots from several precincts. He refused to turn over the records of his office to Talbird and was incarcerated for a lengthy time for refusal to obey a court order to surrender the documents, which he gave up only after the South Carolina Supreme Court refused to release him otherwise. The court also declined to review the canvassing board's decisions in favor of Talbird.[78] Fifteen years after the election dispute, Talbird was swept into another controversy as an eyewitness to the Gonzales-Tillman tragedy. At the time of the trial, Talbird was in his prime: a forty-eight-year-old Washington and Lee–trained lawyer, whose deep-set woeful eyes reflected the seriousness of his testimony, which differed from that of his friend Senator Brown on a pivotal point.

The most significant difference between Talbird's testimony and Brown's is that Talbird placed Tillman and himself in different positions as the trio of legislators walked toward Gonzales immediately before the shooting. Senator Brown had himself walking on the inside nearest the buildings, Talbird in the middle, and Tillman on the outside nearest the street. Talbird also had Brown on the inside, but placed Tillman in the middle and himself on the outside.[79] Such testimony later helped Tillman claim that, when Gonzales turned to his left as he neared the three men, he was not turning away from Tillman on the outside to avoid a confrontation, as he stated in his dying declaration, but was aggressively turning toward Tillman in the middle of the group to confront him in a threatening manner.

Despite the use the defense later made of his testimony, Talbird had the definite impression that Gonzales was turning away from the group to avoid colliding with them. When he first saw Gonzales, he was about ten or fifteen feet from them. When he was about five or six feet away, Tillman said, "How are you Mr. Gonzales?" or "Good morning Mr. Gonzales." According to Talbird, at that point Gonzales, who had been walking on the outside near the Main Street pavement, "turned toward his left, towards the transfer station, as if to pass us on the inside, and I paid no attention to him and he got out of my line of vision." Gonzales had been walking with both hands in his pockets and his overcoat buttoned up. Talbird testified that as Gonzales was making his turn to the left, Tillman said, "'I received your message.' I then looked to my right and saw a glimpse of a pistol in Gov. Tillman's hand, and just then it went off." Gonzales had not replied to any of Tillman's statements to him before the shot. He just continued to turn, but after the shot Talbird saw him take a couple of steps up to the second window of the transfer station on the corner. Talbird's concern was that there be no further violence. He said, "This thing must stop." He did not see a pistol in Gonzales's hands, both of which Talbird believed were now out of his pockets. The editor made no threatening gestures with his hands. Gonzales looked out across Main Street and said, "Here I am; finish me." Tillman was then "going across the street sideways with his eyes turned in our direction. . . . He was walking along with his pistol pointed in this direction (illustrating)." Gonzales said, "I am shot in the stomach; send for a doctor," but Talbird saw only a small tear in his coat.[80] Two men came to Gonzales and helped him back to his office.

Prosecutor Bellinger pressed Talbird about a conversation he had with Tillman later that afternoon at the jail. When Bellinger asked whether Tillman said anything about having considered firing a second shot, the prosecutor was met with a flurry of defense objections. Talbird was finally permitted to testify that Tillman told him he did not fire a second shot because he was afraid of hitting Talbird and because Talbird had said, "This thing must stop."

Talbird was cross-examined by George Croft, whose aim was to minimize any damage Talbird's testimony had done to the defense strategy of arguing that Tillman acted in self-defense in response to menacing gestures Gonzales had made as he approached Tillman and his group. Talbird had told Bellinger on direct examination that he had not seen Gonzales with a pistol immediately after the shooting. But Croft succeeded in narrowing the effectiveness of these answers for the prosecution by getting Talbird to admit that he had not been looking at Gonzales immediately before the shooting. Talbird conceded that at the time of the shot he would not have known if Gonzales had made any threatening gestures with his hands.[81]

Croft asked Talbird if he knew of a bitter feeling Gonzales harbored for Jim Tillman. Talbird replied that neither Gonzales nor Tillman had talked to him about their relationship, but he sensed Gonzales's rancor from his newspaper articles. Croft asked, "Did you know that he [Gonzales] had pursued Mr. Tillman with unabated abuse for a long time?" Talbird replied, "Yes, I do."[82] Croft's questions were in pursuit of the real defense strategy: insinuating that Tillman acted to defend his honor from relentless newspaper criticism, which is not a legal justification for murder. The argument that he acted in defense of his body, which is a legal defense when there is a need to protect oneself from immediate danger, was a mere pretext.[83]

Brown's friend Mrs. Emma C. Melton provided crucial information regarding Gonzales's demeanor and conduct just before the shot was fired.[84] William Watts Ball described her as giving her testimony "in a low voice, with composure and with a tone of certainty."[85] *News and Courier* commentator John Marshall was completely captivated by Mrs. Melton, an attractive and graceful lady in her early forties. She was dressed in the mourning attire of a widow, including a "long black veil [that] swept down from her hat." Her husband, Preston Laborde Melton, owner of a Columbia bicycle company, had died in 1901. Marshall noted that her "fine large dark eyes illumine her face," and her "gentle dignity and poise of manner . . . attracts and charms," while her "demeanor, personality, conduct, inspire regard and confidence" in her testimony.[86] Under questioning by Andrew Crawford, a Columbia lawyer and former judge hired by the Gonzales family to assist Solicitor Thurmond, Mrs. Melton said she worked in the State House as part of the legislature's engrossing department. She told the court that at about fifteen minutes before 2:00 P.M. on January 15, 1903, she left the building hurrying to get to the bank before it closed. She saw Senator Brown, an old friend, walking with Lieutenant Governor Tillman and another man she did not know but had since learned was Senator Talbird. She said Senator Brown was walking inside, closest to the buildings, with Talbird in the middle and Tillman on the outside. Thus she positioned the men the same as Senator Brown had in his testimony, but differently from the defense contentions and Senator Talbird's testimony placing Tillman in the middle.[87] She saw Gonzales coming toward the group. As he neared them, he turned to his left, which would have been away from Tillman as she and Brown had described his position but toward a confrontation with Tillman if he had been in the middle as Talbird and the defense contended. According to Mrs. Melton, when the shot was fired, Gonzales had one more step to take, and he would have been "on a line" with the group and about to pass them on the inside, nearest the transfer station.

Crawford pressed her about Gonzales's appearance and conduct just before the shot. What was his "facial expression," Crawford asked? She said:

A. It was perfectly placid; there was no scowl there; nor was there any glaring at him [Tillman]; there was no indication of danger. I was watching him to speak to him.
Q. Was he looking at this opening [on the inside]?
A. At this opening. He seemed to be absorbed in his thoughts, and I knew unless I caught his eye he would pass me without me getting the opportunity to speak to him.[88]

Mrs. Melton and Gonzales were heading for the same opening on the inside. As Gonzales was looking at and going toward it, the shot was fired. At about the same time, Senator Brown turned his head to speak to her. When she heard the shot, she did not know what it was. It sounded like an explosion under the pavement. She looked down to see if there was any damage to the street. When she saw none, it then occurred to her that it had been a pistol shot. She began to run, and Senator Brown helped her "across the street."

Crawford, who was doing a thorough job in eliciting key points for the prosecution, had a colorful history. He was fifty-five at the time of the trial. As a sixteen-year-old boy, he had served in the Confederate army. After the war, he attended the University of Virginia. He had been active in the Red Shirt movement to restore white rule in South Carolina. Perhaps some of his motivation for taking part in that movement came from his defeat in an 1876 race for probate judge during a time when radical influence remained strong. After the restoration of white rule, he was elected to a probate judgeship and then to the legislature, where he worked to establish a graded school system.[89] He was an effective trial lawyer who knew how to relate to a jury. But in questioning Mrs. Melton he stumbled in one respect. He asked her: "You have described his [Gonzales's] face and his going to this opening; now what was his whole general appearance, the *tout ensemble* of the man?" To which she replied that "he looked perfectly natural." This was a useful point for the prosecution—he did not look like he was gunning for anyone. However, this unnecessary flaunting of his knowledge of French, perhaps inspired by Mrs. Melton's feminine charm, must have fallen strangely on the ears of the jury of farmers and mill hands. The defense consistently did a better job of using language that would not alienate the jury. However, Crawford had a good rapport with Mrs. Melton and gained from her the important statement that she did not see Gonzales making any "demonstration with his hand or his arm."[90]

Cross-examination of Mrs. Melton posed problems for the defense. They needed to undermine her persuasive testimony for the prosecution, but if a woman were treated roughly on the witness stand, it might offend the jury. The defense's approach was to marginalize and belittle her testimony as that of an emotional woman so traumatized by the shooting that her memory was not accurate. Croft insinuated in the way that he framed his questions that she could not have seen everything she purported to remember because, by the time the shot was fired, she was already preoccupied with talking to her old friend Senator Brown. Croft inserted in his questions remarks such as "you became very much excited and shocked," and "you became startled and frightened." She admitted that she had been. During the line of questions in which Croft pointed out the unlikelihood of her being able to see Senator Brown turning to talk to her and simultaneously see what Gonzales did with his hands just before the shot was fired, Croft somewhat condescendingly addressed her as "my dear madam," as if remonstrating with a difficult child.[91]

Perhaps the most effective way of undermining the testimony of a respectable female witness without seeming boorish was to counter her testimony with that of another woman. This is what the defense was able to do several days after Mrs. Melton's testimony when, during the defense phase of the case, it offered the testimony of Mrs. Mary A. Evans, a member of a politically prominent family.[92] John Marshall of the *News and Courier* described her as, "an elderly lady of strong features and pronounced individuality," who spoke in rapid bursts of words.[93] On January 15, 1903, Mrs. Evans had come to Columbia from her home in Newberry to follow the legislature's debate on a bill to regulate child labor. While in Columbia, she was staying at the governor's mansion.[94] When it became obvious that there would be no discussion of the child-labor bill that day, she left the State House and walked down Main Street. Just after she passed the transfer station, she saw Mr. Gonzales walking toward her. Mrs. Evans often wrote newspaper articles on public issues and had met Gonzales at press association meetings. George Croft was conducting the direct examination. He asked her to describe Gonzales's appearance. What she said was drastically different from Mrs. Melton's description of him as "placid" when she saw him a few moments later:

Q. When you passed him did you notice him?
A. I particularly noticed his attitude and facial expression from the fact of what I had seen and heard in the vestibule as I passed out from the State House.
Q. What did you notice about his face as peculiar?
A. A very strange expression, one that looked vindictive and like a tragedy to me.
Q. You spoke of his attitude. How did he have his hands?
A. In his coat pocket; seemed to be pressed. In his overcoat—it was dark, very dark blue or black. It was not a light coat.
Q. Well now in reference to his right hand when you passed him?
A. It was in his coat pocket sir. I saw nothing but I thought, may I be permitted to say what I thought?
Mr. Bellinger: We object.
Q. How did it appear to you?
A. I thought he had a weapon.
Mr. Bellinger: We object to that.
By the court: Yes, sir.
The witness: I felt anxious and worried.
Mr. Croft: Q. Why?
A. Because of the expression of his face and what I heard in the vestibule that Mr. Gonzales had been looking for him [Tillman] at the State House.[95]

Under cross-examination by Bellinger, Mrs. Evans explained what she meant by saying that what she had heard in the vestibule had made her anxious. While walking through the vestibule, she heard two well-dressed gentlemen she did not recognize, since their backs were turned to her, discussing Gonzales's having been in the State House looking for Tillman. She said that "their remarks attracted my attention instantly because I had read those editorials and as a daughter, a child of the state, I was shocked." The ineffective cross-examination did not neutralize this testimony, which was so damaging to the prosecution. It served only to give it further emphasis.

Several things are notable about this remarkable testimony. The witness was allowed to speculate, to give her impression when she had no reliable knowledge upon which to base it. She did not see Gonzales with a weapon. She only thought he had one. In giving vent to this speculation, she was permitted to repeat a conversation she overheard between two men she could not identify. This was blatant hearsay that did not even rise above the level of rumors. Judge Gary usually kept a tight rein on such testimony. Most remarkably, this testimony equates writing harsh editorials with harboring murderous intent.[96] But when Bellinger objected, the judge did not ask for argument or issue a ruling. He simply said ambiguously—"yes, sir."[97] Bellinger was clearly outmaneuvered by defense counsel and a nimble, runaway witness and got no help from a judge who temporarily abdicated his role. In this manner the shaky self-defense theory was allowed to gain the illusion of substance in the eyes of the jury. Despite Mrs. Evans's speculation that Gonzales may have had a pistol in his pocket, even though she "saw nothing," no gun was ever found on him.[98]

Mrs. Evans's adamant defense of Tillman and attribution of murderous intent and action to Gonzales seems to have been inspired by a deep resentment of the editor. What could be the origin of this resentment? It could have been inspired by the rough treatment her son received in the *State*. Her son was Hubert Henry Evans, usually called "Hub" or "H. H.," in political circles. He was a director and sometime chairman of the governing board of the State Dispensary, the government monopoly of liquor sales championed by Ben Tillman when he was governor.[99] During Hub Evans's tenure, rumors of corruption swirled about the board.[100] Mrs. Evans probably resented stories published in the *State* just over a year before she gave her testimony. They made Hub look corrupt and buffoonish. When a story in the *Greenville Daily News* accused Evans of profiting improperly from his directorship, living lavishly—sporting diamonds and buying real estate—he went to Greenville and accosted editor J. K. Blackman, who had risen from a sick bed to hear his complaint. The *State* reported that Evans hit Blackman from behind, beat him to unconsciousness, and while he was unconscious placed Blackman across his knees and spanked him. The report alleged that Blackman suffered a brain concussion and was partially paralyzed for a time.[101] In 1906, after he had left the dispensary board and was seeking to return to the legislature, Hub Evans struck-up a Jim Tillman–like tune when he claimed martyrdom owing to rough newspaper treatment for supporting Ben Tillman. But he said the newspapers were too frightened to brand him a thief.[102] Mrs. Evans's testimony was payback for the mauling given her boy and was a major ingredient in the antipress strategy of the defense.

The bystanders who rushed to aid Gonzales immediately after the shooting had a unique perspective about his reaction to the attack. Just before the shot was fired, J. F. Sims, a farmer, was crossing Main Street at the corner of Main and Gervais, walking toward the transfer station.[103] He saw Tillman and two other men at the corner walking down Main away from the State House. Apparently Sims was not paying any particular attention to them and did not see Gonzales. When he heard the shot, he looked up and saw Tillman pointing a pistol at Gonzales and backing away from him. Sims recalled: "As the pistol fired, Mr. Tillman said 'I received your message, sir.'" When Sims first saw Gonzales, the editor was standing facing Tillman. Gonzales then went around the corner to Gervais. For a while he clung to the corner post of the transfer station. Both his hands were at his side. The prosecutor asked:

Q. State to the jury whether you saw him make any effort to draw anything out of his pockets or use his pistol.
A. None whatever.
Q. Did you see any pistol there?
A. No. sir.[104]

Sims said he walked up to Gonzales and "asked him if he was hit. He said, yes, that he had a mortal wound. I asked what he would like me to do. He said take me to my wife." When he could not find a hack to take Gonzales home to his wife, he and Mr. La Motte helped him walk back to the *State* office. He walked on Gonzales's right side. The prosecutor asked:

Q. You walked close to him?
A. Yes sir.
Q. Did you feel anything in his pocket?
A. No sir.
Q. State to the jury whether he had on gloves or not?
A. He did.
Q. When were those gloves taken off?
A. After he was taken to the office of the State.
Q. Did you take them off?
A. I assisted in taking them off.[105]

As they were walking back to the *State* office, Sims thought Gonzales seemed fairly strong at first, "but I noticed the further we went the more weight he put on me." When they got to the *State* office, Gonzales was put on the floor with a pile of newspapers under his head. On cross-examination, Sims acknowledged that he did not see Gonzales before he heard the shot, and could not say whether or not he made any "demonstration" with his hands.[106] Of course it would be hard to believe that someone on whom no gun was ever found would make a pointless "demonstration," feigning the drawing of a gun. Such a person would have to have a death wish or a macabre sense of humor.

A. Gamewell La Motte was the other Good Samaritan to come to Gonzales's assistance. La Motte was a Columbia architect who spoke with unusual precision in stating distances. He testified that on January 15, 1903, he was "standing about 27 yards up Main Street on the same side of the street as the transfer station where the shooting occurred, with my back toward the corner where it occurred, talking to two gentlemen standing at the outer edge of the pavement."[107] He heard a "sharp report," which he thought was a "torpedo on the track." At first both Gonzales and Tillman had their backs turned toward him, but then Tillman turned around and La Motte saw the pistol in his right hand. The pistol had a "long slender blue barrel." Tillman continued to stare at Gonzales and moved sideways across Main Street to the city hall. La Motte turned his attention to Gonzales. When he saw Sims go to his aid, he followed. He described Gonzales: "I judged from Gonzales' appearance, he was very white and very unsteady and walking very slowly. I judged that he had been shot." He took Gonzales's left arm and Sims his right arm, and they walked with him back to the *State* office. At the office they were met by Mr. M. C. Wallace of the *State* staff and Dr. W. J. Murray, a wholesale druggist with a shop next door. They helped Gonzales lie down with a pile of newspaper as a pillow. He and Dr. Murray opened Gonzales's clothes and someone, La Motte believes it was Mr. Wallace, helped Gonzales take off his coat, which was spread on the floor for him to lie on. Doctors soon began to arrive, including Drs. Coward, Griffith, Taylor, Babcock, and Kendall. La Motte remained by Gonzales's side until just before he was taken to the hospital. When he was helping to loosen Gonzales's clothes and observing the overcoat being removed, La Motte neither saw nor felt a weapon on Gonzales. On cross-examination by Nelson, La Motte admitted he had not searched every pocket of Gonzales's clothing for a gun, but he felt sure that, if one had been present, he would have noticed it. The weapon that

Mrs. Evans, with her gossip-fueled imagination "thought" was there, failed to materialize, even though Gonzales and his clothing were handled extensively by Sims, La Motte, many doctors, law-enforcement officers, and staff members of the *State.*[108] Of course one of these individuals could have found a gun and made off with it, but there were so many people standing around watching that such speculation is difficult to credit. Shortly after the shooting, a pistol owned by Gonzales was found, not on his person but locked in his desk at the *State* offices. Gonzales's assistant, James Hoyt, who was present when the pistol was found, described it as "dusty and rusty," in poor working order, and thus showing no sign of recent use.[109]

The eyewitnesses whose testimony has been described so far saw events immediately before or after the shooting and did not see the killing itself. One who saw the shooting was Cladius Murray Lide, a busy young building contractor.[110] At about 1:45 P.M. on January 15, Lide left his office on Main Street in the "second block above [north of] the State Office [1220 Main St.]" on his way home for dinner. He was walking south in the direction of the State House and on the "left-hand side of Main Street." Just above the bookstore at 1248-1250 Main Street, Lide came across a blind beggar, who gave him some Bible verses that he read and threw away. As Lide got to Murray's drugstore just south of the *State*'s office, he came up behind Mr. Gonzales, who was also walking in the direction of the State House. Lide soon saw Mr. Tillman and two other men walking north from the State House toward Gervais Street. Tillman was on the outside of this group of three, Lide said, the one nearest the Main Street pavement. Gonzales was still in front of Lide. He turned from the outside toward the inside, nearest the buildings. Lide described the crucial events: "when I got about the front of the billboard next to the transfer office, I saw Mr. Tillman throw up his arm and shoot." Lide "did not see whether he drew his pistol or not, just saw the shot, and instantly this man, a sort of light-haired man, who I was afterward told was Senator Talbird, jumped between Mr. Gonzales and Mr. Tillman and threw his hands up this way against Mr. Tillman's face and said, 'This thing must stop' and Tillman had [his] pistol over the shoulder of this gentleman moving it back and forth this way several times, as if he was trying to get a chance to shoot again." Lide was questioned intensely about what Gonzales did with his hands, to see whether he made any provocative movements that would lend credence to the defense theory that Gonzales acted as if he were drawing a gun on Tillman, thus justifying Tillman's shooting in self-defense. The solicitor asked:

Q. What did you see Mr. Gonzales do with his hands just before or just about the time that Mr. Tillman shot him?
A. Nothing at all. He had them in his pockets as far as I could see from the back. He seemed to be holding his overcoat around him that way (indicating).
Q. See any pistol?
A. No.
Q. See him have a weapon of any kind?
A. No sir.
Q. Did he make any demonstration?
A. No sir; kept his hands in his pockets all the time until after these gentlemen [Sims and La Motte] took hold of his arms.[111]

On cross-examination, Nelson pounded Lide with a barrage of questions about the position of Gonzales's hands in his pockets just before Tillman shot him. Could they have been deep in the pockets as if Gonzales were thrusting a hand downward to draw a pistol? Lide was under the impression that Gonzales's thumbs were out of his pockets so he could hold his overcoat more closely about him on that chilly January day.[112]

At about five or ten minutes before 2:00 P.M. on January 15, seventeen-year-old August Schideman, an employee of the Carolina Glass Company, was riding his bicycle south on Main Street toward the State House. He said that, when he was about twenty feet from the transfer station, "I just happened to turn my head over that way and saw Mr. Tillman have his pistol up; never saw him raise it, and I saw the shot fired in an instant."[113] When the shot was fired, Tillman "was standing a little to the side of the corner of Gervais Street on the outer edge." Gonzales was "just south of the transfer station door" and "northeast" of Tillman. "Mr. Gonzales was making to the transfer station north of Tillman and had not passed him yet." Gonzales's side was turned toward Tillman when the shot was fired. This was contrary to the defense assertions that Gonzales was charging straight ahead at Tillman. Furthermore Schideman answered, "No Sir," when prosecutor Andrew Crawford asked, "Did you see him [Gonzales] make any demonstration with his hands or anything of that sort toward Tillman?" Like several others, Schideman heard Tillman say, "I received your message," just as the shot was fired. Crawford probed Tillman's conduct just after he fired the shot:

Q. After Col. Tillman fired the first shot what did he do with his pistol?
A. His hand went down by his side, he stepped around and Mr. Gonzales was kind of leaning up on the side of the transfer station, murmuring something; and Mr. Tillman raised his pistol again as if he was going to fire, and that time I turned my head, because I thought he was going to shoot again.[114]

No second shot was fired, and defense attorney Croft drew attention to this, and his contention that a second shot could easily have been fired, as proof of Tillman's moderation.[115]

Congressman Wyatt Aiken testified that he was walking with Fred Dominick ahead of Tillman and his associates and turned to look back after he heard the sound of the shot. He saw Tillman backing away from the scene of the shooting holding a "blue steel" revolver in his hands.[116] What makes Aiken's testimony intriguing is not what little he saw of the aftermath of the shooting, but his insight into the conduct of both Tillman and Gonzales in the hour just before the killing. He had pleasant casual conversations first with Gonzales and then with Tillman, which stand in eerie contrast with the violence that took place shortly thereafter. Both Gonzales and Tillman congratulated Aiken on his election to Congress. Aiken introduced Gonzales to some other newspaperman that he did not know. Aiken's description of Tillman during their conversation in the State House, only a few minutes before Tillman shot Gonzales, is most surprising. Defense counsel George W. Croft on cross-examination asked Aiken about Tillman:

Q. His manner was perfectly quiet and natural?
A. Yes, sir. I thought so. I was really impressed with Mr. Tillman's appearance that day. I remember speaking of it afterwards; I thought he seemed to be perfectly cool and sober; I knew he had been in the habit of taking a drink occasionally. I have taken drinks with him.[117]

A few minutes later Aiken and Dominick were walking north on Main Street away from the State House when they passed Gonzales walking in the opposite direction. Only a few minutes earlier Aiken had had a pleasant conversation with Gonzales. This time, although Aiken said hello to Gonzales, the editor sailed right past him as if he did not see him. He walked straight ahead as if lost in thought. He and Dominick looked back and saw Tillman and his group and Gonzales nearing each other. Aiken turned to Dominick and said, "in a joking way 'You want to see if those fellows are going to embrace.'" A few moments later they heard the shot.

The above were the main eyewitnesses to the shooting who were presented by the prosecution. It was the prosecution's plan to present a multidirectional view of the killing. Some of the witnesses on the periphery merely confirmed bits and pieces of what the key witnesses saw. J. R. Allen was the city auditor with offices in the city-hall complex in the front of the Columbia Theatre building on the northwest corner of Main and Gervais, opposite the corner on which the transfer station was located. Just before the shooting, Allen saw Gonzales walking toward the corner with his hands in his pockets but with his thumbs out clutching his coat close about him. This contradicted the defense's theory that Gonzales was plunging his hands into his pockets just before the shot was fired so that Tillman could reasonably have feared that Gonzales was about to draw a weapon. Allen did not see the shooting itself because, as Gonzales continued to walk toward the corner, Allen's view was blocked by a streetcar. Immediately after the shooting, he saw Senator Brown escorting Mrs. Melton to safety and saw Tillman emerge from behind a streetcar with a gun in his hand.[118] Allen was subjected to a withering cross-examination by Nelson for staring idly out of his office window when he should have been working for the benefit of the taxpayers. Nelson questioned whether Allen could have observed Gonzales's hands so clearly from a narrow opening in his window across the street from the shooting.[119] But the heart of the defense did not rest on such minute scrutiny of vantage points.

5.

THE DEFENSE CASE

When the defense began its case, it had several aims: to show that James H. Tillman had reason to fear N. G. Gonzales because he had threatened to attack Tillman, that Gonzales made "demonstrations," aggressive movements, just before the shooting that prompted Tillman's reasonable fear that he was about to be shot and needed to shoot his would-be assailant first in self-defense, and that Gonzales's harsh and relentless editorials criticizing Tillman gave credence to the threats and attacked Tillman's honor and integrity beyond the point of endurance. Stripped of its light dusting of self-defense camouflage, the real defense was that the stinging editorials justified the killing. The defense treated the editorial words as if they had the force of blows delivering a remorseless verbal pistol whipping that justified a lethal response to salvage Tillman's honor.

The defense testimony began with witnesses called to show Gonzales's hatred for Tillman. Such testimony would make claims that Gonzales had threatened Tillman with death or serious bodily harm more believable. Miss Mary Julia Roper was the first witness in implementation of this design.[1] W. W. Ball described Miss Roper as "a young woman of good presence and bearing."[2] In the *News and Courier,* August Kohn described Miss Roper's entrance into the courtroom: "she was veiled but it could be seen that she was a bright young blonde."[3] Miss Roper had come from New York City, where she was a practicing nurse, to testify. In early July 1902, during the bitterly fought gubernatorial campaign, Miss Roper had been the head nurse at a Spartanburg hospital when Captain Ralph Elliott, N. G. Gonzales's uncle, was being treated there for what became his last illness.[4] During Mr. Gonzales's visits to his uncle, Miss Roper had several pleasant conversations with Mr. Gonzales on a variety of subjects, one of which was James H. Tillman, to whom Miss Roper was indirectly related by marriage. She told Gonzales of her great admiration for Tillman, but Gonzales said that "he was not in favor of Mr. Tillman being a candidate for governor." She said Gonzales called Tillman "a coward," "a villain," and "a gambler." She said Gonzales asked her if she "considered Tillman a brave man; I told him I certainly did; He said he did not; that he had made Mr. Tillman show the white feather [back down from a fight] twice, that Col. Tillman had challenged him to two duels, which he did not acknowledge and that Col. Tillman had no more resentment than to come in the hotel lobby and offer him a cigar which he declined."

Such criticism did not amount to threats. It was the kind of pointed criticism often used in American political campaigns. Under cross-examination by G. Duncan Bellinger, Miss Roper rallied to Tillman's defense, almost to the point of gushing praise. She said, "I told him [Gonzales] that I was very fond of James H. Tillman." She was proud of having defended Tillman against such a formidable opponent and eagerly sought Tillman's praise for having done so. She admitted that she was grateful to James H. Tillman and Senator Tillman for helping her get a position with the U.S. Army and denied ever having heard James Tillman threaten Gonzales.[5]

Although Miss Roper's testimony had Gonzales lodging harsh criticism of Tillman rather than threatening him, the defense produced other witnesses who claimed to have heard Gonzales making pointed threats to do serious physical harm to Tillman. The prosecution was sometimes able to cast doubt on the weight that should be given to such testimony. T. D. Mitchell boasted of a casual acquaintance with N. G. Gonzales; they occasionally passed on the street and exchanged greetings.[6] One night in September 1902, during the gubernatorial campaign, between the first primary and the run-off, Mitchell was prompted by some recent editorials by Gonzales to go up to him on the street as Gonzales was turning from Main onto Gervais Street and to say that he thought it was "about time you would let up on old Jim." The prosecution objected to this testimony as irrelevant and hearsay, but the court permitted it as laying a foundation for testimony about a threat. Mitchell said that Gonzales replied that he would continue to criticize Tillman as long as he offered himself as a candidate for public office. He said that he had proved on several occasions that Tillman was a "cur," like a worthless dog who barked aggressively, but who, when hit, would just slink away. In essence Mitchell was testifying that Gonzales had accused Tillman of being a coward. Mitchell quoted Gonzales as saying about Tillman, "Well I could slap his face and he would not resent it." Gonzales accused Tillman of not standing up for himself when another editor, a man named Ed DeCamp, confronted him with face-to-face accusations in Gaffney that he was a liar and a deadbeat. Gonzales's alleged tirade against Tillman culminated with the following statement: "If he ever bats his eyes at me I will fill him so full of lead that he will not be able to tote it off." Mitchell said he passed this threat along to Tillman so he could be on guard.[7]

Bellinger's cross-examination reeked with sarcasm and disbelief that such a conversation had ever taken place. He asked questions that elicited a picture of Mitchell as a rolling stone who changed jobs and residences often. At the time of the trial he was a painter, but he had been a detective for the Southern Railway. He admitted that he initiated the conversation with Gonzales and that before the encounter he and Gonzales had exchanged only greetings. Bellinger questioned whether as talented a writer as Gonzales would have used as clumsy a phrase as "tote it off." He was skeptical that Gonzales would unburden himself so candidly to someone who was at most a casual acquaintance. Mitchell was unable to say whether anyone else was present when he informed Tillman of Gonzales's threats. In sum Bellinger pictured the entire conversation as a figment of Mitchell's maladroit imagination. But despite Mitchell's questionable credibility, his testimony fortified both major prongs of the defense strategy: he provided evidence of Gonzales's threats, which supported claims that Tillman could reasonably have feared harm and needed to act in self-defense, and he supported the antipress strategy by testimony that portrayed Gonzales as a reckless and brutal editorial writer who vowed to continue his attacks.

As the defense case proceeded, the belligerence of the threats Gonzales was overheard to have made against Tillman, increased. A. J. Flowers was a young man of twenty-six who had been a member of the regiment Tillman commanded during the Spanish-American War. His loyalty to his former commander obviously continued. During the summer of 1902, while Tillman was touring the state as a gubernatorial candidate, Flowers was working as a conductor for the Columbia Electric Street Railway Company.[8] N. G. Gonzales was a frequent passenger on his streetcars. Sometime late in the summer, probably in September, Flowers saw Gonzales gossiping with three other men about the election. They were seated in the rear smoking section of the car. As he approached the men to collect their fares, Flowers heard Gonzales assailing Tillman's candidacy and declaring the steps he was willing to take to prevent Tillman from becoming governor. Flowers said, "I heard him tell them that if he did not succeed in defeating Mr. Tillman in the governor's office that he would never be seated, because he would kill the rascal."[9] He did not tell Tillman of the conversation until long after the shooting, when on August 15, 1903, Flowers sent a letter to Tillman expressing his somewhat reluctant willingness to testify in his defense. Several factors make the relevance and veracity of the testimony questionable. First, since Tillman was not told of the conversation until long after the shooting, one may question its relevance with regard to determining the reasonableness of Tillman's fear of harm from Gonzales.[10] Furthermore the contingent nature of the statement significantly diminished its threatening quality. The killing was to take place only if Tillman were elected governor, and there was no other means to prevent his taking office. Since Tillman was not elected, the contingency did not occur, and presumably the threat dependent on it was over. Another feature of Flowers's testimony seems odd. He stated that Gonzales and his three companions got on the streetcar at Lady Street, rode a complete circuit of the route, and got off again at Lady Street. In other words their only purpose for taking the car appears to have been a joy ride giving Gonzales a chance to deliver impromptu rants based on his editorials and to mutter dark threats against Tillman. Such a pointless frolic seems unlikely given the busy editor's character.[11]

However, Flowers's testimony produced a clash among the lawyers that vindicated his testimony against a prosecution attempt to discredit him and showed the superior professional skills of the defense attorneys. Several days after Flowers's testimony, the prosecution had a chance to rebut defense evidence. They called Alfred Wallace, the superintendent of the Columbia Electric Street Railway Company, to undermine Flowers's reliability and trustworthiness as a witness.[12] Wallace testified that Flowers's reputation for veracity was bad, that he would not believe what Flowers said under oath, and that Flowers had assured him that he had no information about the Tillman case. The prosecution made an attempt to use Wallace's testimony to introduce records of the Columbia Electric Street Railway Company showing that Flowers had not worked on the cars he said he was in charge of on the days he said he heard Gonzales's threats.

The defense convinced Judge Gary that, as head of the company, Wallace was not the actual keeper of the records and that his lack of knowledge meant he was not competent to testify as to the reliability with which they were maintained. Instead of the boss, who did not soil his hands with the quotidian task of record keeping, the clerk who maintained them was needed.[13] The bookkeeper, A. H. Montieth, was summoned. As the person who made the actual entries, he was considered the proper one to vouch for the records.[14] During his testimony a dispute arose as to whether the proper records were the summary entries in the books or the trip slips from which they were made. This made quite a difference since the books showed Flowers had not worked when he said he did, but the trip slips showed that he had. The judge ruled in favor of the trip slips, and Flowers was vindicated.[15] Thus the energetic and meticulous defense preparation was rewarded, and the prosecution was embarrassed in open court. Although such disputes may seem merely technical, they can have a significant impact on the jury's trust in each side's case.

Other defense witnesses depicted Gonzales as making serious threats in casual conversations. P. W. Hughes said he had gotten to know N. G. Gonzales years earlier, when Hughes was a deputy sheriff in Edgefield, and Gonzales, as a reporter for the *Charleston News and Courier,* came to Edgefield to cover a murder trial.[16] Hughes said he came to Columbia in July 1902, during the gubernatorial campaign, to see his daughter. He was walking down Main Street with several other men, one of whom was named Stroud, when Gonzales came along and stopped to question Stroud about how the Mill District voters were tending in the campaign. Stroud said he thought Mill District opinion was mixed, but Colonel Tillman seemed to be leading. At that point Hughes interjected himself into the conversation and asked Gonzales "had he not done Col. Tillman a great injustice, writing those pieces in the paper, and he said no. He said, 'the black-legged gambler will get greater injustice than that after the election, and it ought to be lead.'" Hughes never told Tillman about the threats.[17]

As the potency of the defense evidence of Gonzales's threats against Tillman increased, the reliability of the evidence presented to prove the threats diminished, but the effect on the prosecution's case was devastating anyway. Victor B. Cheshire was another loyal member of Tillman's Spanish-American War regiment who told his old commander that he was in danger.[18] Cheshire said that, when the political cavalcade rolled into his hometown of Anderson, he went to hear the candidates speak and told Jim Tillman that he had information indicating that Tillman had better be on the lookout for Gonzales. He told Tillman that recently he had been on a train returning to Anderson from a trip to Newberry when he fell into a conversation on politics with W. H. Geer, a traveling subscription agent for the *State* newspaper. Geer and Cheshire had both been in the army during the Spanish-American War, and the question arose as to whether "we army boys" were going to support Jim Tillman again as they had in his successful campaign for lieutenant governor. During the course of an argument between Geer and Cheshire over Tillman's merits, Geer told Cheshire that N. G. Gonzales was going around armed and looking for Tillman. So Cheshire told Tillman "that a representative of the State told me that Mr. Gonzales carried a gun for him and that he had better not jump on him with a stick for if he did he would get the hell shot out of him." The reference to a "stick" was Cheshire's addition to Geer's remarks. Cheshire thought that Tillman had a right to take a stick, or even a gun, to Gonzales because of the critical editorials he had written about Tillman.[19]

Cheshire's testimony provoked a combative argument by counsel as to its admissibility. The prosecution contended that Cheshire's testimony was hearsay because he was not testifying about matters within his knowledge but about gossip passed on by Geer. Geer was not then under examination, so the source of his information was unknown. It could be triple hearsay or greater. Geer may not have observed an armed Gonzales looking for Tillman; he may have heard about it from somebody who heard about it from someone else. Such information is unreliable. You cannot know whether it is true. If a person were permitted to fire a preemptive shot on the basis of what might be unreliable rumors, the level of violence in the community could greatly increase.[20] The supposed object of threats should have the duty to check first on whether they really came from the party against whom he is warned before he acts against that party.[21] Eventually the argument took on a racial tinge. In an effort to show the unreliability of evidence that may have reached the court through several hands whose accuracy is unknown, Prosecutor Andrew Crawford said that "at last it may be traced from an ignorant darkey, we will say, who is venal, willing to be bought, then the defendant under these circumstances with that statement coming from a hundred people, possibly way out yonder, will be permitted to shoot a man down on sight when there is no necessity and the thing is false."[22]

Ultimately Judge Gary ruled for the defense. Cheshire's testimony about Geer saying that Gonzales was carrying a pistol for Tillman could be admitted.[23] To Gary it did not matter whether or not it was true that Gonzales was carrying a gun for Tillman. The statement was not being introduced to prove that Gonzales was carrying a gun, but as evidence that the conversation was passed along to Tillman. It would have had an impact on how much danger Tillman thought he was facing, and it would help the jury determine "whether or not he believed his life was in danger, and for that purpose and that purpose alone, I admit the testimony."[24] A few days later, when the prosecution was permitted to rebut defense evidence, it called W. H. Geer to the stand.[25] Geer testified that he remembered a political conversation with Cheshire on the train, but he never told Cheshire that Gonzales was carrying a pistol for Tillman.

J. A. White was called "Captain" according to the southern custom of honoring people who had served in the military, especially the Confederate army, by addressing them throughout life with their army rank. The defense spent a considerable amount of time bolstering White's credibility by having him recite his Confederate service record, which had lasted from the "beginning to the end" of the Civil War.[26] His credibility was also buttressed by parading his salt-of-the-earth family connections, including one to Solicitor Thurmond by marriage. White was from Tillman's hometown of Edgefield. When this ritual concluded, White was asked about what he saw on January 14, the day before the shooting, while he was at his job as doorkeeper to a Senate committee at the State House. He was seated next to the door he guarded. With him was Richard H. Holsenback, another a key defense witness. A man came up to them and asked where Jim Tillman was. When White said he did not know, the man said, "I suppose he is off neglecting his duty as usual." The man said Tillman "was a pretty sorry man, a coward, and he had made him show the white feather, a time or two, and he would make him do it again." White did not know the man, but Holsenback told him it was N. G. Gonzales.[27]

This testimony was offered in support of the defense theory that Gonzales was stalking Tillman and taunting him with remarks questioning his courage—and that this verbal meanness characterized both Gonzales's everyday conversations and his newspaper writing. The "made him show the white feather" remark—and particularly the closing comment that he would "make him do it again,"—was meant to show that Gonzales was threatening to accost Tillman and force him to defend himself or back away from a fight and be exposed as a coward. Prosecutor G. Duncan Bellinger objected to parts of the defense's direct examination of White on the grounds that defense counsel George Croft was improperly leading the witness by asking questions that suggested the answer Croft wanted. The objection backfired on Bellinger by provoking White to make a comment that made the prosecutor look like a bully who preyed on the afflicted. White misconstrued the objection by thinking it was about the slowness of his answers. An exasperated White angrily told Bellinger, "I am going to say it all if you give me time. I stammer in my speech and can't talk fast."[28] Bellinger was again maneuvered into looking like an arrogant bully with regard to the next witness when in fact Bellinger seems to have been guilty of nothing more than a mild case of pomposity. But Bellinger's cross-examination did expose White's deep indebtedness to Tillman, who had gotten White the job as a Senate doorkeeper.

The next witness turned out to be one of the most dangerous to the prosecution, a wily, though crude, verbal guerrilla fighter with a cunning instinct for baiting lawyers. Richard H. Holsenback was also from Tillman country, Edgefield County.[29] Holsenback said that on January 14, the day before the shooting, he was in the State House talking to Captain White, who was at his post as doorkeeper, when N. G. Gonzales asked White where Tillman was. Holsenback confirmed White's testimony that Gonzales accused Tillman of neglecting his duties, bragged about having made Tillman "show the white feather" on several occasions, and said that he would do so again.[30] Holsenback added that he had come to Columbia to seek a job as a doorkeeper and that he had asked for Tillman's help. He saw Tillman that evening and told him what Gonzales had said about him.

The next day, January 15, Holsenback was again in the State House until the Senate adjourned. After the adjournment, he left, and as he was going down the steps, he saw Senator Brown, Lieutenant Governor Tillman, and Senator Talbird ahead of him walking toward the corner of Main and Gervais Streets. Just behind them was a woman dressed in black (Mrs. Melton dressed in widow's mourning attire). Holsenback hurried to catch up with Tillman and the two senators, who were walking three abreast with Senator Brown on the inside nearest the building, Senator Talbird on the outside nearest the Main Street pavement, and Lieutenant Governor Tillman in the middle. In giving these three positions, Holsenback agreed with Senator Talbird's testimony and the testimony Tillman gave later and disagreed with that of Senator Brown and Mrs. Melton, both of whom put Tillman on the outside, Talbird in the middle, and Brown on the inside. Holsenback saw Gonzales walking on Main Street toward the State House. As he neared Tillman and his group, Gonzales turned to his left. According to Holsenback, Gonzales could have passed the group by going to his right around Senator Talbird on the outside, but instead he turned to his left, which put him on a path toward Tillman in the middle of his group. When Brown fell back to talk to the lady, Tillman was on the inside. As he made this left diagonal turn toward Tillman, Gonzales "rushed his hand in his pocket." Croft asked Holsenback: "Brushed it down in his pocket? A. Yes, sir sort of shoved it back this way (indicating)." He heard Tillman say, "I got your message." Croft had struck gold. He continued:

Q.: What did you expect?
A.: I expected to see him shoot Col. Tillman every second.
Mr. Bellinger: We object.
The Court: Just tell the facts.
By Mr. Croft: Q. He shoved his hand down in his pocket as he was going across diagonally?
A.: Yes, sir.[31]

Holsenback provided the defense with what it needed most. By his positioning of Tillman in the middle, Gonzales's move to his left became not an attempt to avoid Tillman by going away from him but an aggressive move toward him. And by saying that as Gonzales, made the turn he "rushed" or "shoved" his hand further into his pocket, Holsenback had Gonzales appear to reach for a gun, the exact "demonstration" the defense needed in order to create the impression that Tillman's shooting Gonzales was an act he reasonably believed necessary to save his life when considered in the context of the threats against him that the preceding witnesses had described Gonzales as making.

But not even Holsenback saw Gonzales actually produce a gun, and one was not found on him. Croft continued:

Q. At the shot of the pistol what became of Mr. Gonzales?
A. He turned and walked up, sort of against the wall and sort of walked around the corner and leant up against it.

Holsenback testified that Tillman shot only once even though he could have shot again without hitting Senator Talbird. Talbird ran up to Tillman and Gonzales and said, "This must stop." But at first Talbird was not directly between Tillman and Gonzales, and Tillman had a clear field of fire for a second shot. This testimony was an attempt to show that Tillman was exercising self-restraint, using only such force as was necessary to protect himself.

Holsenback watched as Tillman backed away from the scene of the shooting, around a streetcar to the opposing corner of Main and Gervais where the opera house was. Then a man (officer Boland) came up and took him away. Holsenback followed Gonzales and those helping him back to the *State* newspaper office. He stood outside until Gonzales was taken out of a side door and placed in a covered wagon that served as an ambulance.

On cross-examination Bellinger found Holsenback a combative, resentful witness. He could not read, and he wanted to take advantage of every opportunity to prove that he was smarter than the high-priced lawyer who was questioning his word. He skillfully played to the boisterous crowd of rustic Tillman supporters who camped out in front of the courthouse and filled the rough-hewn benches. Holsenback tried to turn the tables on Bellinger by putting the lawyer rather than himself on the defensive. When Bellinger tried to impeach Holsenback by showing bias toward Tillman because he was obligated to Tillman for providing him with jobs, Holsenback said it was Tillman who was obligated to Holsenback for helping him in his campaigns. Then Holsenback went on the attack and accused Bellinger of being nothing but a politician himself, who met with Holsenback to seek his support when he ran for Congress. Bellinger denied any such conversation. Holsenback was clearly enjoying his role as a countrified court jester pricking the dignity of the august lawyer.

Bellinger tried to get Holsenback to admit that he could not have seen the shooting because he had told others that, when the shooting occurred, he was at the foot of the capitol steps rather than near Tillman and his group. Holsenback did not change his story.[32] Bellinger tried to depict Holsenback as someone who would swear to anything, whether true or not, if it was necessary to get a friend acquitted from a murder charge. He tried to get Holsenback to admit to having told a friend, R. A. Temple, that if a man named Boatwright criticized him, Temple could kill him; then if Temple were tried, Holsenback would "swear him out of it." Holsenback denied having said any such thing.

During the cross-examination, Bellinger unwisely gave Holsenback an opportunity to repeat and expand on the statement, made during direct examination, that he expected Gonzales to shoot Tillman. The cross-examination testimony on this issue includes this exchange:

Q. We were talking before dinner about your reason for believing that Mr. Gonzales was going to shoot Mr. Tillman?
A. Yes, sir.
Q. What reason did you give for it?
A. From his talk in the lobby.
Q. That was the only reason?
A. Yes, sir, and what I heard other people speak about him, about in the newspaper. I cannot read myself.

Q. You could not read those editorials at all?
A. No, sir but I heard others speak about them.[33]

Like Mrs. Mary Evans's earlier testimony, this statement by Holsenback used rumor and conjecture to strengthen the plausibility of Tillman's self-defense arguments, placing Gonzales's editorials in the position of real villain and Tillman in the more sympathetic role of victim.

The cross-examination degenerated into petty personal bickering between Holsenback and Bellinger and between Bellinger and defense attorneys Nelson and Johnstone. When Holsenback denied ever having said that at the time of the shooting he was at the State House steps rather than at the scene of the killing, and when defense counsel accused Bellinger of bullying an illiterate witness, Bellinger charged the sly, defiant witness of improper "bearing" toward him. He also accused the Tillman claque in the audience of mocking him by laughter and accused the defense counsel of fiendish, unprofessional delight in his embarrassment.

Holsenback's testimony was the highpoint of his life. His death was tragic and had ironic echoes of his testimony. In 1907 his roadside lounging was interrupted by a man named Thompson, with whom Holsenback had quarreled over money. Thompson demanded that Holsenback retract insulting remarks he was rumored to have made about Thompson. The two men pelted each other with insults, and Thompson struck Holsenback with a buggy whip. When Holsenback's hand moved toward his hip, Thompson shot him, claiming that it looked as though Holsenback was going for a gun, forcing Thompson to defend himself. Thus Holsenback died as the result of an act having an eerie similarity to the killing for which his testimony provided a self-defense justification—and perhaps provided encouragement for those inclined toward similar acts.[34]

The prosecution did not fare much better with the next witness, M. C. Lorick.[35] Under questioning by defense counsel Patrick Nelson, Lorick said he grew up in the Dutch Fork area of Lexington County, but at the time of the shooting he lived in Columbia and had been unemployed about two months. Since then he had found work at Richland Mills. He had earlier been a farmer. On the afternoon of January 15, he had been on his way home to dinner when he decided to linger awhile in front of the opera house near the northwest corner of Main and Gervais. He had been there about half an hour watching the passing scene when he saw Gonzales walking on Main Street toward the capitol and Tillman and two other men walking slowly on Main in the other direction.

Gonzales was on the right of the sidewalk as viewed from Lorick's perspective. Tillman was in the middle of his group of three. When Gonzales was about four or five feet from Tillman's group, he turned to the left and tried to pull his right hand out of his coat pocket. Just after Gonzales moved his right hand, Lorick heard a gunshot. He saw Tillman with a pistol in his hand, sidestepping away from the scene. Tillman's eyes quickly scanned in an arc in front of him and returned to stare intently at Gonzales, apparently searching for some sign that Gonzales would retaliate. Soon after Tillman had retreated across the street, Officer Boland came up and arrested Tillman. While Tillman was making his armed withdrawal from the scene, Gonzales "looked like he was kind of weak, sort of staggered off to the transfer station. I do not know whether he was right against the corner but he was right close to the corner, leaning up."

Lorick went home, quickly ate dinner, and returned to Main Street, stationing himself outside the *State* office, where a large crowd had gathered. He was unable to get close because of police crowd control, but he was able to see Gonzales being taken out a back door and placed in an ambulance, which left for the hospital. Lorick's testimony fortified Tillman's self-defense strategy in several respects. Like Mrs. Mary Evans, Senator Talbird, and Holsenback, Lorick placed Tillman in the middle of his group rather than on the outside as several prosecution witnesses had done. This strengthened Tillman's contention that Gonzales's turn to the left meant he was charging at Tillman, rather than trying to avoid him. In addition Lorick described Gonzales as making a movement with his right hand that Tillman could have interpreted as drawing a pistol. But Lorick did not say he saw Gonzales with a pistol, and the movement Gonzales made with his hand was ambiguous enough that there could be many explanations other than drawing a pistol.

On cross-examination Bellinger tried with some success to depict Lorick as a lazy, shiftless character whose testimony was not to be believed. Even his presence at the scene was suspicious or open to doubt. Bellinger pressed Lorick to tell where his income came from. The witness said he had been a farmer but admitted he had not farmed in three years. He evaded specifying any other source of income. Lorick could not explain why he was standing around on the street corner for so long. The questioning involved this testy sparring:

Q. Who were you talking to at the time of the shooting?
A. I was not talking to anybody.
Q. You were by yourself?

A. Yes, sir.
Q. What were you doing over there?
A. I had been up the street every day when I was not doing anything.[36]

The further the questioning went the clearer it became that Lorick's main occupation was standing on the street corner, interrupted only by meals. As with several others subjected to Bellinger's hard-driving cross-examination, the witness's answers took aim at the lawyer. Lorick accused Bellinger of being just as big of a loafer as he was. He said to the prosecutor, "Do not you loaf the biggest portion of your time—only when you can get money out of some man." The defense attorneys accused Bellinger of prying into the private financial affairs of a man in humble circumstances. They insisted that such questioning was not relevant to the case. However, the judge allowed it so long as it was aimed at testing the veracity of the witness rather than merely seeking to humiliate him.

Lorick seethed under these probing questions. When Bellinger scoffed at Lorick's lack of knowledge about Columbia streets, as if to cast doubt on Lorick's claim that he lived there, Lorick snapped back, "no matter about that. I will put something on you to make you 'shamed of [*sic*] the court if you don't quit."[37] As the witness left the stand, he made threatening comments to Bellinger.[38]

6.

TILLMAN'S TESTIMONY

Tillman's defense counsel had skillfully orchestrated its witnesses to lay a predicate for their self-defense strategy and to show by the defendant's testimony that he had suffered relentless criticism in the *State* newspaper, edited by the deceased, but it was up to Tillman himself to convince the jury that reasonable doubt about his guilt existed even though witnesses had seen him shoot Gonzales, an unarmed man. A personal explanation of why he acted was needed. The 1895 Constitution of South Carolina guaranteed that no person "shall be compelled in any criminal case to be a witness against himself."[1] Sometimes a defendant who testifies can convict himself with his own words, or he can—by arrogance or clumsiness—so alienate a jury as to make its members seek a reason to convict him. But a jury that does not hear from the defendant may feel snubbed, insulted, and suspicious. Tillman and his attorneys decided that he should testify. He took the stand "at six minutes to five o'clock" on Thursday, October 8, 1903.[2]

The newspapers provided colorful accounts of Tillman striding to the witness chair. John Marshall of the *Charleston News and Courier* reported: "The prisoner at the bar rose slowly to his great height, a little darker glow coming to his face, a little more set expression coming to his rugged features, a little less listlessness in his carriage and conduct than have marked his mien at other times. Striding forward deliberately to the clerk's desk he took the oath and ascended the stand. Once seated he composed himself in face and figure and awaited Col. Croft's questions as calmly as though he were about to decide some

James H. Tillman conferring with lawyer George W. Croft as friends look on. Illustration by W. H. Loomis. *New York World,* October 10, 1903, 5. Courtesy of the American Newspaper Respository Collection, 1856–2004. David M. Rubenstein Rare Book and Manuscript Library, Duke University.

knotty point of parliamentary law rather than to seek to justify the tragedy that has challenged his liberty or his life."[3]

The *New York World* noted that Tillman, experienced trial lawyer that he was, positioned the witness chair so that he more directly faced the jury.[4] He seemed to welcome rather than shrink from the chance to tell them his story. He was pleased to see the courtroom crowded with supporters and those who had been witnesses for the defense. The paper said that, when Tillman took the stand, he stood up and "ran his hand through his hair and quickly walked to the clerk's desk where he was sworn."[5] The *Atlanta Constitution* noted, "It was just one hour before adjournment that his counsel asked that the defendant be called. With perfect self-composure he arose from his seat among his attorneys and placed himself at the clerk's desk to take the oath."[6] Tillman consistently won good marks from the press for being clear and articulate. In the *State* W. W. Ball observed: "The prisoner bore himself with calmness and his replies to Congressman Croft, his law partner and leading counsel, were well expressed so far as the use of words is concerned. His resonant voice was easily heard throughout the courtroom. . . . The demeanor appeared as that of one who deemed himself a greatly persecuted man and at the same time was still resentful."[7]

Croft deftly led Tillman through the minefield of his testimony.[8] Their first goal was to establish rapport with the jury by briefly recounting Tillman's life story in an informal way as if he were being introduced to them in a social setting. He stated that he was born in Edgefield as the eldest son of the late George D. Tillman, a long-time congressman from South Carolina. After finishing college, the defendant said, he went to Winnsboro to read law under his brother-in-law, Osmund W. Buchanan, then a lawyer and legislator, later a judge, and now one of Tillman's defense attorneys.

How the Quarrel Began

After this brief personal introduction, Tillman plunged into the thicket of his bitter personal relations with N. G. Gonzales. While in Winnsboro, Tillman wrote an article for the local paper under the "nom de plume 'Fair Play.'" In the article he charged that N. G. Gonzales, then a correspondent for the *Charleston News and Courier,* "had misrepresented a speech which Capt. Tillman, now Senator Tillman, had made before the March convention and I took occasion to correct it." The testimony does not enlighten us as to dates, but the controversy largely took place in April and May 1890.[9] When N. G. Gonzales attempted to find out the name of the writer, Tillman at first refused to reveal his identity because "I did not care to get in any newspaper controversy and my friends advised me for that reason not to give the name but when Mr. Gonzales wrote a very bitter attack upon me I did give my name and established it as well as I recollect in the Winnsboro News and Herald or Herald and News. I do not remember which it was"[10] Croft asked, "So it is not correct to say that you withheld your name? Tillman responded, "No sir, it is absolutely false." It seemed important to Tillman to refute the impression that he cowered behind his pen name.

It is interesting to note that the first blow in this newspaper war of words was struck not by Gonzales but by Tillman. To picture Tillman as a helpless little man overawed by a press lord, as a person who had no access to the press, is misleading. Later Tillman's testimony revealed another incident in which he was the aggressor in a newspaper.

After describing the "Fair Play" incident, Tillman moved on to his next clash with Gonzales, who had deeply resented references in the Winnsboro articles to him as a "wily Spaniard."[11] When Tillman's Uncle Ben was elected governor in 1890, the ambitious nephew attended the inauguration on December 4 and wanted desperately to attend the state ball, the social event of the year. Attendance at such events would signal his membership in the political and social elite, but to attend he needed to become a member of the prestigious private club that sponsored the event. He obtained endorsements of his candidacy from former governor John C. Sheppard and other prominent members but reckoned without the simmering resentment of the one he had branded a "wily Spaniard." Tillman's friends informed him that Gonzales, a member, had organized a blackball against him, and they recommended that Tillman withdraw. He did, and his hopes of attending the state ball were dashed.[12]

Croft tried to picture this social embarrassment as a cruel disappointment to a young man. When he asked Tillman his age at the time, Tillman answered that he had been born on June 27, 1869, but an encyclopedia entry states the year of his birth as 1868.[13] He would have been twenty-one (or twenty-two) at the time of the blackballing incident, thirty-three (or thirty-four) at the time he shot the man he thought had stymied his hopes for the governorship, and thirty-four (or thirty-five) at the time of the trial. Tillman said the incident provoked him to send a challenge to Gonzales, through Mr. George Legare, to meet him in Augusta, Georgia, where they could have a duel without violating the South Carolina prohibition of the practice. Gonzales wanted Tillman to put the challenge in writing, as was customary under John Lyde Wilson's *Code of Honor* (1858), but Tillman did not do so for fear of it getting publicized and embarrassing his uncle the governor. Although he got no acceptance from Gonzales, Tillman went to Georgia. Gonzales did not show up, and he failed to respond to Tillman's demand that he pay Tillman's hotel bills.[14] Perhaps an implication intended by this testimony was that, since Gonzales would not allow him to vindicate his honor by engaging in a gentlemanly duel, Tillman, after continued affronts, was driven to a unilateral attack.[15] A further point of the testimony may have been to show that Gonzales's enmity toward Tillman started before he held public office, and thus Gonzales's bitter criticism could not be justified as a garden-variety commentary on one seeking or occupying public office. It was personal revenge that served no public purpose.

Croft's questions then returned to Tillman's newspaper career. Tillman said, "I was in the newspaper business for a considerable time."[16] He viewed himself as a superior newspaperman because, unlike other South Carolina journalists whom he did not name, he was energetic enough to search for the facts. One of the papers he worked for was the *Atlanta Constitution.* He also sent "telegraphic correspondence" to the *Columbia Journal.* For a time, he served as a correspondent in Washington, D.C., reporting on events in the nation's capital as they affected South Carolina and Georgia. One of those reports led to another clash with Gonzales. Early in Grover Cleveland's second term, which began in 1893, Tillman reported on the chances of South Carolinians getting federal appointments. Gonzales was seeking an appointment as consul general in either Shanghai, China, or Rio de Janeiro, Brazil. Tillman wrote that Gonzales was not expected to get the appointment. This turned out to be correct, but Gonzales seemed to be deeply offended that this negative information was publicized. This led to a confrontation in the lobby of the Metropolitan Hotel, a favorite haunt of southerners visiting Washington, D.C. Tillman frequented the lobby to pick up news of interest to southerners, and he and Gonzales "had some hot words there." The next day Tillman bought some cigars in the lobby and offered them to fellow southerners, including Gonzales, who rudely spurned that friendly gesture. This incident shows Tillman exercising the power of the press and not being victimized by it. In about 1894 he returned to Edgefield and left journalism for the practice of law, becoming a partner of George Croft, who was now examining him.

Tillman told the jury that his first public position was a nonelective one, service in the Spanish-American War. At the outset of the war in 1898, he volunteered his services to the governor, who appointed Tillman lieutenant colonel of the First South Carolina Regiment. This was a considerable plum for a young man of twenty-nine with little experience. The regiment never made it to Cuba, but they repeatedly sought assignment to an active combat role. This lack of combat glory must have galled the ambitious Tillman, especially in light of the fact that his personal gadfly, N. G. Gonzales, had served as a lieutenant on the staff of a Cuban rebel general during that war.[17] Tillman complained that, when Gonzales returned from Cuba and resumed his editorial duties at the *State,* he became sharply critical of Tillman's military service with his regiment, which by then had returned to Columbia from deployment in Jacksonville, Florida.[18] Tillman accused Gonzales of launching a personal vendetta against him and seeking to have him criminally charged, first in civilian court and then in a court-martial. This arose out of an incident in which a faithful Tillman family retainer, a black man named George Johnstone, who had accompanied Tillmans to war for generations, had been abused by some "Negro boys" who stole "a very fine pistol" that Tillman had given "old George." Many of the officers and men of the regiment were fond of "old George" and resented his humiliation by the thieves, so they took immediate extralegal action. Tillman admitted being involved, saying that "we took those negroes and whipped them—gave them a pretty good beating." He could not understand why a newspaper would be interested in the conduct of a high-ranking state-militia officer who had participated in assault and battery. It was a private matter for the regiment, or better still, a private matter for the Tillmans concerning one of their servants. Gonzales interfered by urging civilian prosecution before a magistrate, and when that case was dismissed, he urged holding a court-martial, which did not take place.

In his testimony Tillman complained that Gonzales continued his editorial campaign to denigrate Tillman's military service by accusing him of letting personal ambition dominate his decisions as commander and acting inconsistently by first leading a petition drive to have the regiment disbanded as the war neared an end and the opportunities to gain combat glory vanished and then, when he became colonel of the regiment on the death of its commander, by reversing course and demanding that the unit be kept on active duty. Tillman still brooded over the unfairness of such a characterization. He felt he had kept the interests of the enlisted men, who needed to return home to their jobs, farms, and families, uppermost on this issue.

The final item in Tillman's litany of complaints about Gonzales's treatment of his Spanish-American War service concerned Tillman's proposal to the military authorities in Washington that he be permitted to organize a company of Indian scouts with himself as commander. He proposed that the group serve in the Philippine Islands. Tillman admitted that army officials had rejected the idea because they were fearful of teaching "those Indians our method of warfare and the president [President McKinley] told me frankly he was afraid they would get over there and go to scalping some of us." What rankled Tillman was not so much this official rejection of his pet idea but Gonzales's holding up this attempt to serve his country to ridicule as the wild product of an overheated imagination. Tillman complained to the jury that Gonzales "had me depicted in warpaint, Chief of the Chippemonks and Groundhogs," tribes he invented to make Tillman look like a buffoon.[19] One lampoon, which the *State* borrowed from the *News and Courier,* said that Tillman, "attired in a horse blanket and tail feathers . . . would cut a figure in the van of battle that should be an inspiration to patriotic poets and artists for all time to come."[20]

Despite Tillman's parade of complaints in his testimony, the *State*'s coverage of his military service was not entirely negative. It printed highly laudatory dispatches from his regiment's soldiers. A letter from William Banks said that Tillman's soldiers "fairly idolize their battalion commander."[21] In another dispatch, describing the debate on whether the regiment should be disbanded or go to Cuba, Banks said the men went to Tillman's tent, asked for a speech, and when he complied with "another red hot speech," carried him around camp on their shoulders.[22]

A few weeks before the regiment was mustered out, late in the fall of 1898, Tillman made a speech after a concert by the unit's band in Columbia. In it he complained that the regiment had been "maligned by Penny-a-liner-editors who were living on the fat of the land while the soldiers of the regiment were sweltering under the hot sun and feasting on hard tack."[23] He singled out the *State* as being consistently prejudiced against the First Regiment while praising the Second.[24] This picture, like Tillman's testimony, is incomplete. When the regiment was mustered out, the *State* published several items praising the unit as the first to volunteer and as an outfit that had grown from a group of untrained civilians into a well-honed unit.[25] And when Tillman received a vindication of sorts in the magistrate's court's dismissal of the charges against him in the whipping case because the court considered them not of "such serious character" as to warrant trial in general sessions court, that action received as much coverage as the original allegations.[26] The court's dismissal may reveal an attitude that black against black crime, such as theft of the pistol, is not significant enough to justify the court's attention, and thus can be dealt with by the kind of extralegal "justice" used by Tillman and his kangaroo court of soldiers.

After describing his military career in the Spanish-American War, Tillman's testimony focused on his political career and what he perceived to be Gonzales's vindictive treatment of him in campaigning for or serving in public office.[27] Tillman entered politics in 1900 with his election as a delegate to the Democratic National Convention and his race for lieutenant governor. The launch of Tillman's political career offered a tempting feast to Gonzales. He did not wait long before digging in.

Tillman's Attack on the Editorials

Tillman charged that Gonzales began to hurl false accusations against him from the moment he entered politics. Tillman said Gonzales accused him of betraying Senator Ben Tillman, by working against his uncle in political campaigns. Tillman claimed Gonzales damaged his reputation as lieutenant governor by saying that as presiding officer of the Senate he arrogantly treated the members like wayward children needing his firm dictatorial hand. Tillman argued that both charges were obviously false but that Gonzales recklessly made them anyway.[28]

Here the prosecution woke up. During Tillman's testimony, the prosecution saw its case rapidly going down the wrong road. Rather than focusing on the shooting itself and whether Tillman acted in self-defense while reasonably fearing immediate serious bodily harm, the case had begun to focus more and more on whether the editorials went too far in criticizing Tillman. Harsh words, no matter how critical, do not justify murder.[29] But now the case had begun to focus on how harsh the editorials were and whether such harshness was justified. Under freedom of speech standards, this decision is to be made by the speaker, in this case newspaper editors. This is especially true when the object of the criticism is a candidate for public office.[30] But if the case was headed down the wrong road, the prosecution had helped head it in that direction. At the request of the defense, the prosecution had produced a comprehensive file of *State* editorials published in 1902 that mention Jim Tillman. But it chose to introduce them as part of its own case because it believed the critical nature of the editorials would help to prove Tillman had a motive for murder, that he had formed a malicious intent prior to committing the act.[31] This may have been the narrow ground on which the judge admitted the testimony into evidence, but the focus was the fairness of the editorials. It would be small wonder then if the jury thought that was what it was deciding, not whether the elements of murder and self-defense had been met.[32]

Judge Gary directed Tillman and his counsel to focus his testimony on the editorials on whether they showed that Gonzales harbored such "extreme malignity" toward Tillman that it—together with the threats that Gonzales had been reported as making and his movements at the scene of the shooting—would create a reasonable fear of impending physical harm in the accused that would justify his shooting in self-defense.[33] In pursuance of making this showing, Tillman contended that Gonzales's editorials had accused him of financial dishonesty. He was unfairly accused of not promptly turning over money he had collected for a Confederate monument to the women's organization sponsoring the fund drive, and he was accused of misapplying money he had received from his clients. Tillman claimed that these charges were without foundation and that he had successfully disproved them by evidence, such as a receipt from the monument committee, but Gonzales continued to berate him.[34]

Tillman's testimony next addressed the editorials that he contended unfairly charged him with embarrassing the state by unilaterally attempting to revoke an invitation to President Theodore Roosevelt to come to South Carolina to present an ornamental sword to Major Micah Jenkins, who had been in Roosevelt's "Rough Rider" unit during the Spanish-American War. Tillman asserted that he was only trying to protect the honor of the state and his uncle, Senator Ben Tillman, when Roosevelt rudely revoked an invitation to the senator to attend a White House dinner for Prince Henry of Prussia. Roosevelt rescinded the invitation because Ben Tillman had engaged in a fist fight on the Senate floor with the other South Carolina senator, John L. McLaurin, after Tillman accused McLaurin of accepting a bribe and McLaurin called him a liar. Tillman struck the first blow against McLaurin, a former follower who had become too independent and had committed the cardinal sin among South Carolina Democrats: cozying up to the Republicans.[35] When Jim Tillman blundered onto the scene by coming to Uncle Ben's rescue by unilaterally revoking the invitation to the president to visit South Carolina, this action caused panic among state dignitaries, who did not want to insult the president and provoke people throughout the country to boycott the commercial exposition at which Roosevelt was to speak. A rival fund purchased a more glittering sword for Major Jenkins, and state officials reinvited the president, who ultimately came to the state and presented the second sword to his old comrade in arms. All this inspired Gonzales to sarcasm. One editorial, published in the *State* on February 28, 1902, at the height of the Jenkins sword controversy, warned people throughout the country not to be misled by the lieutenant governor's antics. It said Jim Tillman did not represent "any reputable element" in South Carolina, dismissed him as a "chronic notoriety seeker," and called his solo revocation of Roosevelt's invitation an "act of boorishness."[36] A March 2, 1902, editorial, "A Finisher for Jim Tillman," called Tillman's unilateral withdrawal of Roosevelt's invitation an "affront" to both the president and the state he falsely claimed to represent in the matter.[37]

The *State* in essence called Jim Tillman a liar when it said his claim that subscribers to his fund had asked him to withdraw the invitation was false. Some of the most insulting language in the *State* did not originate in that paper but was reprinted from the *Washington Post,* which quoted what it called an old Spanish proverb that "declares it to be a waste of lather to shave an ass." Then the *Post* even more pointedly observed: "The Honorable Jim Tillman has placed himself in the also brayed class."[38] Tillman complained in his testimony that Gonzales had "blackguarded" him so often he could not keep count.[39] One such reference occurred when the paper compared Major Jenkins, a genuine hero, to the "blackguards" "that we may occasionally elect."[40] Tillman and defense counsel George Croft were particularly incensed by other unfavorable comparisons of Jenkins with Tillman, such as: "the soldier and the swashbuckler" and the "gentleman and the ruffian," but the *State* credited the *Charleston Evening Post* with inventing these comparisons.[41] Tillman had a habit of blaming every critical remark on the *State* even when it was merely reprinting comments made in other papers, such as the *Washington Post* or the *Charleston Evening Post.* But the *State* could pick up metaphors created by other papers and exploit them. One example is the *State*'s use of the *Washington Post*'s comparison of Tillman to a jackass. One editorial in the *State,* "Another Bray—and Another Coming," discusses Tillman's tendency to be a "notoriety" seeker and slams both Tillman's role in the Jenkins affair and his failure to get deployed out of the country during the Spanish-American War.[42] The editorial sarcastically refers to Tillman as "that hero of Smith's branch camp" and concludes that the publicity he was receiving was not the laudatory comments he hoped for, but "even an ass in a colonel's uniform might flinch at the instant recognition, the country over, of his voice when heard in a bravura passage."[43]

Tillman's testimony and the arguments of his counsel interspersed throughout that testimony contended that Gonzales's editorials were so extreme that they were not protected by freedom of the press, and thus Tillman could attack their author, who refused to cease the abuse. Most of the articles Tillman denounced in his testimony fit well within a newspaper's core function in a democracy: criticizing government officials and candidates for office so that voters can make intelligent choices.[44]

Free Speech Precedents

The need for vigorous criticism of officials and candidates was hardly a novel concept developed by Gonzales. Such ideas were germinating even before the Revolution and the writing of the Constitution. Much earlier, in 1720, *Cato's Letters* circulated throughout the American colonies, including South Carolina. This work by John Trenchard and Thomas Gordon, argued that the government officials who waged the fiercest wars against the press were most likely those whose misdeeds were being exposed in print. The authors noted that all liberty, whether property rights or others, depended on the vigilance of the press to expose government officials and candidates who endangered freedom.[45] The John Peter Zenger case provided a widely celebrated and dramatic example of safeguarding the freedom of the press in its role of exposing official abuse of power despite heavy-handed attempts to suppress publication, intimidate, and imprison an editor. Zenger, a New York editor, was arrested and tried in 1735 on a charge that he committed seditious libel by accusing the colonial governor of official misconduct in attempting to manipulate elections and judicial proceedings. At Zenger's trial the jury, inspired by the free-expression arguments made by defense counsel Andrew Hamilton, brought in a verdict of not guilty despite the defense's admission that Zenger had published the offending material and despite the judge's instructions that the truth of the writing was not a defense. In effect the jury nullified a law that was hostile to freedom of the press and embraced Hamilton's argument that unless we have "the liberty—both of exposing and opposing arbitrary power (in these parts of the world, at least) by speaking and writing the truth," other liberties will be lost.[46] Such ideas influenced the formation of the constitutional rights of freedom of speech and of the press. An influential architect of those rights, James Madison, observed that "the right of electing members of the Government constitutes more particularly the essence of a free and responsible government. The value and efficacy of this right depends on the knowledge of the comparative merits and demerits of the candidates for public trust, and on the equal freedom, consequently, of examining and dismissing these merits and demerits of the candidates respectively."[47]

Madison argued that government action inhibiting robust, even harsh, unpleasant debate about candidates "repressed that information and communication among the people which is indispensable to the just exercise of their electoral rights."[48] And in a system of separation of powers, where government branches act as checks and balances on each other, a vigilant press helps each branch to stay informed about the activities of the others. Free speech provides a means to air grievances against the government that might otherwise be expressed by violent means. In this manner free speech contributes to, rather than undermines, the stability of the government.

An 1803 commentary on the developing American approach to free expression came from Virginia's St. George Tucker, an eminent jurist in both state and federal courts. As a law professor at the College of William and Mary, Tucker was one of the earliest scholars to write a systematic study of the constitutional law of the new federal union and its states.[49] He saw a more robust role for freedom of expression than the fragile, cramped right envisioned by Tillman's testimony and arguments by his counsel.[50]

Tillman and his attorneys repeatedly argued that Gonzales had abused freedom of the press by expressing opinions and not merely stating facts. Tucker left no doubt that to him, if it were to play a useful role to keep the electorate in a democracy informed, free expression must encompass the right to state opinions as well as facts. Opinions are often necessary to give facts a framework that lends them cogency and force. Tucker was following a path blazed by Benjamin Franklin, who noted in his 1731 essay "Apology for Printers" that, if opinions were eliminated, there would be little left for newspapers to say. He observed "that the business of printing has chiefly to do with mens [*sic*] opinions; most things that are printed tending to promote some, or oppose others." In this same vein he argued "that if all printers were determined not to print anything till they were sure it would offend nobody, there would be very little printed."[51] One passage in the essay became a motto posted on newspaper office walls around the country: "Printers are educated in the belief that when men differ in opinion, both sides ought equally to have the advantage of being heard by the public; and that when truth and error have fair play, the former is always an overmatch for the latter."[52] But while Franklin thought newspapers could print offensive opinions as a part of public discourse, he believed they should avoid stooping to personal vendettas. Tillman's testimony showed that he thought he had been subjected to such abuse.[53]

In 1799 another early commentator, George Hay, wrote an attack on the constitutionality of the short-lived Sedition Act of 1798, which was aimed at punishing newspapers that were critical of the administration of President John Adams during a time of tense relations with France. Hay, like Tucker, emphasized the importance of giving newspapers the right to express opinions as an essential part of keeping the electorate informed. He contended that "surely freedom of the press, which is the medium of all publications, will not permit a man to be punished, for publishing any *opinion* on any subject." He argued that protecting the expression of facts but not opinions would erect a line demarcating free from banned expression that would be impossible to administer because "the difficulty of distinguishing in many cases between fact and opinion, is extremely great."[54] A late-twentieth-century scholar applied the science of linguistics to free-expression analysis and came to a conclusion similar to Hay's earlier statement. Frederick F. Schauer observed that "most speech will contain some elements of fact, some of inference, some of emotion and some of value judgment," and thus it is difficult to separate one of these elements from the rest and banish it from the protection given free expression.[55]

An eminent South Carolina scholar and combative political figure held a similar belief regarding the importance of opinions. Thomas Cooper, president of South Carolina College in 1820–33, was a doctor, a scientist, a lawyer and the compiler of a scholarly collection of his state's statutes and constitutions. But in an earlier incarnation as a northern newspaper editor vigorously advocating the cause of Thomas Jefferson's Republicans during the Sedition Act of 1798, he was prosecuted, convicted, and jailed for "false, scandalous and malicious writing" defaming the administration of President John Adams. In an 1830 essay on liberty of the press, Cooper looked back on that experience and argued that the clash of opinions was an essential ingredient in the search for truth.[56] The view that the expression of opinion was a protected liberty because it was an essential part of the meaningful criticism of government and candidates, continued to prevail in constitutional scholarship available at the time of the Tillman trial.[57] But in the trial itself, especially during Tillman's testimony, it was treated like rank heresy. St. George Tucker anticipated and refuted such belittling of freedom of the press long before it was made by Tillman's lawyers.

Tillman Attacks the Editorials

Tillman's defense attorneys contended that freedom of the press was an inferior species compared to the vigorous freedom of speech they were exercising in court. Tucker observed that a vigorous freedom of the press was just as important as freedom of speech. The impatience of audiences required that speeches be relatively short. But useful criticism of the government sometimes demanded lengthy exposition such as only the press could deliver. Tucker noted that speeches could be heard by only limited numbers, but newspapers, with their ability to produce many copies, could reach the larger audience necessary if criticism of government was to be effective.[58] Public officials and candidates in a democracy should expect intense examination and criticism that sometimes grows harsh. If the official cannot take it, he should resign rather than attempt to curb the speech. Limiting criticism of government, officials, or candidates, undermines democracy and brings on "oligarchy, aristocracy, or monarchy."[59] To be sure influential commentators, such as United States Supreme Court justice and constitutional scholar Joseph Story, cautioned against interpreting the concept of free speech and press as embracing an unbridled right. In his 1833 treatise, Story argued that the right of free expression did not "allow to every citizen a right to destroy, at his pleasure, the reputation, the peace, the property, and even the personal safety of every other citizen."[60] But Story clearly thought that injury to such interests by an abusive press should be redressed by legal means rather than by "resort to private vengeance," such as "assassinations."[61] It is unlikely that Story's parsimonious view of free expression would countenance the violent self-help Tillman engaged in.

Tillman's testimony showed that he was especially bitter about articles scrutinizing his conduct as lieutenant governor and candidate for governor. Tillman was furious when Gonzales published an editorial lamenting the fact that only one man's life stood between Lieutenant Governor Jim Tillman and the executive mansion.[62] Particularly rankling to Tillman was criticism of his performance as presiding officer of the Senate when he was lieutenant governor, and much of his testimony focused on trying to discredit Gonzales's ridicule of his conduct in that role. A notorious incident occurred in February and March 1902, just before Tillman began his run for governor. The timing of the embarrassing publicity could not have been worse. The Senate was considering a bill that would have expanded the laws requiring the enclosure of farm animals to prohibit trespass of one's domestic fowl upon another's land. Enclosure laws can be deeply divisive issues in agricultural states. In the midst of a vigorous debate on the proposal, a senator moved that consideration of the bill be postponed indefinitely. When senators attempted to debate the motion, Tillman ruled that such a motion was nondebatable. A senator who was stifled by this ruling sought to appeal it to the floor for a vote that could overrule the presiding officer. But he was persuaded to pursue a less confrontational route, and the matter was referred to the rules committee to determine if such motions were debatable. The committee reported that the motions were debatable, and the report was accepted by the Senate.[63]

It was Tillman's response to these actions of the Senate that provoked Gonzales to turn his investigative reporting skill toward the incident, and it was Gonzales's articles on this action, that led Tillman to complain in his testimony that his record as presiding officer had been unfairly condemned in the paper. Just after the committee's report and the Senate's adoption of it, Tillman inserted in the Senate record a statement that claimed endorsement of his ruling from the Olympian gods of parliamentary law: "The chair respectfully cites the committee to Jefferson's manual and heartily commends it to the committee on Rules for diligent study. Since making the ruling the chair has taken the occasion to inquire of the two highest parliamentarians of this country as to the correctness of the same, and is much gratified to learn that it is sustained by them.

Of course the interpretation placed on the rule by the committee on Rules will henceforth be observed, however much at variance it may be with parliamentary law."[64]

Gonzales was not content to take Tillman's word as to the nature of his communications with "the two highest parliamentarians of this country." These august experts were D. B. Henderson, speaker of the U.S. House of Representatives, and Senator William P. Frye, often presiding officer of the U.S. Senate. Tillman also contacted Thomas B. Reed, former speaker of the U.S. House of Representatives and author of a leading manual on parliamentary law.[65] Gonzales telegraphed Henderson and Frye seeking copies of Tillman's query to them and their replies. He published the results of this exchange in an article organized like a legal brief with lettered exhibits.[66] Both the presiding officers Tillman consulted informed him that, while *Jefferson's Manual* was silent on the issue, a motion to postpone indefinitely was debatable under the rules of both houses of the U.S. Congress. Former speaker Reed merely sent Tillman a copy of his book on parliamentary rules, which clearly states that motions to postpone indefinitely are debatable "inasmuch as an affirmative vote on this motion may decide the main question, the merits of the question must be open for discussion."[67] To Gonzales this correspondence proved that Tillman had lied to the Senate when he told it the authorities he had consulted sustained him. What the state needed was not an expert in the arcane points of parliamentary procedure but an honest man.[68]

The defense introduced into evidence a 1901 editorial to fortify Tillman's testimony that Gonzales had not dealt fairly with his term as lieutenant governor.[69] This satirical piece mounted a feigned defense of Lieutenant Governor Tillman against criticism from other papers that he spent too much time away from his official duties covertly betting large sums of money on gamecock fights held at various obscure country locations. The article said being lieutenant governor did not take much time. It largely involved presiding over the Senate, and when it was not in session, he was free to spend his time "in such labors and diversions as may seem to him becoming, rational and elevating." Then, satirizing not only Tillman but also the somewhat pompous style of constitutional-law authorities, the article concluded that Tillman did not violate article XVII, section 8, of the South Carolina Constitution of 1895, which prohibited state officials from "gambling or betting on games of chance." The editorial concluded that Tillman was not gambling since that involved risking something of value, and the main thing he was risking was his reputation, which no one would consider a thing of value. A man of Tillman's large but fragile ego could not stand such mockery. His honor had been held up to ridicule.

Tillman's testimony showed that his pride was deeply wounded by articles questioning his political and moral courage. His political courage was questioned when the *State* reprinted articles from the *Anderson Daily Mail* and the *Florence Times* in which the author, D. H. Russell, said Tillman ran away from a debate in the gubernatorial campaign by using the phony excuse that his sister was gravely ill and he needed to rush to her side. Tillman especially resented these charges because he said his sister was in fact ill and died after lingering for some months.[70] These articles were doubly offensive to a man of Tillman's masculine swagger because the passage quoted from the *Florence Times* accused him of "taking a great refuge in the petticoats in this campaign."[71] Gonzales reprinted the Florence and Anderson stories to show that the *State* was not the only paper critical of Tillman, and his critics included D. H. Russell, who had been a staunch Ben Tillman supporter. James H. Tillman complained repeatedly that the *State* attacked the way he lived, his personal life, rather than confining its criticism to his conduct as an official and candidate. An examination of the editorials introduced into evidence by both sides reveals that the vast majority of editorials from the *State* dealt with Jim Tillman as an official or a candidate. The articles involving his sister's illness come close to dealing with his personal life, but even they primarily involve his conduct as a candidate. Still Tillman's testimony on these articles seemed to flow from a deep well of resentment because they not only questioned his courage but also intruded on what he considered a delicate family matter.

But some support for the claim that editorials in the *State* encroached on what Tillman and his lawyers considered the forbidden topic of his family life can be found in an August 11, 1902, article, "The Truth in Pursuit of a Candidate." This article, written in the closing days of the hard-fought gubernatorial campaign, focused on the paper's claim that Jim Tillman made false charges of oppression by newspapers, with the *State* as the archvillain. In denying Jim Tillman's charge that the *State* had once accused Senator Ben Tillman of wife beating, the article said: "The home life of B. R. Tillman is unassailable, and it would be to the credit of the nephew if he were half as decent in his personal relations as the uncle whose name he is disgracing."[72] This vaguely worded passage makes no specific accusations against James H. Tillman and is not part of a sustained discussion of his family life. It claims to be a refutation of false charges against the paper made by Jim Tillman. But he and his defense counsel seemed to view it as a poisonous innuendo that Jim Tillman beat his wife, and thus it was enough to drive an honorable man to justifiable homicide.

Also galling to Tillman, and prominently mentioned in his testimony, were a series of articles questioning his physical courage. Gonzales dangerously taunted Tillman for his failure to fight to vindicate his honor and compared him unfavorably to Senator Ben Tillman, who had fought Senator John L. McLaurin on the U.S. Senate floor. This taunting series began with a July 25, 1902, editorial, "Grit and Steel," which arose from a disagreement between Jim Tillman and Edward Hope "Ed" DeCamp, editor of the *Gaffney Ledger* as well as of a magazine appealing to followers of gamecock fighting.[73] In his paper DeCamp accused Tillman of taking out advertising in the magazine but not making prompt payment of the bill. DeCamp called Tillman "a gambler, a liar and a drunkard."[74] When Tillman denounced the DeCamp article in a Gaffney speech during his gubernatorial campaign, DeCamp suddenly appeared on stage and repeated the charges to Tillman's face. Pictures of DeCamp taken late in his life showed a crusty-looking, white-haired old man with fierce eyes and a drooping mustache that made him look like Mark Twain in old age. At the time of the confrontation, DeCamp was only thirty-seven with his hair and mustache still dark, but his eyes were already fierce; they must have bored right through Tillman's bravado. Instead of hitting the man who called him a liar, as his uncle had done in the Senate, Tillman calmly asked for evidence to back up the charges and patiently examined what was offered. Rather than complimenting Jim Tillman for displaying the patience and restraint that many would have found admirable in a public official, Gonzales scoffed at him for not having shown the fighting spirit that Ben Tillman's nephew and a true son of Edgefield should have shown. Gonzales recommended that Edgefield adopt DeCamp as a truer example of its fighting spirit than "the patient Jim."[75] Gonzales pointedly observed that DeCamp, even though he had called Tillman a liar to his face, continued to walk around Gaffney "quite whole of body" while Tillman continued his "courageous serenity."

DeCamp had been a compositor at the *State* when it printed its first issue in 1891 and rose to become pressroom foreman before moving on to edit and then buy the *Gaffney Ledger.* He continued to maintain close ties with N. G. Gonzales, and shortly after his campaign platform clash with Jim Tillman, he wrote Gonzales asking "can't you assist me in getting several affidavits from people in Columbia regarding Jim's character, especially his drinking and gambling." DeCamp continued to track Tillman's activities because he resented his "sarcasm and insults" about the paper.[76] One Gonzales biographer concluded that one result of this correspondence was that Gonzales furnished DeCamp with information charging Tillman with mishandling funds he had raised for a Confederate monument.[77] The information fueled accusations that Tillman was tardy in turning the money over to the organizers of the fund drive. Tillman adamantly denied the allegations in his testimony at his murder trial.

The *State*'s coverage of the Gaffney encounter with DeCamp was not a one-shot affair but a veritable barrage of jeering commentary, which—as Tillman's testimony showed—deeply wounded his pride. Gonzales returned to the theme again and again in scoffing at Jim Tillman for not having the physical courage to fight DeCamp. Perhaps the most stinging of these follow-up articles on the DeCamp incident was one published on July 28, 1902, "Two Tillmans–A Contrast," in which the *State* compared the meek nephew Jim to the feisty Uncle Ben.[78] It contrasts Jim's "lamb-like exit" from the confrontation in which DeCamp called him a liar with the conduct of Senator Tillman when called a liar by McLaurin. The article quotes the Associated Press as saying that Senator Tillman "sprang with tiger-like ferocity at his colleague" and explained that "no man could hold up his head in decent society should he, being near enough to answer the lie with a blow, not give it." Jim Tillman explained his more measured response to DeCamp's provocation: "As Lieutenant Governor and an officer of the law a street brawl would have been most unbecoming. My hands were tied. Prometheus [in the Greek legend] when bound had his vitals eaten by vultures." This reasoned explanation is admirable, but then Jim Tillman waxed melodramatic by comparing himself to Christ: "they may crucify me upon a cross of slander but God in heaven knows it is as unjustifiable as when they pinioned to the cross the lonely Nazarene."

The important point here is that Gonzales jeered at his future assassin for not choosing a violent course of action when he was called a liar. The article pointedly says that "if you accept the deliberate declaration of the uncle you must find that the nephew, having acted as he did at Gaffney, can never 'hold up his head in decent society'!" Even such mocking words cannot justify a murder, especially when printed a year and a half before the killing, but it was a dangerous game Gonzales was playing—baiting an emotional man who obviously hated him.[79] Now that Tillman viewed himself as a tragic figure of historical dimensions, first comparing himself to Prometheus, the hero of Greek legends who was punished by angry gods for bringing fire to mankind, and then comparing himself to Christ, who was punished not for his own sins but those of others, we find a man who saw himself in such grandiose terms that he was unlikely to tolerate much belittling treatment.[80]

As we consider these stinging editorials and Tillman's testimony about how they affected his state of mind concerning danger posed by Gonzales, it is important to understand that this was not a one-way flow of invective. Tillman gave as good as he got, and the gubernatorial campaign gave him a wonderful platform from which to attack Gonzales. This was not a case of the helpless little man being beaten by the brutish paper. In his testimony Tillman described how he defended himself and launched offensive strikes of his own.

> Q. [by George Croft] Mr. Tillman in your speeches, particularly in Columbia and Yorkville, I believe you did state plainly what you thought of Mr. Gonzales?
>
> A. Yes sir. I never missed any occasion to state plainly and openly what I thought of him. I stated it on every stump in South Carolina.[81]

Apparently Gonzales kept as careful a count of the names Tillman called him as Tillman did of the insults he received from Gonzales. In an article titled "Partly Personal and Partly Political," Gonzales recalled some of the labels Tillman had applied to him over the course of their relationship. These included: "Ransy Sniffle," "Cuban pony," and "treacherous [or wily] Spaniard."[82] In this piece Gonzales answered Tillman's charge that Gonzales was not man enough to agree to a duel with Tillman in Georgia, where they could fight legally. Gonzales said Tillman never challenged him. He only ambiguously asked through an intermediary what his reply would be if Tillman did issue a challenge. Gonzales said his reply was that if Tillman issued the challenge, he would then consider how to respond.[83]

One of the insulting names Tillman hurled at Gonzales, "Ransy Sniffle," is obscure, but it reveals much about Tillman's attitude toward Gonzales. Ransy was a character in "The Fight," a story in Augustus Baldwin Longstreet's 1835 *Georgia Scenes.*[84] Ransy was an inveterate gossip who devoted his time to stirring up trouble between formerly friendly neighbors. Longstreet wrote that his character "never seemed fairly alive except when he was witnessing, fomenting or talking about a fight," but he avoided participating in the fight himself.[85]

Tillman Denies Premeditation

Tillman's testimony about Gonzales's stinging editorials and his description of the history of the feuding between the two, cast Gonzales in the villain's role and diverted the case from Tillman's actions on the fatal day and the days leading up to it. But the case could not be diverted forever. After dealing with the editorials and trying to picture himself as the victim rather than the assailant, Tillman's testimony turned to refuting some of the damaging aspects of the prosecution's case. It was important for him to undermine testimony that showed him planning Gonzales's death well in advance of the shooting rather than just reacting to the sudden need to defend himself against aggressive action by the deceased. Charles J. Terrell had testified that, as he and Tillman were on a train traveling to Columbia in the fall of 1902, Tillman flourished a pistol while talking boisterously about killing Gonzales. Tillman denied that any such conversation ever took place. He described Terrell as an enemy who had written belligerent editorials about him. Tillman asserted that he would never unburden himself to such a person, who could be expected to twist anything he said. He did remember the train trip, but he said he spent most of the time talking to the manager of a quarry that he owned and not about Gonzales.[86]

Tillman made a systematic attempt to contradict or discredit any testimony that depicted him as fantasizing about killing Gonzales long before his fatal act. He denied confiding in Major Dick Anderson at Grice's livery stable in Edgefield that he would strike back at Gonzales if he could find a way to get at him. He charged that R. G. Arthur, the prosecution witness who had testified about Tillman's livery-stable statements, was not worthy of belief. Arthur had defaulted on a bond he took out as salesman for the Singer Sewing Machine Company, and he disliked Tillman because he was his attorney in Singer's successful suit against him.[87]

Dr. Edward C. "Ned" Adams was Tillman's close friend, but the young physician's testimony about a Columbia hotel-room meeting Tillman had with his supporters near the end of his 1902 gubernatorial campaign was extremely damaging to the defendant. Adams had described Tillman as already bragging, five months before the shooting, about his plans to get Gonzales. Now that he was on the witness stand, Tillman had to defuse that testimony. He agreed that the atmosphere in his room at the Wright Hotel in Columbia was tense and frenetic. People rushed in and out with the latest rumors, often about what

Gonzales had been saying. But Tillman's testimony in his own behalf was almost as damaging as Adams's testimony had been. He stated: "Somebody came in the room and told me about some new rumor what Mr. Gonzales would do to me and I made the remark that *if* he attempted to do that, I don't think I said as Dr. Adams said, 'snuff his light out,' but God damn him, I would kill him, I think."[88] But the word *if*—not used by Dr. Adams—does make the statement less bellicose because it makes the killing contingent on Gonzales's acting first. On this point Tillman's testimony and that of Cole Blease are in agreement.

Cole Blease stoked the anger of the hotel-room group when he read from a stack of Gonzales's editorials. In one Gonzales called Tillman's posturing about fighting him "mock theatricals." Tillman said his response was "that *if* it was 'mock theatricals' and he attempted to carry out the threats, or his purpose to have me assassinated there that night, in the opera house, it would be one of the damndest tragedies in the history of South Carolina."[89] This was also similar but significantly different from what Dr. Adams, testifying as a prosecution witness, had said he heard in that hotel-room meeting of political cronies. Again Tillman introduced the contingent word *if* to show he would use force only if Gonzales placed him in danger or acted first. He removed, "God," from the curse to clean up the remarks. Some listeners who might have been barely tolerant of a hardy "damndest" might have blanched when God's name was added. This would change vulgarity into blasphemy, and he had already committed that transgression once in his testimony.

As the hotel caucus continued, the conversation turned to the rumors that Gonzales was going to pack the opera-house meeting in Columbia with an assassination squad that would get Tillman. During the editorial reading, Tillman showed greatest anger at the articles accusing him of faking his sister's illness in order to dodge a joint campaign appearance with his opponents. Tillman seethed at the editorial that accused him of slinking away from a fight with Ed DeCamp when DeCamp accused Tillman of lying and not paying his debts. These editorials accused him of failing to live up to the *beau ideal* of manly honor.

"I Was Expecting Him to Shoot"

So far Tillman's testimony had been packed with fulminations against Gonzales and his editorials and the evils of a runaway press, but there had been little about the shooting itself. This was all part of the strategy of making the victim into the aggressor and using the harsh editorials as an emotional, if not legal excuse, for the killing. But at last Tillman's testimony came to the days just before the shooting. He arrived in Columbia just before the early January 1903 meeting of the legislature, where he was to preside over the Senate until the new lieutenant governor was inaugurated. When he arrived, his head was full of rumors that Gonzales was going about Columbia armed and waiting for him. On Wednesday, January 14, the day before the shooting, Tillman presided over the Senate briefly and then turned the gavel over to the president pro tempore, former governor John C. Sheppard. Tillman went to his State House office, where he was visited by Captain White, the doorkeeper, who reported to him that Gonzales had been lurking about the Senate chamber and committee rooms looking for Tillman and bragging about having made him show the white feather. Tillman returned to the Caldwell Hotel, where he was staying, and found Richard Holsenback, whom he had been helping to apply for a job with the speaker of the house. Holsenback reported to Tillman that Gonzales had been searching for him at the State House.

Tillman testified that, when he was in Columbia, he took care to be armed at all times. When one of his pistols was broken and being repaired, he borrowed a weapon. When he left the State House on Thursday, January 15, he was carrying two pistols. These were the Luger magazine pistol and a Colt .38 caliber pistol. As he was leaving the State House, he was joined by Senators Talbird and Brown. They crossed Gervais Street to its northeast corner with Main Street. As they were crossing the street and nearing the streetcar transfer station on the corner, he saw Gonzales "some distance down the street," walking toward them and "looking at me very intently." Senator Talbird was on Tillman's left as they walked along at a "leisurely" pace. Tillman said, "Mr. Gonzales was walking along rapidly, his overcoat was very tightly buttoned, both his hands in his pockets, and I never took my eye off of him, nor did he take his eye off of me." Tillman explained that his Luger magazine pistol was not in his hip pocket as some witnesses claimed but in a custom-made shoulder holster that he called a "shoulder sling." Although he had no pistol in his pants hip pocket, he did have one in the left rear pocket of his overcoat. Tillman said, "That is where I drew my pistol from." As Gonzales drew near, "I reached back there and cocked my pistol," and "just before Mr. Gonzales got to me he *cut across toward me.* I said, 'Mr. Gonzales I got your message,' and fired."[90] Tillman claimed that Senator Talbird was walking on the outside, nearest the curb, but there was plenty of room between Talbird and the curb for Gonzales to pass. There was no need for Gonzales to cut over toward him. Thus Tillman claimed, he interpreted Gonzales's turn toward him as an aggressive move. Here again we have one of the fundamental differences between defense and prosecution testimony. Most prosecution witnesses placed Tillman on the outside and Talbird in the middle, so that Gonzales's turn to his left was away from Tillman and an attempt to avoid a confrontation. But most defense witnesses had Talbird on the outside, and Tillman in the middle of his group of three, so that Gonzales's turn to his left was toward Tillman and made it appear as though he were forcing a confrontation. This last interpretation would make it reasonable for Tillman to act in self-defense.

At the heart of Tillman's self-defense case were Gonzales's movements and the position of his hands. Tillman described what he saw: "The thumbs of both of his hands were outside of his overcoat pocket until he started to cut across the sidewalk coming directly towards me, and then the thumb of his right hand disappeared in his pocket and it happened almost directly in three or four seconds after that I was expecting him to shoot and I said 'I got your message and fired.'"[91]

Thus Tillman's testimony turned what could have been a random movement into a menacing gesture. When his defense counsel asked him what message he referred to, he replied that it was the conversation Gonzales had had with Captain White and Richard Holsenback, which they reported to him. He may have been referring to the part of the conversation in which Gonzales was said to have boasted about having made Tillman show the white feather and bragged that he would make him do so again. So what Tillman was saying by shooting is in essence: "I heard that you said I was too much of a coward to fight. This proves I'm not." But, in the context of his self-defense argument, he seemed to refer to Gonzales's white feather statement as if it were another threat—a challenge that said Gonzales was armed and looking for Tillman, and Tillman had better be ready to fight. Seen in that light, and together with his allegations that Gonzales changed course to confront him and thrust his right hand into his pocket as if going for a gun, it could justify drawing his pistol and shooting.

Tillman said that, immediately after he fired, Senator Talbird came between him and Gonzales and said, "This thing has got to stop right here." Tillman said that "Mr. Gonzales came out past me to the corner. He never did take his hands out of his pockets."[92] Tillman testified that he did not shoot a second time "because Mr. Gonzales did not return my fire. I was expecting him to." He did not hear Gonzales say, "Shoot again you coward," as one of Gonzales's dying declarations asserted. Shortly after Gonzales went around the corner to the Gervais Street front of the transfer station, he came back around to Main Street and looked down that street in the direction of the *State* office. Tillman said, "I thought I would be attacked from that quarter, and that is what made me side step off the sidewalk. I did not want to be shot in the back." This sounds as if Tillman expected a gang of *State* staff members to come charging him with guns blazing. Tillman said of the *State* office, "I had heard about that office up there being a kind of arsenal."[93] Tillman had a habit of predicting that teams of assassins were coming for him. Remember his fear that Gonzales had arranged for the opera house to be packed with assassins at the last appearance of gubernatorial candidates in Columbia the previous August. That never happened; nor did a gang of assassins burst out of the *State* office. Much, if not all, of the danger existed only in Tillman's mind and was based on wild speculation. It should not have been considered a valid predicate for self-defense claims.

Tillman testified that he sidestepped across Main Street, where he was met by police officer George E. Boland, who arrested him. Boland was dressed in civilian clothes, but Tillman apparently recognized him as an officer. Boland asked him "what was the matter and I told him I had shot Mr. N. G. Gonzales." So, in addition to the testimony of many eyewitnesses, here was a clear confession by Tillman just after the event, which he repeated on the stand. His original statement did not contain any caveats such as "I shot him because he was pulling a gun on me." Tillman said that the shooting had created pandemonium with "much excitement there, large crowd gathering, people running and rushing about." He said he surrendered quietly and went with Boland to the "police station back of the opera house."

Tillman's defense counsel then asked where Tillman's pistols were and what he did with them at the time of the arrest. His answers created confusion and contradicted statements he had made earlier in his testimony. He answered that one pistol was in his hands and the other was in "my right-hip pocket." Earlier he had emphatically denied that there was a pistol in either hip pocket. He had testified that he drew a pistol from the left rear pocket of his overcoat, not a hip pocket of his pants. This would have meant that the pistol he used to shoot Gonzales came from the left rear coat pocket. But Tillman's remarks now seem to suggest that the pistol in his hand, the one he used, was the magazine pistol taken from the shoulder-sling holster. Of course he could have moved the pistol from one pocket to another, but this would have been pointless. When pressed by his counsel, he clarified that the pistol in his hand, the one he gave up at the scene to Boland, was the "long pistol," "the magazine pistol." He said that it was this Luger that he had used on Gonzales. This Luger magazine pistol taken from the shoulder-sling holster emerges from the confusing welter of Tillman's testimony as the most likely candidate for being the fatal weapon. But one fact is undeniable: Tillman shot Gonzales. He gave the pistol in his hands to Officer Boland, but he was reluctant to do so. He looked at the crowd and told Boland that he "didn't like to give it up. I didn't want to be butchered, and I didn't know who were my friends and who my enemies. There was intense excitement and I didn't know what time anything else would break out."[94] Here again he drew a picture of assassins lurking everywhere. But none appeared.

At the police station Chief Owen Daly calmly took charge. Seventy-two-year-old Daly was a veteran police officer who had been born in Dublin, Ireland, had immigrated to this country with his family, and had served in the Confederate army before going into law enforcement. According to Tillman's testimony, Chief Daly said, "Well, governor I will have to search you," but Tillman told him that there was no need for a search; he had another pistol, which he pulled out of his pocket and turned over to the chief. Tillman and his lawyers labored hard to create a picture that, once the pesky editor was out of the way, Tillman returned to being the very model of a law-abiding citizen.

Tillman did not have to face the police alone. Moral and legal support was on hand almost instantly after the arrest. As Tillman explained in his testimony, his brother-in-law Osmund W. Buchanan had come running up just after Tillman had surrendered to Boland on the street and turned the magazine pistol over to him. Tillman said Buchanan, "was very much excited and came rushing up and said he was unarmed and said he wanted to borrow the pistol I had turned over to the policeman from him." Here again was fear of those predatory newspapermen supposedly lurking everywhere. Again they never appeared. Buchanan ended up performing the more mundane function of contacting defense attorney Patrick Nelson and asking him to meet with Tillman. Nelson hurried to the station house, where he conferred with Tillman in an upstairs room.

Among Tillman's friends who visited him at the jail was legislator Spann Dowling, whom Tillman sent to find out Gonzales's condition, to find out where the bullet had hit Gonzales. In Tillman's testimony this was presented as if Tillman had been concerned about Gonzales and was hoping that the wound was not fatal. Earlier Dowling had testified as a prosecution witness that Tillman had said, if he hit Gonzales where he aimed, he was a dead man. But now Tillman said he had not aimed at all; things were happening too fast for that.

As defense counsel George Croft closed the direct examination of his client, he could look back on testimony that was sprawling, meandering, full of backing and filling of points forgotten, and then finally covered. But in large part Tillman's testimony was thorough and effective. It had painted a picture of Tillman as an aggrieved victim, pushed beyond his limits of endurance by vindictive, relentless editorials and finally forced to defend himself against an armed enemy who patrolled the streets looking for an opportunity to shoot him. Perhaps it was not enough to convince a neutral observer, but it might be enough to provide those inclined in his favor anyway with a peg on which they could hang an acquittal.

Cross-Examination of Tillman

It was now up to prosecutor G. Duncan Bellinger to destroy that flimsy excuse for acquittal. But Bellinger's cross-examination began badly. Bellinger's questions retraced the history of Tillman's relationship with Gonzales, and thus gave the defendant an opportunity to repeat his grievances against Gonzales as a bullying editorial writer. Bellinger did get Tillman to reel in some of his sweeping accusations that Gonzales was the source of all his problems. Tillman admitted that Gonzales had not personally caused his arrest in the Spanish-American War incident when he was accused of encouraging the whipping of some "Negro" boys accused of stealing a pistol from George Johnstone. Others had filed the complaint that led to the arrest. Tillman's complaint did not relate to Gonzales's conduct but his editorials.[95] He further admitted that he had started the bitterness between the two by using rough language, including ethnic slurs, in his 1890 articles in the Winnsboro paper, when he had called Gonzales a "wily Spaniard" and "a man of treacherous breed." He admitted that the verbal abuse was not one sided. Bellinger asked, "you say that every where you went you abused Mr. Gonzales." He replied that he had castigated him "pretty well on every stump in South Carolina" during the 1902 gubernatorial campaign. Bellinger continued in this vein: "He denounced you and you denounced him." Tillman responded, "Yes Sir." Tillman attended all but one of the forty-eight stump meetings during the 1902 campaign and denounced Gonzales at each one. He complained that he was still unable to defend himself against Gonzales's attacks because the newspapers ignored his statements. He charged that there was a newspaper conspiracy of silence, a pact not to criticize other newspapermen. He blamed his defeat in the race for governor on newspaper criticism; he contended that he was the only candidate subjected to such stinging condemnation. But he finally admitted that Gonzales was not the sole source of such criticism, that many others had joined in the attacks. This was a major admission. Previously the defense had created the picture that attacks on Tillman were the aberrant act of Gonzales pursuing a solitary mission of vengeance on a worthy public figure who was admired and respected by everyone else.[96]

Tillman told Bellinger he had told many people that the bad blood between Gonzales and himself was so bitter that he expected the two would have a shootout when they crossed paths in Columbia. Accordingly he had armed himself. During cross-examination Tillman's testimony on the identity and origin of the two pistols he carried at the time of the shooting was as confusing, evasive, and contradictory as it had been on direct examination. He first said he bought the Luger magazine pistol the year before the shooting, but then said he had gotten it, or one like it, from his brother, a regular army officer. The other pistol belonged to Mr. Leon Williams, and he had borrowed it while the Luger was having its magazine repaired the day before the shooting. He had not returned it after getting the Luger back because the person who was returning it for him could not find Williams. Bellinger caught Tillman in a contradiction regarding his reasons for having the pistols at the time of the shooting. At one point he said that, when he was cleaning out his office at the end of his time as lieutenant governor, he found the pistols there and was carrying them back to his hotel when he chanced upon Gonzales on Main Street. But at other times he said he was usually armed in Columbia because of his fear that Gonzales would attack him.[97] Despite Tillman's bobbing and weaving—and sometimes genuine confusion—the picture that emerges from his testimony is that he was usually armed in Columbia and was constantly on the lookout for Gonzales.

Bellinger pressed Tillman to explain why he assumed Gonzales was also armed when they came face-to-face on January 15. As they neared the curb, Tillman said he saw Gonzales looking at him intently. This alarmed him enough that he put his hands on his gun, and when Gonzales turned and walked diagonally toward him and thrust his hands deeply into his pockets, Tillman thought he saw a gun in one pocket. At that point he fired and said, "I got your message." His language here is significant. Bellinger asked, "Did you in any of your statements say you saw the pistol in Mr. Gonzales' pocket?" Tillman replied, "I thought I saw one." This is not a claim that he saw a drawn pistol, one in plain sight. At most it is a claim that he saw an outline of a pistol covered by the coat, which would be hard to distinguish from Gonzales's hand, which was already partly in his pocket. We are still left with the impression that Tillman killed an unarmed man, who merely put his hands further into his overcoat pocket on a winter day. Senator Talbird had testified that Tillman said "good morning" to Gonzales just before firing his pistol. Tillman denied saying those words, which would have made him look exceptionally cold-blooded or as if he were trying to feign cordiality to put Gonzales off his guard. Viewed in either way, such a greeting would have made the shooting look more like a planned event than a defensive act by a man in fear of losing his life. At this point Bellinger maneuvered Tillman into an improbable, suspect answer. He asked Tillman why Senator Talbird would have remembered him wishing Gonzales "good morning" if he never did that? Tillman answered, "He must have heard me say good morning to some other gentlemen. I did not say good morning to Mr. Gonzales." But Tillman could not remember to whom he spoke. He said he often saw many friends around the transfer station and had a habit of greeting them cordially.

Bellinger then asked: "How could you have spoken to somebody else when you were watching the man whom you expected to shoot you every second?" Tillman answered, "Certainly—it was not a 'good morning' in wasting any time, do not understand me that way; just simply 'good morning.'" It is hard to believe that Tillman was simultaneously wishing "good morning" to someone at the transfer station on his right, talking to Talbird, whom he insisted was on his left, and watching Gonzales's every move, including his hand movements and the expression in his eyes. It is more likely that it was indeed Gonzales to whom Tillman spoke and that he was trying to put the newspaperman off his guard by appearing to be cordial.

Tillman remembered Gonzales saying just after he shot him "'well, I guess you have finished me up', or he might have said, 'well, finish me up.'" Bellinger pointed out that Senator Talbird remembered Gonzales's words as having been, "Here I am finish me."[98] In one of his dying declarations, Gonzales claimed he said "shoot again you coward." Since Tillman had cast himself as the heroic defender of his honor and family name, it is unlikely he would have admitted to having his noble act referred to as one of cowardice.

Tillman's testimony continued for some time—with the questioning switching back and forth between the defense counsel and the prosecution—but no new ground was covered. Bellinger's cross-examination of the defendant was thorough and probing, but it landed no major blows. Tillman was caught in occasional inconsistencies and made minor admissions, but the major pillars of his defense remained intact: he had been pushed beyond the breaking point by relentless editorials and was forced to defend himself against an enemy he thought was about to draw a gun on him. Although the first pillar was not a legal defense, and the second appeared to the discerning to be flimsy and contrived, they were enough to convince those eager to be convinced.

The defense called additional witnesses to back up Tillman's assertions that he had good reasons to fear harm from Gonzales. One of these witnesses was W. T. Hyatt (sometimes spelled Hite).[99] The head fireman at the State House, he was not in charge of putting out fires but of maintaining the steam-heat system. Hyatt claimed that he knew N. G. Gonzales by sight and that on the second day of the legislative session in January 1903, the day before the shooting, he saw Gonzales by one of the doors on the Senate side of the State House talking to another man. Hyatt said that, when Gonzales bent over to spit into a cuspidor, he saw a small pistol, possibly a .32 caliber, sticking out of his right hip pocket. Hyatt said he had then instructed George Johnstone, the longtime Tillman family servant, to tell James H. Tillman that Gonzales had been spotted in the State House armed with a pistol. The prosecution objected to this last point as hearsay on the grounds that Hyatt was testifying about a conversation between Johnstone and Tillman that he had not heard. The defense withdrew the questions as to what Johnstone told Tillman, but they had already had Tillman testify that he heard about the incident from Johnstone, and there was no point in a lengthy legal argument on a point that had already been made.

Prosecutor Andrew Crawford succeeded in making Hyatt and his testimony look absurd. He cast doubt over whether Hyatt had seen Gonzales using a spittoon and exposing a gun when he bent over. Hyatt could not say whether Gonzales had spit "white" or had spit tobacco. Doubt was cast on whether the man he saw was Gonzales. When asked how tall the man was, Hyatt said the man was about four and a half feet tall. Crawford sarcastically remarked that this would make him "shorter than Napoleon the Great."[100] Hyatt said that the man he thought was Gonzales wore neither a mustache nor glasses. Pictures of Gonzales typically show him with both. Hyatt could not describe the man's clothes or the color of his eyes.

The defense continued in its effort to prove that Gonzales was a dangerous man and thus that Tillman was reasonable in interpreting Gonzales's action on January 15 as posing a serious immediate threat to him of death or serious bodily injury so that he was justified in shooting in self-defense. They called Richland County Clerk of Court J. Frost Walker, who was directed to bring with him records of Gonzales's 1886 arrests on charges of carrying a concealed weapon. Prosecutor Andrew Crawford objected to the introduction of these records on the grounds that they were too old to be relevant to this case. Any violent tendencies they might have shown in Gonzales in 1886 may have been long since eliminated from his makeup. However, Solicitor Thurmond, as chief prosecutor, overruled him and withdrew the objection, presumably because of a fear that the prosecutors could be accused of attempting to cover up vital evidence if they opposed the use of the records. This permitted defense counsel Patrick Nelson to present evidence of a series of tense confrontations between Gonzales, then working for the *Charleston News and Courier,* and the owners and staff of the *Columbia Register.* In February 1886 Gonzales had pleaded guilty to possessing a concealed weapon, was fined ten dollars, and ordered to forfeit the weapon to the county.[101] Gonzales claimed the weapon was for self-defense. Thomas J. La Motte, a reporter for the *Columbia Register,* published an article that Gonzales considered as, "reflecting on me."[102] Gonzales's affidavit in mitigation of punishment claimed that the Calvo family, who owned the *Register,* thought that he had abused La Motte over the incident, and in retaliation Charles A. Calvo, Jr., had confronted Gonzales outside his office and attempted to beat him with a cowhide whip. Gonzales drew his pistol and used it as a club to beat off Calvo's attack. Gonzales thought he acted with great restraint since he could have shot Calvo. Gonzales said, "after Mr. Calvo was disabled I delivered my pistol to Sheriff Rowan."

Gonzales's affidavit said that later that same day, his friend J. D. Pickard came to his office and said that W. B. Calvo, brother of the man who attacked Gonzales with the cowhide whip, was looking for him to avenge his brother's beating. W. B. Calvo had just returned from the West, where he had earned a reputation for being wild. Pickard advised Gonzales to go armed if he ventured out of the office. He loaned Gonzales a pistol when he had to go to talk with the sheriff about the first incident. As Gonzales was walking down Main Street, a man approached him, identified himself as W. B. Calvo, cursed him, and reached for his hip pocket as if he were drawing a pistol. Gonzales drew his own pistol and hit Calvo in the head with the muzzle. A bystander and a policeman separated the men and took the weapons from them both. Gonzales was fined for this incident as well as the first. He claimed that he did not usually go armed and did that day only because of a volatile situation with the Calvos.[103]

Even though Gonzales's concealed weapons convictions were seventeen years old, they were still a potent addition to the defense arsenal. They sent the jury the message that Tillman's fear of Gonzales carrying a weapon was not a paranoid fantasy or a convenient invention to justify killing Gonzales, but a reasonable fear born of the victim's past conduct. To the prosecution the import was quite different. The records were too old to mean anything about Gonzales's conduct in January 1903. In addition they showed Gonzales acting to defend himself when attacked rather than habitually going armed as Tillman did in Columbia, Finally these old records showed Gonzales in both incidents using the pistol as a club rather than shooting the assailant. Gonzales's response had been proportional to the threat. But still this last major evidence from the defense, focusing on the petty feuding of Columbia newspapers in the past, may have made the jury of farmers and mill hands look askance at the lofty claims of freedom of the press arrayed against the honor of the Tillman name.

Now that both sides had completed their principal cases, each was given the opportunity to attack the credibility of the other's witnesses. The prosecution immediately began to produce witnesses to controvert defense testimony, or show that defense witnesses were not worthy of belief. Much of this rebuttal testimony attacked the character of Richard Holsenback whose eyewitness testimony had been pivotal to the defense effort to show that Gonzales was the aggressor who had searched for Tillman and then made provocative moves that looked like he was drawing a gun. The prosecution hoped to convince the jury that Holsenback was a chronic liar, who had made up his testimony to curry favor with the Tillmans, who could help him get a government job. Several of the witnesses who testified against Holsenback found their own character for truth and veracity attacked on cross-examination.[104]

The prosecution launched a similar attack on the character of another vital defense witness, T. D. Mitchell. Mitchell had seriously damaged the prosecution's case by testifying that he heard Gonzales threaten Tillman. To rebut that testimony, the prosecution called Captain John D. Livingston, who testified that he had known Mitchell for twenty years in Orangeburg, and that his reputation for truth and veracity was so bad that he should not be believed even when under oath.[105] The defense's cross-examination of Livingston reignited the bitterness that remained after the struggle to restore white rule after Reconstruction. Defense counsel Patrick Nelson interrogated Livingston at length about his support of a white Republican congressional candidate in the 1894 race. The candidate's name was Thomas B. Johnston, but he was erroneously referred to in the trial as Tom Johnson. Johnston ran against white Democrat Dr. J. William Stokes, for a congressional seat representing the Seventh District, which comprised Lexington, Orangeburg, Sumter, Colleton, Berkeley, and Richland Counties. The South Carolina secretary of state certified the returns as showing Stokes the winner by a substantial margin, but Johnston protested the result in the United States House of Representatives, which under article I, section 5, of the United States Constitution had the right to "be the Judge of the Elections, Returns and Qualifications of its own Members." The majority report of the committee to which the House referred the issue declared Stokes the winner, and the minority report pronounced Johnston the winner. However, committee chairman S. W. McCall of Massachusetts made a successful proposal that the seat be declared vacant. Although it was clear that the election was invalid because many qualified black people had been denied access to the ballot, it was unclear how they would have voted and in what numbers.[106] For that reason there was no reliable basis for declaring a winner. Seven years later a bitter aftershock of this dispute reverberated in the Tillman trial.

Nelson's questions about Livingston's political affiliations were designed to brand the witness as an outsider, one whose standards were so different from those of the community in which he lived that he was not worthy of belief. The prosecution objected to this line of questioning as not relevant to either the facts of the case or the credibility of the witnesses. Nelson argued that it was relevant to determining whether the witness was of good character for truth and veracity because one who adopted political affiliations outside his group was suspect. He said that "this is to show who he is. Whether he is a white man living in a white community backing a white man or a black man, or a black man living in a white community backing a white man, or who is he."[107]

There was a racial element to the concept of manly honor. Livingston was white, and the candidate he backed, Tom Johnston, was white, but Johnston was a Republican, a member of a party that was viewed as courting black votes and opposing the return of white rule during Reconstruction and its aftermath.[108] The defense contention was that no honorable man would engage in such a shameful betrayal of one's group. Bellinger continued to object to questioning Livingston about his political affiliation. He argued that a witness could be attacked on the basis of his lack of "veracity," or that "his memory is bad," or that what he says is "inaccurate," but not on the basis of his political affiliation.[109] He charged that "too much extraneous matter has already been brought in here in reference to social conditions, factional politics and religions, and we make our protest."

But Judge Gary ruled that this line of questioning was proper. He said that "generally speaking Mr. Bellinger I think your view the correct one, but under our peculiar condition down here, it may affect a man's character—I will not say anything further before the jury. I will not say what I intended to say before the jury but I think this is competent."[110] Sometimes the trial seemed to be as much a test of political strength as it was a factual inquiry. It was directed toward affirming political values more than principles of justice. Those who stood in the way of the dominant values were marginalized as outsiders. Just as Livingston was depicted as an outsider because of his political affiliations, Gonzales, the "wily" or "treacherous Spaniard," was pictured as an outsider because of his ethnic background.

The large array of prosecution witnesses attacking the credibility of key defense witnesses was matched and exceeded by the defense, which presented a large number of Edgefield witnesses who testified that they had known Richard Holsenback for many years and that he had a good reputation for truth and veracity.[111] Again party affiliation was raised; this time by the prosecution. J. B. Odom, the Edgefield postmaster was called by the defense. He testified that he had known Richard Holsenback for twelve years and that he had a good reputation for truth and veracity. On cross-examination the prosecution asked Odom his party affiliation. He answered that it was Republican. Earlier that same day, the defense had attacked the prosecution character witness John D. Livingston as not being worthy of belief because he had supported a Republican congressional candidate, but now the defense objected to the prosecution's question about party affiliation, accusing the prosecution of inconsistency since it opposed similar questions to Livingston. The prosecution responded that, since the judge had ruled such questions proper, it was free to ask them. The defense then tried to distinguish Odom from Livingston by asking him questions designed to show he was a Republican in the national sense, like President Theodore Roosevelt, and not a Republican in the local sense, which connoted one who worked against the cause of maintaining white supremacy.[112]

Again the trial degenerated into a political jousting match rather than a quest for justice. The closing days of testimony, in which the prosecution attacked the credibility of defense witnesses and the defense attacked the credibility of the prosecution witnesses, amounted to little more than a swearing contest and probably did more to pit neighbor against neighbor in the Edgefield community than it did to cast light on the case. Once this imbroglio of character attacks had ceased, the trial proceeded to the closing arguments and the judge's instructions to the jury.

7.

THE CLOSING ARGUMENTS

Having the burden of proof, the prosecution made the first of the closing arguments. Solicitor J. William Thurmond began by emphasizing the grave duty facing the jurors. To him the case was a tragedy as well as a contest in a court of law. He noted that the jury had two pictures before it. The first showed that "a young man of intellect and magnetism is on trial for his life: he is of excellent family. You have the other picture of an able and courageous man, who is dead, leaving a widow, an empty chair at his table which will never be filled again."[1]

The Prosecution: Proving Murder and Defending a Free Press

Thurmond was clearly concerned about the laxity of juries in criminal cases and felt it necessary to advise the jury on its duties. But this he did in the informal manner of a friend giving advice rather than in the hectoring tones of a superior. He reminded them that they had "sworn upon the Holy Evangelist . . . to discharge your duty regardless of the consequences." Their duty was to "enforce the law, the law made by the Anglo-Saxon race," the "law of Christianity and education." Enforcement of the law is essential to protect all of our rights, including the right to own property, the right "to control your own children," and the right to protect one's family. Thurmond ingratiated himself to the jury at the same time that he instructed it. He said that he could tell by the "intelligent faces" of the jurors that they understood their responsibilities. He told the jury that the state had to prove that the defendant is guilty beyond a reasonable doubt. This did not mean that an acquittal could be based on a "fanciful doubt"; it must be based on a "strong, substantial doubt" as to the defendant's guilt; a doubt "must arise upon the testimony or upon the insufficiency of the testimony as given in this case." Thurmond noted that the defendant contended that since he acted in self-defense, he should not be held accountable for the death. The burden, said Thurmond, was on the defendant to prove that he acted in self-defense. He had to prove that he was "without fault in bringing on the difficulty." It was not enough to prove the deceased had threatened him in the past. The question was "what occurred at the time" of the shooting? The deceased had to have made a "demonstration," an action that signaled imminent danger of "serious bodily harm or death"; and there had to be "no reasonable means of escape," so that a "prudent man," a man of "ordinary firmness," would believe that the other party was "about to attack" with "some dangerous weapon" and that Tillman had to use deadly force to defend himself.

Thurmond was unconvincing when he tried to explain why, if so much emphasis was placed on events immediately prior to the shooting, the court's time had been lavished on reading editorials. He said that "they were put in to give the jury some light, to let the jury understand all the surrounding circumstances, to let the jury understand perfectly the relations existing between these two men, to let them understand everything about the trouble that has so long brewed between these two men; that is what they were put in here for." Both the prosecution and defense had introduced editorials from the *State*. The prosecution used them to show that their harsh comments about Tillman gave him a motive for murder and that, because of them, Tillman began contemplating the killing long before it happened. The defense used the editorials to show why he had to act to save his honor and his family's reputation. Whatever the reasons, the dominating role the editorials played in the trial turned it into a forum on the fairness of the *State*'s editorial policy, and Thurmond's explanation of why he so readily allowed the trial to be focused on them is not persuasive. But Thurmond did give a cogent review of the testimony concerning the shooting itself. He pointed out that far from provoking a violent confrontation, Gonzales sought to avoid one. The prosecution witnesses, with the exception of Senator Talbird, placed Tillman on the outside of his group of three, near the street, so that when Gonzales changed course to the left, he was going away from Tillman, not toward him. None of the prosecution witnesses saw Gonzales making any "demonstration," such as a movement of his right hand as if he were drawing a weapon. Thurmond noted that Gonzales had kept his gloves on throughout the encounter. If he had intended to draw a weapon, he would have taken them off to make shooting easier and more accurate. Thurmond's most telling point was based on the fact that Gonzales was unarmed. Neither of the men who assisted him back to the *State* office after he was shot, none of those who handled his clothing, none of those who touched his body when laying him on his office floor, none of the physicians who examined him in the office or in the hospital, found a weapon. Thurmond asserted that the absence of a weapon made it a certainty that Gonzales had made no demonstration. Thurmond asked, "Wouldn't he have been a fool to have attempted to draw nothing from his pocket? Would a man of any sense, would a man of any reason, have made an effort as if to draw a pistol, when he had none, and when he was right at Mr. Tillman, as I say had nothing in his pocket. Would a reasonable man do that? Why, of course not, he would not have done it."[2] This is probably the crucial factual point in the case. This argument was never effectively answered by the defense.

Thurmond argued that Gonzales could not have tried to pull a gun out of his pocket and shoot Tillman because there was no reason for him to do that. Thurmond asked: "Why would Mr. Gonzales want to have any trouble with him? He had opposed him politically. Mr. Tillman had been defeated. Mr. Gonzales had accomplished his purpose, so he no longer could have had any feeling against Mr. Tillman. He desired to do him no harm. He had triumphed, as it were, and there was no reason why he should make any further effort or why he should make any effort at all to do anything whatever toward Mr. Tillman then."[3] Thurmond attempted to show that the killing was not a spur of the moment reaction to Gonzales's movements but an act planned well in advance. When his wife asked Tillman where he would be staying in Columbia, Tillman said it might be in the penitentiary. This statement, asserted Thurmond, showed Tillman was contemplating an act that might land him in prison. Getting his gun repaired the day before the shooting showed he planned the killing carefully. Of course having the gun repaired is also consistent with Tillman's self-defense argument that he needed a gun in good working order to protect himself against an attack by Gonzales.

Thurmond attacked defense witnesses who painted a much different picture, especially those who said they saw Gonzales plunge his right hand into his pocket as if he were going for a gun. He argued that M. C. Lorick could not have seen such a slight movement from his position across the street. The streetcars clustered around the transfer station, the milling crowd, and those walking with and behind Tillman, as well as those walking behind Gonzales, would have blocked his view. Lorick was not a believable witness.

Thurmond used similar arguments against the other defense eyewitness, Richard Holsenback, asserting that he could not have seen what he claimed to have seen from his vantage point. Thurmond pointed out that Holsenback said Tillman and his group were forty yards away and almost at the site of the shooting when he first spotted them, but he somehow managed to catch up with them before the shooting and observe it closely. Holsenback could not have run that fast, Thurmond told the jury, and he commented that "whether he [Holsenback] was dreaming or not is a question for you." Thurmond then listed the prosecution's eyewitnesses: Mrs. Melton, Mr. Lide, Mr. Young, Mr. LaMotte, Mr. Sims, Mr. Aiken, and Mr. Bomar and pointed out that they were respectable members of the community with no reason to lie. He asked why the jury should believe the incredible tales told by Holsenback and Lorick, both street-corner loungers, against the testimony of such worthy people.

Thurmond returned to the subject of the editorials. By now he must have realized that the positions of the parties had been reversed by effective defense strategy. Gonzales, not Tillman, had been portrayed as the aggressor; Tillman had been portrayed as the innocent victim of an abusive press that had so assaulted his honor that he was forced to take drastic measures to defend himself. Gonzales had been placed on trial—and with him the right to a free press. Thurmond had to speak in defense of both. He noted that the Constitution of South Carolina contained a strong guarantee of freedom of the press.[4] Thurmond noted that "two of my distinguished friends on the other side had a hand in making the constitution which guarantees the freedom of the press. The excellent fundamental law of this land allowed freedom of speech and freedom of the press."[5] The members of the defense team who had been delegates to the 1895 South Carolina constitutional convention were former congressman George Johnstone and former state senator Cyprian Melanchthon Efird.[6] By mentioning their involvement, Thurmond demonstrated that freedom of the press was not a dangerous, foreign concept, but one previously embraced by the defense attorneys, who should not be permitted to so quickly condemn a vigorous press. Freedom of the press, Thurmond argued, was "one of the greatest bulwarks of American rights."[7] We use it to defend against encroachments on our other rights. Thurmond pointed out the importance of a free press to our form of government, saying that "the freedom of the press has always been regarded as a necessity to the republican form of government. It is regarded so today. It was so regarded when this country, you might say, was in its swaddling clothes. It has been protected from time immemorial to the present time."[8]

Not only did Thurmond have to defend freedom of the press for his argument to be persuasive in a case where editorials had been put on trial, he had to defend Gonzales. This was not a legal requirement but a practical one that had to be met to win over the jury. The defense had demonized Gonzales at length. Thurmond met this challenge squarely. Gonzales should be praised rather than condemned. He was an honest man who told his readers the straight story as he saw it. In doing so, he sometimes had to be blunt. Imparting information and opinions in a direct manner, without meaningless double-talk, is a valuable function in a democracy whether you agreed with the opinion or not. Thurmond said:

> Gentlemen of the jury you always admire an open, honest man who tells you what he thinks. It is seldom you can get a man—I won't say it is seldom—it is so often that men in public places will not express to you their real thoughts and real opinions of matters of importance. It is frequently a difficult matter, even to get from a strong, vigorous, able man his opinions of men, his opinions of measures, his genuine, his real thoughts. But here was a man who expressed himself fearlessly on every subject, and whether you agreed with him or not, or whether he erred or not, you must admire the manly manner in which he always took a stand one way or another, in whatever confronted the people of South Carolina.[9]
>
> It is from the clash of the differing views of such frank and honest people that the voter in a democracy gets the information and debate needed in deciding how to vote.[10]

Thurmond closed as he began with an admonition to the jury to do its duty. He did not say that their duty was to convict. He told the jurors that they had to act with knowledge that "your acts will have their effects upon posterity for years and eternity."[11] He reminded the jurors that someday everyone would be called before God to answer for their acts. Thurmond was confident that the jurors would approach their decision with the care and seriousness that it deserved because he felt "satisfied that as manly men" they would perform their duties and "discharge them well."

Thurmond had been laboring under a strain created by his duty to the state to present a strong case as prosecutor and by an obligation created by his friendship and political camaraderie with the Tillmans, to not abuse them in discharging his duty to the state. With this closing argument, he completed his duty and turned over the responsibility to the jury. He said, "I feel that the State has done its duty fully in this matter gentlemen of the jury, so far as regards my responsibility. I now shift that upon your shoulders." Both sides frequently invoked the importance of being manly. Thurmond appeared satisfied that he too had been a "manly man."[12]

The Defense: Fighting the Press to Protect Honor

In accordance with the custom of alternating prosecution and defense arguments, the next closing argument was by defense attorney George R. Rembert.[13] Rembert was a twenty-eight-year-old lawyer who had just been admitted to the bar. He had served as a member of Jim Tillman's Spanish-American War regiment and had shown his loyalty to his commander and his unit by writing a letter to the editor of the *State* that sharply condemned what he considered was unfair criticism of the regiment by an "editorial writer seated in a snug office" far from the rough camp life the unit had experienced. This comment ignored N.G. Gonzales's service during the war on the staff of a Cuban revolutionary general under conditions that his biographer described as "arduous" rather than "snug." Apparently this bitterness toward the press remained at the time of his closing argument.[14] Rembert had a "gift" for sarcastic condescension and presenting suppositions as if they were hard facts, and he used this talent to depict the press as a dangerous force whose freedom should be carefully circumscribed.

Rembert's basic argument was that law did not control human nature; human nature controlled law. God had given us a sense of honor and pride and had imbued us with a compulsion to protect it. No man should be punished for obeying that compulsion. Law cannot "forbid a man to do that which human nature compels in the protection of his honor, in the protection of his manhood, in the protection of his life."[15] Here again we see the emphasis placed by both sides on the principle of manliness. As other defense attorneys did in this case, Rembert directly addressed an individual juror, the foreman. "Would you Mr. Foreman, like to be convicted for any act of yours which God in the creation of the universe eight thousand years ago made impossible for you not to do?" To complete the picture Rembert had to demonize Gonzales as having pursued Tillman with "unrelenting venom" that assaulted his honor, manliness, home, and family. In light of this, said Rembert, Tillman's act was not only defensible, it was compelled by God. He told the jury that

> if you find that the defendant has endured this torture at the hands of the deceased, if you find that his name has been blackened, his honor stained, and insults heaped upon him too heavy to be borne, if you find by all this and through all this that the impulse of human nature compels this defendant as he thought to clear his name in the eyes of the public, to defend the soul of his honor, the strength of his manhood, the heart of his home, if you find this, then eight thousand years of human nature, fifteen centuries of Anglo-Saxon manhood, three centuries of American freedom, and three hundred years of Southern honor, and an eternity of justice stands between you and the prisoner at the bar, and demands at your hands his vindication.[16]

So not only did God command the defendant to act the way he did but so did the weight of all human history. Thurmond had been ambiguous about how he thought the jury should decide the case. He had said they should decide as their consciences dictated after careful consideration of the facts. But Rembert and the other defense counsel left no doubt: the jury not only should, but was compelled by God and history, to acquit.

Rembert attacked the editorials and the prosecution claims that they were protected by the constitutional principle of liberty of the press. But Rembert apparently considered freedom of the press to be an insignificant bauble when weighed against the loftier value of honor and the need to protect manliness. Displaying an unusually restricted view of freedom of the press, he argued that it covered only the statement of facts and that the statement of opinions was not protected. Readers should be left to draw their own conclusions, he argued. If not, liberty would become license and that would lead to anarchy and cheap-shot attacks on the reputations of worthy men. Yes, Rembert acknowledged, the record of a public official was subject to comment. But somehow Rembert believed there could be commentary without opinion. When the editorial writer stated a conclusion, Rembert claimed, rather than merely setting forth facts, "this makes him a thief, this makes him a coward, this makes him a liar, these conclusions are personal on the part of N. G. Gonzales and personally he must be held responsible for them."[17] Presumably Rembert meant it was all right to hold Gonzales responsible by killing him rather than by suing him, or by letting Tillman's speech on the political stump counter Gonzales's speech in the paper. Rembert's line drawing between facts and conclusions is impossible to carry out because facts and conclusions fade imperceptibly into each other. Furthermore Rembert was violating his own rule. He was drawing conclusions when he called Gonzales a thief, a liar, and a coward. He said the editorials attacked Tillman's personal life but gave no examples. Here again, he presented the jury with his conclusions. But perhaps he thought his free-speech rights as an attorney were greater than those of a newspaper. In his arguments on the facts of the shooting Rembert presented suppositions as facts even though he presented no supporting evidence.

Rembert attacked the prosecution's attempts to undermine the credibility of the defense witnesses who said they heard Gonzales threaten to kill Tillman. He quite properly criticized the clumsy prosecution attempt to impeach defense witness A. J. Flowers, the streetcar conductor, by trying to show that Flowers did not work on the days he said he heard Gonzales make a threat against Tillman. This blew up in the prosecution's faces when the work records vindicated Flowers. Rembert effectively established a bond between the jury and Flowers by describing him as a "plain country boy," who had been in Tillman's regiment in the Spanish-American War and had loyally come to the aid of his colonel. Rembert described Flowers's face as being "as honest as the sunlight of God."

The prosecution impeachment witnesses had to be demonized as thoroughly as Gonzales had been. T. D. Mitchell, a key defense witness, had testified that in a casual street conversation with Gonzales, the editor had spoken of killing Tillman. He had been impeached by Captain Livingston, who said he would not believe him under oath. But Rembert quickly painted Livingston as a person of low character. He had informed on Mitchell by turning him in for violation of the fish and game laws. But the sure test of a man's character was his political affiliation. Rembert branded Livingston's testimony as worthless by telling the jury to "wrap it up in little packages, lay it there and mark it a Republican who has a grudge against him [Tillman]." Rembert dismissed all the witnesses called to impeach defense witnesses as being unworthy of belief by saying: "wrap them all up in one package, write upon them 'animosity against James H. Tillman,' and cast them in the waste basket."

Richard Holsenback was probably the most important defense witness because not only did he testify that he had heard Gonzales making threatening remarks against Tillman, but he also said that he had witnessed the shooting and that it happened as a response to Gonzales's aggressively turning to confront Tillman and moving his right hand deeper into his pocket as if to draw a weapon. Rembert fortified Holsenback's credibility by pointing out that he had stuck by his story through hours of withering cross-examination by one of the most skilled lawyers in the state. Rembert argued that a "man who cannot read or write" could not endure such abuse on the witness stand unless "he had that back of him which was grander than all of it, the truth."

The most stubborn fact confronting the defense was that Tillman shot an unarmed man. As Solicitor Thurmond pointed out, why would an unarmed man be so foolish as to make a motion that looked as though he were drawing a gun, when he did not have one and was facing his worst enemy? Rembert dealt with this problem by assuming that Gonzales was armed. He presented supposition as fact even though he offered no supporting evidence. He asked: "Do you think for one moment that we for the defense concede that N. G. Gonzales did not have a weapon in that pocket?" Later he said more pointedly, "The defense claim he was armed."[18]

Although Rembert presented no evidence and while many prosecution witnesses who touched Gonzales or his clothing shortly after the shooting found no gun, he argued that evidence the prosecution could have presented, but did not, might have contained proof that Gonzales had a gun. Rembert hinted darkly that the prosecution suppressed such evidence because it would have been damaging to its case. He asked why the verbatim version of Gonzales's dying declaration, which had been taken down in shorthand by Robert Lathan, was not introduced into evidence. Rembert speculated that this document could have contained an admission by Gonzales that he had a weapon.

Yet Lathan had included the content of this dying declaration in an affidavit he made for Tillman's bail hearing. The complete affidavit had been published in the *State,* and it was widely known that it contained no admission by Gonzales that he was armed.[19] Here again Rembert was violating the severe limits he had placed on freedom of speech: he was not merely stating facts; he was drawing conclusions—and fanciful ones at that.

Rembert argued that Tillman was forced to shoot Gonzales because he had no other recourse. Not only was his life in danger, but his honor was being defiled. He was "Tortured day by day, week by week, month by month and by a man who builds around himself the impregnable barrier of the law and refuses to fight you face to face with weapons you both can hold, who behind closed doors distorts your every act and with consummate cunning makes every act seem a crime. Behind closed doors he stabs your honor with a weapon he has which you have not."[20] In other words, because Gonzales would not violate the law against dueling and fight him, Tillman was free to shoot Gonzales, especially if he shoved his hands in his pockets. Here Rembert repeated the canard that Gonzales had the means to reach the public with his message because he edited a paper, but Tillman had no means to answer. Yet the animosity between them had started with Tillman's article in the Winnsboro paper, and it continued in part because of articles Tillman wrote while a newspaper correspondent in Washington. Tillman also had a wonderful means to tell his side of the argument in his campaign speeches, and he constantly took advantage of that forum. Rembert himself noted this fact when he said, "James H. Tillman stung Gonzales on every stump in South Carolina." The picture of Tillman as the innocent party pummeled by an overwhelming bully is unconvincing.

Rembert made use of an ethnic stereotype in depicting Gonzales as a malicious force that Tillman had reason to fear, implying that Gonzales's tempestuous Cuban blood could lead to sudden or elaborately plotted violence: that "the hatred of his hot blood is in him." But Rembert's penchant for overheated rhetoric did not mean that he was ineffective in the meticulous factual analysis that is sometimes necessary in attacking an opponent's case. He raised legitimate questions about how Mrs. Melton could have so closely observed Gonzales's facial expression just before the shooting and almost simultaneously have carried on a conversation with her friend Senator Brown.

In order to dramatize Tillman's victimization at the hands of the avenging editor, Rembert sought to build up Tillman's credentials as a pillar of the community by offering a strained comparison of him to the Good Samaritan, a person sympathetic to the suffering of others and devoting himself to alleviating their pain.[21] This was an odd label to place on a man who did not stop to tend the wounds of his victim, but Rembert did not shrink from making it. In this comparison Rembert made particular reference to Tillman's service as regimental commander in the Spanish-American War. Gonzales had belittled this service by focusing articles on incidents such as the whipping of the black teenagers accused of stealing George Johnstone's pistol in camp. But Rembert noted that, because of Tillman's concern for their welfare, he had been so beloved by his men that they had presented him with a ceremonial sword.

Rembert skillfully played on emotions of the jury, including their natural desire not to do harm. He pictured Tillman's "aged mother," whose hair has been "whitening beneath the tortures her son has suffered." Rembert told the mother that her son would be coming home to her soon to comfort her in her declining years. He drew a poignant picture of Tillman's small daughter wondering when her father would come home and said, "I feel I could say to her. 'Be

The defendant's wife, Mamie Norris Tillman, in the courtroom. Illustration by W. H. Loomis. *New York World,* October 10, 1903, 5. Courtesy of the American Newspaper Respository Collection, 1856–2004. David M. Rubenstein Rare Book and Manuscript Library, Duke University.

of good cheer, you won't lose your papa little one. He is coming home again.'" Then he turned to Tillman's wife, whose marriage to Tillman had been rumored to be a stormy one, and said, "I think of his noble wife, who has stood by him so nobly in this great trouble and by her every act brands as a lie the many tales of scandal which have breathed into the public mind, I feel I can say to her, 'your troubles too are ended. Not one bit of scandal will again darken your life.'" He said that he felt he could tell the members of Tillman's old army regiment that they would be spared the ignominy of having their commander convicted and that "their colonel still may draw in honor the sword they gave him." And he felt confident that Tillman's distinguished kinsman, his uncle and substitute father, Senator Ben Tillman, would be spared seeing a stain on the family name. Having worked his way through a long list of people he was sure would be spared the pain and humiliation a conviction would bring, Rembert reached the loftiest beneficiary of the acquittal that he was sure would come: the state of South Carolina. He said, "I think of South Carolina and know how he has served her and how he has loved her. I feel that I can say to her 'Old State, you need such sons to love and serve you still, and when I look at him and see how he has suffered, I feel I can say to him, beholding the justice reflected in your eyes, rejoice, your suffering is ended; your vindication is at hand. Tomorrow will witness your welcome home.'"[22]

Maudlin though this closing argument was, it was effective in giving the jury a justification for acquittal: it would relieve the suffering of Tillman, his family, and his friends. Of course this argument ignored the feelings of the Gonzales family and the added suffering a lawless and violent society, in which the laws against murder are lightly spurned, would bring on future victims because potential assailants would be encouraged by an acquittal.

The Prosecution: Criticizing Candidates Is a Right

It fell to another young attorney, Gonzales's cousin William Elliott, to give the prosecution's answer to Rembert's scathing remarks about N. G. Gonzales and the evils of a licentious press. Thirty-one at the time of the trial, Elliott was a University of Virginia–trained lawyer, which made him one of the few lawyers involved in the case to have a law-school education. In years following the Tillman trial, Elliott enjoyed a diverse corporate practice, representing cotton mills, electrical utilities, banks, and the State of South Carolina in important cases. He became general counsel and then president of the State Company, which published the newspaper that had been edited by N. G. Gonzales. Elliott's closing argument is noted for its eloquent defense of freedom of the press.[23]

To Elliott, Rembert had been spinning a fantasy, putting words into Gonzales's mouth and attacking imaginary editorial dragons. Elliott had conducted the marathon reading of the *State* editorials in order to have them admitted into evidence. He said: "Mr. Gonzales never spoke of the riff-raff of the cotton mills . . . but I say he is the best friend the cotton mill people of South Carolina have ever had."[24] This was important because the defense had pictured the deceased as an enemy of the cotton-mill worker and Tillman as their champion. There were several cotton-mill workers on the jury. Elliott also contended that Gonzales never called Tillman a "cur" in an editorial. The defense, he said, had never produced an editorial in which Gonzales referred to Tillman with that term. This too was important because the defense argued that such harsh language had stained Tillman's honor and abused him to the point where he could endure no more and had to strike back. If the abuse was less than the defense portrayed it to have been, that argument would falter.

The defense had argued that Gonzales's editorials had gone beyond the dissection of Tillman's public acts, the sort of scrutiny that all public officials and candidates must endure, and had invaded his home life, publishing scandalous material about his family and the way he treated them. Elliott denied this accusation as well: "It is false. It is absolutely without a scintilla of foundation and I again challenge counsel on the other side to show me one word, one single word, by which Mr. Gonzales entered the home of the defendant James H. Tillman."

It was part of the defense strategy throughout the trial to picture Gonzales as the enemy of everyone named Tillman, including Senator Ben Tillman, and thus the enemy of the senator's supporters. As they did with the defendant, his attorneys attempted to show that the newspaper's scrutiny had gone beyond the senator's public acts to include his personal life. Again Elliott denied the charge and challenged the defense to produce even one editorial in which Ben Tillman's personal, rather than his political, conduct had been attacked in the paper. The defense never produced any convincing evidence that the private life of either James H. or Benjamin R. Tillman had been invaded. But they were permitted to repeat the charge so often without backing it up that the jury may have been convinced.

Elliott answered defense claims that the prosecution had failed to produce certain evidence because it would be damaging to the prosecution's case. Where was the verbatim shorthand account of Gonzales's dying declaration taken in the hospital by Robert Lathan? Was it hidden from the jury because it contained an admission by Gonzales that he was armed and searching for Tillman with the idea of killing him? Elliott explained that the prosecution had chosen to produce Dr. Babcock's account of the dying declaration instead of Lathan's because the defense would attack Lathan's version as biased because it came from Gonzales's secretary, whereas everyone would recognize Babcock as unbiased. The defense also accused the prosecution of failing to call all the eyewitnesses to the shooting. Elliott replied that they had called all the eyewitnesses they could find, and if the defense knew of others, they were free to call them as their witnesses.

The defense had tried, with some justification, to depict Gonzales as a person who could be violent, and had used the fight he had had with Calvo years earlier as an example. Elliott deftly turned this accusation against the defense. He compared the restraint Gonzales showed in the Calvo incident with Tillman's conduct. Gonzales had merely hit a man with his pistol when the man had attacked him, whereas Tillman had shot a man who had merely put his hand in his pocket on a winter day. The defendant had the advantage. He "had the drop" on Gonzales. He had his gun and was ready before Gonzales. All he needed to do was warn Gonzales not to move. He did not need to kill him.

Elliott argued that "Mr. Rembert admits what we have suspected all along, that the plea of self-defense in this case is a fiction." He contended that Tillman killed Gonzales not to save his own life, but as "vengeance" for the stinging editorials.[25] That is why the prosecution introduced the editorials into evidence: to prove that vengeance was the real motive and that the self-defense arguments were a mask behind which revenge could hide. The self-defense plea was absurd: "The idea that a man with the intelligence of James H. Tillman should stand before you and say that he found it necessary to kill a brave man because he wiggled his thumb at him is not worthy of serious discussion. If the time has come in South Carolina when a man has been shot in his tracks for wiggling his thumbs—the defendant says himself that's all—then indeed is our manhood debased."[26] Again the concept of "manliness" or "manhood" was pivotal, more important than the technicalities of a murder case. The defendant claimed he had to act to preserve his honor, a key ingredient of manliness.

Elliott sought to build an aura of manliness around Gonzales. He was proud to be a member of the same family as this brave man, explaining that Gonzales's mother was Harriet Rutledge Elliott before she married Ambrosio José Gonzales, who had moved to the United States from Cuba in 1848. The genes of a Cuban revolutionary leader and a South Carolina aristocrat mingled in their offspring.[27] The roots of the Elliott family extended back two hundred years into South Carolina's history. Many members of the family had fought and died for South Carolina. But no one in the "present generation" had had the privilege of giving his life for his state until N. G. Gonzales was shot: "He offered up his life for what he believed was right, true, honest and fair, and I am proud that I am a kinsman of a man who in the hour of tragedy could look his slayer in the face and say as he said 'Here I am finish me.'"[28]

Elliott's staunch defense of freedom of speech and of the press was a much needed antidote to the disparaging remarks directed at those rights by the defense. He noted that, not only did the United States Constitution protect freedom of speech and the press from encroachment by the federal government, but South Carolina constitutions, from the first state constitution in 1778 through the then-applicable Constitution of 1895, protected those rights.[29]

Elliott argued that the freedoms of speech and the press were essential rights without which other rights could not survive, saying that "every other right under the law amounts to nothing, absolutely nothing, unless you can say what you please about those who make our laws, about those who are our officers and candidates for office."[30] If a citizen could not keep watch on the law makers and criticize what they do, they could pass laws encroaching on everything from our right to vote, to our right to freedom of worship, to our right to be free from unreasonable searches and seizures. All Gonzales did was criticize the public acts of Tillman as an official and a candidate. But the defense claimed that there was abuse of the freedom of the press. Although Elliott denied that such abuse occurred, he said that, even if it did occur, the remedy was not shooting the editor, an act that not only took the life of one writer and silenced his voice forever but also was likely to intimidate others into silence when what was needed was a thorough airing of official conduct. The first remedy available to a man who is unjustly attacked in the press is public opinion. Elliott noted that "you gentlemen, all honest men, all citizens, all voters, know that if a man is unjustly attacked, false accusations brought against him, that there is an uprising of public sympathy to support that man and damn his accusers; that no man dare raise his head in public print in false accusation. You know that if a man is slandered, immediately the sympathy of the whole community goes out to him."

Elliott noted that George Washington and Thomas Jefferson had been vilified by political enemies, but neither resorted to murder as a means of defending his name. He gave an example of Jefferson's conduct when he was accused of stealing money. The remedy Jefferson used was letting speech counter speech rather than a violent response. He showed vouchers and other proof of how he had used the money he was accused of misappropriating. Elliott offered John C. Calhoun as another example. He had been subjected to withering insults by abolitionists, but he never shot anyone. Here again speech countered speech. Calhoun answered his critics by logic and eloquence, so that, when he died, a leading abolitionist and statesman, Daniel Webster, eulogized his political opponent as a man of "exalted patriotism." The kind of public forum used by Jefferson and Calhoun, Elliott pointed out, would have been available to an official and candidate such as Tillman.

If letting his speech answer that of his critics would not have been effective, Tillman still had other remedies available. Elliott contended that "this defendant could have sued N. G. Gonzales for libel. He could have gone in a courthouse and sued him on the civil side of the court for libel. He could allege 'you said untrue things of me and you must answer the consequences' and a jury could sit as a court of honor. Under the constitution in such a case they are the sole judges of the law and fact; and no such right is given anywhere else in the law, to any citizens, for any wrong."[31] Elliott anticipated defense arguments contending that economic realities would have rendered a libel case an empty remedy. Perhaps N. G. Gonzales did not have enough money to pay a judgment, Elliott answered, but even if that had been the case, "would not the fact that a jury of his countryman had said 'you have slandered and falsely accused a fellow citizen,' would not that have been judgment enough for any man."[32] Elliott recognized that the defense might offer further economic arguments as to why a libel case would have been an ineffective remedy for Tillman. Bringing such a case would be expensive. But Elliott answered this anticipated defense argument by saying, "I venture to say that the trial would not have been half as long, or the expense half as great as in this case, and James H. Tillman would have been vindicated, and would not have had the blood of his fellow man on his hands." Elliott even held out the possibility that Tillman could have instituted a criminal libel prosecution against Gonzales, which could have resulted in his being jailed, perhaps even if Gonzales had proved his charges were true, if the jury were convinced that he had made his damaging statements with a "bad heart" or "base motive." Such criminal prosecutions, controversial even then, are now considered constitutionally suspect and required to meet very rigorous standards.[33] A criminal libel prosecution would not have been an attractive course for Tillman because the South Carolina Constitution, and a 1901 case, made it clear that a criminal-libel defendant could introduce proof of the truth of his assertions in his defense.[34] This might have given Gonzales as a defendant a chance to give even more publicity to his charges. The defense also could have pointed out that criminal-libel actions had not proved to be effective instruments for vindicating those who claimed injury by the press. As noted earlier, the 1875 criminal libel case brought against Charleston editor Francis Warrington Dawson at the instigation of Sheriff C. C. Bowen did not result in vindication of the complainant but in a hung jury.[35] The defense could have also noted that the 1892 criminal-libel complaint filed against N. G. Gonzales by offended attorney G. W. M. Williams never went to trial and provoked additional mocking comments by Gonzales.[36] But Elliott's message was that legal remedies, though far from perfect, surely were preferable to violent self-help.

Elliott contended that, not only were critical editorials no justification for murder, but it was also significant that many of the newspaper comments objected to most loudly by the defense as damaging Tillman's honor did not originate with Gonzales, but were first made in other papers and merely quoted by the *State.* He gave as an example an article comparing Tillman to an ass. "Also Brayed Class," which sarcastically argued that it was a waste of time to "shave an ass," originated in the *Washington Post.* Elliott noted that Tillman in his testimony, and the defense lawyers in their arguments, seemed particularly incensed by a charge that Tillman had fled from a campaign appearance with opposing candidates, falsely claiming that his sister was ill, an excuse the defense called valid because she was in fact ill. Elliott noted that this charge was originally made in the *Florence Times,* and he argued that many allegations that Tillman was a habitual liar came from an Anderson paper. He noted that Tillman had murdered none of these editors. Tillman's hatred for Gonzales was so warped and bitter, Elliott charged, that he blamed all his problems on Gonzales even when others had caused them.[37]

Elliott demonstrated that his arguments defending the freedom of the press were not novel. They were deeply rooted in South Carolina's constitutional traditions. The historic case of *Mayrant v. Richardson* (1818) stated in no uncertain terms that freedom of speech included the right to examine a candidate's credentials and offer *opinions* about them and his conduct.[38] This precedent effectively refuted the defendant's oft-made argument that the rights of free speech and press are limited to a laconic recitation of facts and do not include the proffering of opinions. This case endorsed the need for a particularly vigorous exchange of views with regard to candidates. One who offered himself for public office did not insulate himself from public criticism; he opened himself to it. Such scrutiny was essential for the electorate to reach informed decisions about how to cast their ballots in a democracy. Justice Abraham Nott, speaking for the South Carolina Constitutional Court of Appeals in *Mayrant v. Richardson,* put it in this fashion:

> And I am not aware of any principle of Law or Constitution, by which a person proclaiming himself a candidate for Congress, becomes so far elevated above the common level of mankind, as to entitle himself to any exclusive privilege. On the contrary, when one becomes a candidate for public honors, he makes *profert* of himself for public investigation. All his pretensions

> become subjects of inquiry and discussion. He makes of himself a species of *public property,* into the qualities of which every one has a right to inquire, and of the fitness of which, every one has right to judge and give his *opinion.* The ordeal of public scrutiny, is many times a disagreeable and painful operation. But it is the result of that *freedom of speech* which is the necessary attribute of every free government, and is expressly guaranteed to the people of this country by the constitution.[39]

One of the leading constitutional-law treatises available at the time of the Tillman trial, Henry Campbell Black's *Handbook of American Constitutional Law* (1895), states that federal and state constitutional provisions guaranteeing freedom of speech and the press are "designed to insure freedom for the expression of *opinion*" and that this freedom of expression "protects the individual against governmental oppression on account of his honest criticism of public men, measures or affairs."[40]

The *Mayrant* case's strong endorsement of the right to criticize candidates strengthened Elliott's free-press arguments, but in another way it was a double-edged sword that weakened his position. Elliott offered a libel action as a peaceful alternative to murder. Because *Mayrant* involved dismissal of a candidate's slander action against one who had criticized his mental capacity for public office, the case could be considered to undermine the viability of that peaceful alternative. The court concluded that a candidate for public office opened himself up to criticism. However, the court said, the right of freedom of speech is not a "Telemonian Shield" offering complete protection from slander and libel suits. Such suits might be viable when the injurious words were false and malicious and attacked his "private character" or "domestic tranquility" rather than his public acts.[41]

Elliott closed by admonishing the jury that, if they rendered a not-guilty verdict, vindicating Tillman's blatant act of vengeance at the expense of an editor's life and the exercise of our prized right of a free press, it would make South Carolina and its justice system look absurd in the eyes of the rest of the country. The jury would be saying that "we a jury of true and lawful Lexington citizens, preferring to have dishonest and corrupt men in public office, rather than have their character and reputation and fitness discussed, render a verdict of not guilty."[42] But any vindication of Tillman from such a verdict would be an illusion. His honor and reputation would not be restored. The criticism would not stop just because one man had been stopped. Freedom of the press would suffer a blow, but it would remain vigorous, "for the time has not yet come when Anglo-Saxons can be deterred by the fear of death from doing their duty, and though he may slay a hundred critical editors there would yet be another to step in where the last man fell."[43]

The Defense: Denouncing Candidates Is Not a Right

The defense reply to Elliott's eloquent argument on behalf of freedom of the press was given by former congressman George Johnstone, who had an unusually cosmopolitan educational background. He had not only studied at the State Military Academy in South Carolina but also at the University of Edinburgh in Scotland for three years. After returning to South Carolina and studying law, he was admitted to the bar and practiced in Newberry. He served one term in Congress in 1891–93 but failed to be renominated. He was a delegate to the South Carolina constitutional convention that passed the article I, section 4, provisions in the Constitution of 1895, guaranteeing freedom of speech and the press. Six years after the Tillman trial, Johnstone served as president of the South Carolina Bar Association.[44]

The view of freedom of the press Johnstone presented in his closing argument was even more grudging than that offered by his younger defense colleague George Rembert.[45] Like Rembert, Johnstone did not think freedom of speech or the press protected the expression of opinions, and he tightened the screws of this limitation even further. Newspaper commentary that contained denunciations of a candidate was not protected; Johnstone said: "I deny your right to descend into mere denunciation."[46] Johnstone's view would have rendered editorials toothless and pointless. Without such critical commentary, accounts of political campaigns and the acts of public officials would be bland pabulum indeed rather than the hard information the electorate needs in deciding how to vote. Furthermore Johnstone contended that Gonzales's editorials were often unprotected by freedom of the press because they were malicious and dealt with Tillman's private life. Johnstone gave as an example a May 11, 1902, editorial in the *State* that, he claimed, accused Tillman of wife beating.[47] None of the editorials introduced by the prosecution or the defense substantiated this assertion, and Elliott's closing argument had already vehemently denied that Gonzales wrote editorials about James H. Tillman's domestic life.

Johnstone dismissed the peaceful alternative that Elliott had suggested. A lawsuit was impractical because of the expense. He directly addressed two jurors:

Defense attorney George Johnstone. Courtesy of the South Caroliniana Library, University of South Carolina, Columbia, S.C.

"Take you Mr. Foreman, take you Mr. Jumper, let a powerful paper of the country denounce you day after day, year after year, and then sue him. Where is the money with which you are to sue, where are the attorneys through whom you are to sue? If you are rich enough sue me, if you are powerful enough sue me, if not stand still and take it."[48] The implications of this line of argument are startling: murder is all right because it is cheap. Such reasoning places no value on a human life. But even under cold cost-accounting standards, the argument makes little sense. Using information from officials, the *News and Courier* estimated that the Tillman trial would cost $6,000. Richland County would bear that expense despite the transfer of venue to Lexington County.[49] The article concluded that the cost had risen from the roughly $3,500 that would have been spent if the case had remained in Richland. By committing the act necessitating the trial and then insisting on a change of venue, the defendant did not save the state any money by choosing the supposedly cheap remedy of murder for his grievances. The venue change required travel and lodging expenses for witnesses who had to go to the new location. The murder and the ensuing trial were not cheap for the Gonzales and Tillman families. In addition to expenses incurred by the state, the defendant retained many attorneys during the trial and pretrial periods.[50] The Gonzales family hired attorneys to assist Solicitor Thurmond.[51] It is unlikely that a civil libel case would have necessitated such a large array of eminent attorneys. Tillman's lengthy incarceration cost the county government a considerable amount as well.

Johnstone argued that N. G. Gonzales had not practiced what his kinsman William Elliott now preached. When Gonzales had his disputes with the *Columbia Register* and its owners and staff, he did not bring lawsuits. He armed himself. Elliott, said Johnstone, would deny Tillman the same option.[52] Gonzales had taunted Jim Tillman and called him a coward when he did not fight Gaffney editor Ed DeCamp, who had insulted him. Gonzales did not say Tillman should have brought a defamation case; Gonzales said Tillman should have fought DeCamp. But Tillman carried his dispute with Gonzales beyond a fistfight to the extreme measure of murder.

Johnstone contended that the code under which Tillman lived required him to defend his good name against Gonzales's verbal savagery. Any man who stood such abuse and did not act to avenge himself would not be respected.[53] Any man who allowed himself to be pummeled in this fashion would be an "Ishmaelite," an outcast, a wanderer welcome nowhere.[54] This was too heavy a price to pay for freedom of the press. Here Johnstone made an allusion to the biblical story in which Abraham, at the instigation of his wife Sarah on the birth of their son Isaac, disowned his son Ishmael, whose mother was the slave Hagar. Ishmael became an outcast and wanderer, the fate that would have befallen Tillman, Johnstone said, if he had not been manly enough to defend his honor.[55]

But Johnstone repeatedly undermined his picture of the poor, put-upon, victimized Tillman with no recourse but murder, by noting that Tillman replied to Gonzales's invectives with stinging criticism from the campaign stump, including the Columbia city hall speech at the end of his campaign for governor. Johnstone asked the judge to charge that Tillman had such a right of reply. He asked the judge to charge "that when one man assaults another with words the other man has the right to answer back in words. He is not to stand back like a whipped cur and skulk and not open his mouth."[56] But no one had denied Tillman the right to reply with words. That was his proper remedy, and as a prominent politician with a campaign forum, he was in a position to exercise it effectively. If he had stopped with a verbal reply, he would not have been on trial for murder.

Although his attack on what he regarded as a licentious press formed the core of his argument, Johnstone did not ignore the testimony of the eyewitnesses to the shooting. His task was to build-up those who had seen events in a way that fortified Tillman's self-defense strategy and to marginalize those who supported the prosecution argument that Gonzales took no actions that created a reasonable apprehension of danger from Tillman. Johnstone treated Richard Holsenback, whose testimony had supported Tillman's version of events, as if he were a folk hero. Johnstone made the illiterate but sly office seeker into a symbolic everyman who stood up to the bullying cross-examination of the arrogant former attorney general G. Duncan Bellinger and got the better of him.

Johnstone had to marginalize the testimony of Mrs. Melton, who said that Gonzales appeared benign rather than fierce just before the shooting and that he turned to avoid, rather than to confront, Tillman. Johnstone did this by treating her as a sincere, but confused, dainty little woman, who could not be expected to observe correctly such masculine matters as murder because her tea-party-in-the-parlor life had not given her experience. Johnstone strutted before the all-male jury and cast a disdainful look at the ladies in the courtroom. He observed of women in general, "They are made for scenes of love and they know nothing about war, or war combat." He said of Mrs. Melton in particular, "She has been accustomed to the drawing room and to all [?] the elegancies and refinements of it [?] and she evidently has drawn around her, wherever she may be the most [?] courtly and most elegant. She is unsuited to a scene of strife, and as soon as the pistol cracked, Mrs. Melton went where ladies generally go, to the drawing room and the parlor."[57] Johnstone rather boorishly asked for a pistol so that he could "get amongst these ladies here and I want as a matter of experiment to get [?] out a pistol, raise it and let it crack, and you will never have seen partridges scatter quicker than these ladies will do." There is no indication that Johnstone actually performed this experiment. At any rate Johnstone argued that a man of Tillman's "honored name" should not be convicted and confined "within the walls of the penitentiary and consort him there with Negro ruffians and criminals" on the testimony of a woman, especially when her vantage point was from behind Tillman and his associates so that she could not have seen all of the things she claimed to have seen.

Johnstone set himself up as a mind reader in order to discredit the testimony of another prosecution witness, Claudius Murray Lide, who had been walking just behind Gonzales at the time of the shooting. Rather than witnessing just the aftermath of the shooting, as some others did, Lide had testified that he saw Tillman fire the gun. He was also sure that Gonzales made no aggressive moves with his hands. Johnstone said Lide, an energetic young building contractor, whom he pictured as a mover and shaker in the business community, could not be relied on as an accurate observer because his mind was probably on his next business deal. In addition to being a building contractor, the busy Lide was active in engineering, architecture, and agricultural businesses.

In his peroration Johnstone, like Rembert, pulled out all the emotional stops, reminding the jury that it held the reputation of an "honored name" in its hands. He further asked the jurors to think of Tillman's wife and child: "Remember in this room anxious hearts will await you and around yonder door infant feet will play and infant feet stand ready to carry to a mother's heart as sweet a message as was ever whispered into human ears since the message of peace was first breathed upon the world from the infant lips of the little babe at Bethlehem." Johnstone showed no embarrassment at elevating a Tillman acquittal to the same level of importance as the birth of Christ, nor did he seem to realize that he had attributed to the newborn baby Jesus the message of peace the Bible attributes to the Heavenly Host.[58]

The Prosecution: The Editorials Had Ceased

Thirty-two year old Edward Lee Asbill of the Lexington County Bar gave a brief but forceful closing argument for the prosecution.[59] Asbill emphasized that the editorials critical of Tillman should not be considered a justification for the killing. Because they had ceased five months before the killing, Tillman could not argue that shooting Gonzales was the only way to stop the abuse. It had already stopped.

Asbill contended that all men should be treated as equals under the law. The jury should not give Tillman a free pass because of the lofty position he had held and the political glitter reflected on him by his powerful uncle.

The Defense: A Spiteful Editor Abused His Freedom

Chief defense counsel Patrick Henry Nelson's closing argument added his forceful voice to the attack on the press in general and the *State* in particular, accusing them of unleashing a feeding frenzy of hate against Jim Tillman. Nelson contended that, although a vigilant press was needed in a democracy to evaluate the fitness of candidates for office, such commentary ceased to be protected free speech when it was undertaken with the purpose of injuring the individual rather than supplying information to inform the electorate.[60] Nelson viewed freedom of the press as a privilege rather than a firm right, and the privilege disappeared if the author did not have the proper attitude. Nelson's vague standard gave no guidance to editors who could not discern how their attitude might be viewed by myriad readers. Determining an author's or an editor's purpose or intent is a notoriously subjective matter. The editor could think that his intent in criticizing a public official is to provide a public service by informing the electorate of the quality of its government, but the target of his barbs may think the editor is motivated by pure spite. Nelson did not say who was to be the judge—the editor, the target of the criticism, an objective reasonable man, the conglomerate view of the public, or what. A cautious editor might decide not to give the public needed information if he is afraid of being second-guessed later by someone who viewed an article he thought was a public service as a personal attack instead. Viewed in this manner, freedom of the press is a slender reed upon which to lean. It may hold or collapse in an unpredictable fashion.

By arguing that speech made with the purpose of causing personal injury was not privileged and was subject to a libel action, Nelson admitted the existence of a peaceful remedy for Tillman.[61] But he quickly dismissed that alternate remedy. He argued "why resort to the weapon and kill him? Why not sue the State Company for libel? Gentlemen, it has been somewhat against the traditions of our people and our country to bring a libel suit for any defamatory language or slander or abuse against you."[62] If he had brought a suit, James H. Tillman would have betrayed his code of honor; he would have been hiding behind judicial robes rather than fighting like a man.

Nelson's closing argument was characterized by displays of personal acrimony toward opposing counsel. His sharpest barbs were aimed at the private attorneys hired by the Gonzales family to assist the official prosecutor, Solicitor Thurmond. Nelson told the jury, "Ah! Gentlemen, there is something more than the prosecution in this case being conducted by the state's officer. It is being conducted by private individuals who are selling their talents for gold." His implication was that prosecutors paid by the family who owned the *State* were turning the case into an extension of that paper's persecution of Jim Tillman. His strongest ire was directed at G. Duncan Bellinger, who had roughed-up Richard Holsenback, the witness the defense was touting as a symbolic everyman, a witness who backed up the self-defense theory with his eyewitness testimony and was also the type of person jurors could identify with. Part of the defense strategy was to make the case look like oppression by the rich and powerful, represented by the *State* newspaper and Bellinger, against the common man, represented by Holsenback, the salt-of-the-earth Lexington jury, and their champion Jim Tillman. Nelson also turned his scorn on prosecutor William Elliott for his vigorous defense of freedom of the press and trying to picture the arrogant editor as the friend of the mill worker and farmer when he actually held them in contempt because they supported the Tillmans at the ballot box. Nelson did an effective job of making Gonzales appear to be the aggressor, reviewing the violent episodes in Gonzales's past, including his feud with the rival newspaper clan the Calvos. Nelson painted Jim Tillman as a would-be peacemaker who made overtures of friendship to Gonzales that were brusquely spurned.

A highly unusual feature of Nelson's closing argument is that the judge permitted him to use jurors, including the foreman, in demonstrations. In one reenactment, he sought to discredit Mrs. Melton's eyewitness testimony that, as Gonzales approached Tillman's group, his facial expression was benign, not aggressive, and he made no movement with his right hand that might have suggested he was drawing a weapon. Nelson had the foreman stand up, look at his face, and see if he could simultaneously see Nelson's hand movements at his side. Nelson argued that this could not be done. Of course you could look quickly at one and then the other. Tillman claimed to have observed both Gonzales's hands and his facial expressions. So perhaps it was not impossible after all. Nelson also pointed out that by the time the shot was fired, Mrs. Melton had been distracted by Senator Brown, who engaged her in conversation. Like the other defense attorneys, he sought to marginalize Mrs. Melton's testimony as that of a mere woman, but one, he hastened to add, for whom he had the greatest respect. He told the jurors that they had to ask themselves, "whether a woman placed in those circumstances can remember accurately everything that occurred." Would not she be too overcome by emotion to remember clearly?

Nelson used another juror in a demonstration to refute the rumors that Tillman had shot Gonzales in the back. He enlisted a juror to show the location of entry and exit wounds. Nelson asked the juror to raise his hand as if he were firing a pistol. Then Nelson illustrated on his own body where the entry and exit wounds were. Such use of jurors in demonstrations during closing arguments was undoubtedly an effective way to get the points across to the jury, but it damaged the impartiality of the proceedings to permit the defense lawyers to co-opt the jurors as part of their case. Yet it provoked no objections from the prosecution.

Each defense closing argument was designed to end with a reminder to the jurors that a conviction of James H. Tillman would in a sense be not only a conviction of the defendant but also of the highly vaunted Tillman name. Previous defense closings had focused on the joy an acquittal would bring to the accused's wife and daughter and the anguish a conviction would cause. Focusing on the damage to the defendant's mother and to the memory of his father, the late congressman George D. Tillman, Nelson spoke of the "devotion of the old gray-haired mother." He noted the father's status as a revered redeemer, one of those who rescued South Carolina from black and carpetbagger rule. Nelson said the father was "the man who in '76 stood by the side of [Wade] Hampton, [Matthew C.] Butler and [Martin W.] Mart Gary, helping to redeem this State from Negro domination and rule, the man who after that was sent to congress and served there ably, an ornament to the state, an ornament to the nation, for

18 years and then retired to private life."[63] Nelson also extolled George Tillman's service in the state constitutional convention of 1895, noting he was so revered that he was called the "Grandest Roman of them all." Nelson asked, "Can the son of such a man, the son of such a mother be a murderer?" In a final oratorical flourish, Nelson answered. No! You cannot call the son of such people a murderer just "because he killed one Narciso Gener Gonzales." This statement came close to saying that Tillman's name was more important than Gonzales's life.[64]

The Prosecution: A Planned Murder, Not Self-Defense

In Andrew Crawford, a former probate judge, the prosecution had on its team an orator who first gained renown as a leader of the paramilitary Red Shirts, the group that spearheaded the return of white rule by intimidating black voters. Crawford was remembered by fellow lawyers as an eloquent speaker who had lent his debating skills as well as his military ability to the cause of restoring white dominance during the 1876 gubernatorial campaign, in which their candidate, Wade Hampton III, was elected governor.[65] A history of the Richland County Bar describes Crawford and chief defense counsel Patrick Nelson as among the small group of lawyers who handled "the best of the criminal cases." The two lawyers were "great cronies," who after work swapped "news and gossip" as they "partook of cheering refreshment."[66] Even though he gained fame as a political orator during the turbulent days of 1876, Crawford's closing argument was one of the most professional ones in the trial. It was largely free of the personal feuding with opposition attorneys, the political posturing, and the appeals to prejudice that characterized some of the other closing arguments.[67]

A major focus of Crawford's argument was demonstrating that the prosecution had proved the mental element, malice aforethought (premeditated malice), necessary to a conviction for murder.[68] The case law available at the time of the trial says, "Malice is a term of art importing wickedness and excluding a just cause or excuse."[69] The South Carolina Supreme Court had held that "wherever there is a previously formed intention to kill, it cannot be excused by a provocation at the time of the homicide."[70] Since Tillman's lawyers were trying to prove that Gonzales provoked Tillman's self-defensive action by appearing to reach for a gun, the prosecution hoped to neutralize that strategy by a strong showing of malice aforethought.

So Crawford sought to demonstrate how the prosecution had proved that Tillman had "a previously formed intent" at the time of the killing. To do this he relied on several points brought out by the prosecution during the trial. An expert on architectural measurement had testified, displaying a map to demonstrate that, when Tillman exited the State House just before the shooting, he probably could have seen as far as the office of the *State* newspaper, and he would have seen Gonzales coming up Main Street from that office toward him. If he were truly afraid of Gonzales, Crawford said, Tillman would have changed direction to avoid Gonzales. The fact that Tillman had continued down Main Street toward Gonzales proved he had already formed an intent to kill.[71] The defense itself had helped prove malice aforethought by constantly harping on how much Tillman had been offended by the stinging criticism of him in the editorials. Gonzales threw verbal brickbats at Tillman in the pages of the *State* during the entire 1902 campaign. Tillman had brooded for months over this long series of affronts. As Crawford pointed out, witnesses said Tillman had told them that whenever he was in Columbia he prowled the streets looking for Gonzales. Tillman did not kill Gonzales because of the victim's hand movements on January 15. Tillman killed the editor pursuant to a settled intent. For a man intent only on defending himself, Tillman was overarmed. He had two pistols; one was a gun that was then a rare and exotic weapon for Columbia: a German Luger magazine pistol. He had had the foresight to send that pistol out for repairs the day before the killing. He had bragged about his plans for Gonzales in a hotel-room meeting with his political cronies. He was going to "snuff his light out," to shoot him down "like a mad dog." Even his "Good morning Mr. Gonzales" greeting moments before shooting, was a calculated attempt to put Gonzales off his guard. With this array of evidence, "a previously formed intention," said Crawford, had been proved many times over.

Crawford was equally methodical in rebutting the defense team's insinuations that Gonzales was armed at the time of the killing, even though no gun had been found on him, and no one had seen him with a gun at that time. The one possible exception was Mrs. Evans, who had a vague impression of seeing a bulge in his coat pocket that she thought could have been a gun. Crawford carefully reviewed the testimony of all the witnesses who had touched or examined Gonzales's body or clothing after the shooting. This included the testimony of the bystanders who had helped him back to his office, of people at the office who handled his coat, and of physicians who examined him.

Even though most of his argument was focused on the facts rather than appeals to prejudice, Crawford could sometimes be just as maudlin as the defense attorneys who had closed their arguments with poignant allusions to Tillman's wife, mother, and child. Crawford said that "methinks I see silhouetted against the skies over the cemetery a widow, the form of a sweet woman bending upon the new-made grave, and as she speaks through me, she asks not for vengeance, but for justice."

Crawford had a talent for capturing the weaknesses of the defense case in a pungent phrase. He said accepting the defense argument that murders were justified just because the victim insulted the perpetrator would mean that "every home in South Carolina would be a charnel house." He called Tillman a "walking arsenal" for prowling the streets of Columbia armed with two pistols and looking for Gonzales. The *News and Courier* gave Crawford's closing argument some of its highest marks. It said Crawford "went into the argument with his whole soul and really made a superb speech" and added that finding a "real orator [was] exceedingly rare" and that Crawford had proved he had "in him the stuff of which orators are made."[72]

The Defense: Gonzales "Brought about His Own Destruction"

Tillman's law partner, George Croft, had pursued a slash-and-burn, take-no-prisoners strategy throughout the trial. A key element of this approach was vilification, which was the main theme of his closing argument: vilification of Gonzales, vilification of prosecutors who had gotten under his skin, vilification of prosecution witnesses whose testimony was particularly damaging, and vilification of the press in general and the *State* in particular. Croft's biggest target was Gonzales: "I believe Mr. Gonzales was an element of discord, a firebrand; he arrayed father against son, and brother against brother and neighbor against neighbor, and kept us asunder for long years."[73] Arguing that Gonzales "brought his own destruction upon himself," Croft made killing Gonzales sound like a public service, like pest removal, but then covered the act with a thin veneer of self-defense.

Croft recognized the need for a free press, he said, but carrying it to the point of the personal insult was going too far. He asked the jury "would any man have a right to brand you as a thief, a coward, a blackguard, debauchee, corrupt, disgraceful and a dishonor to your family and your countrymen?" This question follows the defense theme that freedom of speech and press encompassed only inoffensive expression. Such a grudging, skinflint scope for freedom of expression would leave unprotected much of the roughhouse, brawling political speech of the Tillman era, including that of the titular family.[74]

Croft asserted that Gonzales had been duly warned about his likely fate if he continued with his venomous attacks. The warning, Croft said, came from the treatment of other editors around the country who spewed hatred in their papers: "I know of no man in free America who has with unbridled license slandered his fellow man but what sooner or later he met his fate."[75] He gave an example of a San Francisco editor who was "so denunciatory of his fellow man that he died with his boots on because of his slander." These remarks probably referred to an 1880 incident in which Charles de Young, editor of the *San Francisco Chronicle,* was shot and killed by the mayor's son in revenge for vituperative editorials against the mayor. The killer was acquitted. This was the basis for Croft's implication that vicious editors were an outlaw species who could be shot with impunity. But the case furnished a poor example for Croft since the de Young case was starkly different from the Gonzales-Tillman affair. De Young's editorial attacks were more personal than Gonzales's, and de Young, unlike Gonzales, had been the first to use violence when he shot the mayor while he was still a candidate and popular preacher. De Young believed that the preacher had insulted his mother by alleging that he was the product of "bawdy house breeding."[76] Croft also pointed to a Texas editor who suffered a similar fate. With these well-known examples before him, Gonzales should have known what destiny awaited him if he continued to wield his paper as a weapon of personal revenge rather than in its proper role of informing the public about the job performances of public officials. In other words Gonzales knowingly asked for his tragic end and he got it; he, not Jim Tillman, was to blame.

Croft could have fortified his point that Gonzales had only himself to blame by noting that the *State* had applauded the shooting of a journalist for besmirching the reputation of a young lady. In this 1902 episode, editor Frederick Marriott of the *San Francisco News Letter* was shot by two politically and socially prominent "clubmen." The Columbia paper gave its story on this incident a headline that said "Slanderous Editor Deservedly Shot."[77] Here was Gonzales approving the gun-barrel censorship that was later practiced on him. Marriott recovered and attempted to persuade prosecutors to charge the assailants with crimes. But the authorities shrank from bringing charges, probably because of the perpetrators' political influence. Faced with timidity in the criminal-justice system, Marriott had to look to a civil suit for damages. He recovered sixteen thousand dollars.[78]

The Texas incident to which Croft referred was the 1898 shooting in Waco of William Cowper Brann, editor of an internationally circulated magazine that was appropriately named, the *Iconoclast.* But there were significant differences between the Gonzales-Tillman case and Brann's. The Texas editor was not so much engaged in the core free press function of informing voters about government officials and candidates as he was attacking privileged institutions and individuals. He repeatedly attacked the Baptist-affiliated Baylor University for conduct that he thought was sexual immorality and that he believed exposed female students to abuse. He tried to bury the school and its respected president with an avalanche of invective that went even further than anything Gonzales published. Brann called the university a "manufactory of ministers and Magdalenes [prostitutes]" and "worse than a harem." Brann was killed by a man whose daughter attended Baylor and who perhaps thought the editor was accusing all Baylor female students of loose morals. In the Waco incident, both the editor and his assailant were armed and both were killed in a shoot-out. Thus the editor's killer was not crowned a champion of the downtrodden by a jury acquittal as Croft hoped his client would be.[79]

Croft seemed to argue that it was proper to criticize an official's public acts and public character, but not his personal traits, such as his lack of truthfulness, temperance, or of courage. But the line between public and personal is impossible to draw. What part of a candidate's character can be criticized if his lack of truthfulness, temperance, honesty, and courage are out of bounds? Croft was not above a few vengeful personal comments himself. He lashed out at young William Elliott, calling him Gonzales's "cousin attorney" and saying that the freedom of speech doctrine he espoused was "fiendish" and "corrupt."[80] Somehow it was improper for Elliott to call Jim Tillman corrupt, but it was all right for Croft to say that Elliott's doctrine was corrupt. The corrupt doctrine Croft attributed to Elliott was saying that "a newspaper man has a right to say anything about anybody." This was a considerable misrepresentation of the strong but temperate defense of freedom of the press found in Elliott's closing argument.

When it came to discrediting certain prosecution witnesses, Croft's vilification strategy lost whatever qualities of cool, professional sarcasm it possessed. He approached with bitter, festering anger prosecution witnesses Captain August Fischer and Captain John D. Livingston, called to discredit defense witness T. D. Mitchell, who had testified that he had heard Gonzales threaten Tillman. Fischer and Livingston had testified that Mitchell was not a person of good character for truth and veracity and that they would not believe what he said under oath. For Livingston, Croft reserved one of the most lethal and derisive words in the southern vocabulary: *scalawag.* Croft defined the term for jurors who were too young to remember the 1876 campaign to return white rule, explaining that "a scalawag was a white man so measly, so poor that he quit his race and joined the darkies to put the Negro government above the white. Oh, look at Livingston! He is not here, but I would say it if he was here, didn't he look like a scalawag. Didn't he look like he had been drawn through a stove pipe and beat with a soot bag."[81]

At one point during his closing argument, Croft moderated his strategy of vilification but only slightly. During the trial he had sought to marginalize the testimony of the distinguished journalist August Kohn, who had witnessed Gonzales's dying declaration, by sending signals to the jury that Kohn was not one of "us"—not part of the Christian community. When Kohn would not say, as Croft wanted him to during cross-examination, that he had personal knowledge of Gonzales's hating Tillman, Croft asked Kohn if he would swear to God that he was telling the truth. Kohn answered "yes," but Croft was not satisfied. He asked the Jewish Kohn if he would swear "before God and the Living Christ." When Kohn would not do so, reasonably concluding that swearing by God was enough, Croft had succeeded in marginalizing Kohn's testimony as coming from a man who was not one of "us" and not worthy of belief.[82]

Croft finally realized that this anti-Semitic ploy had its dangers. He tried to make amends, but he could not quite make himself go all the way. He first directly addressed Kohn, who was sitting in the courtroom covering the trial for the *News and Courier.* Croft bluntly told Kohn that he did not owe him an apology for the cross-examination, but he wanted to make it clear that he believed in freedom of religion. He noted that "the Great God has made mankind in thousands of religions."[83] He recognized the Jews as a "great race" who had given us many of our traditions. He recited a pantheon of distinguished Jews whom he admired, including Lord Beaconsfield (Benjamin Disraeli), the former British prime minister, and Judah P. Benjamin, a Confederate cabinet member. But Croft still thought that Kohn had personal knowledge of Gonzales's enmity toward Tillman and that Kohn should have admitted it.

Croft concluded by urging the jury to "be proud of your manhood." In saying this, he was attempting to stiffen the spines of the jury so that they would be courageous and bring back a verdict of acquittal even though it might cause an uproar and subject them to criticism, perhaps even to ridicule.

The Prosecution: Even the Powerful Must Obey the Law

Having the burden of proof, the prosecution is traditionally given the envied position of making the last closing argument. G. Duncan Bellinger, the most experienced and tenacious of the prosecutors, made the last argument.[84] Bellinger began by ingratiating himself with the jury. He complimented them on being members of the white race, saying: "I will use good Anglo-Saxon words, clear in their meaning to you and to me, clear to you who are as I understand, of true Anglo-Saxon blood, perhaps as pure and unmixed as can be found in America today."

Bellinger said that he regretted having to argue against the son of his old friend, the late congressman George Tillman and "the nephew of the man whom I have supported ever since I entered public life." It was a clever tactic of the prosecution and the Gonzales family that they had chosen as a private attorney to assist the solicitor a prominent lawyer who was also a staunch supporter of Ben Tillman. This ploy was designed to help neutralize defense accusations that trying Jim Tillman was part of a plot to smear the senator. Despite his regrets at finding himself prosecuting the son and nephew of old friends, Bellinger had proved to be an aggressive prosecutor with a battering-ram style.

Bellinger first addressed himself to some of the petty personal slurs aimed at him by the defense attorneys. He noted that the chief defense attorney, Patrick Nelson, had insinuated that he and the other private attorneys assisting the prosecution were paid from a fund organized by northern newspapers and that these attorneys had sold their "talents for gold." He denied this allegation and said the privately paid prosecutors were paid by Ambrose Gonzales, a "hard working" man who started from nothing after the war and made his own money. Bellinger said that everybody, even lawyers, had to make a living. Nelson himself had been paid to prosecute "white men in other counties." Bellinger and Nelson had displayed professional jealousy throughout the trial.

Defense attorney Johnstone took the highly unusual step of interrupting an opponent's closing argument. He asked Bellinger a question on a point that the defense had hammered at again and again. Why had not the prosecution introduced the verbatim version of Gonzales's dying declaration taken stenographically by Robert Lathan? What was the prosecution trying to hide? Bellinger gave the same answer the prosecution had given the many times the defense had raised the question before. If the prosecution had attempted to use the Lathan version rather than Babcock's version, which was used, the defense would have objected that it was not trustworthy because it had come from a biased source, Gonzales's own secretary.

Bellinger was acting as clean-up man for the prosecution—responding to defense arguments that had muddied the prosecution's case. He noted Croft's charge that William Elliott had claimed a sweeping freedom of the press allowing newspapers to say anything they wanted to about anybody. Bellinger denied that Elliott had asserted such an unlimited freedom of the press and noted that he had specifically recognized that lawsuits for defamation could be brought in case of abuse. Tillman, Bellinger said, should have taken advantage of such legal redress rather than murder.

The most significant part of Bellinger's argument concerned the contradictions between the testimony of the eyewitnesses to the shooting, specifically that of prosecution witness Mrs. Melton, who had said Gonzales tried to avoid confronting Tillman, and defense witness Richard Holsenback, who said the editor had changed direction so as to confront Tillman. Bellinger said that the conflict in the testimony of the two witnesses should be resolved by believing Mrs. Melton.

Bellinger intimated that either Holsenback did not see the shooting and claimed to have done so only to ingratiate himself with Tillman or that Holsenback could have been part of a conspiracy to place him at the scene of the crime in advance so the defense would have a witness guaranteed to have seen the shooting in a way most advantageous to their side. Bellinger did not explicitly state this last theory but gave enough hints that we can tell what he meant. He gave no evidence in support of this theory—only his distrust of the slippery Holsenback. He said that "this ubiquitous man Holsenback who was there whenever you would want him, and it seems from a question I asked [while cross-examining him] that it is his custom to be anywhere there is a homicide. I say take out Holsenback or decide he is unworthy of belief, and what have you got."[85]

Why should such a chameleon-like witness be believed instead of the respectable Mrs. Melton? Bellinger asked—who do you believe? "Mrs. Melton with the face of a Madonna—Holsenback, thank God he has no prototype, and thank God I am informed—he will have no progeny—put them against each other."

While he was making his closing argument, Bellinger was interrupted repeatedly by several members of the defense team, including Croft, Nelson, and

Johnstone. The judge did nothing to control this highly unusual conduct, but perhaps the interruptions were understandable in light of Bellinger's dark hints about a conspiracy.

In conclusion Bellinger urged the jury to hold James H. Tillman responsible for his own actions—not to let him off because of his famous name. His father, George Tillman, his uncle Ben Tillman, and another uncle, Confederate hero James Tillman, were venerated by many, but they were not on trial. Jim Tillman fired the fatal shot, and he must stand in the harsh light of his own actions rather than the glow cast by his family name. The jury must do its duty to the state: "The time has come in South Carolina when the jurors must decide whether they are going to protect our women and our children, the future wives, the future progeny of our boys, or whether the civilization, and religion of our state must go down, strangled in human blood. . . . I hope Divine power will sustain you in that room and give you courage to save our state from impending ruin."[86] In this last argument, Bellinger pointed directly at questions that had lurked beneath the trial's surface throughout but had only been circled warily before: would James H. Tillman be treated more leniently because of his powerful political connections, or more severely, or in a fashion similar to other men who claimed to have acted in defense of their honor or life? The trial now approached the endgame: the judge's charge to the jury, the jury deliberations, and the verdict.

8.

THE VERDICT

The last stage of the trial before jury deliberations was the charge to the jury by Judge Frank Gary.[1] The question in the minds of many was whether the man the Tillmans fondly called "Cousin Frank" would favor the defendant in instructing the jury on the law.

The Jury Charge: Self-Defense and the "Appearance" of Danger

Judge Gary began by telling the jurors that he would instruct them only as to the law that they should apply to the facts. The jury had the exclusive prerogative to determine the facts. Prior to the adoption of the South Carolina Constitution of 1868, judges could charge juries on the facts in a case as well as on the law. But the 1868 Constitution forbade judges to charge on the facts, permitting them only to "declare the law" and to "state the testimony" in an impartial manner. The 1895 Constitution removed even the modest power to "state the testimony," and in an even more pointed effort to ensure that the judges did not usurp the fact-determining role of juries, it mandated: "Judges shall not charge juries in respect to matters of fact, but shall declare the law." Since the South Carolina Supreme Court was vigorous in policing this limitation on judicial authority, Gary was wise to adhere to it scrupulously.[2]

Exercising his duty to instruct the jury on the law, Judge Gary told them that in considering whether or not Tillman was guilty of the murder charge against him, they should know that there are three types of homicide: justifiable, excusable, and felonious. A justifiable homicide was one performed pursuant to

Judge Frank Gary when he was serving in the United States Senate, 1908–9. Courtesy of the Library of Congress.

a legal duty, such as an official executing someone sentenced to death by a court. An excusable homicide could be an accidental killing committed by a person performing a lawful act or a killing by someone defending himself.[3] Felonious homicides were the only ones punishable by law. These were of two types: murder and manslaughter.

As Gary explained, "Murder was defined by statute to be killing of [any person] a human being with malice aforethought, either express or implied."[4] Gary said that "malice may be defined to be an evil spirit—a depraved and wicked spirit."[5] Expressed malice was "where one person kills another with a sedate, deliberate, meant and formed design, such formed design being evidenced by external circumstances, which discover the inward intention, such as lying in wait, antecedent menacing, threats, former grudges, and concerted schemes to do somebody harm." He described manslaughter as the "killing of a human being in sudden heat and passion and upon sufficient legal provocation." If a defendant was found guilty of the less serious offense of manslaughter rather than murder, it was one of the law's "charities," arising out of a "tender regard for the frailties of our nature" and recognizing that "under certain circumstances we are liable to be so far transported beyond ourselves that we act from passion and not from reason." But if "sufficient time elapses" between the provocation and the killing for the passion to cool, the perpetrator will be guilty of murder.[6]

Gary told the jury that it should focus on the following questions: "Has N. G. Gonzales been killed? Did James H. Tillman kill him? If so under what circumstances was the killing done? Was the killing felonious, such as the law punishes for? If so, was it murder or manslaughter, or was the killing excusable?"[7] The pivotal point in the judge's charge concerned the defendant's plea of self-defense. Judge Gary told the jury that if the defendant was successful in proving that he acted in self-defense, then the killing was excusable, and the jury should bring in a verdict of not guilty. The key idea underlying self-defense, Gary said, was "necessity; that is, that it was necessary to take the life of a fellow man to save one's own life or to avoid serious bodily harm." To establish successfully that he acted in self-defense, the defendant had to prove "that he was without fault in bringing on the difficulty" between the parties; "that he believed at the time that he was in danger of receiving serious bodily harm, or losing his own life"; "that it was necessary to take the life of his assailant" to avoid his own death or bodily harm; "that a reasonable man, a man of ordinary firmness, courage, prudence and reason, situated as he was, would have come to a like conclusion"; and that there was no other likely means for avoiding the defendant's death or serious bodily harm than killing the assailant.

The prosecution had the burden of establishing the elements of murder beyond a reasonable doubt, but the defendant had the burden of proving self-defense by a preponderance of the evidence. The beyond-a-reasonable-doubt standard that the state had to meet was the toughest level of proof required by law; preponderance of the evidence was still a demanding standard but not as high as that required of the state. Judge Gary defined a reasonable doubt, charging that "it is not a vague, whimsical, [?] weak, imaginary doubt but is a strong substantial, well founded doubt growing out of the evidence." He noted that preponderance of the evidence "means the greater weight of the evidence."[8] He told the jury to picture a scale as weighing the evidence. If the side of the scale "in favor of the plea bears down the testimony against it, it outweighs it. It preponderates and the plea is established."

The judge instructed the jury that it could choose as the form of its verdict either: "guilty of murder, guilty of murder with a recommendation to mercy, guilty of manslaughter, or not guilty." The second option could be used if the jury found the defendant guilty of murder, but concluded that he did not deserve the "extreme penalty of the law," death. He said the recommendation of mercy, "will, of itself, reduce the punishment from death to imprisonment for life in the penitentiary."

In addition to his general charge, Judge Gary considered several requests from the prosecution and defense that specific points in their favor be included in the instructions. These requests were presented in a manner that would be considered strange to a person familiar with modern procedure, in which such requests are considered out of the presence of the jury and the judge later presents those requests that he accepts to the jury as his own without attribution to either side. In the Tillman case, the attorneys were permitted to present their requests to the judge in the presence of the jury as part of their closing arguments. The judge repeated these requests during his charge to the jury, stated which side they came from, announced which ones he accepted and rejected, and gave the reasons why. It would be difficult to conceive of a system more likely to confuse, and sometimes prejudice, the jury. Instructions, often couched in arcane legal language, are difficult for lay jurors to understand to begin with. If jurors are given multiple versions of the law on several points, the confusion would likely be compounded. In explaining why he accepted some requests and rejected others, the judge's opinion on the facts of the case could seep through, thus degrading his impartiality. In addition the judge's aura as the authority figure controlling the proceedings is reduced since the jury is presented with a variety of voices declaring the law in an oracular manner.[9]

One of the most crucial decisions by Judge Gary in determining which proposals for jury charges to accept concerned the plea of self-defense. Gary granted a defense request to charge that one could kill to defend himself, even when there was "no actual danger," if it "*appeared* to him at the time" that there was a danger and if the situation would have *appeared* to a "man of ordinary firmness and reason" to be so dangerous that he had to take the life of the deceased to save his own life, or save himself from serious bodily harm.[10] This was an important victory for Tillman because the jury could now acquit on the basis of his self-defense contentions, even though no actual danger to him existed from the unarmed Gonzales. Under this standard the jury was permitted to find that it could reasonably have *appeared* to Tillman that such danger existed because Gonzales's threatening messages and his hand movements made it *appear* as if he were going for a gun.[11] The judge gave the charge again and again with slightly different wording, thus giving the point unusual prominence. Whether the danger would have appeared to exist in the eyes of a hypothetical person of ordinary reason and firmness was to be judged under "all the circumstances."

Judge Gary defined "all the circumstances" with such breadth that he gave the defense another victory in the maneuvering to gain favorable jury instructions. The term embraced "the feeling and disposition the deceased bore towards the defendant, as evidenced by his past conduct and attitude, together with any threats that may have been made against defendant." This allowed the jury to focus not just on all the circumstances at the time of, and just before and after the shooting, but on the entire history of the long Tillman-Gonzales relationship. Thus all the social offenses committed by Gonzales—from refusing to accept a cigar from Tillman in the Washington hotel lobby to engineering the blackballing of Tillman from private-club membership—could be combined with Gonzales's critical editorials and taunting remarks about Tillman's lack of courage to show that Gonzales hated Tillman and, as shown by his threats, was bent on killing him. This charge made it too easy to justify killing someone who had been highly offensive but not dangerous in the sense of posing a serious physical threat. The judge also granted prosecution requests for instructions, including one asking the judge to charge that "a mere threat" was not enough to justify killing in self-defense unless it was also accompanied by a "demonstration" on the part of the deceased at the time of the killing that showed him making movements to harm the defendant.[12] But the judge's charges regarding the appearance of harm were of such breadth, and were so often repeated like a litany, that they tilted the jury instructions in favor of the defense. As the jurors received the case and began deliberations, these points must have dominated their thinking.

Another dominating issue received no attention whatsoever in the judge's charge. That is the issue of the scope of freedom of the press. Had Gonzales's editorials gone too far? Were they too harsh, too opinionated, and too personal? Much time was lavished on these points during the trial even though their relevance was arguable. As noted earlier, abusive editorial language is no legal justification for murdering an author. Absence of these points from the judge's charge was consistent with self-defense being the pretended focal point of the trial when the real issue was the nature of the editorials. This permitted the trial to do real damage to freedom of the press while seeming to deal with it only incidentally. After the instructions, the jury began its scrutiny of the facts of the case amid the meandering path of the law and the political crosscurrents that swirled around the case.

Jury Deliberations: Two Mavericks

The jury got the case at 1:42 P.M. on October 14 and deliberated for more than nineteen hours on the fourteenth and fifteenth. The jury sessions were nominally secret, but much information wafted over the transom anyway. The first ballot was taken at about 2:00 P.M. on the fourteenth, and it produced a 10-2 vote for acquittal.[13] From then on, arguments in the jury room focused on attempts by the majority to persuade the two mavericks to switch their votes to not guilty to provide the required unanimity. The jury spent a tense, "uncomfortable night."[14] The jurors were given no accommodations or "bedding" for sleeping, but the sheriff permitted them to sleep. Some remained awake to keep the pressure on the two hold-outs. At about five the next morning the first switch occurred. J. B. Jumper joined the majority side, voting for acquittal after he and juror Milton Sharpe had struggled against the strong tide for acquittal by arguing in favor of a manslaughter conviction. Jumper, a mill worker, was described by *News and Courier* reporter and trial witness August Kohn as a "pale looking" young man.[15] At 10 A.M. on October 15, Milton Sharpe, a farmer, yielded to the majority, and the unanimous vote of twelve necessary for acquittal was achieved.[16] Sharpe had been ill earlier in the trial and the several days duration of that illness had almost caused a mistrial. When the unanimous vote had been achieved, the foreman, George Koon, a former county supervisor and farmer, knocked on the door of the jury room and asked for pen and ink.[17] This sent a signal throughout the close-knit Lexington community that a verdict was imminent, and the courtroom began to fill, particularly with hundreds of Tillman well-wishers.

These Tillman partisans expected a verdict of acquittal and were prepared for it. According to one account, they stationed Tillman supporters, including "dead shots," who could act immediately if an acquittal led to an attempt on Tillman's life. An out-of-town telegrapher, imported to help with the increased traffic expected from the verdict announcement, was startled to find himself closely watched by Tillman guardians because he was a stranger to them.[18]

Judge Gary directed that the defendant be brought into court, and runners were sent to find the attorneys for both sides. Defense counsel quickly assembled, but only Solicitor Thurmond could be located from the prosecution side. The courtroom crowd waited in edgy suspense while officials hunted for G. Duncan Bellinger and Andrew Crawford. Finally, in exasperation, Judge Gary directed that the verdict be read, but in doing so he warned that he would tolerate no outburst.[19]

Judge Gary asked jury foreman Koon if the jury had reached a verdict. When he replied "yes," he was directed to turn the verdict forms over to the clerk. The clerk said: "James H. Tillman, stand up." The *New York World* reported that at this point "Tillman rose to his feet pale but self-possessed. So tense was the feeling that only the rustling of the papers in the clerk's hand could be heard." Then the clerk gave the official pronouncement: "We the jury find James H. Tillman not guilty."[20]

The judge's admonition that the verdict should be greeted with calm was obeyed by many people, but several Tillman supporters yelled with delight. At least one shouted "Hurrah for Old Jim Tillman." The judge ordered that supporter's arrest, but he dodged his pursuers and escaped into the crowd.[21] One of the most delighted persons to hear the verdict was Tillman's eighty-four-year-old African American servant, George Johnstone. Tillman was receiving the congratulations of a crowd of his supporters when he noticed the ecstatic old family retainer off to the side of the crowd. Tillman immediately left the group, and he and Johnstone embraced. The *New York World* described this emotional greeting as the only time Tillman broke out of his shell of preternatural calm. Tillman and his attorneys thanked the jury. Later that day the jury attended a victory celebration at an apartment kept by Tillman's lawyers.[22]

There was something odd about the crowd in the courtroom when the verdict was announced. There were no ladies present. Rumors about possible attempts to assassinate Tillman if he were acquitted, and expectations that crude and boisterous comments would be made about the verdict no matter what its nature, had driven the ladies to more refined surroundings. Tillman's mother, Mrs. George D. Tillman, awaited the verdict at her hotel. When she heard the result, she began to walk toward the courthouse. Her son, who had been released from custody by Judge Gary, met her on the street as he was walking toward her hotel. Mother and son warmly embraced. Tillman's wife had been waiting for him in the parlor in the part of the jailhouse that served as a residence for the jailer and his family. After their reunion, she joined him to walk toward his mother's hotel.[23] Another account tells a different story of a more restrained reunion between husband and wife. The *New York World* said that, after Tillman and his mother met and hugged on the street, they walked to the hotel, where Tillman's wife awaited him on the plaza. She had not rushed eagerly to the jail. This account said husband and wife did not embrace but coolly shook hands as if they were distant acquaintances rather than partners in the intimate relationship of marriage.[24] Senator Ben Tillman was not present when the verdict was announced. He had been in the courtroom during closing arguments, which no doubt signaled to the jury his great interest in the case. But he had to leave because of his wife's injury in a carriage accident.[25]

Amid the celebratory events that followed announcement of the not-guilty verdict, Jim Tillman still had to deal with some of the sordid details of the trial and the shooting that led to it. Before he left the courthouse, as the paperwork directing his release was being prepared, the clerk of court removed from the evidence drawer the two pistols taken from Tillman at the time of his arrest. But when the clerk tried to return them to Tillman, he "waved both of his hands as if to spurn the offer, and said: 'I never want to see those things again.'" Several people in the crowd of onlookers clamored to gain ownership of the weapons. The Luger magazine pistol went to a Tillman relative who said he planned to place it on exhibit in Augusta, Georgia.[26]

Is There an Explanation for the Verdict?

August Kohn tried to find out the reasoning behind the verdict. Since many people had seen Tillman shoot Gonzales and no weapon had been found on the victim, the verdict defied logic. Interviewing members of the jury, Kohn asked them what the "predominating reason" behind the verdict was.[27] He was told that there was no single reason behind the vote. The original ten-man majority was composed of jurors with a variety of reasons for voting the way they did. However, the two jurors who held out for manslaughter but switched to the majority were said to have done so because the other jurors convinced them Tillman had acted in self-defense when he saw Gonzales make a "demonstration" with his right hand that made it look as if he were going for a gun. Kohn was convinced that the self-defense evidence was so weak that it was a mere "excuse" for a not-guilty vote for jurors who wanted to vote that way for other reasons. Those other reasons flowed from a belief that the press in general, and N. G. Gonzales in particular, had grown too powerful and could attack a man's honor, his prized reputation in the community, with impunity while safely ensconced in an editorial-office sanctuary. Direct evidence that this was a significant feature of the jury's deliberations comes from a letter written by juror W. I. Risinger, a farmer, to the editor of the *Spartanburg Journal,* in which Risinger responded to the paper's criticism of the jury. The letter, which was reprinted in the *State,* is reproduced here as it appeared in the Spartanburg paper, which apparently retained its unusual grammar, capitalization, and spelling:

> Spartanburg Journal
> Spartanburg, S.C.
> Sir.
>
> I have read your article in the columbia state which was an insult to Every Juryman who sits on the Tillman case, not only an insult to that body of men, but to the Judges who was concerned in the case. you are following in the steps of the decease Editor "abusing your liberty." I wish to be polite in this matter and show more wisdom than you did in writing up the Lexington court that tried James H. Tillman. To make my letter brief, I refer you to the annals of History when you will fail to find a single conviction of any man for shooting an Editor. The State and counsel for the same was satisfied with the Verdict otherwise the state could have gone to appeal courts, the

> Masses have accepted the verdict as fair but seemingly the press wants more blood which can be found by walking in the foot prints of N. G. Gonzales. Mr. Gonzales was an able man. but unfortunately he made a great mistake by abusing the liberty of his press. The courts have sustained the defendant by which all law biding citizens should be satisfied. If I was an Editor and not satisfied with the Defendant's acquital and had the grit to follow my pen, I would certainly invite the Defendant to Entertain me [fight a duel] beyond the Georgia lines which would be more patriotic to my fellow man than to sit in my sanctum and abuse him with my pen. In Extending this invitation mention above I would say to my Bro Editor. If I should prove the unfortunate one in the affair not to call it Murder, but suicide by abuse of liberty with the wrong man, now, Mr. Editor with the kindest of feelings towards all Editors will you kindly give this note room in your paper and ask the columbia state to copy same am not hunting a contriversy but will assure the press that any comments made the same will be answered politely.
>
> Very Truly yours
> W. I. Risinger
> Lexington SC—
> 10-21st 1903[28]

The letter espouses the view that editors are a species apart. Unlike others, they are a type of outlaw—and denied the protection of the laws against murder. It does not mention the transparently flimsy self-defense evidence and instead focuses on the jury's belief that Gonzales had abused the freedom of the press; that he was ruining a man's honor and his reputation in the community by firing verbal grapeshot, which could be avenged only by murdering him when he left his editorial bunker. The jury was acting as an ultimate censor, which placed the state's imprimatur of approval on Jim Tillman's deadly act.[29] The juror's mistaken belief that the state could appeal if it was dissatisfied with the verdict discloses an erroneous view by the jury that it need not be rigorous in its review of the evidence since its mistakes could be corrected by an appellate court.

In a sense the Tillman case was viewed as a struggle among competing values: freedom of the press versus the personal honor of a man attacked by the press. To a male member of society, personal honor meant his reputation for being courageous and manly as much as his reputation for honesty and integrity. Freedom of the press was an abstract concept with which the jurors in the Tillman case could not identify. Personal honor, however, was a concept dear to many southerners.[30] Honor probably was the ascendant value to the Tillman jurors.[31] In a sense the fact that the verdict flew in the face of the evidence reflected a wider social problem beyond just the behavior of the Tillman jury. In the years just before the Gonzales killing, jurors in South Carolina had shown a marked reluctance to convict defendants who killed to vindicate their honor. Charles Albert Woods, president of the South Carolina Bar Association, vigorously condemned this tendency in an address to the association that, ironically, was delivered in Columbia on January 15, 1903, the same day as the shooting. Although the speech made no reference to Tillman's shooting of Gonzales and, judging by its careful wording, had been in preparation for some time, the address was highly appropriate to the aftermath of the killing. Woods proved to be a shrewd judge of the immediate past and a prophet of the near future.[32] He observed that frequent killings took place "in real or pretended defense of individual rights or dignity." The killings were encouraged by the ready availability of the "nimble pistol" and "an immunity from punishment indicative of a diseased public conscience." He noted that "it must be admitted that the unpunished crimes of violence, even among the higher classes of society, are quite frequent enough to cause grave concern to every patriot." In a passage that was prophetic of the Gonzales-Tillman verdict, Woods observed that "the law now says to shoot for even grievous insult is murder, but too often public sentiment has allowed the slayer to escape on incredible pleas of self-defense."[33]

The easy availability of the "nimble pistol" that Woods spoke about is seen in the treatment of the indictment for carrying a concealed deadly weapon that was brought against Tillman along with the murder charge. The *New York Times* reported that this charge "was ignored during the trial, and the jury took no action on it."[34] It was treated by the lawyers, judges, and jury as if it did not exist. That carrying a concealed weapon was considered a matter of little consequence was signaled by an 1897 change in the law that substantially lowered the penalty for this misdemeanor charge. It cut the maximum fine from two hundred to one hundred dollars and the maximum jail time from twelve months to thirty days.[35] But the 1897 law required that when a charge of murder with a concealed deadly weapon was brought, it had to be accompanied by an additional count of carrying a concealed weapon, and the jury was required to render a verdict on that count.[36] This mandate was flouted in the Tillman case. Historian Walter Edgar notes that, by the time of the Tillman-Gonzales incident, carrying a concealed weapon had become so common that many considered a pistol to be an essential part of the attire of a well-dressed man. That weapons were not considered mere fashion accessories is seen in the fact that "four members of the state's congressional delegation in the 1890s had killed someone."[37]

In his 1896 study "Homicide in the Southern States," B. J. Ramage observed that "farmers, merchants, bankers, physicians, lawyers, even ministers of the gospel, often slay their fellow man in private warfare, and often after a mock trial are set at liberty, not only with no serious detriment to their reputation, but in many instances increased popularity."[38] The lengthy and turbulent Tillman case was no mock trial, but the quotation accurately catches the mood of the time and place. In a 1906 paper presented to the American Bar Association, Thomas J. Kernan, a Louisiana trial lawyer with wide experience, described several "unwritten laws" that often had significant influence on jury verdicts. One such law, he said, was that in the eyes of jurors "the lie direct, and certain other well known opprobrious epithets, which constitute mortal insult, are each equal to a blow, and any of them justifies an assault."[39] In 1883 Professor F. C. Woodward of South Carolina's Wofford College observed that the mode of settling disputes was in a transitional stage. Reliance on the complex ritual of dueling was gone, but trust in the law courts to provide satisfaction was incomplete. In the transition phase "we have fallen into the present lawless and cruel habit of street fighting."[40]

In 1935 Clemson sociologist H. C. Brearley concluded that those who killed to vindicate their honor were still often acquitted on the basis of spurious claims of self-defense. He quoted an 1890 essay by Harvard's Nathaniel Southgate Shaler, "The Peculiarities of the South," which said: "It has been found impossible to convict men of murder for such crimes, provided the jury is convinced that the assailant's honor was aggrieved and that he gave his adversary notice of his intention to assail him."[41] Jim Tillman's lawyers made it clear in the way they questioned witnesses and the way they shaped their closing arguments, that they were counting on the jury's retention of the attitude that legal remedies were insufficient to repair damage to a proud man whose honor had been pummeled by a man in command of a powerful newspaper who refused to halt the attacks. Only direct action against the editor could enforce the unwritten law, which was in fact a form of lawlessness in which each man defined the law for himself.[42]

Where had this lawless attitude come from? Charles Albert Woods thought it flowed from a deeply ingrained resentment of the law. Southern white men had developed a defiant attitude during and after Reconstruction. Woods concluded that white men had formed the "habit of thought that the law was made to oppress and rob and not protect, that the Federal government was controlled by his relentless enemies, and the state government by thieves whose sole purpose was to prey upon him and his."[43] This resentment of the law probably contributed to the immunity from punishment often enjoyed by killers. The adoption of violence, including murder, as an instrument of policy by those who strove to "redeem" the state for white rule cheapened the value placed on life. Those who followed this course during the time surrounding the 1876 election were more often cast as heroes than as villains.[44] Following this approach, almost thirty years later, Jim Tillman cast himself in the heroic role. With the aid of his lawyers, he became more than a man defending himself against a murder charge. His attorneys dressed him in the shining armor of a paladin of the little man, such as the jurors, defending them, as well as himself, against powerful economic forces symbolized by the press and particularly Gonzales. Even if this enabled him to kill his nemesis and purge his inner demons, the public was the loser. Violent crime was encouraged; a valued life was lost; a vigorous press was mocked by a verdict at odds with the evidence; and public confidence in the impartiality of the judiciary was undermined.

Reactions to the Verdict in Press and Pulpit

Critics were quick and vigorous in denouncing the verdict. National and state newspapers were especially vociferous in criticizing the verdict and the tone of the trial as threats to freedom of the press and respect for human life. Furthermore the verdict was detrimental to the reputation of the court system because the decision exemplified a discriminatory approach to justice in which the rich and powerful were treated more indulgently than others; that is the courts endorsed the crimes of white people while black people were convicted summarily or lynched without being afforded any form of trial whatsoever. The outcome of the Tillman trial was also described as encouraging people to settle their disputes by violent means rather than by the somewhat sublimated combat offered by the legal system.

Northern newspapers had observed the proceeding closely and were quick to react when the verdict reached them. The *Boston Transcript* saw the verdict as a manifestation of a racially biased southern brand of justice and of an upside-down set of values in which honor, seen as public esteem, trumps all other standards, including respect for life. The paper argued that, if the accused had been black, "the mob would have quickly done for him without giving him a chance to state his provocation or plead justification." The paper concluded that the decision sent the incongruous message "that what is diabolism in a negro is chivalry in a white man—in South Carolina."[45] But the *Cincinnati Enquirer* cautioned that the press should not be quick to condemn the verdict since "there is no ground for belief that the Tillman jury was improperly influenced or prejudiced" and the instructions it received from the judge were "fair, clear and honest and impartial."[46]

The *Washington Post* fired a series of short epigrammatic bursts at the verdict, including: "The pistol is mightier than the pen in South Carolina." The paper expressed disdain for a justice system that would produce such a verdict by observing that "Tillman was defended by twelve lawyers. More lawyers than law, it would seem."[47] But in a longer, more nuanced commentary, the *Post* observed that, although the killing was "a bloody and dreadful act" that could not be condoned, it was at least understandable in light of the provocation of Gonzales's stinging editorials and the regional custom of avenging insults by violent action.[48] One of the most cogent comments on the impact of the verdict on the freedom of the press came from pioneering African American historian and archivist Arthur A. Schomburg in a letter to the *New York Times.* Schomburg believed that one of the most important functions of a free press is to serve as an outlet for society's grievances concerning its government so the people can vent these complaints and perhaps provoke correction of them, thereby obviating the need for violent acts against the government. Schomburg was afraid that the killing of such an outspoken editor as Gonzales—and the endorsement of such acts by juries—would intimidate the press into subservience. He argued, "The freedom of the press seems to be in danger of death in South Carolina. One must come to this conclusion after reading the verdict rendered in the Tillman case. The press is like the safety valve of a boiler—always ready to blow through printed papers the abuses or unlawful acts done against the welfare, peace and prosperity of the community. It checks the spirit of anarchy and tyranny, and like the bugle call, is ready to reverberate the sound of danger and bring to the defense of the state the good citizens to remove the oppressor and re-establish the proper conditions of order."[49]

A *New York Times* editorial called the trial result "a false verdict" and asked, "How can the community in which such a thing can happen be called a civilized community?" It predicted that a state that permitted murderers to go free would continue to be among "the least attractive to the immigration either of labor or capital."[50] This was not a welcome prediction for a state struggling to develop its economy.

Joseph Pulitzer's *New York World* reacted with the dire prophecy "that hereafter a free press is impossible in South Carolina" and asserted that the verdict portends "that an editor who criticizes a public official may with impunity be slain in cold blood."[51] The *Chicago Daily Tribune* also found in the verdict a sinister warning "to South Carolina editors that in the future they take their lives in their hands when they criticize their political opponents and that these opponents will go scot free in case of murder." The paper was surprised to find that, despite the chilling message sent by the verdict, the editor of the *Charleston News and Courier* was still "courageous" enough to engage in a war of epithets with Senator Ben Tillman in which the editor accused the senator of writing the paper a letter that was full of crude and false statements.[52] The *Philadelphia Public Ledger* argued that in a democracy, the maintenance of a "civilized state" depended on protecting the right of a newspaper editor to "publish his convictions on public questions," and if this right were not protected, the other functions of government would be less effective because of the reduced scrutiny they would receive from a timid press.[53]

Two religious publications argued that the verdict was a moral and judicial transgression. The *Baptist Courier* of Greenville, South Carolina, was fervent in contending that the verdict lessened the public's confidence in the fairness of the judicial system and encouraged settling disputes by violence rather than in the courts. The *Courier* declared that "political influence, social position and money went very far in securing an acquittal at Lexington," and it contrasted the Tillman verdict with "how summarily the average negro is tried, condemned, sentenced, and punished, always receiving the extreme penalty." The paper recognized that the trial result was a warning shot directed at editors, but it was confident that it would not succeed in frightening the press into becoming a tame instrument of the politicians rather than being tough monitors of their performance. It noted that "the verdict means that no newspaper writer, without danger of assassination, or bodily harm, dare expose a candidate for office, or public officer, whose acts are open already to the public and whose conduct is a matter for public comment. The jury may declare that the man who shot the editor last January did no wrong, but that does not make it so, neither will that verdict still the pens of other editors; they will continue to expose wrongdoing." In the view of the *Baptist Courier,* there had been a double crime: not only the killing of Gonzales but also the severe damage the verdict had committed "against law and order and justice."[54]

The *Southern Christian Advocate,* an official publication of the South Carolina Conference of the Methodist Episcopal Church, also reacted to the verdict with righteous indignation. By letting violent criminals go free, South Carolinians "are sowing the wind and we shall reap the whirlwind, and it will be a bitter harvest" in the form of "mobocracy," which people would resort to when they learn that they cannot rely on the courts to enforce the law. The *Advocate* called on "law-abiding Christian citizens" to create a "moral sentiment that will force our judiciary to mete out justice." Calling the verdict "a blow at the liberty of the press," the *Advocate* predicted that this could lead to a government mired in degradation: "Muzzle the press and our public offices, in many instances, will be filled with unscrupulous, corrupt, intriguing demagogues."[55]

Like the *Baptist Courier* and the *Southern Christian Advocate,* most other South Carolina papers condemned the verdict. The *Spartanburg Journal* called it "probably the most unreasonable verdict that was ever reached in South Carolina." The *Journal* scoffed at the self-defense arguments contending that "there was less to base a plea of self-defense on than in any case that has ever come within knowledge of the writer. The idea of self-defense was, as stated by one of the lawyers, only a fiction and the real defense was that Tillman was justified in killing Gonzales because of the editorial attacks made on him." This defense argument was unconvincing because Tillman "waited five months after the cause for anger [the editorials during the campaign] had been given." The paper blamed the judges who delayed the case and transferred venue so that a jury favorable to the defense could be found. It blamed "a politically prejudiced jury" and defense lawyers who "stooped to arouse the lowest passions of an ignorant and prejudiced jury."[56]

The *Charleston News and Courier* concluded that the legal system had functioned so poorly that "the law has condemned itself." The verdict demonstrated the low value placed on human life compared to even minor items of property: "If Mr. Tillman had taken Mr. Gonzales's pocketbook, he would have been required to pay the penalty prescribed by law; he took Mr. Gonzales's life and a South Carolina jury says that he did nothing to deserve punishment."[57]

The *Johnston News,* published in a town near Jim Tillman's hometown of Edgefield, strenuously argued that the acquittal raised questions about how vigorously an editor could discharge the function of a free press and stay alive. The paper asked, "If a thief, a liar, an incompetent man offers himself for office and it is a fact and known to be truth, must an editor keep this information from the public, and allow such characters to fill the offices of trust and disgrace the State, bankrupt her institutions and bring sorrow to true citizens?" It insisted that such verdicts would destroy public confidence in the courts so that those who have been wronged would not seek redress there but would "become a law to themselves."[58]

As might be expected, the *State* reacted to the verdict with anger, featuring a headline saying "THE FARCE IS ENDED." Beneath this headline, William Watts Ball, a prominent conservative, anti-Tillman South Carolina journalist brought in from another paper to cover the trial for the *State,* penned a stinging appraisal of the case including allegations that key defense witnesses committed perjury. He described the killing and the verdict as an assault on the freedom of the press. He urged his fellow journalist to have courage, saying that "to my brethren of the South Carolina press, let me say that the bullet that felled Gonzales was aimed at us all. It was aimed to still all the hands that dare to write. Never was the pen of Gonzales so sorely needed in South Carolina as it is today. None of us can fill his place. But those of us who are left, shall we hide in bomb-proofs or shall we remember a duty to the trampled decency of South Carolina?"[59] Ball continued to brood over the perplexing question of why liberty of the press ranked so low in the South Carolina pantheon of respected values. In a 1913 address to the South Carolina Press Association, Ball confronted the subject in a speech titled "Freedom of the Press in South Carolina and Its Limitations." He concluded that "we have a state ruled by two widely separated classes," "the one the printed word appeals to; the other is swayed by the spoken word from the lips of the haranguer in campaign years." Because of its low education level, the second group seldom, if ever, reads the paper, and it was easy for demagogic politicians to paint newspapers as sinister forces that abuse the little man of society so brutally that they must be stopped. But despite discouraging events, such as the Tillman verdict, Ball was not personally discouraged. He continued to rail against those he thought pandered to the worst instincts of the public.[60]

Another prickly commentator appeared to be energized rather than intimidated by the verdict. Ed DeCamp of the *Gaffney Ledger,* long a searing critic of James H. Tillman, was undeterred by the verdict. He argued that, despite the verdict, Tillman wore the "mark of Cain." DeCamp also warned those who hoped the killing and verdict would intimidate the press that the newspapers would be as vigilant as ever in ferreting out corruption. He asked "do they think they'll stop the press from exposing well-bred liars, gamblers, thieves and murderers? Not so long as there remains a spark of manhood within the breast of a single man in South Carolina who follows the Fourth Estate."[61]

But a few papers had a more sympathetic view of the verdict. The *Medium,* published in the small town of Abbeville, South Carolina, concluded that, since proper legal procedure had been followed throughout the case, the result should be respected.[62] The *Augusta Chronicle,* published in Georgia but near Edgefield, depicted the reception of the verdict in Lexington as a joyful celebration at which Jim Tillman was treated like a conquering hero by "a throng of admirers." The paper described his mother as tenderly greeting her "stalwart son," depicted his lead attorneys as a "gallant trio," and painted the courtroom scene when the verdict was announced as "just simply a love feast of the defendant's friends." The article exulted that Tillman had emerged from the trial with "his name untarnished and his liberty untrammeled." After this adulatory account, it was not surprising that the *Chronicle*'s editorial position was sympathetic to the trial result and especially to the jury, which the *Chronicle* felt had been unjustly criticized. The paper argued that "the verdict can be accepted without involving any endorsement of the crime itself" and concluded that a jury of honest, reputable citizens could reasonably reach a verdict of acquittal because Gonzales's vicious personal attacks on Tillman went beyond the bounds of good journalism: "When an editor goes into that sort of thing he invites personal violence, indeed almost forces it, and it is to be presumed that he stands ready to meet the consequences." The *Chronicle* asserted that the verdict was best understood as applying not only the written law in the statute books but "the customs of the people and the unwritten laws that have been made by common usage." These customs favor responses such as Tillman's to vicious personal attacks on one's honor.[63]

Many, but not all, observers in other southern states condemned the verdict as encouraging lawlessness and denigrating the value of human life and respect for the law. The *Virginia Law Register,* an astute observer of justice throughout the South, concluded that "the verdict is a source of profound discouragement to all who wish to see the standard at which human life is held in the South materially elevated." However, it limited its condemnation to the jury and exonerated the judges, whom it believed, had behaved admirably in refusing bail and defining the law for the jury in a fair and accurate manner.[64]

University of Tennessee president Dr. Charles W. Dabney spoke to a meeting of Knoxville citizens that had been called to plead with area officials to enforce the law, which in the statute books expressed the lofty sentiments of a civilized society against violence but too often had turned out to be empty, unenforced rhetoric. Dabney called the Tillman case "a travesty of justice" that showed how "the man of influence and wealth goes free, while the poor wretch is punished. Through some influence, which I do not say is, in every instance, money, our judges, our officers, our juries do not enforce the law."[65] Dabney's concern that Tennessee officials were taking an indulgent attitude toward homicide seemed to have been justified by Governor Malcolm Patterson's issuance of a pardon for a prominent political ally, Duncan Cooper, on the same day that his conviction in the 1908 killing of *Nashville Tennessean* editor and former United States senator Edward Carmack was sustained by the Tennessee Supreme Court. Just as Tillman resented Gonzales's abrasive editorials as an affront to his honor, Cooper resented Carmack's stinging accusations of corruption as besmirching his honor, but there is no way to determine whether the 1903 Tillman acquittal definitely encouraged the 1908 killing of Carmack or the governor's politically inspired pardon.[66]

The *Atlanta News* praised the Tillman verdict: "The truth, however, is that the exoneration of the ex-lieutenant governor is a remarkable triumph of passionless justice." It praised the South Carolina jurors: "They considered not the respective records of the two men, nor their respective reputations, but the crime and the provocation therefor—and they rightfully decided that the better man had hounded the worser to a point that justified the worser in his act."[67] The *Times-Recorder* of Americus, Georgia, approved of the verdict because Gonzales's editorials had "goaded" Tillman into taking action to "defend his honor and good name." It warned against a rogue press and argued that "newspapers should be bold and aggressive but they should be fair and respectful."[68] Yet the more influential *Atlanta Constitution* said that, while it was inclined to give some deference to the "histology of the southern ideals of honor, the jealousy of its guardianship and the impulsiveness of self-defense approved by traditions," it did not approve of killing, especially by high officials, who should be examples of respect for the law, when their grievances could be adequately redressed by the courts. The paper concluded, "Life ought to be as sacred and safe in the south as anywhere on earth," and it looked forward to the time when those "high in place or influence will find it hard to hoodwink justice and impossible to escape her avenging sword."[69] The *Memphis News* was most concerned about the precarious legal climate that it believed the case had created for freedom of the press. It noted that "a South Carolina jury has just said that if an editor criticizes a public man, that man is justifiable in killing the editor though the latter be unarmed, and trying to get away from the murderer. If this be the law in South Carolina, the press in that state is no freer than it is in darkest Russia, and human life is of no more value than it is in Dahomey."[70]

At the time the verdict was rendered, A. B. Williams, a veteran South Carolina journalist, was working in Virginia as editor of the *Richmond Leader.* In a balanced, carefully considered editorial titled "Liberty of the Press," Williams drew on his knowledge about editors' attitudes throughout the South. He asserted that it was "not only the right but the duty of a newspaper to consider and criticize the methods, abilities and characters and policies of men in public office or before the public as candidates," using whatever language necessary, but this should be done by focusing on the "facts" rather than "epithets." He considered the consensus among editors to be that Gonzales had gone "too far in assailing Tillman and was intemperate and unnecessarily harsh and bitter," but that the killing could "not be justified on any ground, no matter what the jury may say." Tillman had deviated from the southern traditions governing actions to protect one's honor by waiting until long after the articles that were the provocation had ceased and by not giving the other party "fair notice and an opportunity to defend himself."[71]

The predominant reaction to the verdict was that it had inflicted great damage on law and order, respect for the courts, and confidence in their ability to serve as peaceful and nondiscriminatory instruments for resolving disputes. It may have temporarily reduced the prestige and clout of the press as an effective monitor of public life in South Carolina, but the number and vigor of the newspaper criticisms of the verdict proved that the press would not be intimidated into subservience. Still the courtroom vindication of honor over freedom of the press in a battle of values was deeply troubling.

Tillman's Honor after the Verdict

Did all of this damage to freedom of the press, respect for the justice system and the value in which human life is held, accomplish anything, even from Jim Tillman's narrow perspective? Did it silence his critics? Did it open the way for a revival of his political career now that N. G. Gonzales's mocking voice had been stilled and a jury had vindicated his action as necessary to defend his honor, imperfectly disguised as action necessary to safeguard his life? At first it looked as if his hope of regaining high office could be realized. In its account of the announcement of the not-guilty verdict, the *New York World* revealed: "Before he had been a free man an hour his friends and admirers from Edgefield and surrounding counties were booming him for Governor."[72] Not everyone in Edgefield was swept up in such enthusiasm. The *Edgefield Advertiser* fired a warning shot across the bow of Tillman's resurging political ambitions. It advised "now that James H. Tillman has been relegated to private life the press should withhold further criticism. However, in the future should he aspire to fill public office, then those who mold and shape public sentiment should do their full duty in the premises."[73] Despite this warning, Tillman tested the political waters, but events seemed to conspire against him. The death of Congressman George Croft, Tillman's defense counsel and former law partner, seemed to offer an opportunity for Tillman to occupy the congressional seat that had been held for many years by his late father, George D. Tillman, and he announced his candidacy in mid-March 1904. His candidacy was scarcely launched before it was terminated. Croft's son Theodore, armed with strong support from the people of his hometown, Aiken, announced that he would seek the office.[74]

Two years later, Tillman's congressional ambitions were again aroused and quickly extinguished. This time he pointed to strong local support, but again he failed to run, blaming that archvillain the press and even making vague allusions to the calumnies of N. G. Gonzales. The race began auspiciously for Tillman. The Edgefield County Convention passed an enthusiastic resolution of support stating that Tillman would be the best person to go to the "National House of Representatives" to fight for "our people in the great battle now being waged against corporate greed and corruption in the country." Tillman expressed gratitude for the strong show of support from those "who have known me all my life," but he noted that only "a short while ago I was the victim of calamity and misrepresentation without parallel in this State with the possible exception of another of my name." Since the memories of the nasty pummeling he had been subjected to in his 1902 race for governor because of "misrepresentation" by the press continued to be a source of pain, he decided not to make the race and give his critics a fresh opportunity to hurl epithets at him.[75]

Not only did the verdict not revive his political career, it also did not redeem his honor by ensuring that the public held him in esteem as a courageous, manly, leader. Both the killing and the verdict prompted an angry fusillade of editorials and sermons calling his surprise attack on an unarmed man "cowardly."[76]

Life began to turn sour for James H. Tillman a few years after the trial. His mother died in 1906. His brother-in-law, defense counsel, and law mentor Osmund W. Buchanan was shot in 1908. Tillman's relations with his wife, Mamie Norris Tillman, became strained, perhaps because of his outsized personality, and the Tillmans "were probably living apart" by 1908, the year in which he was stricken with tuberculosis.[77] The disease prompted him to conduct a desperate odyssey in search of a cure. He sought a dry climate in the West. On his departure in 1908, he published a poignant announcement that seemed to contemplate a lengthy, or possibly permanent, absence from his hometown and longtime friends. He stated in part, "in a distant section of the country, in far off California, where it is said all is sunshine and clouds are unknown, I wander in search of health. There among strangers in coming years, if years be left to me, I hope to clasp the hands of many and call them friends—friends such as I leave behind."[78] Like the early Spanish explorers searching for a legendary city of gold in South America, Tillman found no Eldorado of health, friendship, and new beginnings in California. His restless spirit sent him back to South Carolina and finally to Asheville, North Carolina, in further search of health. There on April 1, 1911, he died with only his physician, a nurse, or according to some accounts, a young nephew, present. Mrs. Tillman was probably living with her mother at her family's Edgefield home, Magnolia Dale, a large, white-columned house, where she had been born, a setting that evoked the old South. But rather than brooding in a big mansion, she lived a long life of community service in church and patriotic organizations, including twenty-one years as president of the Edgefield County Historical Society.[79]

By the time of Tillman's death, the supposed wellspring of his misfortune, N. G. Gonzales, had been dead more than eight years. It became apparent as time went on that Gonzales's legacy was more than that of an editor who wrote sharply worded editorials about public officials and candidates and kept voters well-informed about their qualifications, but whose pen sometimes became too bitter, personal, and vengeful. More often he spoke eloquently for civic improvements, such as ending the abuse of child labor, doing away with the exploitative convict-lease system, and stopping lynch-mob justice. He advocated extending the vote to women and improving transportation for Columbia and the state by paving roads and building canals. He spoke of the need to attract industry to diversify the economy and of the dire need to improve education, including the passage of a compulsory school-attendance law. Although, as a creature of his time and place, he continued to believe in white supremacy, he spoke vehemently against the use of fraud and deceit to curb black political participation. Such a legacy of public service through editorials could not be wiped out by killing their author.

The *State,* the newspaper of which N. G. Gonzales was cofounder and editor, lived and flourished under the leadership of his older brother, Ambrose, as president and publisher and his younger brother, William, as editor. They continued to champion many of the causes espoused by their fallen brother, but in the words of historian Lewis P. Jones, they "were more circumspect in expression than the militant N. G. Gonzales had been." Rather than using Tillman's death as an occasion to vent rage against their brother's killer, they marginalized Tillman's life and death by giving him a one-sentence obituary that dismissively stated: "Asheville, N.C., April 1—James H. Tillman, at one time lieutenant governor of South Carolina, died here tonight."[80] For one, who like Tillman, had so assiduously sought celebrity during his life, being reduced to an irrelevancy in a death notice was not a favorable omen that he would be regarded as an historically important figure. Censorship, whether by killing the messenger or otherwise, often backfires on its perpetrator. Jim Tillman's critics—the press, the pulpit, and others—were like the mythical creature the Hydra. Severing one of its heads did not kill it but produced multiple replacements. Unlike Hercules in the myth, Tillman discovered no way to halt this perpetual regeneration of critics. After the announcement of the verdict, new critics appeared and old ones stayed the course, proving the futility of censorship in a climate of proliferating speakers.

NOTES

Chapter 1. An Editor Is Censored

1. McNeely, *Fighting Words,* 128–29, concludes that James H. Tillman was opposed in the 1902 race for governor by "The Daily Mail in Anderson, The Post in Charleston, The Evening Record in Columbia, The Daily Times in Florence, The Gaffney Ledger in Gaffney, The Daily News in Greenville, The Daily Index in Greenwood, The Daily Herald and The Evening Journal in Spartanburg and The Daily Item in Sumter." A description of the location of the shooting is found in Pierce, *Palmettos and Oaks,* 54–60. See also Latimer, *The Story of the* State, 53–57; Moore, *Carnival of Blood,* 101–23; and Montgomery, *Columbia, South Carolina,* 103 (describing the city hall and Columbia Theatre).

2. See Nisbett and Cohen, *Culture of Honor,* xvi, for a definition of the southern sense of honor, in which confrontations among men are described as not referring to "probity of character" but to "status and power." The authors go on to say that honor in the sense that they use it "situates a man socially and determines his right to precedence." It refers to his "strength and power to enforce his will on others" (ibid., 4–5). A man was willing to fight to preserve honor when it had this meaning. He had to prove his manliness. Another scholar has described the southern tradition of honor as focusing more on how others view an individual than on innate standards of right and wrong (see Watson, *Norman and Saxon,* 11). In a chapter titled "Bloody Edgefield," Butterfield in *All God's Children,* 11, describes the meaning and importance of honor in James H. Tillman's home county, observing that "honor became a compelling passion, an overwhelming concern with one's reputation and manliness" and that "it was as intolerable to call a man a liar as to hit or shoot him." Butterfield notes Jim Tillman's outrage at Gonzales for calling him a liar. One aspect of the concept of honor is the reliability of a man in keeping his personal, political, and financial commitments. By calling someone a liar, you undermine his reputation for reliability (ibid., 52–53). See also Mushal, "'My Word Is My Bond,'" 1–26. Hagstette in "Dueling and Identity" emphasizes the significant impact of the printed word in attacking and defending honor and in conducting affairs of honor. He calls our attention (18), to Freeman, *Affairs of Honor,* 132, in which the author says: "Where reputations had such importance, [as in early national politics] a print attack was more vicious—and painful—than we might imagine." Freeman further

notes, "Honor was entirely other-directed, determined before the eyes of the world; it did not exist unless bestowed by others" (ibid., xvi). As the primary mass medium in 1903, newspapers could be devastatingly effective in destroying the public image of a leading figure and thereby severely damaging his honor. Another scholar observes that this focus on public image by elite southern men amounted to an obsession with the "superficial," "the surface of things—with the world of appearances" (Greenberg, *Honor and Slavery,* 3). Pieter Spierenburg concludes, "Honor has at least three layers: a person's own feeling of self-worth, this person's assessment of his or her worth in the eyes of others, and the actual opinion of others about her or him" (*Men and Violence,* 2). James H. Tillman was obsessed with the second element; his view of the assessment of his worth by others who had read Gonzales's attacks. But all three elements are relevant to appraising his actions.

3. *Charleston News and Courier,* January 16, 1903, 1; *New York World,* January 16, 1903, 1; *State* (Columbia S.C.), January 16, 1903, 1; Moore, *Carnival of Blood,* 115–16 (noting the disagreement among witnesses as to whether Tillman bade Gonzales "good morning" before shooting him); Miles S. Richards, "Heyward, Duncan Clinch," in Edgar, ed., *The South Carolina Encyclopedia,* 441 (discussing the man who defeated James H. Tillman for the governorship); see also Jones, *Stormy Petrel,* 297 (noting James Tillman's fourth-place finish). See South Carolina General Assembly, Senate, *Journal of the Senate* (1903 session), 37–38 (noting that a joint assembly of the Senate and House of Representatives met and "opened, tabulated and published" the election returns for the 1902 governor's race). In a letter to members of the Spanish-American War regiment he had commanded, James H. Tillman thanked them for their support in the election and contended that he would have been elected governor if not for the "brutal, false and malicious newspaper attacks headed by N. G. Gonzales." In his introduction to the publication of the letter in the *State,* Gonzales mocked the letter's author as "the precious 'Jim Tillman'" (*State,* September 1, 1902, 4).

4. Trial testimony of arresting officer George E. Boland, September 28, 1903, is in James F. Byrnes's "Stenographic Report" for September 28, 1903, *State,* September 29, 1903, 1. Then a court reporter, Byrnes was hired by the *State* to make a verbatim record of each day's proceedings in the trial. These reports were usually published the next day in the *State* with pagination beginning anew each day. Since no official transcript exists, these reports are the best account of the testimony. Byrnes, who later became a congressman, U.S. senator, U.S. Supreme Court justice, U.S. secretary of state, and governor of South Carolina, was an official court reporter in another circuit, a position he had won in a competitive examination. See Robertson, *Sly and Able,* 22–24. Testimony of James H. Tillman, "Stenographic Report" for October 9, 1903, *State,* October 10, 1903, 2 (denying that Gonzales said "shoot again, you coward"). Jones, *Stormy Petrel,* 298–99. The "shoot again, you coward" statement was recounted by Gonzales in a "dying declaration" he made to his assistant, James A. Hoyt, Jr., which Hoyt described in his trial testimony. See "Stenographic Report" for September 30, 1903, *State,* October 1, 1903, 2. Testimony of Thomas Talbird, "Stenographic Report" for October 2, 1903, ibid., October 4, 1903, 5.

5. Testimony of James H. Tillman, "Stenographic Report" for October 9, 1903, *State,* October 10, 1903, 2–3.

6. Moore, *Carnival of Blood,* 115–16. See also James A. Hoyt, Jr., "The Death of N. G. Gonzales, Editor of the *State,* 1891–1903," a manuscript in the James A. Hoyt Papers, South Caroliniana Library, University of South Carolina, Columbia, S.C. Hoyt wrote his account on the fiftieth anniversary of the shooting. It is reproduced in Latimer, *The Story of the* State, 53–62.

7. Map of downtown Columbia, S.C., August 1904, Map Division, Library of Congress, available at the South Caroliniana Library, University of South Carolina, Columbia, S.C. See the testimony of bystanders J. F. Sims and A. G. LaMotte in "Stenographic Report" for October 2–3, 1903, *State,* October 4, 1903, 5, 9.

8. *Charleston News and Courier,* January 16, 1903, 1, and January 17, 1903, 1 (describing the shooting and Tillman's arrest and confinement). See also Grantham, *The Regional Imagination,* 53–63 (describing the killing of Gonzales and comparing it to "violent scenes" in the politics of other southern states).

9. *Charleston News and Courier,* January 17, 1903, 1, and January 18, 1903, 1.

10.Ibid., January 18, 1903, 1.

11. T. J. Simmons, "Tillman Talks to a Journal Man," *Atlanta Journal,* January 18, 1903.

12. *Charleston News and Courier,* January 25, 1903, 2.

13. "The Gonzales Inquest," ibid., January 23, 1903, 2.

14. Ibid. See also *New York World,* January 23, 1903, 2.

15. *Charleston News and Courier,* January 20, 1903, 1, and January 21, 1903, 1 death and funeral of N. G. Gonzales).

16. *New York World,* January 21, 1903, 1.

17. "In Sackcloth and Ashes," *Charleston News and Courier,* January 21, 1903, 1.

18. *New York World,* January 21, 1903, 1.

19. *Charleston News and Courier,* January 21, 1903, 1.

20. "Another Account," *Charleston News and Courier,* January 20, 1903, 1. Accounts of the marriage of N. G. Gonzales and Lucy (or Lucie) Barron and the death of their daughter are found in Pierce, *Palmettos and Oaks,* 45; In *The Story of the* State, 64–65, Latimer describes Mrs. Gonzales's career as state librarian, the death of their daughter, and Mrs. Gonzales's work in many civic and charitable activities after the death of her husband. See also Jones, *Stormy Petrel,* 184.

21. *New York World,* January 21, 1903, 1.

22. Ibid., 6.

23. Brown, *Strain of Violence,* 67–90; Ford, "Origins of the Edgefield Tradition," 328–30; Butterfield, *All God's Children,* 11–14, 52–53; Burton, *In My Father's House,* 6; Chapman, *A History of Edgefield County,* 34–42, 65–71; Alexander Moore, "Cherokee War (1759–1761)" and "Cherokee War (1776)," in Edgar, ed., *The South Carolina Encyclopedia,* 162–63.

24. Kantrowitz, *Ben Tillman,* 22, 316n25 (citing minutes for 1841, in General Sessions Journal, Edgefield County Judge of Probate Records, 43, 52, 57, South Carolina

Department of Archives and History, Columbia, S.C. The fine was imposed on January 22, 1842 [ibid., 57]). Kantrowitz was unable to confirm reports that the elder Benjamin Tillman had killed a man in 1847 (*Ben Tillman,* 316n25). But see Butterfield, *All God's Children,* 13–14. Genealogical material on the Tillman family in general and James H. Tillman in particular may be found in Stephen Frederick Tillman, *The Tillman Family,* 88–90, and James David Tillman, Jr., *Tillman & Hamilton Family Records,* 3:185–87.

25. Simkins, *Pitchfork Ben Tillman,* 31–33. Simkins discusses gambling and violence by the elder Benjamin Tillman (ibid., 29). See also Butterfield, *All God's Children,* 11–14.

26. Simkins, *Pitchfork Ben Tillman,* 31–33. Butterfield, *All God's Children,* 13, 337, cites the coroner's inquest testimony describing the killing of J. H. (Henry) Christian by George Tillman. See *State v. Body of J. H. Christian,* 121–22. "Stop the Murderer," *Edgefield Advertiser,* July 23, 1856, 3 (reward offered by victim's brothers).

27. Simkins, *Pitchfork Ben Tillman,* 33.

28. Ibid. See also Kantrowitz, *Ben Tillman,* 23–24, 31.

29. Kantrowitz, *Ben Tillman,* 23–24; see also Ford, "Origins of the Edgefield Tradition," for a discussion of George Tillman's political career.

30. Ford, "Origins of the Edgefield Tradition," 341n31, citing Bailey, Morgan, and Taylor, *Biographical Directory of the South Carolina Senate,* 3:1613–15; see also Burton, *In My Father's House,* 51. Brown, *Strain of Violence,* 67–90 (discussing the history of violence in the Edgefield area and its relation to political extremism).

31. See "Tillman, George Dionysius," *Biographical Directory of the United States Congress,* http://bioguide.congress.gov/ (accessed January 28, 2013). For additional biographical material on George D. Tillman, see Chapman, *A History of Edgefield County,* 203–6, and "Tillman, George Dionysius (1826–1901)," in Bailey, Morgan, and Taylor, *Biographical Directory of South Carolina Senate,* 3:1613–14. These sources are in disagreement as to whether George D. Tillman died in 1901 or 1902. The 1901 date given in Bailey, Morgan, and Taylor is supported by the most thorough research. See the affectionate and laudatory obituary written by N. G. Gonzales and published in the *State* on the day after George D. Tillman's death (February 3, 1901, 8).

32. The quotations expressing N. G. Gonzales's affection and admiration for George D. Tillman are found in two letters from N. G. Gonzales, Washington, D.C., to his aunt Emily (Emmie) Elliott, January 25, 1882, and February 5, 1882, Elliott/Gonzales Papers, Southern Historical Collection, Wilson Library, University of North Carolina, Chapel Hill, N.C.

33. Simkins, *Pitchfork Ben Tillman,* 32.

34. See Wilentz, *The Rise of American Democracy,* 688–93, 931n60 (quoting Sumner's speech, describing his caning by Brooks, and reporting the reaction in North and South).

35. In addition to Wilentz, *The Rise of American Democracy,* see McPherson, *Battle Cry of Freedom,* 148–54; Goodwin, *Team of Rivals,* 184–85; and Donald, *Charles Sumner,* 278–309. A leading authority cited by most of the above is Gienapp, "The Crime against Sumner." In letters to J. H. (Ham.) Brooks, dated May 23, 1856, and June 21, 1856, Preston Brooks said he gave Sumner "about 30 first rate stripes," and "the fragments of

the stick are begged for as *sacred relics*" (emphasis in original); Robert L. Meriwether, "Preston S. Brooks." A somewhat sympathetic view of Brooks is taken by Mathis, "Preston Smith Brooks." The influence of the southern concept of honor on the incident is discussed in Watson, *Norman and Saxon,* 1–18.

36. Johnson, *A History of the American People,* 429–30.

37. Benjamin Ryan Tillman, Sr., to Iverson Brookes, August 6, 1844, Iverson Brookes Papers, South Caroliniana Library, University of South Carolina, Columbia, S.C., quoted in Ford, "Origins of the Edgefield Tradition," 336n16.

38. John Hammond Moore recounts this incident in *Carnival of Blood,* 108, 227n13 (citing George Tillman to N. G. Gonzales, February 6, 1895, in N. G. Gonzales Papers, South Caroliniana Library, University of South Carolina, Columbia, S.C.). Gonzales and George Tillman remained on good terms despite the simmering dispute between Gonzales and George Tillman's son and the *State*'s criticism of Senator Tillman.

39. For an account of the wedding, see "Marriage in High Life," *Edgefield Advertiser,* July 1, 1896. Mrs. Tillman's community service is described in her obituary in the *Edgefield Advertiser,* February 7, 1962, 1. Moore, *Carnival of Blood,* 107. Jones, *Stormy Petrel,* 299n45. See "Mrs. Tillman's Sympathy Is Wired Mrs. Gonzales," *Savannah Press,* January 19, 1903, collected in Gonzales-Tillman Scrapbooks (1903), newspaper clippings concerning the murder of N. G. Gonzales and the trial of James H. Tillman, 3 vols., South Caroliniana Library, University of South Carolina, Columbia, S.C.

40. *Charleston News and Courier,* June 27, 1900, 2 (Tillman's bragging about his support from the men in his regiment).

41. Ibid., July 15, 1900, 1.

42. Ibid., July 28, 1900, 1.

43. *Edgefield Chronicle,* July 19, 1900, 4.

44. Ibid., August 23, 1900, 1; *Charleston News and Courier,* August 1, 1900, 1 (Tillman's support for the dispensary and opposition to prohibition while claiming to be a friend of the factory worker).

45. *Charleston News and Courier,* July 17, 1902, 1–2.

46. Ibid., June 27, 1902, 2.

47. *Abbeville Press and Banner,* June 18, 1902, 1; see also *Greenville Daily News,* July 12, 1902, 1.

48. Richards, "Heyward, Duncan Clinch," in Edgar, ed., *The South Carolina Encyclopedia,* 441.

49. *Charleston News and Courier,* August 21, 1902, 1 (noting Tillman's opposition to an old soldiers' home).

50. *Greenville Daily News,* August 17, 1902, 1.

51. W. L. Nicholson to *Edgefield Chronicle,* August 9, 1902, published August 14, 1902, 2.

52. N. G. Gonzales to *Edgefield Chronicle,* August 15, 1902, published August 21, 1902, 2.

53. Ball, *An Episode in South Carolina Politics,* 10–11; Jones, *Stormy Petrel,* 104; Moore, *Carnival of Blood,* 103, 227n3.

54. Jones, *Stormy Petrel,* 104.

55. Ibid., 276–77. For Gonzales's own account of his Spanish-American War service, see Gonzales, *In Darkest Cuba,* 287 (under enemy fire), 304 (arduous marching).

56. Jones, *Stormy Petrel,* 161, 186–241.

57. de la Cova, *Cuban Confederate Colonel,* xx, 54 (Cuban revolutionary), 152–53, 236–40 (Confederate artillery officer).

58. Lawrence S. Rowland, "Elliott, Williams III," in Edgar, ed., *The South Carolina Encyclopedia,* 298. Rowland, Moore, and Rogers, The *History of Beaufort County, South Carolina,* 403–5 (discussing William Elliott III). Jones, *Stormy Petrel,* 3–4 (discussing William Elliott III as a "sportsman and political nonconformist"). See also "Elliott, William (1788–1863): Son of William Elliott (1761–1808)" in Bailey, Morgan, and Taylor, *Biographical Directory of the South Carolina Senate,* 1: 470–73. On the nullification controversy see Ford, *The Origins of Southern Radicalism,* 120–51. Sinha, *The Counterrevolution of Slavery,* 33–61.

59. On N. G. Gonzales's education and upbringing, see Jones, *Stormy Petrel,* 16, 30, 32, 37–41; see also de la Cova, *Cuban Confederate Colonel,* 292 (death of mother), 309–11 (Beaufort, S.C., schooling).

60. Letter from N. G. Gonzales to Emily [Emmie] Elliott, February 17, 1874. The author is grateful to Antonio Rafael de la Cova, author of *Cuban Confederate Colonel,* for calling his attention to this letter. The full text may be found at http://www.latinamericanstudies.org/gonzales/1874–78.pdf (accessed September 16, 2012). See also *Cuban Confederate Colonel,* 317.

61. For a colorful account of the Smalls/Gonzales encounter, see Matthews, "N. G. Gonzales," 84–85 (citing *Charleston News and Courier,* December 14, 1881, and N. G. Gonzales to Emily Elliott, December 25, 1881, Elliott/Gonzales Papers, Southern Historical Collection, University of North Carolina, Chapel Hill). See also Jones, *Stormy Petrel,* 81; Billingsley, *Yearning to Breathe Free,* 158; Miller, *Gullah Statesman,* 135–38 (Smalls's election dispute with George Tillman and fight with Gonzales).

62. Gonzales criticized Lipscomb's firing of clerk M. C. Robertson as politically motivated in "A Sensation in Columbia," *Charleston News and Courier,* May 30, 1883, 1. An unsigned editorial, "A Kick at the Party Platform" (ibid., May 31, 1883, 2), criticized Lipscomb as violating the party platform, which pledged to stop the firing of civil servants except for cause. Gonzales's pro-Thomas account of the Thomas-Lipscomb fight is found in "Blows at the State House" (ibid., September 16, 1883, 1). Lipscomb and Gonzales sent letters to the editor explaining their widely different views of what happened: "Affray at the State House, Secretary of State Lipscomb Gives His Version of the Affair" (ibid., September 19, 1883, 1) and "The Reply of Mr. Gonzales" (ibid.). The *News and Courier* published a comprehensive recapitulation of the event as "The State House Imbroglio" (September 18, 1883, 1). Jones describes the affair in *Stormy Petrel,* 97–98.

63. See "A Lively Day in Columbia: Three Fights between the Bureau and the Register," *Charleston News and Courier,* February 3, 1886, 2; "Keeping Up the Excitement," ibid.; "The Journalists' Rencontre Yesterday," *Columbia Register,* February 3, 1886, 4;

"The Day after the Battle: Columbia Restored to Comparative Quiet," *Charleston News and Courier,* February 4, 1886, 1; "The Columbia Fights: Calvo and Gonzales before Mayor Rhett," ibid., February 9, 1886, 3. The *Columbia Register*'s coverage of the series of fights spans February 2–9, 1886. See also Jones, *Stormy Petrel,* 99–101.

64. Jones, *Stormy Petrel,* 134–35. The Tillman election forced the Gonzales brothers to make career moves that led to their founding the *State* with leading conservative Tillman opponents such as A. C. and J. C. Haskell (ibid., 136–40). See the discussion of Ben Tillman's inaugural address in Simkins, *Pitchfork Ben Tillman,* 169–75. The full text of the address is found in South Carolina General Assembly, House of Representatives, *Journal of the House of Representatives* (1890 session), 129–55.

65. Jones, *Stormy Petrel,* 138.

66. Ibid., 152–53.

67. Ibid. Dr. Sampson Pope was an ardent supporter of Ben Tillman at the time of the melee at the Grand Central Hotel, but later he became just as ardent an opponent. Dr. Pope was the brother of Young J. Pope, who was chief justice at the time of James H. Tillman's trial. See "Pope, Sampson (1836–1906)," in Bailey, Morgan, and Taylor, *Biographical Directory of the South Carolina Senate,* 2:1293–94.

68. *Columbia Daily Register,* November 25, 1891 (saying Dr. Pope was on top during the wrestling match on the floor); *State,* November 25, 1891, 8 (saying N. G. Gonzales was on top).

69. Jones, *Stormy Petrel,* 152 (saying the printers showed up with "side sticks, foot sticks, mallets, column rules, and other printing shop implements").

70. Ibid., 152–53; *Columbia Register,* November 26, 1891.

71. *State,* November 28, 1891, 8; ibid., November 29, 1891, 5.

72. Jones, *Stormy Petrel,* 153.

73. See Nisbett and Cohen, *Culture of Honor,* 50 (discussing experiments finding that southern males felt their manhood would be doubted if they were insulted in front of others).

74. N. G. Gonzales to J. C. Hemphill, March 23, 1889, N. G. Gonzales Papers; a copy made by Mattie Russell in 1959 is available in the Hemphill Family Papers, Perkins Library, Rare Book, Manuscript, and Special Collections Library, Duke University.

75. Francis Warrington Dawson to N. G. Gonzales, July 23, 1885, in Francis Warrington Dawson, Letterpress Book II, May 25, 1884–October 15, 1887, Charleston, S.C., 127–30, Perkins Library, Rare Book, Manuscript, and Special Collections Library, Duke University. The year in which this letter was written is probably 1885, but numbers are unclear and it could be 1883.

76. Ibid. Lee, *History of American Journalism,* 319–22.

77. Matthews, "N. G. Gonzales," 95–96 (citing *Charleston News and Courier,* March 19, 1883, and August 15, 1883).

78. Ibid., 94, 100–101, citing *Charleston News and Courier,* December 13, 1886 (advocating the paving of streets, and January 22, 1885 (advocating building the Columbia Canal).

79. Ibid., 191–93, citing *State,* January 29, 1900, and February 6, 1902, and Davidson, *Child Labor Legislation,* 140 (crediting the *State* in 1902 with being "the most zealous advocate of child labor reform in the South").

80. See "Child Slavery in Our Cotton Mills," *State,* January 29, 1900, 4. Less than a month after Gonzales's death, a weak statute was passed to curb some of the worst child-labor abuses through wage and hour limitations. See act no. 74, February 13, 1903, in South Carolina, *Statutes at Large* (1903), 113–16.

81. A good example of the *State*'s editorial position on women's suffrage is "Women in the Future," *State,* December 11, 1892, 4 (touting women's suffrage as the inevitable wave of the future).

82. Jones, *Stormy Petrel,* 188.

83. *State,* July 3, 1891; ibid., September 8, 1891. See the discussion of these views in Jones, *Stormy Petrel,* 189.

84. Simkins, *Pitchfork Ben Tillman,* 234–60; see also Hendricks, "South Carolina Dispensary System," 176–97, 320–49; Kantrowitz, *Ben Tillman,* 181–97 (discussing the rural-urban conflict in enforcing the controversial dispensary measures); Eubanks, *Ben Tillman's Baby;* and Rita Foster Wallace, "South Carolina State Dispensary," 1–87.

85. Act no. 28, December 24, 1892, South Carolina General Assembly, *Acts and Joint Resolutions* (1892), 62–76.

86. Simkins, *Pitchfork Ben Tillman,* 239–40.

87. Kantrowitz, *Ben Tillman,* 191.

88. Ibid., 189–91.

89. *State,* December 24, 1892; Jones, *Stormy Petrel,* 202.

90. *State,* November 18, 1893; ibid., January 28, 1894; Jones, *Stormy Petrel,* 204.

91. Simkins, *Pitchfork Ben Tillman,* 253.

92. Chapter 105: Of Offences against the Public Peace, section 2582, Governor to Take Possession of Telegraphs, in South Carolina, *General Statutes and the Code of Civil Procedure of the State of South Carolina Adopted by the General Assembly of 1881–82,* 725–26; see also Snowden, *History of South Carolina,* 2:1018–21. This codification incorporates Reconstruction era provisions passed in 1868. See sec. 5 of act no. 40, September 22, 1868, in *The Statutes of South Carolina,* 14: 85–87.

93. *State,* April 2, 1894. Jones, *Stormy Petrel,* 206–7, gives an exciting account of the Gonzales brothers' circumvention of the news blockade. Kantrowitz, *Ben Tillman,* 193–94, discusses the Darlington riots. Another journalist, August Kohn of the *Charleston News and Courier,* circumvented the ban on sending telegrams from the scene of the Darlington riots by going to a nearby town and sending reports to his paper from an office not watched by the troops. See Hennig, *August Kohn,* 110–11.

94. The Diaries of W. W. Ball, vol. 3, December 18, 1916–June 16, 1918, 137–38, Perkins Library, Rare Book, Manuscript, and Special Collections Library, Duke University. See the discussion of Ball's account of the *State*'s circumvention of the censor during the Darlington riots in Matthews, "N. G. Gonzales," 168.

95. David Duncan Wallace, *South Carolina: A Short History,* 626. A good summary of the "Dispensary War" and the *State*'s role in it is found in Edgar, *South Carolina: A History,* 441–43.

96. *State,* May 11, 1895.

97. Ibid.; Jones, *Stormy Petrel,* 222–23.

98. Ibid., art. II, sec. 4(d).

99. The debates in the 1895 constitutional convention are discussed in Underwood, *The Constitution of South Carolina,* 4: 58–109; see especially the discussion of Tillman's participation in the debate (98–106); see South Carolina Constitutional Convention (1895), *Journal,* 28–72; see also *State,* November 1, 1895, 4, for the paper's description of Benjamin Tillman's speech to the convention on the suffrage issue and ibid., 5, for its verbatim account of his speech. See also Kantrowitz, *Ben Tillman,* 224–28, discussing the debate and the position of the *State.*

100. South Carolina Constitution of 1895, art. II, sec. 8 (gubernatorial appointment of county registrars with advice and consent of the South Carolina Senate).

101. *State,* September 24, 1895, 4.

102. Ibid., September 25, 1895, 4. See also Underwood, *The Constitution of South Carolina,* 4:69–75, discussing the *State*'s campaign against the adoption of election machinery that could be easily manipulated.

103. *State,* September 17, 1895.

104. South Carolina Constitutional Convention (1895), *Journal,* sessions of September 18–19, 1895, 154–61. Simkins, *Pitchfork Ben Tillman,* 293–95, discusses the controversy over the new counties and the censure motion. See also Jones, *Stormy Petrel,* 223–24 (citing *Charleston News and Courier,* September 20, 1895).

105. Jones, *Stormy Petrel,* 224 (citing *State,* September 20, 1895).

106. J. J. Negrin, "To the Public," *Charleston City Gazette and Daily Advertiser,* August 23, 1805, 1. See also Fraser, *Charleston, Charleston,* 188–89; Matthewson, "Jefferson and Haiti," 233; Hagy and Van Ruymbeke, "The French Refugee Newspapers of Charleston," 142–44; and McNeely, *Fighting Words,* 19–20.

107. To the Honorable the President and Senate of the State of South Carolina, the Memorial of John James Negrin, November 23, 1805, General Assembly Petitions, no-1886-01, South Carolina Department of Archives and History, Columbia, S.C.

108. Act no. 1860, December 19, 1805, South Carolina, *Statutes at Large,* 5, sec. 2:503.

109. Edgar, *South Carolina: A History,* 328–30. Paquette and Egerton, "Of Facts and Fables." See generally Egerton, *He Shall Go Out Free,* and especially 136–38, 163–69, 211–12. See also Freehling, *Prelude to Civil War,* 53–65, 82–86, 109 (discussing the impact of the Vesey affair on freedom of expression), and Ford, *The Origins of Southern Radicalism,* 117 (noting that the Vesey plot created a fear that the debates about slavery "might foment rebellion in the slave quarters").

110. Howe, *What Hath God Wrought,* 428–30; see also Wilentz, The *Rise of American Democracy,* 410–12; Savage, "Abolitionist Literature," 150, 160–65; and Wyatt-Brown, "The Abolitionists' Postal Campaign."

111. Savage, "Abolitionist Literature," 161.

112. Howe, *What Hath God Wrought,* 429. See also Savage, "Abolitionist Literature," 162–63, and Freehling, *Prelude to Civil War,* 340–43.

113. "Fourth Annual Report . . . January 20, 1836," Massachusetts Anti-Slavery Society, *Annual Report,* 24.

114. See "An Act to Provide for the Peace and Security of This State," act no. 4446, 1859, South Carolina, *Statutes at Large,* 12:768–69.

115. Ibid., sec. 1–4. The reader is cautioned that this 1859 statute is hard to find because of its anomalous printing history. In some compilations it is given a different statute number and page number. See act no. 4445, December 22, 1859, ibid., 12:655–56, and Eaton, *Freedom of Thought,* 130 (discussing this and similar statutes in other southern states). See also "An Act for the Punishment of Certain Crimes against the State of South Carolina," act no. 1860, 1805, South Carolina, *Statutes at Large,* 5, sec. 2: 503 (prohibiting the writing or publishing of inflammatory words or delivering an inflammatory discourse tending to alienate the loyalty of a slave from his master), and "An Act to Restrain the Emancipation of Slaves and to Prevent Free Persons of Color from Entering Into the State; and for Other Purposes," act no. 2236, 1820, *Statutes at Large,* 7, sec. 6:460 (prohibiting white persons from directly or indirectly circulating written or printed matter with intent to disrupt the peace and security of the state by stirring up the slaves).

116. Jack Kenny Williams, "The Code of Honor," 113, 116. See also McNeely, *Fighting Words,* 22–23.

117. The letters, signed "A Nullifier" and titled "To the Hon. A. G. Magrath" [no. 1, 2, 3] are found in the *Charleston Mercury,* September 24, 1856, 2; September 26, 1856, 2; and September 29, 1856, 2. See also "The Affair of Honor between Edward Magrath, Esq. and William R. Taber Jr. Esq." *Charleston Mercury,* October 2, 1856, 2, and *Charleston Courier,* October 2, 1856, 2 (containing Magrath's challenge and Taber's response). Many of these documents are in the James Ward Hopkins Scrapbook, Manuscript Collection, South Caroliniana Library, University of South Carolina, Columbia. Taber's second, Colonel John Cunningham, was also a journalist, and in settlement negotiations he adamantly refused to agree to a retraction by his principal because "it would have been a stultification of him as an editor, and a humiliation of him as a man" (quoted in Fitzsimons, "Hot Words and Hair Triggers," South Caroliniana Library, University of South Carolina, Columbia, S.C., manuscript fiche m.44). When his rejection of the proposed settlement was criticized, Cunningham argued that acceptance would have amounted to "abandonment of the LIBERTY OF THE PRESS." See John Cunningham, letter to John Bellinger, M.D., in "The Late Duel," *Charleston Courier,* December 9, 1856, 1. An exploration of the issues of honor involved in the Magrath-Taber duel is found in Mushal, "'My Word Is My Bond,'" 215–58. Renowned novelist William Gilmore Simms served as an adviser to John Heart in making arrangements for the duel (see Oliphant and Eaves, with additional text by Alexander Moore, *The Letters of William Gilmore Simms,* expanded edition with supplement [1834–70], 6:332–37). A discussion of the duel may be

found in Evarts, "Code Duello," 1–2, 31–37. See also King, *The Newspaper Press,* 154–55, and David Duncan Wallace, *South Carolina: A Short History,* 494–96.

118. Jack Kenny Williams, *Dueling in the Old South,* 30–31 (challenges to duel "dampened the ardor of much of the press"). See also Kibler, *Benjamin F. Perry,* 120–40 (Perry/Bynun duel during 1832 nullification controversy.). The nullification controversies forming the background for the Perry/Bynun duel are discussed in Sinha, *The Counterrevolution of Slavery,* 33–61. Dueling standards are set forth in Wilson, *The Code of Honor.* Antebellum antidueling statutes include "An Act to Prevent the Pernicious Practice of Duelling," act no. 2008, 1812, in South Carolina, *Statutes at Large,* 5:671–72. For amendments to this law, see act no. 2304 of 1823 and act no. 2641 of 1834 in South Carolina, *Statutes at Large,* 6:208, 515. The 1868 S.C. Constitution in art. I, sec. 32, barred duelists and their aiders and abettors from office. An 1880 statute provided for depriving convicted duelists of the right to vote and hold office and gave judges the discretion to sentence duelists and those who aided them to up to two years in prison. Those taking public office had to take an oath that they had not engaged in a duel, or aided those who had, since January 1, 1881, and would not do so while in office. A similar oath was required in art. III, sec. 26, of the original constitution of 1895. See also act no. 410, 1880, in South Carolina General Assembly, *Acts and Joint Resolutions* (1880), 501–2. See Moore, *Carnival of Blood,* 12–28 for a discussion of the notorious July 5, 1880, duel in which Colonel E. B. C. Cash killed William Shannon. This episode may have helped to create the impetus for the passage of the 1880 law. Dueling continues to be prohibited. See S.C. Code sec. 16-3-410 to 460 (430 repealed) in *Code of Laws of South Carolina,* 7A:170–74, and 2011 cumulative supp., 91. See also the current South Carolina Constitution, art. XVII, sec. 1B (disqualifying duelists from holding office).

119. See "A Quarrel of Our Own," *Charleston Mercury,* April 2, 1861, 1, and "The Press and the Law," ibid., August 26, 1862, 1. See also McNeely, *Fighting Words,* 28–32. Telegraph dispatches had to be approved by an officer, and sometimes telegraphers "appointed themselves official censors and delayed sending newspaper stories even when they had been approved" (McNeely, quoting a correspondent in "Felix Gregory de Fontaine," *Knights of the Quill,* 45, 59); Van Tuyll and McNeely, "Robert W. Gibbes: The 'Mind' of the Confederacy," ibid., 95–103, 622–23; *Charleston Courier,* March 21, 1857, 1 (discussing the trial of Gibbes's suit against the mayor); "Triumph of Right and Principle," *Memphis Daily Appeal,* March 25, 1857 (quoting judge's charge); Hatch, *Rights of Corporators and Reporters;* Towery, "Censorship of South Carolina Newspapers"; McPherson, *Battle Cry of Freedom,* 433–36 (martial law orders by General Van Dorn and other Confederate commanders). The orders of Generals Van Dorn and Bragg, and other instances of censorship, are discussed in Reynolds, "Words of War," 97–99. Despite wartime conditions, the *New York Times,* September 7, 1862, reprinted as "A Spicy Correspondence," the tense exchange between *Montgomery Advertiser* editor Samuel G. Reid and General Bragg's staff concerning the arrest of the paper's reporter. See also Sass, *Outspoken,* 34–35 (discussing seizure of the *Courier* by Union forces). King, *The Newspaper Press,* 123–25, discusses the seizure. The problems confronting journalists in the Confederacy are discussed in Mott, *American Journalism,* 329–72.

120. See Zuczek, *State of Rebellion,* 163–65, and Zuczek, "Hamburg Massacre," in Edgar, ed., *The South Carolina Encyclopedia,* 415–16. See also Budiansky, The *Bloody Shirt,* 225–37; Kantrowitz, *Ben Tillman,* 64–71; Simkins, *Pitchfork Ben Tillman,* 61–64, 263, 268, 270–71; Andrew, *Wade Hampton,* 371–72; and Foner, *Reconstruction,* 571–72. An account of the Hamburg Massacre by a journalist who covered the story for South Carolina newspapers in 1876—and included his views in a book written fifty years later—is Alfred B. Williams, *Hampton and His Red Shirts,* 27–32.

121. Clark, *Francis Warrington Dawson,* 53–68.

122. Editorial, "The Bloody Work at Hamburg," *Charleston News and Courier,* July 10, 1876, 2. An article on page 1 under the same title gives a factual account of the Hamburg Massacre.

123. Editorial, "The Hamburg Affray and Its Consequences," ibid., July 11, 1876, 2.

124. Editorial, "The Hamburg Massacre," ibid., July 12, 1876, 2.

125. Editorial, "General Butler," ibid., July 12, 1876, 2.

126. Kantrowitz, *Ben Tillman,* 71. Clark, *Francis Warrington Dawson,* 63–65, discusses a challenge to a duel Dawson received from rival newspaper editor Robert Barnwell Rhett, Jr., a proponent of the straight-out ticket. The challenge resulted in a ritualistic showing of courage as the two editors passed one another on the street, but no shootout took place. See also Alfred B. Williams, *Hampton and His Red Shirts,* 64–65.

127. Editorial, "The Hamburg Riot—Its Origin and Causes," *Charleston News and Courier,* August 14, 1876, 3.

128. The view that Dawson changed his editorial position on the Hamburg Massacre because of threats and intimidation is taken in Budiansky, *The Bloody Shirt,* 245. See also Clark, *Francis Warrington Dawson,* 67.

129. *Charleston News and Courier,* August 14, 1876, 3; see also Clark, *Francis Warrington Dawson,* 60–69, and Kantrowitz, *Ben Tillman,* 71. Budiansky, *The Bloody Shirt,* 244, calls most of the evidence adduced at Aiken "fraudulent."

130. See U.S. Senate Mis. Doc. No.48, 44th Congress, 2d Sess., South Carolina in 1876, Testimony as to the Denial of the Elective Franchise in South Carolina at the Elections of 1875 and 1876 Taken Under the Resolution of the Senate of December 5, 1876, 1:145–60 (testimony of Louis Schiller). See also Budiansky, *The Bloody Shirt,* 237–38.

131. Clark, *Francis Warrington Dawson,* 41–45.

132. Ibid., 44–45. The *Charleston News and Courier* covered the trial in issues published April 20–27, 1875.

133. South Carolina Constitution of 1868, art. I, sec. 7 and 8. Judge J. P. Reed's charge to the jury is found in Conner, *The Libel Cases,* 87–89.

134. The quotation is from art. I, sec. 8, of the South Carolina Constitution of 1868, which Judge J. P. Reed relied on in his jury charge. See Conner, *The Libel Cases,* 87.

135. See Judge Reed's charge, ibid., 88–89.

136. Court documents and newspaper articles relating to the case were collected by defense counsel Conner in *The Libel Cases.*

137. See Moore, *Carnival of Blood,* 84–100; Clark, *Francis Warrington Dawson,* 215–31.

138. Burton, "Race and Reconstruction," 31, 33–34, 51n8. See also Mims, "The Editors of the *Edgefield Advertiser,*" 71–75, and Leonard Todd, *Carolina Clay,* 167, 280n14. The article by James T. Bacon that caused the federal reprisals was "Gen. Wilde and Dr. French," *Edgefield Advertiser,* July 12, 1865, 1. Bacon's article expressing regrets was "I Will Speak Daggers to Him, but Use None," ibid., July 19, 1865 , 1. The title is a variation on a soliloquy in Hamlet, act 3, scene 2, and was apparently intended to assure the federal authorities and local readers that, although the paper used sharp language, it meant no physical harm to anyone. The paper described the editor's confinement and release in "Advertiser Extra, Arrest of Our Editor," August 9, 1865, 1, and "Advertiser Extra, Return of Our Editor," August 16, 1865, 1. See also "Suppressed," *Abbeville Bulletin,* August 10, 1865, 1.

139. South Carolina Constitutional Convention (1868), *Proceedings,* 27–31 (quoting statements in the *Charleston Mercury* caricaturing the delegates).

140. Another account of the action against the *Charleston Mercury*'s journalists taken by the 1868 constitutional convention is found in McNeely, *Fighting Words,* 35. See also Davis, *Rhett,* 552–53, and South Carolina Constitutional Convention (1868), *Proceedings,* 181–83.

141. Ibid. See also Underwood and Burke, *At Freedom's Door,* especially the essays by Underwood, "African American Founding Fathers," 1–35; Gergel and Gergel, "'To Vindicate the Cause of the Downtrodden,'" 36–71; and Smith, "The Reconstruction of Justice Jonathan Jasper Wright," 72–89.

142. South Carolina General Assembly, House of Representatives, *Journal of the House of Representatives* (1868[–69] session), January 15, 1869, 191–93. The 1868 session extended into January 1869 resulting in the inclusion of this 1869 entry in the 1868 volume. See also the editorial "The Expulsion of Our Columbia Reporter," *Charleston News and Courier,* January 18, 1869, 2; "From the State Capital," *Charleston News and Courier,* January 12, 1869, 4 (charging Whipper with attempting to destroy the university for not furnishing him and his family with lodgings during legislative sessions); and a letter to the editor signed with the name "Justice," under the headline "The Expulsion of the Courier Reporter," *Columbia Daily Phoenix,* January 17, 1869, 2, charging that the action of the House showed that it "preferred to grope in the darkness" rather than to admit a reporter "fearless enough to put into public print the truth."

143. South Carolina General Assembly, House of Representatives, *Journal of the House of Representatives* (1874–75 session), March 18–19, 1875, 670–77. See *Columbia Daily Phoenix,* March 18–19, 1875, 2; *Anderson Intelligencer,* March 25, 1875, 2; and Moore, *South Carolina Newspapers,* 203 (describing the *Union-Herald* as "Republican-created").

144. "Pay Up or Go to Jail," *State,* December 20, 1892, 8 (quoting a December 8 article of the same title in the *State*).

145. See "A Ludicrous Finale," *State,* December 21, 1892, 3.

146. Editorial, "Libel and Limbo," *State,* December 20, 1892, 4.

147. Ibid.

148. Editorial, "Libel as a Guilt-Offering," *State,* December 30, 1892, 4.

149. Williams's attempt to instigate a criminal libel prosecution against Gonzales began near the end of 1892, and probably would have received grand jury consideration early in 1893. The report of the attorney general for 1893 indicates that the only Barnwell County criminal libel action considered in 1893 resulted in a "no bill" (failure to indict). The reports at that time did not list case names. The case resulting in a "no bill" is probably Williams's case against Gonzales, but this is not a certainty. See "Report of D. A. Townsend, Attorney-General of South Carolina for the Fiscal Year Ending October 31st 1893," 192–94, available at the University of South Carolina Law School Library, Columbia. Jacob Davis, an assistant to the author, searched Barnwell County Court records on November 14, 2008, and found no further action in the case.

Chapter 2. Pretrial Maneuvers

1. South Carolina Constitution of 1895, art. I, sec. 20. See also *South Carolina Criminal Code in 1902,* sec. 28.

2. *Charleston News and Courier,* February 8, 1903, 1; February 13, 1903, 1; February 20, 1903, 1.

3. *State,* February 20, 1903, 1.

4. *Charleston News and Courier,* February 20, 1903, 1.

5. *State,* February 13, 1903, 1; February 20, 1903, 1; *Charleston News and Courier,* February 13, 1903, 1; February 20, 1903, 1.

6. *State,* February 20, 1903, 1; *Charleston News and Courier,* February 20, 1903, 1.

7. *State,* February 20, 1903, 1.

8. Ibid.

9. *New York World,* February 21, 1903, 6. See also coverage of the bail proceedings in ibid., February 13, 1903, 3.

10. See "Pope, Young John (1841–1911)," in Bailey, Morgan, and Taylor, *Biographical Directory of the South Carolina Senate,* 2:1296–98. With regard to Pope's decisions on the dispensary system, see *McCullough v. Brown,* 41 S.C. 220, 254 (1894) (Pope, J., dissenting from a ruling striking down first dispensary law); but see *State Ex. Rel. George v. Aiken,* 42 S.C. 222 (1894) (Pope, J., voting with the majority to uphold the second dispensary law).

11. *McCullough v. Brown,* 41 S.C. at 254–266 (Pope, J., dissenting).

12. *Charleston News and Courier,* March 3, 1903, 2.

13. Ibid., April 8, 1903, 2.

14. Ibid., April 9, 1903, 1.

15. Ibid., June 25, 1903, 1.

16. But see Sewell, "The Gonzales-Tillman Affair," 56 (stating, without reference to the Pope decision denying bail, that Tillman was out on bail).

17. *Charleston News and Courier,* June 13, 1903, 2.

18. South Carolina Constitution of 1895, art. I, sec. 18.

19. Ibid., art. VI, sec. 2. The reader should note that this citation is to the Constitution as it was organized and worded at the time of the trial in 1903. At this writing, the change of venue provisions are worded differently and are in art. V, sec. 23.

20. Ibid.

21. Ibid. and *South Carolina Criminal Code in 1902,* sec. 2735: See also South Carolina Constitution of 1868, art. V, sec. 2, for the precursor of the 1895 provision. The 1868 provision also provided for a transfer to obtain a fair and impartial trial.

22. South Carolina Constitution of 1895, art. VI, sec. 2, and *South Carolina Criminal Code in 1902,* sec. 2735.

23. *Charleston News and Courier,* June 24, 1903, 1 (quoting affidavit of P. H. Nelson).

24. George W. Croft, Columbia, to Senator Benjamin Tillman, Trenton, S.C., June 9, 1903, in Tillman Incoming Correspondence (series 7, folder 55), Special Collections, Clemson University. Simkins, *Pitchfork Ben Tillman,* 384n41, discusses Senator Tillman's aid in getting the affidavits. A transcription of much of the letter is found in the Francis Butler Simkins Papers, Southern Historical Collection, Wilson Library, University of North Carolina, Chapel Hill. Croft wrote: "There are several parties here [in Columbia] whose affidavits we very much desire. So far we have been unable to get them; but believe that you can be the means of securing them for us."

25. *Charleston News and Courier,* June 23–24, 1903, 1–2.

26. Ibid.

27. Affidavit of James A. Hoyt, Jr., in *Charleston News and Courier,* June 23, 1903, 1 (reproduced verbatim). All the affidavits referred to were printed verbatim.

28. Affidavits of W. E. Gonzales, Ambrose E. Gonzales, James A. Hoyt, Jr., and Paul Brice, ibid.

29. Ibid., 1–2. The wording of the two affidavits was strikingly similar, indicating that they probably had been prepared by prosecution attorneys.

30. Affidavit of William H. Lyles, ibid.

31. Nelson quoted sermon descriptions from the *State,* January 19, 1903. His presentation is described in the *Charleston News and Courier,* June 24, 1903, 1.

32. Affidavit of Senator J. Q. Marshall, *Charleston News and Courier,* June 23, 1903, 1.

33. Ibid. The Rev. Thomas J. Hegarty also noted that the hostility to Tillman right after the killing had diminished and that Tillman had been a popular vote getter in the county (*Charleston News and Courier,* June 24, 1903, 1).

34. Ibid.; affidavit of Senator J. Q. Marshall.

35. See "Marshall, John Quitman (1849–1908)," in Bailey, Morgan, and Taylor, *Biographical Directory of the South Carolina Senate,* 2:1058–59. See also Edgar, *South Carolina: A History,* 462–63, discussing Marshall's sponsorship of child labor legislation and the *State*'s advocacy of such laws since 1898 and crediting the passage of such legislation in 1903 with initiating the Progressive Era in South Carolina.

36. Affidavit of James H. Tillman, *Charleston News and Courier,* June 24, 1903, 1.

37. Affidavit of O. W. Buchanan, ibid.

38. See "Croft, George William," *Biographical Directory of the United States Congress,* http://bioguide.congress.gov/ (accessed January 28, 2013). See also "Memorials, George William Croft," *Transactions of the South Carolina Bar Association,* 1892–1905, 99–100.

39. Affidavit of George W. Croft, *Charleston News and Courier,* June 24, 1903, 1.

40. See "Nelson, Patrick Henry," in Garlington, ed., *Men of the Time,* 327; Rogers, *Generations of Lawyers,* 99, 126, 140; and "Patrick Henry Nelson," South Carolina Bar Association, *Transactions of the Eighteenth Annual Meeting* (1911), 95–96, 159–60 (referring to Nelson as "one of the best advocates who ever practiced at the Columbia Bar").

41. Affidavit of Patrick H. Nelson, *Charleston News and Courier,* June 24, 1903, 1.

42. Argument of Nelson for change of venue, *Charleston News and Courier,* June 25, 1903, 1. Bellinger acknowledged that in *State v. Sullivan,* 39 S.C. 400, 17 S.E. 865 (S.C. 1893), the court concluded a change of venue in a murder case was justified because the sheriff, one of the jury-list compilers in the original jurisdiction, was the half-brother of the deceased. But, Bellinger argued, the procedure for compiling the list had improved since then, so it could be compiled by the other officials charged with the task, while the biased one stepped aside (argument of G. Duncan Bellinger, *Charleston News and Courier,* June 25, 1903, 1).

43. South Carolina Constitution of 1895, art. I, sec. 18, and art. VI, sec. 2.

44. Ibid., art. VI, sec. 2; Argument of G. Duncan Bellinger, *Charleston News and Courier,* June 25, 1903, 1.

45. See "George Duncan Bellinger," in Hemphill, ed., *Men of Mark,* 2:27.

46. *Charleston News and Courier,* June 25, 1903, 1.

47. *State v. Williams,* 13 S.C.L. 383 (S.C. Const. App. 1823).

48. Ibid.

49. See "Osmund Woodward Buchanan," in Hemphill, ed., *Men of Mark,* 2:48.

50. See "Buchanan, Osmund Woodward," in Garlington, ed., *Men of the Time,* 60–61, and "Judge Osmund Woodward Buchanan," in Brooks, *South Carolina Bench and Bar,* 288–89.

51. *Charleston News and Courier,* June 25, 1903, 1.

52. Burton, introduction to Simkins, *Pitchfork Ben Tillman,* xi–xii.

53. See "Military Promotions," *State,* December 7, 1894, 6, accusing the Ben Tillman machine of running a promotion mill for loyal attorneys.

54. See Rogers, *Generations of Lawyers,* 107–9.

55. Watts, *Memoirs,* 61–62. See also Rogers, *Generations of Lawyers,* 108, discussing Watts's comment about electing Tillmanite judges. For biographical material on Judge D. A. Townsend, see J. A. Sawyer, "Memoriam—Daniel Alexander Townsend," in South Carolina Bar Association, *Transactions of the Nineteenth Annual Meeting* (1912), 121–23, and "Judge Daniel A. Townsend," in Brooks, *South Carolina Bench and Bar,* 283–84.

56. David Duncan Wallace, *South Carolina: A Short History,* 626. The criticism of Governor Ben Tillman and John Gary Evans for not going to the scene of the disturbance in Darlington—and of Buchanan for going and complaining about the danger—is found in "Crying for Tillman," *State,* April 3, 1894, 5. See also "At the Seat of War," *State;* April 3, 1894, 1, and "How the Murder Was Done," *State,* April 1, 1894, 5 (describing a deadly clash between dispensary "spies" and a crowd in Darlington); and Simkins, *Pitchfork Ben Tillman,* 247–61.

57. *State,* June 25, 1903, 5.

58. *People v. Sharp,* 5 N.Y. Cr. R. 155 (N.Y. S. Ct. 1886); *People v. Squire,* 4 N.Y. CR. R. 444, 1 N.Y. St. Rep. 534 (N.Y. S. Ct. 1886).

59. *State v. Crafton,* 56 N.W. 257 (Iowa S. Ct. 1893). But see *State v. Williams,* 88 N.W. 194 (Iowa S. Ct. 1901), which says that, when the trial was held four months after the crime, a change in venue was not required because of sensational newspaper descriptions of crime and plans to erect monument to victim.

60. The argument over whether the case of *State of South Carolina v. W. R. Crawford* was a relevant precedent for venue transfer because of newspaper prejudice is found in the *Charleston News and Courier,* June 25, 1903, 1, 5. Since the *Crawford* case was not an officially reported appellate decision, we must rely on a newspaper account. See "Crawford Case to Go to Kershaw County," *State,* April 11, 1899, 8, and "Venue Change," ibid., 4.

61. *Charleston News and Courier,* June 25, 1903, 1; *New York World,* June 25, 1903, 2; *State,* June 25, 1903, 1.

62. See *State v. Jackson,* 110 S.C. 273, 96 S.E. 416 (1918), noting "the inflamed state of the public mind" as necessitating a transfer; *State v. Gossett,* 117 S.C. 76, 108 S.E. 290–94 (1921), citing the "spirit of mob law" in the community as requiring a transfer to ensure the defendant's constitutional rights to due process and equal protection; *State v. Davis,* 138 S.C. 532, 137 S.E. 139, 140 (1927), focusing on the "strong sentiment against, the defendant" as mandating a transfer. It is notable that in these cases media such as newspapers were not specified as provoking the prejudice, which was probably spawned instead by an old-fashioned rumor mill.

63. This two-pronged approach in determining whether media pretrial publicity warrants a change in venue is seen in *Skilling v. United States,* 130 S. Ct. 2896 (2010), a recent U.S. Supreme Court decision. South Carolina cases evidencing this approach include *State v. Evins,* 373 S.C. 404, 645 S.E.2d 904 (S.C. S. Ct. 2007), *cert denied* 552 U.S. 1046 (2007); *State of South Carolina v. Parker,* 381 S.C. 68, 671 S.E.2d 619 (S.C. App. 2008); *State v. Owens,* 293 S.C. 161, 166–67, 359 S.E.2d 275, 278 (S.C. S. Ct. 1987), *cert. denied* 484 U.S. 982 (1987). See also LaFave, Israel, King, and Kerr, *Criminal Procedure,* 6, sec. 23.2:262–89, Whellan, "What's Happened to Due Process among the States?"

64. *New York World,* June 25, 1903, 2.

65. *Charleston News and Courier,* June 25, 1903, 1.

66. South Carolina Constitution of 1895, art. VI sec. 2; *South Carolina Criminal Code in 1902,* sec. 2735.

67. One commentator has traced George D. Tillman's plans for breaking up the overly large Edgefield District into smaller units back to 1853. The plans were derailed for a lengthy period by Tillman's manslaughter charge, the Civil War, the turbulence of Reconstruction, and higher priorities in reconfiguring government after restoration of white rule. See Ford, "Origins of the Edgefield Tradition," 328–34. But the frustrations brought on by such a delay helped to energize the postbellum move for change, especially in the 1895 constitutional convention (ibid.). See also Simkins, *Pitchfork Ben Tillman,* 293–94, and Burton, *In My Father's House,* 14–15.

68. South Carolina Constitution of 1895, art. I, sec. 18.

69. *Charleston News and Courier,* June 25, 1903, 1.

70. Ibid.

71. Ibid. A description of key speeches made by George Tillman to the 1895 constitutional convention is found in Underwood, *The Constitution of South Carolina,* 2: 73–74. Since the official convention record does not give verbatim accounts of speeches, we must resort to newspapers for details. See *State,* October 22, 1895, 2, and October 25, 1895, 2, 5.

72. See the description of Thurmond's background in "Thurmond, J. William," in Garlington, ed., *Men of the Time,* 415–16; see *Charleston News and Courier,* June 25, 1903, 1 (describing Thurmond's argument on the new trial-location issue).

73. In an introduction to Simkins, *Pitchfork Ben Tillman,* xxvii, Burton notes that J. William Thurmond was Ben Tillman's Edgefield attorney and that Tillman influenced both William and his son J. Strom Thurmond, who later became a U.S. senator.

74. *Charleston News and Courier,* June 26, 1903, 1.

75. Ibid., June 27, 1903, 2.

76. Ibid., July 12, 1903, 2, and July 14, 1903, 1; see also *State,* July 14, 1903, 2.

77. Senator Benjamin R. Tillman, Trenton, S.C., July 24, 1903, to Colonel E. B. Hook, Augusta, Ga., Tillman Outgoing Correspondence (series 7, folder 16).

78. Thomas W. Loyless, Augusta, Ga., July 30, 1903, to Senator Benjamin R. Tillman, Trenton, S.C., Tillman Incoming Correspondence (series 7, folder 57). Although both the Tillman and Loyless letters are in the Clemson University Special Collections, the fictitious interview itself could not be found.

79. Ibid. Senator Tillman's attempt to enlist the aid of the *Augusta Chronicle* in creating a favorable public attitude toward his nephew's defense is discussed in Simkins, *Pitchfork Ben Tillman,* 384n42.

80. George W. Croft, Aiken, S.C., to Hon. B. R. Tillman, Trenton, S.C., September 24, 1903, Tillman Incoming Correspondence Collection. (series 7, folder 59).

81. *Charleston News and Courier,* September 5, 1903, 2, quoting verbatim Chief Justice Y. J. Pope's order appointing Judge Townsend to replace Judge Gage.

82. The events leading to the appointment of Frank B. Gary, former speaker of the South Carolina House of Representatives, as special judge to preside in the Tillman trial can be traced in the *Charleston News and Courier,* September 5, 1903, 2; September 12, 1903, 2; September 13, 1903, 1; September 14, 1903, 2; September 17, 1903, 2; September 18, 1903, 2; and September 19, 1903, 2.

83. Telegram from Chief Justice Y. J. Pope to attorney Patrick Nelson, September 17, 1903 (quoted in full in *Charleston News and Courier,* September 18, 1903, 2).

84. South Carolina Constitution of 1895, art. V, sec. 6; *South Carolina Criminal Code in 1902,* sec. 2743–44 (providing for the temporary appointment of special judge by the governor upon the recommendation of the chief justice).

85. *Charleston News and Courier,* September 19, 1903, 2.

86. "Juggling with the Courts," *State,* September 26, 1903, 4.

87. *South Carolina Criminal Code in 1902,* sec. 2744.

88. *State,* September 26, 1903, 4.

89. George W. Croft, Aiken, S.C., to Hon. B. R. Tillman, Trenton, S.C., September 16, 1903. Tillman Incoming Correspondence (series 7, folder 58).

90. Ibid.

91. Ibid.

92. For the work of the 1895 convention in suppressing black votes, see Underwood, *The Constitution of South Carolina,* 4: 58–157.

93. See "Gary, Frank Boyd," *Biographical Directory of* the *United States Congress,* http://bioguide.congress.gov/ (accessed January 28, 2013), and Veronica Bruce McConnell, "Gary, Frank Boyd," in Edgar, ed., *The South Carolina Encyclopedia,* 360.

94. See Budiansky, *The Bloody Shirt,* 222–30, 244–45 (discussing the role of Martin W. Gary in the Redeemer movement); Kantrowitz, *Ben Tillman,* 71–79; Simkins, *Pitchfork Ben Tillman,* 56–57; Burton, *In My Father's House,* 290; Henry H. Lesesne, "Gary, Martin Witherspoon," in Edgar, ed., *The South Carolina Encyclopedia,* 361; and Zuczek, *State of Rebellion,* 167, 174.

95. See this description of the Gary family judges and their participation in this full court (en banc) proceeding in *Traynham v. C. & W. C. Ry. Co.,* 92 S.C. 43 (1912), in Memorial Exercises in Honor of Frank Boyd Gary (1923), 43, 58, South Caroliniana Library, University of South Carolina, Columbia.

96. See *McCullough v. Brown,* 41 S.C. 220 (1894), striking down the Dispensary Act of 1892 (act no. 28 of December, 24, 1892), in South Carolina General Assembly, *Acts and Joint Resolutions* (1892), 62. The *McCullough* case was overruled by *State Ex Rel. George v. Aiken,* 42 S.C. 222 (1894), upholding the Dispensary Act of 1893, act. no. 313 of December 23, 1893, in South Carolina General Assembly, *Acts and Joint Resolutions* (1893), 430. See Rogers, *Generations of Lawyers,* 107–9, which describes the successful effort of the Tillman supporters in the General Assembly to elect judges believed to be sympathetic to the governor's program. See Watts, *Memoirs,* 61, in which Watts, a Tillman supporter elected during that time, noted that "there was a determination then to elect for circuit judges, Tillmanites." One distinguished circuit judge who lost his position in this judicial upheaval was Joshua Hilary Hudson, who noted in his memoir, that he was ousted "owing to the tide in politics by which Governor Tillman and his faction came to power" (Hudson, *Sketches and Reminiscences,* 28).

97. Memorial Exercises in Honor of Frank Boyd Gary, 55–56, quotes extensively from Gary's immigration speech. For a discussion of Athenian democracy, see Fox, *The Classical World,* 210–11.

98. *Charleston News and Courier,* October 1, 1903, 1. See also Memorial Exercises in Honor of Frank Boyd Gary, 51–52.

99. Simkins, *Pitchfork Ben Tillman,* 383, and Moore, *Carnival of Blood,* 117, describe Lexington County as Tillman country.

100. Jones, *Stormy Petrel,* 303.

101. George W. Croft, Aiken, S.C., to Benjamin R. Tillman, Trenton, S.C., September 16, 1903, Tillman Incoming Correspondence (series 7, folder 58). A partial verbatim transcription made by a leading Tillman biographer is found in the Francis Butler Simkins Papers, quoted in Simkins, *Pitchfork Ben Tillman,* 383n38.

102. Simkins, *Pitchfork Ben Tillman,* 383n38, and Moore, *Carnival of Blood,* 117–18, refer to this rumor. In the *New York World*'s version of this undercover jury canvassing, the photographer contacted everyone who had been called for service during the first or second week of the September term of court and showed them pictures of prominent South Carolinians, including N. G. Gonzales and James H. Tillman, as samples of his company's photograph-enlargement work. This large array of pictures somewhat obscured the direct connection of the interviews to the case, which would have been clearer if only the photographs of the victim and accused had been used. See "Sounding Jurors for Jim Tillman, Picture Man Tries to Gain Views as to Guilt or Innocence," *New York World,* September 27, 1903, 2N.

103. Croft to B. R. Tillman, September 16, 1903.

104. *Charleston News and Courier,* September 22, 1903, 1.

105. Ibid.

106. Description based on the W. H. Loomis drawing, *New York World,* September 28, 1903, 3.

107W. H. Loomis drawing, "The Court House at Lexington, S.C.," ibid., September 23, 1903, 3.

108. Loomis drawing, "Senator Tillman in Evidence on Streets of Lexington, S.C.," ibid., September 27, 1903, 2N.

109. Description based on Loomis drawing, ibid., September 29, 1903, 4.

110. *Charleston News and Courier,* October 1, 1903, 1.

111. Ibid., September 22, 1903, 1.

112. Photograph of James H. Tillman, *New York World,* September 21, 1903, 3.

113. Ibid., September 29, 1903, 4.

114. Ibid.

115. Ibid. See General Sessions Journal, 1896–1904, Lexington County, September term 1903, Monday, September 28, 1903, 450, South Carolina Department of Archives and History, Columbia, S.C. The official record merely states that the defendant was brought in from the jail and pleaded not guilty and that the defense announced it was ready for trial.

Chapter 3. The First Round of the Trial

1. *New York World,* September 29, 1903, 4.

2. See "Voir dire," in *Black's Law Dictionary,* 1599.

3. "Stenographic Report" for September 28, 1903, *State,* September 29, 1903, 1.

4. The elimination of these four may have been based on their relationship to the accused or victim because the local paper concluded that no one was dismissed because of "bias or prejudice for or against the prisoner" or of feeling incapable of being "an impartial juror" (*Lexington Dispatch,* September 30, 1903, 4).

5. "Stenographic Report" for September 28, 1903, *State,* September 29, 1903, 1; *Charleston News and Courier,* September 29, 1903, 1; *New York World,* September 29, 1903, 4.

6. *Lexington Dispatch,* September 30, 1903, 4; *Charleston News and Courier,* September 29, 1903, 1; "Stenographic Report" for September 28, 1903, *State,* September 29, 1903, 1–2.

7. *Charleston News and Courier,* September 29, 1903, 1.

8. *Lexington Dispatch,* September 30, 1903, 4.

9. *Charleston News and Courier,* September 29, 1903, 1. The official list of jurors is in General Sessions Journal, 1896–1904, Lexington County, September term 1903, Monday, September 28, 1903, 451. The jury list in the *New York World* (September 29, 1903, 4) differs somewhat in name spellings and occupations. For example it lists Corley as a schoolteacher rather than a cotton-mill operative; Leitzsey is spelled "Lightsey"; Shealey is called "Healy"; and Risinger is spelled "Resinger." See also *Lexington Dispatch,* September 30, 1903, 4, for a complete listing of both accepted and rejected jurors. The official list uses the spellings "Leitzsey" and "Risinger."

10. See "Lexington's Splendid New Bridge, Dutch Fork Joined to Remainder of County by Steel Ties," *State,* February 27, 1911, 10, and "Place Dispensaries, Lexington County Board Will Hold Meetings," ibid., September 27, 1913, 8 (both discussing Koon's political activities).

11. Burton, introduction to Simkins, *Pitchfork Ben Tillman,* xx.

12. "Juggling with the Courts," *State,* September 26, 1903, 4.

13. *Charleston News and Courier,* September 29, 1903, 1.

14. Ibid.

15. For the official list of attorneys, see General Sessions Journal, 1896–1904, Lexington County, September term 1903, 440. Lists of attorneys in the case are found in the *Lexington Dispatch,* September 23, 1903; *Charleston News and Courier,* September 21, 1903, 1, and September 22, 1903, 1; *New York World,* September 27, 1903, 2N; Jones, *Stormy Petrel,* 303; and Moore, *Carnival of Blood,* 117. The listings are inconsistent on Sturkie's initials. "T. C." is probably correct.

16. *Charleston News and Courier,* September 21, 1903, 1, and September 22, 1903, 1.

17. For biographical material on Efird and Sharpe, see "Efird, Cyprian Melanchthon," in Bailey, Morgan, and Taylor, eds., *Biographical Directory of the South Carolina Senate,* 1:460–61,and "Sharpe, William Henry Jr.," ibid., 2:1443–44. Some issues of the *South Carolina Supreme Court Reports,* for which Efird served as reporter, spell his name with two "f's."

18. *Charleston News and Courier,* September, 21, 1903, 1.

19. South Carolina General Assembly, House of Representatives, *Journal of the House of Representatives* (1894 session), 263–64 (Thurmond's nomination of Ben Tillman for U.S. Senate).

20. *State,* August 6, 1897, 8; *Charleston News and Courier,* August 6, 1897, 2. See also *Aiken Journal and Review,* March 31, 1897 (an early account of the Thurmond/Harris shooting); *Edgefield Advertiser,* March 31, 1897, 3 (coroner's inquest in the Thurmond/Harris case); *Charleston News and Courier,* March 26, 1897 (inquest); *Charleston News and Courier,* April 1, 1897 (Thurmond's release on bail, March 31, 1897); *Charleston*

News and Courier, April 12, 1897, 2 (Thurmond affidavit explaining why he shot Harris); *Charleston News and Courier,* August 4–6, 1897, 1–2 (Thurmond's trial and acquittal). The incident is also described in Bass and Thompson, *Ol' Strom,* 27.

21. "*State*'s Survey," *State,* August 8, 1897, 4.

22. Simkins, *Pitchfork Ben Tillman,* 531–35.

23. Bass and Thompson, *Ol' Strom,* 25.

24. Ibid., 26. See also "Thurmond, J. William," in Garlington, ed., *Men of the Time,* 415–16.

25. Garlington, ed., *Men of the Time,* 415; Bass and Thompson, *Ol' Strom,* 25.

26. J. W. Thurmond, Edgefield, S.C., to Hon M. L. Smith, Camden, S.C., October 24, 1903, and June 29, 1903 (both letters requesting that Thurmond's copy of "Clark's Criminal Law" be sent); and Thurmond to Smith, December 17, 1902 (requesting background information on railroad-consolidation case). These letters are available in the J. W. Thurmond Papers, South Caroliniana Library, University of South Carolina, Columbia.

27. See generally Thurmond, *Thurmond's Key Cases.*

28. Garlington, ed., *Men of the Time,* 415.

29. Bass and Thompson, *Ol' Strom,* 29.

30. *New York World,* September 27, 1903, 2N (discussing political considerations in the selection of counsel).

31. Jones, *Stormy Petrel,* 303. The other prosecutors were also retained by the family, with the possible exception of William Elliott, a Gonzales's relative, whose arrangement is not clear.

32. On the Broxton Bridge lynchings and Bellinger's role as prosecutor see "An Ugly Lynching," *State,* December 6, 1895, 1; "Truth and Duty," ibid., December 10, 1895, 4 (a minister's letter to the editor condemning the lynchings); "Now for the Verdict," *State,* February 25, 1896, 1 (describing the Walterboro trial for the murder of the mother); editorial, "A Double Shame," *State,* February 22, 1896, 1 (condemning the acquittal in first trial); "The Shame of the *State,*" *State,* March 3, 1896, 1 (a collection of newspaper editorials from around the state, most of which condemn the verdict in first [Walterboro] trial); "Strong Case Made Out," *State,* October 29, 1896, 1 (describing the second, Aiken case); and "Acquitted! Jury Finds Those Charged with Broxton Bridge Horror Not Guilty," *State,* October 30, 1896, 1.

33. South Carolina Constitution of 1895, art. VI, sec. 1 (arbitration); sec. 2 (change of venue); sec. 3 (uniform rules of pleading); sec. 4 (public laws); sec. 5 (code commissioner); sec. 6 (holding officials who permit lynching responsible).

34. *New York World,* September 27, 1903, 2N.

35. Underwood, *The Constitution of South Carolina,* 4:109; South Carolina Constitutional Convention (1895), *Journal,* 487.

36. See "George Duncan Bellinger," in Hemphill, ed., *Men of Mark,* 2:25–28; see also "George Duncan Bellinger" in Richland County Bar Association, *History of the Bar of Richland County,* 57–59.

37. R. Beverly Herbert gave this description of Bellinger in Richland County Bar Association, *History of the Bar of Richland County,* 159–60.

38. "Nelson, Patrick Henry," in Garlington, ed., *Men of the Time,* 327.

39. Richland County Bar Association, *History of the Bar of Richland County,* 159.

40. Ibid., 95–96.

41. Rogers, *Generations of Lawyers,* 126–27, 140.

42. David Duncan Wallace, *The History of South Carolina,* 4:899. The picture described is in South Carolina Bar Association, *Transactions of the Eighteenth Annual Meeting* (1911), n.pag.; see also Garlington, ed., *Men of the Time,* 327. The W. H. Loomis drawing is in *New York World,* October 3, 1903, 3.

43. *New York World,* September 27, 1902, 2N.

44. *Edgefield Advertiser,* August 11, 1897, 2.

45. Rogers, *Generations of Lawyers,* 126.

46. See "Croft, George William," *Biographical Directory of the United States Congress,* http://bioguide.congress.gov/ (accessed January 28, 2013).

47. See "George William Croft," in South Carolina Bar Association, *Transactions of the Twelfth Annual Meeting* (1905), 99–101.

48. Drawing by W. H. Loomis, *New York World,* October 3, 1903, 3.

Chapter 4. The Prosecution's Case

1. See the charge of Judge Frank Gary, which states: "10. A man may curse another in the vilest manner, using the most abusive language, and yet that in law is no legal provocation. I charge you that" ("Judges Charge," *State,* October 15, 1903, 5). See also *State v. Jackson,* 32 S.C. 27, 10 S.E. 769, 771 (S.C. S. Ct. 1890).

2. "Stenographic Report" for September 28, 1903, *State,* September 29, 1903, 1.

3. Burke, "A History of the Opening Statement."

4. Burke notes the lack of an opening statement in the Tillman case, ibid., 55.

5. Testimony of Officer George Boland, "Stenographic Report" for September 28, 1903, *State,* September 29, 1903, 1–2.

6. Testimony of Sheriff W. H. Coleman, ibid., 2.

7. Evidence on the chain of custody of the bullet was even more confusing because it was presented out of sequence: the sheriff got the bullet from George Kohn, but the sheriff's testimony was presented first. Further confusion occurred when Kohn said he got the bullet from some young man he did not know, who found it on the street (ibid.).

8. Witnesses involved in this inquiry were J. F. Walker, Richland County clerk of court and several staff members of the *State* who had seen what Gonzales had been wearing on the day he was shot. These included James A. Hoyt, Lewis Wood, and M. C. Wallace (ibid., 2).

9. Testimony of Dr. Legrand Guerry, "Stenographic Report" for September 29, 1903, *State,* September 30, 1903, 1.

10. Ibid. On the standards for admitting medical testimony about the cause of death, see *State v. Terrell,* 46 S.C.L. (12 Rich.) 321, 327–29 (S.C. CT of App. 1859). See

also Underhill, *A Treatise on the Law of Criminal Evidence,* 372–73 (discussing evidence admissible to prove the "cause and manner of death").

11. Greenleaf, *A Treatise on the Law of Evidence,* 1, sec. 155–61: 245–53. Because it was the leading treatise available at the time of the Tillman case, I have used this text to explain the dying declaration exception to the rule against admission of hearsay evidence. See also Underhill, *A Treatise on the Law of Evidence,* 138–47, and Park, Leonard, Orenstein, and Goldberg, *Evidence Law,* sec. 9.42: 368–71.

12. See Greenleaf, *A Treatise on the Law of Evidence,* 1, sec. 155–59: 245–50.

13. Ibid., 247.

14. Ibid., 246. See *State v. Terrell,* 46 S.C.L. (12 Rich.) 321, 329 (S.C. Ct. App. 1859), in which the court admitted a dying declaration by someone other than the person whose death was the subject of the prosecution when the declarant's death arose from the same event.

15. Greenleaf, *A Treatise on the Law of Evidence,* 1, sec. 155: 245.

16. Ibid., 247. Key South Carolina cases setting forth the standards for admitting dying declarations that were available at the time of the Tillman trial are *State v. Terrell,* 46 S.C.L. (12 Rich.) 321, 329 (S.C. Ct. App. 1859), *State v. Bannister,* 35 S.C. 290, 14 S.E. 678 (S.C. S. Ct. 1892); *State v. Johnson,* 26 S.C. 152, 1 S.E. 510 (S.C. S. Ct. 1887), *State v. Nance,* 25 S.C. 168 (S.C. S. Ct. 1886), 1886 W.L. 2491 (S.C.); *State v. Gill,* 14 S.C. 410 (S.C. S. Ct. 1881), 1881 W.L. 5841 (S.C.); *State v. Washington,* 13 S.C. 453 (S.C. S. Ct. 1880), 1880 W.L. 5655 (S.C.); *State v. McEvoy,* 9 S.C. 208 (S.C. S. Ct. 1878), 1878 W.L. 5322 (S.C.); *State v. Leggett Quick,* 49 S.C.L. (15 Rich.) 342, (S.C. Ct. App. 1868), 1868 W.L. 2622 (S.C.); *State v. Ferguson,* 20 S.C. L. (2 Hill) 619 (S.C. Ct. App. 1835), 1835 W.L. 1418 (S.C. App.). The United States Supreme Court case quoted is *Mattox v. United States,* 146 U.S. 140, 152 (1892). For a discussion of the South Carolina law, including how standards have changed over time, see Collins, *South Carolina Evidence,* 418.

17. "Stenographic Report" for September 29, 1903, *State,* September 30, 1903, 1.

18. Testimony of Dr. D. S. Pope, ibid., 1–2.

19. Ibid., 1–2.

20. Testimony of Dr. L. A. Griffith, "Stenographic Report" for September 29, 1903, ibid., September 30, 1903, 5.

21. Testimony of Dr. B. W. Taylor, "Stenographic Report" for September 30, 1903, ibid., October 1, 1903, 1.

22. Testimony of Dr. L. A. Griffith, "Stenographic Report" for September 29, 1903, ibid., September 30, 1903, 5.

23. Testimony of Dr. Taylor, "Stenographic Report" for September 30, 1903, ibid., October 1, 1903, 5.

24. Testimony of Dr. J. H. McIntosh, ibid., 1.

25. Ibid.

26. Testimony of Dr. C. W. Barron, ibid., 2.

27. Ibid.

28. Judge Gary's rulings, ibid., 2–3.

29. Ibid., 2. See the definition in Greenleaf, *A Treatise on the Law of Evidence,* 1, sec. 156: 245. According to Greenleaf, the declaration must be "made in extremity, when the party is at the point of death." *Black's Law Dictionary* defines "in extremis" as "in extreme circumstances" or "near the point of death."

30. "Stenographic Report" for September 30, 1903, *State,* October 1, 1903, 2–3. See Kahn, *South Carolina Evidence Handbook,* 98, which states that "the length of time the declarant lives after making the dying declaration is immaterial. But see *Mattox v. U.S.,* 151, which says the length of time between the dying statement and death is relevant, but the key factor is whether the declarant believed at the time he made the statement that death was impending.

31. Testimony of James A. Hoyt Jr., in "Stenographic Report" for September 30, 1903, *State,* October 1, 1903, 2.

32. Ibid.

33. Testimony of Dr. J. W. Babcock, ibid., 2–3.

34. Ibid.

35. See closing defense argument by Patrick Nelson, in "Stenographic Report" for October 13, 1903, *State,* October 14, 1903, 3.

36. See Kristin M. Harkey, "Lathan, Robert," in Edgar, ed., *The South Carolina Encyclopedia,* 536–37. See also Sass, *Outspoken,* 53, 100–101 (reprinting the Pulitzer Prize editorial). In a February 17, 1903, letter to Lathan, Ambrose Gonzales said that his "dear brother" N. G. had been "very fond" of Lathan and that Ambrose valued "your sterling qualities of heart and head," Robert Lathan Papers, South Carolina Historical Society, Charleston, S.C.

37. Affidavit of Robert Lathan, dated February 11, 1903, published in the *State,* February 20, 1903, 1–2. Lathan's affidavit containing his stenographic version of N. G. Gonzales's dying declaration is also reproduced in Latimer, *The Story of the* State, 62–63.

38. Lathan affidavit, *State,* February 20, 1903, 1–2.

39. Testimony of Dr. J. W. Babcock, "Stenographic Report" for September 30, 1903, *State,* October 1, 1903, 2–3. A leading authority on evidence law as it existed near the time of the trial noted that for an expert to be examined on a subject, it should be established that the witness has "special practical acquaintance with the immediate line of inquiry" (Wharton, *A Treatise on the Law of Evidence in Criminal Issues* [1880], sec. 408, 320). Dr. Babcock was a distinguished physician, but it is questionable whether he had the requisite "practical acquaintance" with the behavior of bullets. But see *State v. Terrell,* 46 S.C.L. (12 Rich.) 321, 327–29 (S.C. Ct. of App. 1859), permitting testimony based on respected medical books when three of five doctors testifying had no direct experience with the poison allegedly causing death. See also Underhill, *Treatise on the Law of Criminal Evidence,* sec. 312: 372–73 (a doctor can testify as to the direction of a blow). In *Spring Company v. Edgar,* 99 U.S. 645 (1878), the U.S. Supreme Court decided that the competency of experts to testify was to be determined by the trial judge and that decision would not be reversed unless the ruling was manifestly erroneous. See also Kahn, *South Carolina Evidence Handbook,* 61–68. For biographical material on Dr. Babcock, see Peter

McCandless, "Babcock, James Woods," in Edgar, ed., *The South Carolina Encyclopedia,* 39.

40. Testimony of Dr. B. W. Taylor, "Stenographic Report" for September 30, 1903, *State,* October 1, 1903, 5. On the use of hypothetical questions with expert witnesses, see Wharton, *A Treatise on the Law of Evidence in Criminal Issues* (1880), sec. 418: 329–30.

41. Testimony of James H. Tillman, "Stenographic Report" for October 9, 1903, *State,* October 10, 1903, 2.

42. Testimony of Dr. C. W. Barron, "Stenographic Report" for September 30, 1903, ibid., October 1, 1903, 2.

43. See "August Kohn," in Hemphill, ed., *Men of Mark,* 4:169–72.

44. Ibid., 170.

45. Hennig, *August Kohn,* 111.

46. Jones, *Stormy Petrel,* 204–7. Edgar, *South Carolina: A History,* 441–43.

47. Testimony of August Kohn, "Stenographic Report" for September 30, 1903, *State,* October 1, 1903, 3.

48. "Stenographic Report" for October 1, 1903, ibid., October 2, 1903, 1.

49. Testimony of August Kohn, ibid., 1.

50. *Charleston News and Courier,* October 3, 1903, 1.

51. Closing argument of Patrick H. Nelson, "Stenographic Report" for October 13, 1903, *State,* October 14, 1903, 2, and closing argument of George W. Croft, "Stenographic Report" for October 14, 1903, in the *State,* October 15, 1903, 2.

52. Closing argument of George W. Croft, ibid.

53. See Hemphill, ed., *Men of Mark,* 4:169–72. W. W. Ball described Kohn's calm demeanor on the witness stand in "New Testimony of Importance . . . Mr. Kohn Steady under Severe Cross Examination," *State,* October 3, 1903, 1.

54. Testimony of W. F. Stieglitz, "Stenographic Report" for September 29, 1903, *State,* September 30, 1903, 4. The stenographic report is inconsistent in spelling the name of the witness, sometimes spelling it "Stieglitz" and sometimes "Steiglitz." Biographical material on Frederick H. Dominick may be found in the 1940 edition of *Who's Who in America,* 785; and in *Biographical Directory of the United States Congress,* http://bioguide.congress.gov/ (accessed January 28, 2013).

55. Testimony of Dr. S. T. D. Lancaster, "Stenographic Report" for September 29, 1903, *State,* September 30, 1903, 4.

56. Testimony of W. B. Gause, ibid.

57. Testimony of R. G. Arthur and R. M. Broadwater, ibid.

58. Testimony of C. J. Terrell, "Stenographic Report" for October 2, 1903, *State,* October 3, 1903, 2.

59. Ibid.

60. W. W. Ball was not then a regular staff member of the *State.* The newspaper had brought him in to cover the trial in an effort to demonstrate that its coverage was impartial. Every day Ball wrote an introduction to the verbatim record of the trial. See his description of Dr. Adams in the *State,* October 3, 1903, 1. Highlights of Adams's

testimony are in a box on page 1, and the verbatim account is on pages 2–3 in the "Stenographic Report."

61. Testimony of Dr. E. C. L. Adams, "Stenographic Report" for October 2, 1903, *State,* October 3, 1903, 2–3. See also the box in column one of the first page.

62. Ibid.

63. Constitution of 1895, art. I, sec. 11 (removal of officer for dueling) and art. III, sec. 26 (an incoming officer must swear that he has not engaged in a duel).

64. Constitution of 1895, art. XV (impeachment), art. III, sec. 27 (removal of officers for incapacity, misconduct, or neglect of duty).

65. Testimony of Cole Blease, "Stenographic Report" for October 8, 1903, *State,* October 9, 1903, 1–2.

66. See William V. Moore, "Blease, Coleman Livingston," in Edgar, ed., *The South Carolina Encyclopedia,* 79–80.

67. This picture accompanies the rather hagiographic account of his life in David Duncan Wallace, *The History of South Carolina,* 4:963–64.

68. See the photographs of Blease in William V. Moore, "Blease, Coleman Livingston," in Edgar, ed., *The South Carolina Encyclopedia,* 79, and David Duncan Wallace, *The History of South Carolina,* 4:962.

69. *State,* July 19, 1892, 4, and July 23, 1892, 4. See also Jones, "The Word War," 4–12, 52–55; Burnside, "The Governorship of Coleman Livingston Blease," 1–10; and Blease's inaugural address, in South Carolina General Assembly, House of Representatives, *Journal of the House of Representatives* (1911 session), 86–91 (denouncing the press and calling for stronger criminal libel laws).

70. Testimony of Cole Blease, "Stenographic Report" for October 8, 1903, *State,* October 9, 1903, 1.

71. Ibid. (emphasis added).

72. Ibid. (emphasis added).

73. Ibid., 2. The South Carolina Constitution of 1895, art. I, sec. 17, guarantees the right against self-incrimination.

74. Testimony of Cole Blease, "Stenographic Report" for October 8, 1903, *State,* October 9, 1903, 2.

75. Ibid.

76. For the details of Senator George Washington Brown's life, see Bailey, Morgan, and Taylor, eds., *Biographical Directory of the South Carolina Senate,* 1:205.

77. Testimony of Senator G. W. Brown, "Stenographic Report" for October 2, 1903, *State,* October 3, 1903, 3.

78. The Talbird/Whipper election dispute court decisions are *Whipper et al. v. Talbird et al.,* 32 S.C. 1, 10 S.E. 578 (S.C. Sup. Ct. 1890), holding that Whipper could not appeal the decisions of the state board of canvassers upholding the county board's determination that the ballots from certain precincts should not be counted and that Talbird was elected probate judge); *In re Whipper,* 32 S.C. 5, 10 S.E. 579 (S.C. Sup. Ct. 1890), upholding trial court's rejection of Whipper's petition to be released from jail by habeas

corpus procedure and continuing his confinement until he turned over the records to Talbird. The fusion ticket on which Talbird ran and the election dispute are discussed in Billingsley, *Yearning to Breathe Free,* 192–93, and Miller, *Gullah Statesman,* 186 (statement by Thomas Miller that Smalls and Talbird worked together to defeat Whipper). See also Lawrence S. Rowland, "Whipper, William J.," in Edgar, ed., *The South Carolina Encyclopedia,* 1019–20. Biographical material on Talbird is found in Bailey, Morgan, and Taylor, eds., *Biographical Directory of the South Carolina Senate,* 3:1578; Snowden, *History of South Carolina,* 5:229. See also "Thomas Talbird," in Hemphill, ed., *Men of Mark,* 1:394–95. Whipper's view of the election dispute is found in Whipper, *An Account of the Beaufort County Election.* A Whipper descendent, Carole Ione, has written about the election controversy in *Pride of Family,* 193–94.

79. Testimony of Senator Thomas Talbird, "Stenographic Report" for October 2, 1903, *State,* October 4, 1903, 5. Although Talbird's testimony was presumably part of the October 2 "Stenographic Report," it was not published in the *State* until October 4, 1903, because of space limitations.

80. Ibid.

81. Ibid.

82. Ibid.

83. Self-defense law in South Carolina as it existed near the time of the Tillman trial is discussed in *State v. Turner,* 29 S.C. 34, 6 S.E. 891 (S.C. S. Ct. 1888). The court adopted the following standard: "Now, self-defense, as defined by Mr. Greenleaf, (Volume 3, 14th ed. sec. 116), is 'where one is assaulted upon a sudden affray, and, in the defense of his person, where sudden and immediate suffering would be the consequence of waiting for the assistance of the law, and there was no other probable means of escape, he kills his assailant'" (ibid., 893). See also *State v. Bodie,* 33 S.C. 117, 11 S.E. 624 (S.C. S. Ct. 1890), discussing when a homicide is justifiable or defensible with particular emphasis on the standards for proving self-defense; and *State v. Jackson,* 32 S.C. 27, 10 S.E. 769 (S.C. S. Ct. 1890), stating that earlier threats are not enough to justify a killing in self-defense; there must be, at the time of the killing, some demonstration by the deceased that he intended to execute the threat.

84. Testimony of Mrs. Emma C. Melton, "Stenographic Report" for October 3, 1903, *State,* October 4, 1903, 10–11.

85. W. W. Ball, "Story of a Tragedy Told by a Woman," *State,* October 4, 1903, 9.

86. John Marshall, "Trial of Jas. H. Tillman: Mrs.'s Melton's Testimony," *Charleston News and Courier,* October 4, 1903, 1.

87. Testimony of Mrs. Emma C. Melton, "Stenographic Report" for October 3, 1903, *State,* October 4, 1903, 10–11.

88. Ibid., 10.

89. See "Andrew Crawford," in Richland County Bar Association, *History of the Bar of Richland County,* 68–70.

90. Testimony of Mrs. Emma C. Melton, "Stenographic Report" for October 3, 1903, *State,* October 4, 1903, 10.

91. Ibid., 10–11.

92. See Testimony of Mrs. Mary A. Evans, "Stenographic Report" for October 8, 1903, *State,* October 9, 1903, 2.

93. *Charleston News and Courier,* October 9, 1903, 1.

94. Testimony of Mrs. Mary A. Evans, "Stenographic Report" for October 8, 1903, *State,* October 9, 1903, 2.

95. Ibid.

96. See Greenleaf, *A Treatise on the Law of Evidence,* 1, sec. 98: 182: "But it is requisite that, whatever facts the witness may speak to, he should be confined to those lying within his own knowledge, whether they be things said or done, and should not testify from information given by others, however worthy of credit they may be." See also Greenleaf, sec. 430(i), 527 (evidence of an "impression" held by a witness is not admissible when he or she had "no actual observation or source of knowledge at all").

97. Comment by Judge Frank Gary during the testimony of Mrs. Mary A. Evans, *State,* October 9, 1903, 2.

98. Testimony of Mrs. Mary A. Evans, ibid.

99. Eubanks, *Ben Tillman's Baby,* 149–177. H. H. Evans's election to the Dispensary Board in 1900, when he was a member of the legislature, the body which chose the directors, is recorded in "Session Lists 1692–1973," *Biographical Directory of the South Carolina House of Representatives,* 473.

100. See Eubanks, *Ben Tillman's Baby,* 166–67 (reproducing the April 14, 1906, affidavit of Brevard D. Miller accusing Evans and another director, L. J. Williams, of giving a contract to Carolina Glass Company in exchange for company stock).

101. *State* stories recounting H. H. Evans's spanking of editor J. K. Blackman are "Hub Evans Spanked a Greenville Editor," *State,* July 8, 1902, 1; "He Says Hub Evans Hit from Behind. Editor of Greenville News Makes Statement," *State,* July 9, 1902, 1; "Hub Evans Detained," *State,* July 9, 1902, 8; "As Seen by a Parson," *State,* July 12, 1902, 6; and "Greenville News to Indict Hub Evans," *State,* July 13, 1902, 13.

102. "Hub Evans Defends State Dispensary," *State,* August 1, 1906, 1.

103. Testimony of J. F. Sims, "Stenographic Report" for October 2, 1903, *State,* October 4, 1903, 5.

104. Ibid.

105. Ibid.

106. Ibid.

107. Testimony of A. G. La Motte, "Stenographic Report" for October 3, 1903, *State,* October 4, 1903, 9. The *Lexington Dispatch,* October 7, 1903, 4, noted that La Motte went by his middle name, Gamewell, and that his profession was architect, which may explain the unusual precision with which he stated distances.

108. Testimony of Mary Evans, "Stenographic Report" for October 8, 1903, *State,* October 9, 1903, 2.

109. Affidavit of James A. Hoyt, Jr., February 11, 1903, available in N. G. Gonzales Papers.

110. Testimony of C. M. Lide, "Stenographic Report" for October 3, 1903, *State,* October 4, 1903, 9–10.

111. Ibid.

112. Ibid. An added difficulty in interpreting Lide's testimony about the position of Gonzales's hands, whether they were in or out of his overcoat pockets, is that the court reporter (or the lawyers) sometimes used Tillman's name when they probably meant Gonzales.

113. Testimony of August Schideman, "Stenographic Report" for October 3, 1903, *State,* October 4, 1903, 10.

114. Ibid.

115. Ibid.

116. Testimony of Wyatt Aiken, "Stenographic Report" for October 2, 1903, *State,* October 4, 1903, 5.

117. Ibid.

118. Testimony of J. R. Allen, ibid., 5–6.

119. J. S. Young, a "car-caller" at the transfer station, heard the shot, looked up, and saw Tillman with a gun and Gonzales leaning against the corner post. Young did not see Gonzales with a gun. Testimony of J. S. Young, ibid., 6. Arledge Lyles, a fifteen-year-old boy, ran a cigar and fruit store in the transfer station. He was watching a workman install wiring in the shop when he heard the shot. He saw Tillman with a pistol pointed at Gonzales. Gonzales's right hand was in his pocket with his thumb out. He had no gun and made no "demonstration" toward Tillman. Then he clutched his stomach. Two men came up and helped him back toward the *State* office. Testimony of Arledge Lyles, ibid.

Chapter 5. The Defense Case

1. Testimony of Miss Mary Julia Roper, "Stenographic Report" for October 3, 1903, *State,* October 4, 1903, 11, 13.

2. W. W. Ball, "The Story of a Tragedy Told by a Woman: First Witness for the Defense," *State,* October 4, 1903, 9.

3. *Charleston News and Courier,* October 4, 1903, 1.

4. Testimony of Miss Mary Julia Roper, "Stenographic Report" for October 3, 1903, *State,* October 4, 1903, 11, 13.

5. Ibid.

6. Testimony of T. D. Mitchell, "Stenographic Report" for October 7, 1903, *State,* October 8, 1903, 1–2.

7. Ibid.

8. Testimony of A. J. Flowers, ibid., 2.

9. Ibid.

10. See Wharton, *A Treatise on the Law Evidence in Criminal Issues* (1912), 2, sec. 757 and sec. 912: 1507, 1707. While threats not communicated to the defendant may sometimes be used with regard to establishing self-defense, they normally should not be used in the absence of an overt aggressive act by the deceased and proof that the defendant was "in apparent imminent danger" at the time of the collision (ibid., 1507).

11. Testimony of A. J. Flowers, "Stenographic Report" for October 7, 1903, *State,* October 8, 1903, 2.

12. Testimony of Alfred Wallace, "Stenographic Report" for October 10, 1903, *State,* October 11, 1903, 9–10.

13. See Wharton, *A Treatise on the Law of Evidence in Criminal Issues* (1912) 2, sec. 527: 1107. Railroad records are best presented through the testimony of the person who made the entries.

14. Testimony of A. H. Montieth, "Stenographic Report" for October, 10, 1903, *State,* October 11, 1903, 10.

15. Ibid. The judge concluded that summaries of records could be used when the records are voluminous, but in this case the trip slips apparently were not voluminous, and there were questions about the accuracy of the summaries that could be resolved only by looking at the original trip slips with the assistance of a person intimately familiar with the manner in which the records were kept. See Wharton, *A Treatise on the Law of Evidence in Criminal Issues* (1912) 2, sec. 527e: 1107. See also Park, Leonard, Orenstein, and Goldberg, *Evidence Law,* sec. 15.12: 609 (discussing the admission of summaries of voluminous records); and Wigmore, *A Treatise on the System of Evidence in Trials at Common Law,* 2, sec. 1230: 1473 (noting that summaries could be used when records are voluminous but the mass of records should be available when accuracy of the summary is questioned).

16. Testimony of P. W. Hughes, "Stenographic Report" for October 7, 1903, *State,* October 8, 1903, 2–3.

17. Ibid., 3. Much of what Hughes said about Gonzales's threats was confirmed by the testimony of A. J. Blalock, Hughes's son-in-law, who was present during the same conversation. Testimony of A. J. Blalock, ibid.

18. Testimony of Victor B. Cheshire, ibid., 3, 5.

19. Ibid.

20. See the arguments by Solicitor Thurmond and prosecutors G. Duncan Bellinger and Andrew Crawford, ibid., 3.

21. See the argument of Solicitor Thurmond, ibid., 3, citing *State v. Jackson,* 32 S.C. 27, 10 S.E. 769 (S. Ct. of S.C., 1890), and prosecutor Crawford, citing Wharton, *A Treatise on the Law of Evidence in Criminal Issues.* Although the record does not specifically say so, Crawford was probably citing the 1880 edition of Wharton, sec. 757: 614–16.

22. Argument of prosecutor Crawford against admitting controversial evidence of threats, ibid., 3.

23. Ibid. Ruling of Judge Frank Gary admitting controversial evidence of threats Gonzales supposedly made concerning Tillman.

24. Ruling of Judge Gary, ibid., 3. But see Wharton, *A Treatise on the Law of Evidence in Criminal Issues* (1912), 2, sec. 757: 1507, which concludes that evidence of such threats by the deceased should not be admitted in the absence of an overt act of attack by the deceased and evidence that the defendant was in "apparent imminent danger" at the time of the clash.

25. Testimony of W. H. Geer, "Stenographic Report" for October 10, 1903, *State,* October 11, 1903, 10.

26. Testimony of J. A. White, "Stenographic Report" for October 8, 1903, *State,* October 9, 1903, 3.

27. Ibid.

28. Ibid.

29. See Testimony of Richard H. Holsenback, ibid., 3, 5. The reader is advised that the stenographic report is inconsistent in its spelling of this witness's name. This makes finding material about him difficult. The spelling "Holzenback" is also used fairly often. The spelling used in this book is the one in the official General Sessions Journal, 1896–1904, Lexington County, September term 1903, October 8, 1903, 455.

30. Testimony of Richard H. Holsenback, "Stenographic Report" for October 8, 1903, *State,* October 9, 1903, 3.

31. Ibid.

32. Ibid.

33. Ibid., 5.

34. See "Holsenback's Slayer Made His Escape," *State,* April 16, 1907, 1; and "Dick Halsonback Shot in Heart," *State,* April 15, 1907, 1.

35. Testimony of M. C. Lorick, "Stenographic Report" for October 8, 1903, *State,* October 9, 1903, 5.

36. Ibid.

37. Ibid.

38. *Charleston News and Courier,* October 9, 1903, 1.

Chapter 6. Tillman's Testimony

1. South Carolina Constitution of 1895, art. I, sec. 17. For a case interpreting the art. I, sec. 17, right against self-incrimination near the time of the Tillman trial, see *Town Council of Crosshill v. Owens,* 61 S.C. 22, 39 S.E. 184 (S.C. S. Ct. 1901). In that case a pharmacist was convicted of selling intoxicating liquors though he insisted that he did so only for medical purposes and in small amounts. The defendant was called by the prosecution and was its only witness. The South Carolina Supreme Court, in an opinion by Justice Pope, reversed the conviction, concluding that the defendant was compelled to testify against himself. It did not matter that he did not object to testifying. The prosecution violated his rights by calling him. A defendant has a right to ask to be sworn and testify in his own behalf, but the defendant made no such request. See also *State v. Atkinson,* 40 S.C. 363, 372, 18 S.E. 1021, 1025 (S.C. S. Ct. 1894), holding that the use of evidence obtained by compelling the defendants to furnish it is cured when the court instructs that such evidence be stricken and that the jury should not consider it. Under art. I, sec. 18, of the Constitution of 1895, the accused has a right "to be fully heard in his defense by himself or by his counsel or by both."

2. W. W. Ball, "The Defendant Takes the Stand," *State,* October 9, 1903, 1.

3. *Charleston News and Courier,* October 9, 1903, 1.

4. *New York World,* October 9, 1903, 4.

5. Ibid.

6. *Atlanta Constitution,* October 9, 1903, 1.

7. *State,* October 9, 1903, 1. For another account of the Tillman testimony, see *Lexington Dispatch,* October 14, 1903, 4. The *Dispatch* says Tillman "gave his testimony in a clear, distinct voice audible throughout the court room and appeared perfectly at ease." See also *Edgefield Chronicle,* October 15, 1903, 1.

8. Testimony of James H. Tillman, "Stenographic Report" for October 8, 1903, *State,* October 9, 1903, 6.

9. Jones, *Stormy Petrel,* 288; Moore, *Carnival of Blood,* 105.

10. Testimony of James H. Tillman, "Stenographic Report" for October 8, 1903, *State,* October 9, 1903, 6.

11. Simkins, *Pitchfork Ben Tillman,* 382.

12. Moore, *Carnival of Blood,* 106. Testimony of James H. Tillman, "Stenographic Report" for October 8, 1903, *State,* October 9, 1903, 6. Simkins, *Pitchfork Ben Tillman,* 169, states that the inauguration of Benjamin Tillman as governor was on December 4, 1890.

13. See Alexia Jones Helsley, "Tillman, James Hammond," in Edgar, ed., *The South Carolina Encyclopedia,* 962, which states that Tillman was born on June 27, 1868. Moore, *Carnival of Blood,* 227n10, concludes that 1869 is the correct year of Tillman's birth because he gave that date under oath in the trial and it is so stated on his tombstone.

14. Testimony of James H. Tillman, "Stenographic Report" for October 8, 1903, *State,* October 9, 1903, 6.

15. For a discussion of the wide acceptance of using violence as a means of upholding one's honor in the South, particularly South Carolina, see Wyatt-Brown, *Southern Honor,* 366–68, and Cash, *The Mind of the South,* 73–74. Cash contended that many nineteenth-century southerners believed violent retaliation against the perpetrator was the only way a serious affront to one's honor could be vindicated. This slowed the development of police powers as a means of controlling violence.

16. Testimony of James H. Tillman, "Stenographic Report" for October 8, 1903, *State,* October 9, 1903, 6.

17. See Gonzales, *In Darkest Cuba.*

18. Testimony of James H. Tillman, "Stenographic Report" for October 8, 1903, *State,* October 9, 1903, 6.

19. Ibid.

20. "The Nation's Opportunity," *State,* September 16, 1899, 3 (reprinted from the *Charleston News and Courier*). See also, "The Great Chief of the Chipmunks," *State,* September 21, 1899, 4, and "Heap Much Big Chief," ibid., September 20, 1899, 3.

21. Letter from William Banks, "Dispensation for Deserters, Excellent Advice to Friends of Men Who Have Left; with Our Boys at Panama Park," *State,* August 19, 1898.

22. William Banks, "First Regiment Wants to Be Free," *State,* August 25, 1898. In the fluid context of the debate on whether the regiment should disband and go home or go to Cuba for noncombat duties, it is unclear whether this gesture is one of agreement with Tillman's speech or an attempt by the men to persuade him to their point of view.

23. "Tillman on Columbia," *State,* October 30, 1898.

24. Ibid.

25. See "Goodby, to the First South Carolina," *State,* November 12, 1898, and, "Its Record Is Now Ancient History," ibid.

26. Compare "Whipping Post at Camp Geiger," *State,* October 6, 1898, with "Colonel Tillman's Case Dismissed," ibid., October 8, 1898.

27. Testimony of James H. Tillman, "Stenographic Report" for October 8, 1903, *State,* October 9, 1903, 6.

28. Ibid.

29. *State v. Jackson,* 32 S.C. 27, 10 S.E. 769, 771 (S.C. S. Ct. 1890), holding that "it is well settled that no words, however violent or threatening in their character, will justify even a battery, much less a homicide, unless they are accompanied with some act—some offer or attempt to do violence, to the person of another."

30. See *Mayrant v. Richardson,* 10 S.C. L. (1 Nott and McC.) 347 (S.C. Const. App. 1818), 1818 W.L. 915 (recognizing the constitutional right to criticize candidates). See also Emerson, *The System of Free Expression,* 668 (noting: "Traditionally the press has operated in the classic laissez-faire pattern"), and Meiklejohn, *Free Speech,* 26–27, 88 (emphasizing that free speech and press are essential in a system of self-government in order to inform voters about issues and candidates and that such commentary must sometimes be vigorous and offensive). State constitutional law was the controlling authority with United States constitutional law being merely persuasive authority since the Bill of Rights, including the free speech and press provisions, had not yet been held applicable to the states. See *Barron v. The Mayor and City Council of Baltimore,* 32 U.S. (7 Pet.) 243, 250–51 (1833) and *Livingston's Lessee v. Moore,* 32 U.S. (7 Pet.) 469, 551–52 (1833). The free press clause of the First Amendment of the U.S. Constitution was held by the U.S. Supreme Court to have been incorporated for application against the states by the due process clause of the Fourteenth Amendment in 1931, well after the events in the Tillman case. See *Near v. Minnesota,* 283 U.S. 697 (1931), incorporating freedom of the press for application against the states through the Fourteenth Amendment.

31. See the comment by Judge Gary on the state's introduction of editorials to prove malice, "Stenographic Report" for October 9, 1903, *State,* October 10, 1903, 1.

32. The jury's attention was focused on the editorials for an entire day when they were introduced into evidence by prosecutor William Elliott, who read the voluminous file word for word. See "Stenographic Report" for October 1, 1903, *State,* October 2, 1903, 1 and following. The *State*'s publication of the editorials resumed on October 3, 1903, 9, and October 4, 1903, 6, and following. This first batch of editorials was from 1902 and often focused on Tillman's campaign for governor. Additional editorials were introduced as part of the "Stenographic Report" for October 8, 1903, *State,* October 9, 1903, 9. These are from 1898 (Spanish-American War), 1901 (cockfighting patron as lieutenant governor), and 1902 (dealing with both Senator Benjamin R. Tillman and Lieutenant Governor James H. Tillman.) The last set of editorials, those read on October 8, were introduced for the defense.

33. Remarks by Judge Frank Gary, "Stenographic Report" for October 9, 1903, *State,* October 10, 1903, 1.

34. Testimony of James H. Tillman, ibid.

35. Ibid. See also Simkins, *Pitchfork Ben Tillman,* 8–12, 385–90, and Kantrowitz, *Ben Tillman,* 254–55.

36. Editorial, *State,* February 28, 1902, reprinted as part of the trial evidence in *State,* October 2, 1903, 1 (also reprinting a March 1, 1902 editorial, "The Protest of Charleston," noting the concern that Tillman's actions would discourage people from attending the commercial exposition in Charleston).

37. Editorial, "A Finisher for Jim Tillman," originally published in *State,* March 2, 1902, and reprinted as part of the trial evidence, *State,* October 2, 1903, 1.

38. Ibid., 9 (quoting the *Washington Post* comparison of Jim Tillman to an ass).

39. Testimony of James H. Tillman, "Stenographic Report" for October 9, 1903, *State,* October 10, 1903, 1.

40. See "A Finisher for 'Jim Tillman,'" reprinted in *State,* October 2, 1903, 1.

41. *State,* October 2, 1903, 9, reprinting an editorial from *State,* March 5, 1902, crediting an unfavorable comparison of Jim Tillman to Major Micah Jenkins to the *Charleston Evening Post.*

42. *State,* October 2, 1903, 9, reprinting an editorial from *State,* March 8, 1902, "Another Bray—Another Coming," as part of the trial evidence.

43. Ibid. Although the editorial comments on observations made in Augusta and Florence papers, these statements originate in the *State.*

44. *Mayrant v. Richardson,* recognizing a constitutional right to criticize candidates. See also *Reid v. Delorme,* 4 S.C. L. (2 Brev.) 76 (S.C. Const. App. 1806), 1806 W.L. 333. In discussing the right to petition the legislature for redress of grievances, a liberty cognate with freedom of the press, the court recognized a broad right to criticize public officials even when the criticism was offensive to third parties as well as the official. In *Black v. State Co.,* 93 S.C. 467, 77 S.E. 51 (S.C. S. Ct. 1913) free expression was both a winner and a loser because both sides asserted that constitutional right. The plaintiffs had opposed a candidate endorsed by the *State* newspaper for the Columbia, South Carolina, city council. When the *State*'s favorite lost, it published editorials criticizing the plaintiffs for conducting an "unfair," "insidious," last minute "whisper" campaign against its candidate. The plaintiffs' defamation suit against the paper was allowed by the South Carolina Supreme Court to continue despite the defendant's attempt to have it halted by demurrer. The Supreme Court decision was based more on technical procedural grounds than constitutional reasoning, but its effect was to vindicate the voters' right to criticize candidates at the expense of the paper's right to criticize the voters who injected themselves into campaigns. A barely articulated premise of the decision seems to have been that the paper's editorials went beyond attempting to refute the plaintiffs' reasons for opposing the paper's candidate and vengefully tried to destroy the plaintiffs' business by holding them up to ridicule. A well-reasoned dissent by Justice Richard Cannon Watts argued that, since the plaintiffs had thrust themselves into the campaign, a matter of

public interest, the "plaintiffs had occupied a quasi public position, and their conduct was subject of fair and bona fide criticism by a public newspaper" (77 S.E. 59 [Watts, J., dissenting]). On remand the jury awarded the plaintiffs twenty thousand dollars, of which fifteen thousand was remitted after the trial judge threatened to order a new trial, thus prodding the plaintiffs to agree to the reduction. The newspaper appealed, but this reduced award was approved by the South Carolina Supreme Court (99 S.C. 432, 83 S.E. 1088 [S.C. S. Ct. 1914]).

45. Gordon, "Of Freedom of Speech." See also the discussion of the essay titled "Of Freedom of Speech" in Levy, *Emergence of a Free Press,* 109–14; and Ramsay, *The History of the American Revolution,* 1:29, which notes that "those fashionable authors, who defended the cause of liberty, Cato's Letters," etc. "were common in one extreme of the colonies, while in the other, histories of the Puritans, kept alive the remembrance of the sufferings of their forefathers."

46. Alexander, "The Trial of John Peter Zenger," 397, 416. See also Rutherfurd, *John Peter Zenger;* Alexander, *A Brief Narrative;* Linder, "The Trial of John Peter Zenger"; Lee, *History of American Journalism,* 39–43; and Rosenberg, *Protecting the Best Men,* 35–39.

47. Madison, "Report on the Virginia Resolutions," 141, 145.

48. Ibid., 145. See also Ketcham, *James Madison,* 401–2.

49. See "St. George Tucker (1752–1827)," *Encyclopedia Virginia,* http://www.encyclopediavirginia.org (accessed September 16, 2012).

50. Tucker, "Of the Right of Conscience."

51. Franklin, "Apology for Printers," *Pennsylvania Gazette,* June 10, 1731, *Writings,* 171–77. See paragraphs 2, 5, and 8 for quotations. This essay is discussed in Isaacson, *Benjamin Franklin,* 66–68. See also Brands, *The First American,* 115–116. Benjamin Franklin as a printer and editor is discussed in Thomas, *The History of Printing in America,* 1:233–39.

52. Franklin, "Apology for Printers," *Writings,* 172. See also Isaacson, *Benjamin Franklin,* 66.

53. See Franklin, "Apology for Printers," *Writings,* 173, and Franklin's "Autobiography" (ibid., 1398), in which he stated, "In the conduct of my newspaper I carefully excluded all libelling and personal abuse, which is of late years become so disgraceful to our country." Franklin's career as a journalist is discussed in Burns, *Infamous Scribblers,* 67–96.

54. Hay, *An Essay on the Liberty of the Press,* 41–42, 44 (emphasis added). See also Wortman, preface to *A Treatise Concerning Political Enquiry,* iv (discussing the importance of "freedom of speech and opinion") and Wood, *Empire of Liberty,* 308–12 (discussing the arguments of Hay and Wortman against the Sedition Act of 1798).

55. Schauer, "Language, Truth and the First Amendment," 263, 279n64.

56. Cooper, *A Treatise on the Law of Libel,* 42–47. See also Malone, *The Public Life of Thomas Cooper,* 111–49. Sedition Act of July 14, 1798, 1 United States Statutes at Large, chap. 74, 596–97. Rosenberg discusses the Sedition Act in *Protecting the Best Men,* 82–99.

57. See for example Black, *Handbook of American Constitutional Law,* sec. 164: 472–73, and Cooley, *A Treatise on the Constitutional Limitations,* 596. The Cooley treatise

concludes that not only the United States Constitution but those of the states provide "a shield of protection to the free expression of opinion in every part of our land."

58. Tucker, "Of the Right of Conscience," 382–83.

59. Ibid., 381.

60. Story, *Commentaries on the Constitution of the United States,* sec. 993, 703.

61. Ibid.

62. Testimony of James H. Tillman, "Stenographic Report" for October 9, 1903, *State,* October 10, 1903, 1.

63. The main contours of this controversy can be followed in the Senate records, but they are not as detailed as one would wish. See South Carolina General Assembly, Senate. *Journal of the Senate* (1902 session). The pertinent discussions involve H. R. 562-The Kibler Bill, the proposed expansion of the stock enclosure law. See the *Journal* for February 4, 1902, 246 (motion by Mr. Henderson to indefinitely postpone), February 6, 1902, 270 (issue of whether motions to postpone indefinitely are debatable under rules of S.C. Senate), February 12, 1902, 326 (rules committee reports that motions to postpone indefinitely are debatable under S.C. Senate rules and the Senate adopts the report).

64. South Carolina General Assembly, Senate, *Journal of the Senate* (1902 session), 326.

65. See Reed, *Reed's Rules.* The copy of this book that Reed sent to Tillman and autographed for him is available in the law library at the University of South Carolina, Columbia.

66. "James H. Tillman Proved a Falsifier by Senator Frye and Speaker Henderson," *State,* March 24, 1902, 1, 5. A follow-up article became a part of the trial evidence on October 1, 1903, and was reproduced as part of the "Stenographic Report" for that date in the *State,* October 2, 1903, 9, under the title "The Exposure of Jim Tillman."

67. Reed, *Reed's Rules,* sec. 122: 87.

68. In a later article, "Tillman Tacitly Confesses Guilt," *State,* June 16, 1902, 4, Gonzales accused Tillman of trying to cover up his lies to the South Carolina Senate by inserting a statement in the *Journal of the Senate of South Carolina* claiming that the telegrams from Frye and Henderson had shown "a wide difference of opinion among them" and that this was what he had represented to the Senate. This later statement, "A Question of Personal Privilege," was inserted in the *Journal of the Senate of South Carolina* for February 14, 1902, 362–63. To Gonzales this revised statement was a cover-up that compounded the original falsification. The N. G. Gonzales Papers contain several items related to this controversy. One is a statement given by Paul M. Brice, editor of the *Columbia Evening Record,* to N. G. Gonzales in which Brice says he interviewed Senator Whiteford Blakeney, chairman of the Rules Committee, who also said he had been in communication with Frye and Henderson, who told him that the advice they had given Tillman was not as Tillman had represented it. The file also contains copies of correspondence from Frye and Henderson with regard to questions Gonzales had raised about Tillman's practices in appointing senators to conference committees. Brief accounts of the Senate ruling controversy and the enmity the articles created between Gonzales and Tillman, are found in Moore, *Carnival of Blood,* 110–11, and Jones, *Stormy Petrel,* 292–93.

69. This editorial is "We Plead for a Sporting Statesman," *State,* June 22, 1901, reproduced as part of the "Stenographic Report" for October 8, 1903, *State,* October 9, 1903, 9.

70. Testimony of James H. Tillman, "Stenographic Report" for October 9, 1903, *State,* October 10, 1903, 2.

71. *State,* October 3, 1903, 9 (reprinting as part of the trial evidence "An Animated Falsehood," *State,* August 23, 1902).

72. "The Truth in Pursuit of a Candidate," *State,* August 11, 1902, reprinted as part of the trial evidence, *State,* October 4, 1903, 6. This editorial was apparently introduced at the trial on Thursday, October 1, 1903, but the *State* claimed that it was "accidentally omitted" from the "Stenographic Report" for that day. See the *State,* October 4, 1903, 5.

73. "Grit and Steel," originally in *State,* July 25, 1902, reprinted as part of the trial evidence in *State,* October 2, 1903, 10.

74. Ibid. See "A Mere Incident," *Gaffney Ledger,* July 25, 1902, 4. In this follow up to his campaign-platform confrontation with Jim Tillman, Ed DeCamp again called Tillman "a liar, a gambler, and a drunkard," added the charge that he was a "demagogue," and called his supporters "howling partisans who would not listen to the truth."

75. "Grit and Steel," *State,* October 2, 1903, 10.

76. Edward Hope DeCamp, *Gaffney Ledger* editor, to N. G. Gonzales, July 25, 1902, N. G. Gonzales Papers. The Decamp-Gonzales correspondence and their relationship is discussed in Matthews, "N. G. Gonzales," 220–21. DeCamp's background and the clash with James H. Tillman are discussed in McNeely, *Fighting Words,* 140–41.

77. Matthews, "N. G. Gonzales," 221.

78. "Two Tillmans—a Contrast," *State,* July 28, 1902 (reprinted as part of the trial evidence in *State,* October 2, 1903, 10).

79. Gonzales was still harping on Tillman's failure to fight DeCamp as the Democratic gubernatorial primary neared an end. See "The Finish of Jim Tillman," *State,* August 23, 1902 (reprinted as part of the trial evidence, *State,* October 3, 1903, 9).

80. See Hamilton, *Mythology,* 22 (Prometheus prefigures Christ as savior of mankind), 85–87 (Prometheus created mankind), 87–99 (Prometheus was punished by gods for bringing fire to mankind). See also Bulfinch, *Bulfinch's Mythology,* 17 (Prometheus making man in the image of the gods and bringing fire to man).

81. Testimony of James H. Tillman, "Stenographic Report" for October 9, 1903, *State,* October 10, 1903, 2.

82. "Partly Personal, Partly Political," *State,* July 31, 1902, and reprinted as part of the trial evidence, *State,* October 2, 1903, 10.

83. Ibid.

84. Longstreet, "The Fight," *Georgia Scenes,* 53–64.

85. Ibid., 55, 64. See also Nimeiri, "Play in Augustus Baldwin Longstreet's *Georgia Scenes*" (discussing Ransy Sniffle as troublemaker).

86. Testimony of James H. Tillman, "Stenographic Report" for October 9, 1903, *State,* October 10, 1903, 1–2.

87. Ibid.

88. Ibid. (emphasis added).

89. Ibid. (emphasis added).

90. Ibid. (emphasis added).

91. Ibid.

92. Ibid., 2.

93. Ibid. No proof was ever offered that the *State* office was "a kind of arsenal," as Tillman claimed he had heard.

94. Ibid.

95. Cross-examination of James H. Tillman by G. Duncan Bellinger, ibid., 2–3.

96. See W. W. Ball, "The Defendant Takes the Stand," *State,* October 9, 1903, 1 (discussing Tillman's claims that he was persecuted mostly by the *State*).

97. Testimony of James H. Tillman, "Stenographic Report" for October 9, 1903, *State,* October 10, 1903, 3.

98. Ibid.

99. Testimony of W. T. Hyatt, ibid., 5.

100. Ibid.

101. Testimony of J. Frost Walker, ibid.

102. Gonzales's affidavit on the 1886 concealed-weapons charge, introduced during Walker's testimony, ibid.

103. Ibid.

104. The attempts by the prosecution and defense to attack each other's key witnesses through other witnesses attacking their character, and the defense's attempts to *rehabilitate* witnesses by *positive* testimony about their credibility, are found in the "Stenographic Report" for October 10, 1903, *State,* October 11, 1903, 9–11, 13.

105. Testimony of J. D. Livingston, ibid., 9.

106. See Report of the Committee on Elections, no. 3, 54th Congress, 1st Session, House of Representatives, report no. 1229, April 13, 1896, *Thomas B. Johnston v. J. William Stokes,* (majority recommendation for Stokes, 14; minority recommendation for Johnston, 95). See also "South Carolina Seat Vacated," *New York Times,* June 2, 1896, 2 (describing the House of Representatives vote to declare the seat vacant). There has been some confusion as to Johnston's race, but scholars and records clearly show that he was white. See Work et al., "Some Negro Members of Reconstruction Conventions," 63, 88 (listing Thomas B. Johnston as a white member of the S.C. House of Representatives elected in 1876); see also Woody, "Behind the Scenes in the Reconstruction Legislature," 233, 254n110 (listing Thomas B. Johnston, merchant as a Sumter County representative in the S.C. House in 1872 and 1877). The 1870 United States Federal Census records list T. B. Johnston of Mayesville, Sumter, South Carolina, as a white male of thirty-five born in Ireland in about 1835. The 1890 Veterans Schedules record lists him as having served for five years during the Civil War on the Union side. He was discharged as a captain. Both records are available at ancestry.com (accessed August 9, 2006).

107. Argument on the cross-examination of J. D. Livingston, "Stenographic Report" for October 10, 1903, *State,* October 11, 1903, 9.

108. See Foner, *Reconstruction,* 603 (southern attitude toward the Republican Party). See also Ayers, *The Promise of the New South,* 8–9 (comparing the positions of the Democratic and Republican Parties at the time of the Redeemer movement). One historian notes, "For South Carolina whites, a Republican state government would never have legitimacy; it might have power, but not authority" (Zuczek, *State of Rebellion,* 49).

109. *State,* October 11, 1903, 9.

110. Ibid.

111. "Stenographic Report" for October 10, 1903, ibid., 11, 13.

112. Ibid.

Chapter 7. The Closing Arguments

1. Closing argument by J. William Thurmond, "Stenographic Report" for October 12, 1903, *State,* October 13, 1903, 1–2.

2. Ibid.

3. Ibid.

4. Constitution of South Carolina, 1895, art. I, sec. 4, states, "The General Assembly shall make no law respecting an establishment of religion or prohibiting the free exercise thereof, or abridging the freedom of speech or of the press; or the right of the people peaceably to assemble and to petition the Government or any department thereof for a redress of grievances." This wording is not identical to that in the First Amendment to the United States Constitution but tracks it closely.

5. Closing argument by Thurmond, "Stenographic Report" for October 12, 1903, *State,* October 13, 1903, 2. The reference to the "fundamental law" is to the First Amendment of the United States Constitution.

6. See "Johnstone, George," *Biographical Directory of the United States Congress,* http://bioguide.congress.gov/ (accessed January 28, 2013); David Duncan Wallace, "Cyprian Melanchthon Efird," *The History of South Carolina,* 4:813–14; and "Efird, Cyprian, Melanchthon (1856–1941)," in Bailey, Morgan, and Taylor, *Biographical Directory of the South Carolina Senate,* 1:460–61.

7. "Stenographic Report" for October 12, 1903, *State,* October 13, 1903, 2.

8. Ibid.

9. Ibid.

10. See Lewis, *Make No Law,* 53; Lewis, *Freedom for the Thought We Hate,* 37–38; and Meiklejohn, *Free Speech,* 25, 27, 38–40, 56, 59–61, 88.

11. Closing argument by Thurmond, "Stenographic Report" for October 12, 1903, *State,* October 13, 1903, 2.

12. Ibid.

13. Closing argument by defense attorney George R. Rembert, ibid.

14. "George Robert Rembert," Richland County Bar Association, *History of the Bar of Richland County, 1790–1948,* 104–5. "Defending the Men," letter to the editor from Sergeant George R. Rembert, Co. K, First S.C. Infantry, *State,* September 9, 1898, 3. Jones, *Stormy Petrel,* 275–78, describes the Spanish-American War service of N. G.,

Ambrose, and William E. Gonzales. William Gonzales's service in Cuba was occupation duty in 1899 and less arduous than his brother's.

15. Closing argument by Rembert, "Stenographic Report" for October 12, 1903, *State,* October 13, 1903, 2.

16. Ibid.

17. Ibid.

18. Ibid.

19. Affidavit of Robert Lathan on Gonzales's dying declaration, *State,* February 20, 1903, 1–2. This document is reproduced in Latimer, *The Story of the* State, 62–63.

20. Closing argument by Rembert, "Stenographic Report" for October 12, 1903, *State,* October 13, 1903, 2.

21. The story of the Good Samaritan is set forth in Luke 10:30–37.

22. Closing argument by Rembert, "Stenographic Report" for October 12, 1903, *State,* October 13, 1903, 2–3.

23. Biographical material on William Elliott may be found in Richland County Bar Association, *History of the Bar of Richland County,* 75–76; see also Pierce, *Palmettos and Oaks,* 145–50; Latimer, *The Story of the* State, 179–81; Wallace, *The History of South Carolina,* 4:978.

24. Closing argument of William Elliott, in "Stenographic Report" for October 12, 1903, *State,* October 13, 1903, 3.

25. Ibid.

26. Ibid.

27. Jones, *Stormy Petrel,* 3–10. See also Gonzales, foreword to *In Darkest Cuba,* 7–26, and Aaron W. Marrs, "Gonzales, Narciso Gener," in Edgar, ed., *The South Carolina Encyclopedia,* 383. For a biography of N. G. Gonzales's adventurous father, see de la Cova, *Cuban Confederate Colonel.* See also Jones, "Ambrosio José Gonzales."

28. Closing argument of Elliott, "Stenographic Report" for October 12, 1903, *State,* October 13, 1903, 3.

29. The Constitution of March 26, 1776, was more concerned with delineating abuses of the British Crown, and erecting an emergency government structure, than defining civil liberties. The Constitution of 1778 began the fuller development of civil rights in the state's fundamental laws. See South Carolina Constitution of 1778, art. XLIII: "That the liberty of the press be inviolably preserved." The South Carolina Constitution of 1790, art. IX, sec. 6, states: "The trial by jury, as heretofore used in this state, and the liberty of the press shall be for ever inviolably preserved." The South Carolina Constitution of 1861, art. IX, sec. 6, states: "The trial by jury, as heretofore used in this State, and the liberty of the press, shall be forever inviolably preserved." See also the South Carolina Constitution of 1865, art. IX, sec. 7: "The trial by jury, as heretofore used in this State, and the liberty of the press, shall be forever inviolably preserved." The South Carolina Constitution of 1868, art. I, sec. 7: "All persons may freely speak, write and publish their sentiments on any subject, being responsible for the abuse of that right; and no laws shall be enacted to restrain or abridge the liberty of speech or of the press." The South

Carolina Constitution of 1895, in effect at the time of the Tillman trial, states in art. I, sec. 4: "The General Assembly shall make no law respecting an establishment of religion or prohibiting the free exercise thereof, or abridging the freedom of speech or of the press; or the right of the people peaceably to assemble and to petition the Government or any department thereof for a redress of grievances."

30. Closing argument of Elliott, "Stenographic Report" for October 12, 1903, *State,* October 13, 1903, 3.

31. Ibid. Art. I, sec. 21, of the South Carolina Constitution of 1895 says: "In all indictments or prosecutions for libel, the truth of the alleged libel may be given in evidence, and the jury shall be the judges of the law and the facts."

32. Closing argument of Elliott, "Stenographic Report" for October 12, 1903, *State,* October 13, 1903, 3.

33. To be valid, criminal libel statues must meet tough standards. As Federal District Judge Joseph F. Anderson, Jr., put it in *Fitts v. Kolb,* 779 F. Supp. 1502 (D. S.C. 1991), in striking down a 1912 South Carolina criminal libel statute: "no criminal liability for libel may be imposed in connection with the discussion of public affairs unless the publisher of a falsehood knows it was false at the time it was published or had a reckless disregard of whether it was false or true. The South Carolina criminal libel statute lacks the high degree of protection afforded free expression by the actual malice standard, and allows the imposition of criminal penalties with no showing that the publisher knew the information being published was false or had a high degree of awareness of its probable falsity." (citing U.S. Supreme Court cases *New York Times v. Sullivan,* 376 U.S. 254 (1964). *Garrison v. Louisiana,* 379 U.S. 64 (1964). *Bleckley News Corporation v. Hanks,* 389 U.S. 81 (1967). *Curtis Publishing Co. v. Butts,* 388 U.S. 130, 134 (1967)). See Gregory C. Lisby, "No Place in the Law," in which the author argues that criminal libel prosecutions are antithetical to our system of free expression because "Its purpose is to chill speech. It does not promote the equality of persons or of ideas" (435). See Lewis, *Make No Law,* 154–55, 167, 183–84, 192. The danger of permitting criminal libel prosecutions in light of their intimidating effect on free speech is discussed in Emerson, "Toward a General Theory," 877, 924, which observes that "it can hardly be urged that maintenance of peace requires a criminal prosecution for private defamation." The harm to reputation can be redressed by a civil suit not carrying the risk of criminal fines or imprisonment.

34. South Carolina Constitution of 1895, art. I, sec. 21 (stating that "the truth of the alleged libel may be given in evidence"). See also *State v. Brock,* 61 S.C. 141, 39 S.E. 359 (S.C. S. Ct. 1901). In *Brock* Justice Pope said in his lead opinion that truth was a complete defense, but Chief Justice McIver said it served only to disprove malice. Two other justices concurred in reversal of a criminal libel conviction without comment.

35. Conner, *The Libel Cases,* 89–90. See also Clark, *Francis Warrington Dawson,* 44–45.

36. See the discussion in chapter 1 of this book of the criminal libel case filed by G. W. M. Williams against N. G. Gonzales in 1892.

37. Closing argument of William Elliott, "Stenographic Report" for October 12, 1903, *State,* October 13, 1903, 3.

38. *Mayrant v. Richardson,* 10 S.C. L. (1 Nott and McC) 347, 1818 W.L. 915 (S.C. Const. App. 1818), upholding the right to criticize candidates and offer opinions as well as facts about them.

39. Ibid. Most of the italics are in the original. The italics for "opinion" were added by the author. The *Mayrant* case is discussed by William Elliott in "Stenographic Report" for October 12, 1903, *State,* October 13, 1903, 3.

40. Black, *Handbook of American Constitutional Law,* sec. 164: 472–73 (emphasis added). See also Cooley, *A Treatise on the Constitutional Limitations,* 596.

41. *Mayrant,* 10 S.C.L. (1 Nott and McC) 347.

42. Closing argument of Elliott, "Stenographic Report" for October 12, 1903, *State,* October 13, 1903, 3.

43. Ibid. A version of William Elliott's closing argument may be found in the South Caroliniana Library at the University of South Carolina, Columbia. That version does not contain Elliott's responses to defense attorney George Rembert's argument (which immediately preceded his), which are found in the "Stenographic Report."

44. See "Johnstone, George," *Biographical Directory of the United States Congress,* http://bioguide.congress.gov/ (accessed January 28, 2013). Johnstone served as president of the South Carolina Bar in 1909. Tillman's defense team included two other attorneys who had been, or would be, bar president. George W. Croft was president in 1901, and Patrick H. Nelson in 1911–12. See Rogers, *Generations of Lawyers,* 126.

45. Closing argument by defense attorney George Johnstone, "Stenographic Report" for October 12, 1903, *State,* October 14, 1903, 9.

46. Ibid.

47. Ibid. The editorials put in evidence by the defense are reprinted in "Editorials Read for the Defense," *State,* October 9, 1903, 9–10.

48. Closing argument of George Johnstone, "Stenographic Report" for October 12, 1903, *State,* October 14, 1903, 9.

49. "The Capitol of the State: The Tillman Trial from a Financial Point of View," *Charleston News and Courier,* June 27, 1903, 2.

50. *Charleston News and Courier,* September 22, 1903, 1, and September 25, 1903, 2 (listing defense counsel).

51. *Charleston News and Courier,* September 22, 1903, 1, listing five attorneys assisting the solicitor. These were private attorneys, but it is not clear whether all were paid by the Gonzales family. William Elliott, Jr., a Gonzales relative, may not have charged for his services.

52. Closing argument of George Johnstone, "Stenographic Report" for October 12, 1903, *State,* October 14, 1903, 9.

53. Wyatt-Brown, *Southern Honor,* 356–57 (noting that would-be leaders had to show their willingness to fight to defend their honor).

54. Closing argument of Johnstone, "Stenographic Report" for October 12, 1903, *State,* October 14, 1903, 9.

55. Ibid. See also Genesis 21:9–21, which describes Ishmael's becoming an outcast, the fate defense counsel George Johnstone said Tillman sought to avoid. But note that

Ishmael's fate was not so stark as Johnstone described it. God watched over him, and he became the father of a nation.

56. Closing argument of Johnstone, "Stenographic Report" for October 12, 1903, *State,* October 14, 1903, 9–10.

57. Ibid. Some of the words are partially obscured by spots. When this occurs and the correctness of the word used is in doubt, a question mark in brackets has been inserted.

58. In Luke 2:13–14 the heavenly host announces peace on earth at the birth of Jesus Christ.

59. Closing arguments of prosecutor E. L. Asbill, "Stenographic Report" for October 12, 1903, *State,* October 14, 1903, 1. Asbill delivered his argument just after Johnstone's, but through an editorial fluke, Asbill's argument and several other defense arguments were printed in the *State* before Johnstone's.

60. Closing argument of defense attorney Patrick H. Nelson, "Stenographic Report" for October 13, 1903, *State,* October 14, 1903, 2–3. Nelson cited McClain, *A Treatise on Criminal Law* as authority for his view that freedom of the press was limited in a political context to commentary about candidates that is made to inform the public, rather than to injure the individual (see sec. 1050–52, 214–18). This treatise does not say that intentionally injurious comments justify the murder of an author, but this seems to be what the defense argument is implying. Furthermore Nelson's quotation focuses on a passage discussing freedom of the press as "understood in England," ignoring the South Carolina Constitution and the American tradition.

61. The role of malice, or spite, in making commentary vulnerable to defamation suits is discussed in two authorities used in South Carolina during the decades just before and after the Tillman case. See Odgers, *A Digest of the Law of Libel and Slander,* 32–42. Although originally written by a British legal scholar, this work was highly influential on American treatises such as Newell, *The Law of Defamation,* 566–78. An example of a case using these authorities is *Black v. State Co.,* 93 S.C. 467, 77 S.E. 51 (S.C. S. Ct. 1913).

62. Closing argument of Patrick H. Nelson, "Stenographic Report" for October 13, 1903, *State,* October 14, 1903, 2–3.

63. Ibid.

64. Ibid., 3. Several authorities discuss this pantheon of "Redeemers," the Tillmans' place in it, and George D. Tillman's role in the constitutional convention of 1895. See Budiansky, *The Bloody Shirt,* 223–26; Foner, *Reconstruction,* 570–75 (on the role of Wade Hampton, Matthew C. Butler, and Martin W. Gary as "Redeemers" during and after the 1876 campaign); Simkins and Woody, *South Carolina During Reconstruction,* 564–69; Kantrowitz, *Ben Tillman,* 53–60 (discussing the roles of George D. Tillman, M. C. Butler, and M. W. Gary in fighting Reconstruction); Simkins, *Pitchfork Ben Tillman,* 56–69 (discussing the campaign of 1876); Underwood, *The Constitution of South Carolina,* 4:75, 93, 119 (examples of George Tillman's actions in the 1895 constitutional convention); ibid., 2:73; Paul R. Begley, "Butler, Matthew Calbraith," in Edgar, ed., *The South Carolina Encyclopedia,* 111; Henry H. Lesesne, "Gary, Martin Witherspoon," in Edgar,

ed., *The South Carolina Encyclopedia,* 361; and Robert K. Ackerman, "Hampton, Wade, III," in ibid., 421–23. To regain white rule, Butler and Gary embraced the so-called Edgefield plan of destroying black voting strength by fraud, intimidation, and violence while Hampton, the gubernatorial candidate whose election signaled the return of white rule, counseled against such tactics. See the excellent recent biography by Andrew, *Wade Hampton,* 379. However, it would seem to be easy for Hampton's policy of "force without violence" to be transformed into violence by less cautious followers (ibid., 386–91). Simkins, *Pitchfork Ben Tillman,* 156, argues that Hampton was unaware of some of the more drastic tactics that had been used to bring him to power in 1876. See also Zuczek, *State of Rebellion,* 159–92 (discussing the "Redeemer" movement in general).

65. "Andrew Crawford," in Richland County Bar Association, *History of the Bar of Richland County, 1790–1948,* 69. See the discussion of the role of the paramilitary groups in the campaign of 1876 and related events in Budiansky, *The Bloody Shirt,* 221–54.

66. Richland County Bar Association, *History of the Bar of Richland County,* 96–97, 149.

67. Closing argument of Andrew Crawford, "Stenographic Report" for October 13, 1903, *State,* October 14, 1903, 3, 5.

68. *South Carolina Criminal Code in 1902,* chap. 9, sec. 108, defined murder as "the killing of any person with malice aforethought, either express or implied."

69. Annotation to ibid., citing *State v. Doig,* 31 S.C.L. (2 Rich.) 179 (1845).

70. Annotation to ibid., citing *State v. Sullivan,* 43 S.C. 205; 21 S.E. 4 (1895). See also Wharton, *A Treatise on the Law of Evidence in Criminal Issues* (1880), sec. 734: 589 (stressing the importance of proving intent rather than relying on theoretical presumptions, such as that the mere act of the killing gives rise to a presumption of malicious intent, since such presumptions do not always stand up during a hard fought case.)

71. Closing argument of Crawford, "Stenographic Report" for October 13, 1903, *State,* October 14, 1903, 3, 5.

72. *Charleston News and Courier,* October 14, 1903, 1.

73. Closing argument of George W. Croft, "Stenographic Report" for October 13–14, 1903, *State,* October 15, 1903, 1.

74. For some rough Ben Tillman campaign rhetoric that might not be protected speech under the limited view of free speech espoused by James H. Tillman's defense counsel, see Ben Tillman's remarks about ministers who opposed his liquor policies (Simkins, *Pitchfork Ben Tillman,* 378).

75. Closing argument of Croft, "Stenographic Report" for October 13, 1903, *State,* October 15, 1903, 1–2.

76. McKee, "The Shooting of Charles de Young," 271–84 ("bawdy house breeding" quote, 281).

77. *State,* September 5, 1902, 1.

78. The Marriott shooting is discussed in a biography of Hiram Johnson, Marriott's lawyer in the civil suit and later California governor and U.S. senator (Weatherson and Bochin, *Hiram Johnson,* 12). See also McKee, "The Background and Early Career of Hiram Warren Johnson."

79. See Carver, *Brann and the Iconoclast,* 140–41, 178–80.

80. Closing argument of Croft, "Stenographic Report" for October 13, 1903, *State,* October 15, 1903, 1.

81. Ibid., 2. See Rubin, *South Carolina Scalawags,* xii ("a scalawag, on the other hand, was a white southerner who joined with former slaves and voted for the Republican Party, thus incurring the enmity of his Democratic and white supremacist neighbors"), and Foner, *Reconstruction: America's Unfinished Revolution,* 297–99 (discussing the role of "scalawags" in Reconstruction politics). Foner notes that most white southerners considered "southern-born white Republicans" to be "lepers" in the community, "even more reprehensible than the hated carpetbaggers," and that they were "castigated by their opponents as 'white Negroes'" (ibid., 297). See also Zuczek, *State of Rebellion,* 53, 71–72, 153 (describing the contempt with which many white South Carolinians held scalawags).

82. Cross-examination of August Kohn by George W. Croft, "Stenographic Report" for October 2, 1903, *State,* October 3, 1903, 1. Both Nelson and Croft participated in the cross-examination.

83. Closing argument of George W. Croft, "Stenographic Report" for October 13–14, 1903, *State,* October 15, 1903, 2.

84. Closing argument of G. Duncan Bellinger, ibid., 2–3.

85. Ibid., 3.

86. Ibid.

Chapter 8. The Verdict

1. Charge to the jury by Judge Frank Gary, "Stenographic Report" for October 14, 1903, *State,* October 15, 1903, 3, 5 (hereafter "judge's charge).

2. Ibid., 3. See Figg, "Limitations on Trial Judge's Commenting," 215. Examples of cases enforcing the constitutional provisions forbidding judges to charge juries as to the testimony are *State v. White,* 15 S.C. 381, 1881 WL 5906 (S.C. S. Ct, 1881) and *State v. Green,* 48 S.C. 136, 26 S.E. 234 (S.C. S. Ct. 1897). For a discussion of the historical diminution of the power of judges to charge the jury on the facts, see *Norris v. Clinkscales,* 47 S.C. 488, 25 S.E. 797 (S.C. S. Ct. 1896). The constitutional provisions quoted are South Carolina Constitution of 1868, art. IV, sec. 26, and South Carolina Constitution of 1895, art. V, sec. 26 (renumbered in 1985 to be art. V., sec. 21).

3. Judge's charge, 5.

4. Ibid. Judge Gary's definition of murder is a near quote of section 108 of chapter 9 in the *South Carolina Criminal Code in 1902.* Where he deviated from the code language, I have placed the statutory language in brackets. For an example of proper instructions to a jury on a murder charge, see Anderson, *South Carolina Requests to Charge,* 35–38. See also McAninch, Fairey, and Coggiola, *The Criminal Law of South Carolina,* 85–86 (discussing the definition of murder).

5. Judge's charge, 5. This definition is similar to one used in *State v. Doig,* 31 S.C.L. (2 Rich.) 179, 182 (1845), in which the court said that "malice is a term of art, importing wickedness and excluding a just cause or excuse."

6. Judge's charge, 5.

7. Ibid.

8. Ibid. A question mark in brackets has been inserted where the print in the record is not clear.

9. See Judge Gary's discussion of the lawyers' request for charges in ibid. For examples of requests for charges by counsel, see requests by prosecutor Andrew Crawford in "Stenographic Report" for October 13, 1903, *State,* October 14, 1903, 3, and by defense counsel Patrick Nelson, in ibid., 1–2.

10. Judge's charge, 5 (emphasis added). In his discussion of the judge's charge to the jury on self-defense, Judge Ralph King Anderson, Jr., notes: "A defendant in a self-defense case, has the right to act on appearances" (Anderson, *South Carolina Requests to Charge,* 457–58); see also McAninch, Fairey, and Coggiola, *The Criminal Law of South Carolina,* 537–50, which states: "If a person reasonably believes he is in danger of death or serious bodily harm, then he is entitled to defend with deadly force if it appears reasonably necessary." (546). A highly regarded South Carolina circuit judge, L. D. Lide, who was on the bench from 1938 to 1948, compiled his charges into Judge Lide's Notebook, University of South Carolina Law Library, Columbia. His instructions were much respected by other judges, and his notebook was used by later judges. He based his charges on historical as well as contemporary case law. His self-defense charge is set forth on page 78 and is similar to the charge used by Judge Gary, but Lide did not go to the extreme Gary did in making even minor social contacts between victim and assailant relevant to looking at the totality of the circumstances in determining whether the defendant appeared to be in danger. See also Hubbard, *Jury Instructions for Criminal Cases,* 61–85 (jury instructions relating to murder) and 265–297 (self-defense). Professor Hubbard's book is especially helpful in grasping the defense's task in requesting charges on self-defense.

11. Judge's charge, 5.

12. Ibid.

13. *New York World,* October 16, 1903, 4; *Charleston News and Courier,* October 16, 1903, 1 (describing the jury deliberations, the verdict, and the reactions to it immediately after its rendition). See also *Atlanta Constitution,* October 16, 1903, 7.

14. *New York World,* October 16, 1903, 4.

15. *Charleston News and Courier,* October 16, 1903, 1.

16. *New York World,* October 16, 1903, 4; *Charleston News and Courier,* October 16, 1903, 1.

17. *New York World,* October 16, 1903, 4.

18. Ibid.

19. *Charleston News and Courier,* October 16, 1903, 1; *New York World,* October 16, 1903, 4.

20. *New York World,* October 16, 1903, 4. The verdict is recorded in General Sessions Journal, 1896–1904, Lexington County, September term 1903, Thursday, October 15, 1903, 458. The *Augusta Chronicle,* October 16, 1903, 2, described the reaction to the verdict by the pro-Tillman claque in the courtroom as euphoric.

21. *Charleston News and Courier,* October 16, 1903, 1, *New York World,* October 16, 1903, 4.

22. *New York World,* October 16, 1903, 4, *Atlanta Constitution,* October 16, 1903, 7.

23. *Charleston News and Courier,* October 16, 1903, 1.

24. *New York World,* October 16, 1903, 4.

25. Ibid.; *Charleston News and Courier,* October 16, 1903, 1 (indicating that Senator Tillman was not present when the jury verdict was announced); *State,* October 15, 1903, 1 (indicating "Senator Tillman Present during Closing Hours of Trial"); and *Atlanta Constitution,* October 16, 1903, 7 (indicating that Senator Tillman was not present at the announcement of the verdict but was informed by telegram).

26. *Charleston News and Courier,* October 16, 1903, 1. The judge's order releasing Tillman from custody is recorded in General Sessions Journal, 1896–1904, Lexington County, October 15, 1903, 462.

27. *Charleston News and Courier,* October 16, 1903, 1.

28. *Spartanburg Journal,* October 22, 1903, 4. Risinger's letter was probably in response to an editorial published the day after the verdict was rendered. In that editorial the jurors were named in order "to place in the pillory of public scorn and contempt" those responsible for what the paper called "the outrageous verdict rendered yesterday in Lexington" (editorial, "Where the Responsibility Lies," *Spartanburg Journal,* October 16, 1903, 4).

29. *Spartanburg Journal,* October 29, 1903, 8, quoting the *Richmond News Leader,* which makes particularly useful observations on the jury's misconception of its role as permitting it to be a supercensor.

30. Wyatt-Brown, *Southern Honor,* 366.

31. See Nisbett and Cohen, *Culture of Honor,* 39.

32. Woods, "Lawlessness and Patriotism," in South Carolina Bar Association, *Transactions of the Tenth Annual Meeting* (1903), 69–86. Wood's remarks carry extra weight in historical perspective because he later became a distinguished judge, first on the South Carolina Supreme Court (1903), and later on the United States Court of Appeals (1913). See Rogers, *Generations of Lawyers,* 128–29.

33. Ibid., 74–75, 78.

34. See "Acquittal of Tillman," *New York Times,* October 16, 1903.

35. Compare the concealed weapons statutes act no. 251 (no. 34) of February 17, 1897, *South Carolina Statutes at Large, 1897,* 22:423–24, and act no. 362 of December 24, 1880, *South Carolina Statutes at Large, 1880,* 17:447–48.

36. Act no. 251 of 1897, sec. 2. These concealed weapons provisions were codified in the *South Carolina Criminal Code in 1902,* 2 (criminal law), sec. 130–31: 275–76.

37. Edgar, *South Carolina: A History,* 468.

38. Ramage, "Homicide in the Southern States," 213–14, discussed in Ayers, *Vengeance and Justice,* 10.

39. Kernan, "The Jurisprudence of Lawlessness," 450, 452.

40. Ayers, *Vengeance and Justice,* 268, 343, quoting Professor F. C. Woodward, *Nation* 36 (February 22, 1883): 170.

41. Brearley, "The Pattern of Violence," 678, 687. See Brearley, *Homicide in the United States,* 51 (discussing unwritten laws or folkways that were at odds with written homicide laws in the South). The quote from Shaler is found in Shaler, "The Peculiarities of the South," 477, 488. See also McWhiney, *Cracker Culture,* 163 (tendency of juries to acquit on the basis of spurious pleas of self-defense when it was a common practice to go armed).

42. On the "peculiarly Southern disposition to use force to settle personal, sectional and national grievances," see Reed, "To Live and Die in Dixie," 429–430. Hackney, "Southern Violence," 906, 925, attributes the southerner's disposition toward violence to a feeling of persecution by powerful outside forces beyond his control. This attitude removes feelings of personal responsibility and guilt. In 1880 one scholar noted that "measured by relative population, however, we find that murder and manslaughter among the white people of South Carolina to be more than fifteen hundred percent more frequent than among the American-born citizens of New England" (Redfield, *Homicide,* 86).

43. Woods, "Lawlessness and Patriotism," 80.

44. See Budiansky, *The Bloody Shirt,* 221–54; see also Simkins, *Pitchfork Ben Tillman,* 57–69, and Kantrowitz, *Ben Tillman,* 53–79. In "White Supremacist Justice and the Rule of Law" Kantrowitz discusses the historical context that spawned so-called honorable killings. Zuczek, *State of Rebellion,* 159–92, 206–8, discusses the use of violence and intimidation as a means of regaining white rule. See also Andrew, *Wade Hampton,* 369–91.

45. *Boston Transcript,* quoted in *Spartanburg Journal,* October 19, 1903, 3.

46. *Cincinnati Enquirer,* reprinted in *Charleston News and Courier,* October 20, 1903, 5.

47. *Washington Post,* October 17, 1903, 6.

48. *Washington Post* editorial, reprinted in *Greenville Daily News,* October 18, 1903, 6.

49. Arthur A. Schomburg, letter to the editor, *New York Times,* October 18, 1903, 25.

50. See "The Acquittal of Tillman," *New York Times,* October 16, 1903, 6.

51. "South Carolina Is Convicted," *New York World,* October 16, 1903, 6.

52. *Chicago Daily Tribune,* October 21, 1903, 12.

53. The *Philadelphia Public Ledger*'s views are discussed in *Washington Post,* October 17, 1903, 6.

54. *Baptist Courier,* October 22, 1903, 4. For basic facts about the *Baptist Courier* see Moore, *South Carolina Newspapers,* 118, 195.

55. *Southern Christian Advocate* (South Carolina Conference of the Methodist Episcopal Church, South), October 22, 1903, 1. For basic facts about the *Southern Christian Advocate,* see Moore, *South Carolina Newspapers,* 16, 59, 126, 189, 210, 226.

56. See "The Acquittal of Tillman," *Spartanburg Journal,* October 15, 1903, 4, and "Where Responsibility Lies," *Spartanburg Journal,* October 16, 1903, 4.

57. "Not Guilty," *Charleston News and Courier,* October 16, 1903, 4.

58. *Johnston News,* reprinted in *State,* October 23, 1903, 2.

59. *State,* October 16, 1903, 1, 5. Ball's distrust of populist political movements as betraying South Carolina's tradition of rule by an educated elite and his antagonism toward Benjamin R. Tillman for undermining that tradition by his 1890 overthrow of the Bourbons are discussed in Stark, *Damned Upcountryman,* 5, 21, 26, 74, 84–85. See also Holden, *In the Great Maelstrom,* 11–12, 86, 97, 104–5, 109–10 (discussing Ball's conservative political beliefs). In *The State That Forgot,* 15, 149, Ball showed his antidemocratic views by referring to democracy as a "foreign poison." His disdain of the Tillman movement is shown by his reference to it as "The Agrarian Jehad" (ibid., 202).

60. For the text of William Watts Ball's July 27, 1913, address to the South Carolina Press Association, see "The Freedom of the Press in South Carolina and Its Limitations," in *The Editor and the Republic,* 12, 20–21.

61. *Gafney Ledger,* October 20, 1903, 2. For basic facts about the *Gaffney Ledger,* see Moore, *South Carolina Newspapers,* 71.

62. *Abbeville Medium,* October 22, 1903, 2.

63. *Augusta Chronicle,* October 16, 1903, 1 (describing the reaction to the verdict in Lexington). See also two *Chronicle* editorials: "The Chronicle and the Tillman Verdict," ibid., October 20, 1903, 4, and "The Verdict at Lexington," ibid., October 17, 1903, 4.

64. *Virginia Law Register* 9 (October 1903): 567.

65. Speech of Dr. Charles Dabney, quoted in "Travesty of Justice," *Charleston News and Courier,* October 16, 1903, 1.

66. Summerville, *The Carmack-Cooper Shooting,* 1–43, 123. See also Majors, *Editorial Wild Oats,* 139–57.

67. *Atlanta News,* quoted in *Spartanburg Journal,* October 19, 1903, 3.

68. *Americus Georgia Times-Recorder,* quoted in *State,* October 29, 1903, 8.

69. "Verdicts That Cheapen Life," *Atlanta Constitution,* October 16, 1903, 6–7.

70. See "An Everlasting Shame," *Memphis News,* reprinted in *Charleston News and Courier,* October 18, 1903, 14.

71. A. B. Williams, "The Liberty of the Press," *Richmond News Leader,* reprinted in *Greenville Daily News,* October 17, 1903, 5.

72. "Tillman Free and Boomed for Governor," *New York World,* October 16, 1903, 4.

73. *Edgefield Advertiser,* October 21, 1903, 2.

74. "James H. Tillman Up for Congress," *Augusta Chronicle,* March 16, 1904, 2. See also "J. H. Tillman for Congress," *New York Times,* March 16, 1904, 1, and "J. H. Tillman Will Not Go to Congress," *New York Times,* March 18, 1904, 2.

75. "Col. Tillman Will Not Be a Candidate for Congress," *Edgefield Advertiser,* June 6, 1906, 2.

76. Editorials and sermons called Tillman a coward, ruffian, or assassin—or used similarly pejorative terms—for killing Gonzales. Editorials: "The Work of a Ruffian," *Greenville Daily News,* January 16, 1903, 4; "Shoot Again, You Coward!" *Houston Chronicle,* January 17, 1903, 4; "A Cowardly Assassin," *New York Times,* January 17, 1903, 8; "Another Tillman Escapade," *Detroit Free Press,* January 17, 1903, 4; "The Dead and

the Living," *News and Courier,* January 20, 1903, 4; "Fatal Pistol Politics," *New Orleans Daily Picayune,* January 20, 1903, 6; "Tillman, Assassin," *Philadelphia Inquirer,* January 21, 1903, 8; "The Columbia Tragedy," *Bamberg Herald,* January 22, 1903, 2; "A Cowardly Murder," *Sumter Herald,* January 23, 1903, 4; untitled editorial, *Gaffney Ledger,* January 27, 1903, 2; "Acquittal of Tillman," *Spartanburg Journal,* October 15, 1903, 4; "Tillman Acquitted," *Los Angeles Daily Times,* October 16, 1903, 6; "A Travesty on Justice," *Sumter Herald,* October 16, 1903, 3; "South Carolina and Assassination," *Philadelphia Inquirer,* October 17, 1903, 8; "Shame of the Tillman Verdict," *New York Press,* republished in *Charleston News and Courier,* October 18, 1903, 14; "A Disgrace to South Carolina," *Nashville American,* republished in *Charleston News and Courier,* October 18, 1903, 14; "The Aspect of Cold-Blooded Assassination," *Nashville News,* republished in *Charleston News and Courier,* October 19, 1903, 5; "A Standing Invitation to the Murderer," *Norfolk Virginian-Pilot,* republished in *Charleston News and Courier,* October 19, 1903, 5; "What Might Have Been Expected," *St. Paul Pioneer Press,* republished in *Charleston News and Courier,* October 20, 1903, 5; untitled editorial, *Lynchburg Times,* republished in *Lancaster Ledger,* October 21, 1903, 2. Sermons: "Crime and Lawlessness," *News and Courier,*" January 20, 1903, 5 (sermon by Rev. J. A. B. Scherer, St. Andrews Lutheran Church); "Lawlessness in the State," *News and Courier,* January 26, 1903, 3 (sermon by Rev. E. O. Watson, Bethel M. E. Church); "What it Means," *News and Courier,* October 19, 1903, 5 (sermon by Rev. J. S. Moffatt, Chester, S.C.); *Lancaster Ledger,* October 21, 1903, 2 (sermon by Rev. J. W. Powers, Baptist church, Georgetown); "A Time to Speak," *Lancaster Ledger,* October 21, 1903, 2 (letter of the Rev. J. H. Tillinghast, Zion Church, Eastover, S.C.); "Denounced from the Pulpit," *News and Courier,* October 22, 1903, 6 (sermons by W. B. Oliver, First Baptist Church, Florence, and Methodist minister J. G. Beckwith); "The Need of Our Time is a Vision of God," *Lancaster Ledger,* October 28, 1903, 2 (sermon by the Rev. W. C. Winn, Tabernacle Methodist Church, Kingstree, S.C.); "Out Damned Spot," *Gaffney Ledger,* October 20, 1903, 2 (sermon by Rev. C. C. Brown, First Baptist Church, Sumter, S.C.).

77. Moore, *Carnival of Blood,* 122–23.

78. The passage quoted is from "Death Claims J. H. Tillman," *Charleston News and Courier,* April 2, 1911, 1, quoting a 1908 piece from the *Edgefield News.*

79. "Death Claims J. H. Tillman," *Charleston News and Courier,* April 2, 1911, 1 (listing only a doctor and nurse as present at Tillman's death); "Col. Jas. H. Tillman Dies in Ashville," *Newberry Herald,* April 4, 1911, 2 (only physician and nurse present); "James H. Tillman Dead," *Edgefield Chronicle,* April 6, 1911, 5 (reporting the presence of nephew Tillman Bunch at time of death); "Col. Tillman Dying Alone," *Washington Post,* January 17, 1911, 1 (reporting that four months before his death, Tillman was living in a four-room cottage unable to sit up in bed, attended only by a nurse, and out of contact with his family). See also Moore, *Carnival of Blood,* 122–23. For information on Tillman's wife, see "Mamie Norris Tillman (1875–1962)," in Edgefield County Historical Society, "The Spirit of Edgefield." See also "Mrs. M. N. Tillman Claimed by Death." *Edgefield Advertiser,* February 7, 1962, 1.

80. Pierce, *Palmettos and Oaks,* 61–84. The terse death notice for Tillman is in *State,* April 2, 1911, 1. On N. G. Gonzales's editorial legacy, see Jones, *Stormy Petrel,* 245–70, and Matthews, "N. G. Gonzales," 185–95. The editorial direction of the *State* after N. G. Gonzales's death is discussed in Jean Kennedy Todd, "The Editorial Policy of the State." See also Jones, "The Second Epoch of the *State*" (noting that the paper continued to advocate many causes favored by N. G. Gonzales, such as child-labor laws and improved education and transportation, and it continued its opposition to lynching, the dispensary, and mixing of the races).

BIBLIOGRAPHY

Archival Sources

The Diaries of W. W. Ball, vol. 3, December 18, 1916–June 16, 1918. Perkins Library, Rare Book, Manuscript, and Special Collections Library, Duke University, Durham, N.C.

Iverson Brookes Papers, South Caroliniana Library, University of South Carolina, Columbia, S.C.

Francis Warrington Dawson, Letterpress Book II, May 25, 1884–October 15, 1887, Charleston, S.C. Perkins Library, Rare Book, Manuscript, and Special Collections Library, Duke University, Durham, N.C.

Elliott, William. [Speech of William Elliott against James Tillman during the trial of Tillman for shooting N. G. Gonzales], South Caroliniana Library, University of South Carolina, Columbia, S.C.

Elliott/Gonzales Papers, Southern Historical Collection, Wilson Library, University of North Carolina, Chapel Hill, N.C.

Mabel Trott Fitzsimons, "Hot Words and Hair Triggers." South Caroliniana Library, University of South Carolina, Columbia, S.C., manuscript fiche m. 44.

General Sessions Journal, Edgefield County Judge of Probate Records, 1838–1847, typescript. South Carolina Department of Archives and History, Columbia, S.C.

General Sessions Journal, 1896–1904, Lexington County, South Carolina Department of Archives and History, Columbia, S.C.

N. G. Gonzales Papers, South Caroliniana Library, University of South Carolina, Columbia, S.C.

Gonzales-Tillman Scrapbooks (1903), newspaper clippings concerning the murder of N. G. Gonzales and the trial of James H. Tillman, 3 vols., South Caroliniana Library, University of South Carolina, Columbia, S.C.

Hemphill Family Papers. Perkins Library, Rare Book, Manuscript, and Special Collections Library, Duke University, Durham, N.C.

James Ward Hopkins Scrapbook, 1850–1862, Manuscript Collection, South Caroliniana Library, University of South Carolina, Columbia, S.C.

James A. Hoyt Papers, South Caroliniana Library, University of South Carolina, Columbia, S.C.

Robert Lathan Papers, 1898–1970 (25/188/1), South Carolina Historical Society, Charleston, S.C.

Judge Lide's Notebook (unpublished material), University of South Carolina Law Library, Columbia, S.C.

Memorial of John James Negrin, November 23, 1805, General Assembly Petitions, No-1886-01. South Carolina Department of Archives and History, Columbia, S.C.

Memorial Exercises in Honor of Frank Boyd Gary, Judge of the Eighth Circuit, before the Supreme Court of South Carolina (1923), South Caroliniana Library, University of South Carolina, Columbia, S.C.

Savannah Press, Gonzales-Tillman Scrapbooks (1903), newspaper clippings concerning the murder of N. G. Gonzales and the trial of James H. Tillman, 3 vols., South Caroliniana Library, University of South Carolina, Columbia, S.C.

Schomburg Center for Research in Black Culture, New York Public Library, New York, N.Y.

Francis Butler Simkins Papers, Southern Historical Collection, Wilson Library, University of North Carolina, Chapel Hill, N.C.

South Carolina Constitutions of 1776, 1778, 1790, 1861, 1865, 1868, and 1895, South Carolina Department of Archives and History, Columbia, S.C.; South Caroliniana Library and the Coleman Karesh Law Library, University of South Carolina, Columbia, S.C. Unless otherwise specified, references to the 1895 Constitution are to that document as it existed at the time of the trial in 1903.

State v. Body of J. H. Christian, Coroner Inquest Report, July 21, 1856, Edgefield County, South Carolina Department of Archives and History, Columbia, S.C.

J. W. Thurmond Papers, South Caroliniana Library, University of South Carolina, Columbia, S.C.

Tillman Incoming Correspondence (series 7). Special Collections, Clemson University, Clemson, S.C.

Tillman Outgoing Correspondence (series 7). Special Collections, Clemson University, Clemson, S.C.

Newspapers

Abbeville Bulletin.

Abbeville Medium.

Abbeville Press and Banner.

Aiken Journal and Review.

Americus (Georgia) Times-Recorder.

Anderson Intelligencer.

Atlanta Constitution.

Atlanta Journal.

Atlanta News.

Augusta Chronicle.

Bamberg Herald.

Baptist Courier.
Boston Transcript.
Charleston City Gazette and Daily Advertiser.
Charleston Courier.
Charleston Evening Post.
Charleston Mercury.
Charleston News and Courier.
Chicago Daily Tribune.
Cincinnati Enquirer.
Columbia Daily Phoenix.
Columbia Daily Register.
Columbia Evening Record.
Columbia Register.
Columbia Union-Herald.
Detroit Free Press.
Edgefield Advertiser.
Edgefield Chronicle.
Gaffney Ledger.
Greenville Daily News.
Houston Chronicle.
Johnston News.
Lancaster Ledger.
Lexington Dispatch.
Los Angeles Daily Times.
Lynchburg Times.
Memphis Daily Appeal.
Memphis News.
Montgomery Advertiser.
Nashville American.
Nashville News.
New Orleans Daily Picayune.
New York Press.
New York Times.
New York World.
Norfolk VirginianPilot.
Pennsylvania Gazette.
Philadelphia Inquirer.
Philadelphia Public Ledger.
Richmond News Leader.
St. Paul Pioneer Press.
Southern Christian Advocate.
Spartanburg Journal.

State (Columbia, S.C.).
Sumter Herald.
Virginia Law Register.
Washington Post.

Other Primary Sources

South Carolina. *Code of Laws of South Carolina.* Vol. 7A. Minneapolis: Thomson West, 1985.

———. *General Statutes and the Code of Civil Procedure of the State of South Carolina Adopted by the General Assembly of 1881–82.* Columbia: Printed by James Woodrow, 1882.

———. *South Carolina Criminal Code in 1902.* Vol. 2: *Code of Civil Procedure and Criminal Code.* Columbia: The State Company, 1902.

———. *South Carolina Statutes at Large.* Vol. 17: 1880. Columbia: Printed by James Woodrow, 1881.

———. *South Carolina Statutes at Large.* Vol. 22: 1897. Columbia: Printed by Charles Calvo, Jr., 1897.

———. *South Carolina Statutes at Large.* Vol. 24: 1903. Columbia: The State Company, 1903.

———. *The Statutes at Large of South Carolina.* Vol. 5. Edited by Thomas Cooper. Columbia: Printed by A. S. Johnston, 1839.

———. *Statutes at Large of South Carolina.* Vols. 6 and 7. Edited by David McCord. Columbia: Printed by A. S. Johnston, 1839, 1840.

———. *Statutes at Large of the State of South Carolina.* Vol. 12: 1850–61. Columbia: Republican Printing, 1874.

———. *The Statutes of South Carolina.* Vol. 14. Reprint, Columbia: Republican Printing, 1873.

South Carolina at the Elections of 1875 and 1876, [investigation] Taken under the Resolution of the Senate of December 5, 1876. Vol. 1. Washington, D.C.: U.S. Government Printing Office, 1877.

South Carolina Bar Association. *Transactions of the Eighteenth Annual Meeting, January 26 and 27, 1911.* Columbia: R. L. Bryan, 1911.

———. *Transactions of the Nineteenth Annual Meeting, January Twenty-fourth and Twenty-fifth, Nineteen Hundred and Twelve.* Columbia: R. L. Bryan, 1912.

———. *Transactions of the Tenth Annual Meeting of the South Carolina Bar Association, January 15–16, 1903.* Columbia: R. L. Bryan, 1903.

———. *Transactions of the Twelfth Annual Meeting of the South Carolina Bar Association, January 19–20, 1905.* Columbia: R. L. Bryan, 1905.

South Carolina Constitutional Convention (1868). *Proceedings of the Constitutional Convention of South Carolina.* Charleston: Printed by Denny & Perry, 1868.

South Carolina Constitutional Convention (1895). *Journal of the Constitutional Convention of the State of South Carolina.* Columbia: C. A. Calvo, 1895.

South Carolina General Assembly. *Acts and Joint Resolutions of the General Assembly of South Carolina Passed at the Regular Session of 1880.* Columbia: Printed by James Woodrow, 1881.

———. *Acts and Joint Resolutions of the General Assembly of South Carolina, Regular Session, 1892.* Columbia: Printed by Charles A. Calvo, Jr., 1892.

———. *Acts and Joint Resolutions of the General Assembly of South Carolina, Regular Session, 1893.* Columbia: Printed by Charles A. Calvo, Jr., 1893.

South Carolina General Assembly, House of Representatives. *Journal of the House of Representatives of the State of South Carolina Being the Regular Session of 1868.* Columbia: Printed by John W. Denny, 1868.

———. *Journal of the House of Representatives of the State of South Carolina for the Regular Session of 1874–75.* Columbia: Republican Printing, 1875.

———. *Journal of the House of Representatives of the General Assembly of South Carolina Being the Regular Session Commencing November 25, 1890.* Columbia: Printed by James W. Woodrow, 1891.

———. *Journal of the House of Representatives of the General Assembly of the State of South Carolina, Regular Session commencing November 27, 1894.* Columbia: Printed by Charles A. Calvo, 1895.

———. *Journal of the House of Representatives of the General Assembly of the State of South Carolina, Regular Session Beginning Tuesday, January 10, 1911.* Columbia: Printed by Gonzales and Bryan, 1911.

South Carolina General Assembly, Senate. *Journal of the Senate of the General Assembly of the State of South Carolina, Regular Session Beginning Tuesday, Jan. 14, 1902.* Columbia: The State Company, 1902.

———. *Journal of the Senate of the General Assembly of the State of South Carolina, Regular Session Beginning Tuesday, Jan. 13, 1903.* Columbia: The State Company, 1903.

South Carolina, Office of the Attorney General. *Report of D.A. Townsend, Attorney-General of South Carolina, for the Fiscal Year Ending October 31st 1893.* Vol. 1 of *Reports and Resolutions of the General Assembly of the State of South Carolina, Regular Session Commencing Nov. 28, 1893.* Columbia: Printed by Charles A. Calvo, Jr., 1893.

United States Federal Census Records, 1870.

Secondary Sources

Adler, Mortimer J., and Charles Van Doren, *Annals of America,* vol. 1 (1493–1754): 397–417. Chicago: Encyclopaedia Britannica, 1976.

———. "The Trial of John Peter Zenger." In *The Annals of America.*

Alexander, James. *A Brief Narrative of the Case and Trial of John Peter Zenger, Printer of the New York Weekly Journal.* Edited by Stanley Nider Katz. Cambridge Mass.: Harvard University Press, 1963.

Anderson, Ralph King, Jr. *South Carolina Requests to Charge—Criminal.* Columbia, S.C.: South Carolina Bar, 2007.

Andrew, Rod, Jr. *Wade Hampton: Confederate Warrior to Southern Redeemer.* Chapel Hill: University of North Carolina Press, 2008.

Ayers, Edward L. *The Promise of the New South: Life after Reconstruction.* New York: Oxford University Press, 1992; 15th anniversary edition, 2007.

———. *Vengeance and Justice: Crime and Punishment in the 19th Century American South.* New York: Oxford University Press, 1984.

Bailey, N. Louise, Mary Morgan, and Carolyn R. Taylor, eds. *Biographical Directory of the South Carolina Senate, 1776–1985.* 3 vols. Columbia: University of South Carolina Press, 1986.

Ball, William Watts. *The Editor and the Republic: Papers and Addresses of William Watts Ball.* Edited by Anthony Harrigan. Chapel Hill: University of North Carolina Press, 1954.

———. *An Episode in South Carolina Politics.* Columbia, S.C.?, 1915?.

———. *The State That Forgot: South Carolina's Surrender to Democracy.* Indianapolis: Bobbs-Merrill, 1932.

Bass, Jack, and Marilyn W. Thompson. *Ol' Strom: An Unauthorized Biography of Strom Thurmond.* Atlanta: Longstreet Press, 1998.

Billingsley, Andrew. *Yearning to Breathe Free: Robert Smalls of South Carolina and His Families.* Columbia: University of South Carolina Press, 2007.

Black, Henry Campbell. *Handbook of American Constitutional Law.* St. Paul, Minn.: West, 1895.

Brands, H. W. *The First American: The Life and Times of Benjamin Franklin.* New York: Anchor Books, 2000.

Brearley, H. C. *Homicide in the United States.* Chapel Hill: University of North Carolina Press, 1932.

———. "The Pattern of Violence." In *Culture in the South,* edited by W. T. Couch, 678–92. Chapel Hill: University of North Carolina Press, 1935.

Brooks, U. R., ed. *South Carolina Bench and Bar.* Columbia, S.C.: State Co., 1908.

Brown, Richard Maxwell. *Strain of Violence: Historical Studies of American Violence and Vigilantism.* New York: Oxford University Press, 1975.

Budiansky, Stephen. *The Bloody Shirt: Terror after Appomattox.* New York: Viking, 2006.

Bulfinch, Thomas. *Bulfinch's Mythology.* New York: Modern Library, 1993.

Burke, William Lewis, Jr. "A History of the Opening Statement from Barristers to Corporate Lawyers: A Case Study of South Carolina." *American Journal of Legal History* 37 (January 1993): 25–64.

Burns, Eric. *Infamous Scribblers: The Founding Fathers and the Rowdy Beginnings of American Journalism.* New York: Public Affairs, 2006.

Burnside, Ronald D. "The Governorship of Coleman Livingston Blease of South Carolina, 1911–1915." Ph.D. diss., Indiana University, 1963.

Burton, Orville Vernon. *In My Father's House Are Many Mansions: Family and Community in Edgefield, South Carolina.* Chapel Hill: University of North Carolina Press, 1985.

________. Introduction to *Pitchfork Ben Tillman, South Carolinian,* by Francis Butler Simkins, xi–xii. Baton Rouge: Louisiana State University Press, 1944. Reprint, Columbia: University of South Carolina Press, 2002.

———. "Race and Reconstruction: Edgefield County, South Carolina." *Journal of Social History* 12 (Autumn 1978): 31–56.

Butterfield, Fox. *All God's Children: The Bosket Family and the American Tradition of Violence.* New York: Knopf, 1995.

Byrnes, James F., court reporter. "Stenographic Report" of the Tillman trial for September 28–October 14, 1903. *State,* September 29–October 15, 1903.

Carver, Charles. *Brann and the Iconoclast.* Austin: University of Texas Press, 1957.

Cash, W. J. *The Mind of the South.* New York: Knopf, Inc., 1941. Reprint, New York: Vintage, 1991.

Chapman, John A. *History of Edgefield County from the Earliest Settlement to 1897.* Newberry, S.C.: Elbert N. Aull, 1897.

Chiasson, Lloyd, Jr., ed. *The Press in Times of Crisis.* Westport, Conn.: Greenwood Press, 1995.

Clark, E. Culpepper. *Francis Warrington Dawson and the Politics of Restoration, South Carolina 1874–1889.* Tuscaloosa: University of Alabama Press, 1980.

Collins, Danny R. *South Carolina Evidence.* Columbia: South Carolina Bar, 1995.

Conner, James. *The Libel Cases of the News and Courier, The Great Libel Case, Report of the Criminal Prosecution of the News and Courier for Libeling Sheriff and Ex-Congressman C. C. Bowen. The State v. F. W. Dawson.* Charleston, 1875.

Cooley, Thomas M. *A Treatise on the Constitutional Limitations Which Rest upon the Legislative Power of the States of the American Union,* edited by Victor H. Lane. 7th ed. Boston: Little, Brown, 1903.

Cooper, Thomas. *A Treatise on the Law of Libel and the Liberty of the Press: Showing the Origin, Use, and Abuse of the Law of Libel.* New York: G. F. Hopkins, 1830.

Davidson, Elizabeth H. *Child Labor Legislation in the Southern Textile States.* Chapel Hill: University of North Carolina Press, 1939.

Davis, William C. *Rhett: The Turbulent Life and Times of a Fire-Eater.* Columbia: University of South Carolina Press, 2001.

de la Cova, Antonio Rafael. *Cuban Confederate Colonel: The Life of Ambrosio José Gonzales.* Columbia: University of South Carolina Press, 2003.

Donald, David. *Charles Sumner and the Coming of the Civil War.* New York: Knopf, 1960.

Eaton, Clement. *Freedom of Thought in the Old South.* Durham, N.C.: Duke University Press, 1940. Reprint, New York: Peter Smith, 1951.

Edgar, Walter. *South Carolina: A History.* Columbia: University of South Carolina Press, 1998.

———, ed. *Biographical Directory of the South Carolina House of Representatives.* 5 vols. Columbia: University of South Carolina Press, 1974–92.

———, ed. *The South Carolina Encyclopedia.* Columbia: University of South Carolina Press, 2006.

Egerton, Douglas R. *He Shall Go Out Free: The Lives of Denmark Vesey.* Madison, Wis.: Madison House, 1999.

Emerson, Thomas L. *The System of Free Expression.* New York: Random House, 1979.

———. "Toward a General Theory of the First Amendment." *Yale Law Journal* 72 (April 1963): 877–956.

Eubanks, John Evans. *Ben Tillman's Baby: The Dispensary System of South Carolina, 1892–1915.* Augusta, Ga., 1950.

Evarts, Trina J. "Code Duello in the American Southeast: An Evolving Drama." M.A. thesis, University of South Carolina, Columbia, 2000.

Figg, Robert McC., Jr. "Limitations on Trial Judge's Commenting on the Evidence in South Carolina." *South Carolina Law Quarterly* 5 (December 1952): 214–22.

Foner, Eric. *Reconstruction: America's Unfinished Revolution, 1863–1877.* New York: Harper & Row, 1988.

Ford, Lacy K., Jr. *The Origins of Southern Radicalism: The South Carolina Upcountry, 1800–1860.* New York: Oxford University Press, 1988.

———. "Origins of the Edgefield Tradition: The Late Antebellum Experience and the Roots of Political Insurgency." *South Carolina Historical Magazine* 98 (October, 1997): 328–38.

Fox, Robin Lane. *The Classical World: An Epic History from Homer to Hadrian.* New York: Basic Books, 2006.

Franklin, Benjamin. *Writings.* Edited by J. A. Leo Lemay. New York: Library of America 1987.

Fraser, Walter J. *Charleston, Charleston: The History of a Southern City.* Columbia: University of South Carolina Press, 1989.

Freehling, William W. *Prelude to Civil War: The Nullification Controversy in South Carolina.* New York: Harper & Row, 1966.

Freeman, Joanne B. *Affairs of Honor: National Politics in the New Republic.* New Haven: Yale University Press, 2001.

Garlington, J. C., ed. *Men of the Time: Sketches of Living Notables, a Biographical Encyclopedia of Contemporaneous South Carolina Leaders.* Spartanburg, S.C.: Garlington, 1902.

Gergel, Richard, and Belinda Gergel. "'To Vindicate the Cause of the Downtrodden,' Associate Justice Jonathan Jasper Wright and Reconstruction in South Carolina." In *At Freedom's Door: African American Founding Fathers and Lawyers in Reconstruction South Carolina,* edited by James Lowell Underwood and W. Lewis Burke, 36–71. Columbia: University of South Carolina Press, 2000.

Gienapp, William E. "The Crime against Sumner: The Caning of Charles Sumner and the Rise of the Republican Party." *Civil War History* 25 (September 1979): 218–45.

Gonzales, N. G. *In Darkest Cuba: Two Months' Service under Gomez along the Trocha from the Caribbean to the Bahama Channel.* Columbia, S.C.: State Company, 1922.

Goodwin, Doris Kearns. *Team of Rivals: The Political Genius of Abraham Lincoln.* New York: Simon & Schuster, 2005.

Gordon, Thomas. "Of Freedom of Speech: That the Same Is Inseparable from Publick Liberty" (essay no. 15, Saturday, February 4, 1720). In *Cato's Letters,* by John Trenchard and Thomas Gordon, 2 vols., edited by Ronald Hamowy, 1:110–17. Indianapolis: Liberty Fund, 1995.

Grantham, Dewey W. *The Regional Imagination: The South and Recent American History.* Nashville: Vanderbilt University Press, 1979.

Greenberg, Kenneth S. *Honor and Slavery: Lies, Duels, Noses, Masks, Dressing as a Woman, Gifts, Strangers, Humanitarianism, Death, Slave Rebellions, The Proslavery Argument, Baseball, Hunting and Gambling in the Old South.* Princeton, N.J.: Princeton University Press, 1996.

Greenleaf, Simon. *A Treatise on the Law of Evidence,* 16th ed. Vol. 1, edited by John Henry Wigmore. Boston: Little, Brown, 1899.

Hackney, Sheldon. "Southern Violence." *American Historical Review* 74 (February 1969): 906–25.

Hagstette, Todd. "Dueling and Identity: Constructions of Honor Violence in Nineteenth-Century Southern Letters." Ph.D. diss., University of South Carolina, 2010.

Hagy, James W. and Bertrand Van Ruymbeke. "The French Refugee Newspapers of Charleston." *South Carolina Historical Magazine* 97 (April 1996): 139–48.

Hamilton, Edith. *Mythology.* New York: Little, Brown, 1942.

Hatch, J. L. *Rights of Corporators and Reporters: Being a Report of the Case of R. W. Gibbes, Editor of the South Carolinian, vs. E. J. Arthur, Mayor of Columbia, S.C. and John Burdell, Chief of Police.* Columbia, S.C.: Steam-Power Press of R. W. Gibbes 1857.

Hay, George. *An Essay on the Liberty of the Press.* Philadelphia: Aurora Office, 1799. Reprint, New York: Arno/New York Times, 1970.

Hemphill, J. C., ed. *Men of Mark in South Carolina: Ideals of American Life, A Collection of Biographies of Leading Men of the State.* 4 vols. Washington, D.C.: Men of Mark Publishing, 1907–9.

Hendricks, Ellen A. "South Carolina Dispensary System." 2 parts. *North Carolina Historical Review* 22 (April 1945): 176–97; 22 (July 1945): 320–49.

Hennig, Helen Kohn. *August Kohn, Versatile South Carolinian.* Columbia, S.C.: Vogue Press, 1949.

Holden, Charles J. *In the Great Maelstrom: Conservatives in Post–Civil War South Carolina.* Columbia: University of South Carolina Press, 2002.

Howe, Daniel Walker. *What Hath God Wrought: The Transformation of America, 1815–1848.* New York: Oxford University Press, 2007.

Hubbard, F. Patrick. *Jury Instructions for Criminal Cases in South Carolina: Defendants' Requested Instructions.* 2d ed. Columbia: South Carolina Bar, 2001.

Hudson, Joshua Henry. *Sketches and Reminiscences.* Columbia: State Co., 1903.

Ione, Carole. *Pride of Family: Four Generations of American Women of Color.* New York: Summit Books, 1991.

Isaacson, Walter. *Benjamin Franklin: An American Life.* New York: Simon & Schuster 2003.

Johnson, Paul. *A History of the American People.* New York: HarperCollins, 1998.

Jones, Lewis Pinckney. "Ambrosio José Gonzales: A Cuban Patriot in Carolina." *South Carolina Historical Magazine* 56 (April 1955): 67–76.

———. "The Second Epoch of the *State,* 1903–1913." In *South Carolina Journals and Journalists,* edited by James B. Meriwether, 17, 24–31. Spartanburg S.C.: Reprint Co. 1975.

———. *Stormy Petrel: N. G. Gonzales and His State.* Columbia: University of South Carolina Press, 1973.

———. "The Word War between Cole Blease and the Gonzaleses." *South Carolina Illustrated History* 1 (May 1970): 4–12, 52–55.

Kahn, Justin. *South Carolina Evidence Handbook.* Annotated 5th ed. Columbia: South Carolina Bar, 2009.

Kantrowitz, Stephen. *Ben Tillman and the Reconstruction of White Supremacy.* Chapel Hill: University of North Carolina Press, 2000.

———. "White Supremacist Justice and the Rule of Law: Lynching, Honor, and the State in Ben Tillman's South Carolina." In *Men and Violence: Gender, Honor and Rituals in Modern Europe and America,* edited by Pieter Spierenburg, 213–39. Columbus: Ohio State Press 1998.

Kernan, Thomas J. "The Jurisprudence of Lawlessness: A Paper Read before the American Bar Association at St. Paul, August 30, 1906." *Report of the Twenty-Ninth Annual Meeting of the American Bar Association,* part 1: 450–67. Philadelphia: Dando Printing and Publishing, 1906.

Ketcham, Ralph. *James Madison: A Biography.* Charlottesville: University Press of Virginia, 1990.

Kibler, Lillian Adele. *Benjamin F. Perry, South Carolina Unionist.* Durham, N.C.: Duke University Press, 1946.

King, William L. *The Newspaper Press of Charleston, S.C.* Charleston: Lucas & Richardson, 1882.

LaFave, Wayne R., Jerold H. Israel, Nancy J. King, and Orin S. Kerr. *Criminal Procedure.* Vol. 6. Minneapolis: Thomson/West, 2007.

Latimer, S. L. *The Story of the* State, *1891–1969, and the Gonzales Brothers.* Columbia: State Printing Co., 1970.

Lee, James Melvin. *History of American Journalism.* Boston & New York: Houghton Mifflin, 1923.

Levy, Leonard. *Emergence of a Free Press.* New York: Oxford University Press, 1985.

Lewis, Anthony. *Freedom for the Thought We Hate: A Biography of the First Amendment.* New York: Basic Books, 2007.

———. *Make No Law: The Sullivan Case and the First Amendment.* New York: Vintage, 1991.

Linder, Doug. "The Trial of John Peter Zenger: An Account." University of Missouri at Kansas City, Famous Trials Project, http://www.law.umkc.edu/faculty/projects/ftrials/zenger/zengeraccount.html (accessed September 26, 2010).

Lisby, Gregory C. "No Place in the Law: The Ignominy of Criminal Libel in American Jurisprudence." *Communication Law and Policy* 9 (Autumn 2004): 433–87.

Longstreet, Augustus Baldwin. "The Fight." In *Georgia Scenes,* 53–64. Nashville J. S. Sanders, 1992.

Madison, James. "Report on the Virginia Resolutions, January 1800." In *The Founders' Constitution,* vol. 5, edited by Philip B. Kurland and Ralph Lerner, 141–46. Chicago: University of Chicago Press, 1987. Reprint, Indianapolis: Liberty Fund, 2000.

Majors, William R. *Editorial Wild Oats: Edward Ward Carmack and Tennessee Politics.* Macon, Ga.: Mercer University Press, 1984.

Malone, Dumas. *The Public Life of Thomas Cooper, 1783–1839.* Columbia: University of South Carolina Press, 1961.

Massachusetts Anti-Slavery Society. *Annual Report Massachusetts Anti-Slavery Society.* 10 vols.: 1833–42. Westport, Conn.: Negro Universities Press, 1970.

Mathis, Robert Neil. "Preston Smith Brooks: The Man and His Image." *South Carolina Historical Magazine* 79 (October 1978): 296–310.

Matthews, Linda McCarter. "N. G. Gonzales, Southern Editor and Crusader, 1858–1903." Ph.D. diss., Duke University, 1971.

Matthewson, Tim. "Jefferson and Haiti." *Journal of Southern History* 61 (May 1995): 209–48.

McAninch, William Shepard, W. Gaston Fairey, and Lesley M. Coggiola. *The Criminal Law of South Carolina.* 5th ed. Columbia: South Carolina Bar, 2007.

McClain, Emlin. *A Treatise on Criminal Law as Now Administered in the United States.* 2 vols. Chicago: Callaghan, 1897.

McKee, Irving. "The Background and Early Career of Hiram Warren Johnson, 1866–1910." *Pacific Historical Review* 19 (February 1950): 17–30.

———. "The Shooting of Charles de Young." *Pacific Historical Review* 16 (August 1947): 271–84.

McNeely, Patricia G. *Fighting Words: The History of the Media in South Carolina.* Columbia: South Carolina Press Association, 1998.

McNeely, Patricia G., Debra Reddin van Tuyll, and Henry H. Schulte, eds. *Knights of the Quill: Confederate Correspondents and Their Civil War Reporting.* West Lafayette, Ind.: Purdue University Press, 2010.

McPherson, James M. *Battle Cry of Freedom: The Civil War Era.* New York: Oxford University Press, 1988.

McWhiney, Grady. *Cracker Culture: Celtic Ways in the Old South.* Tuscaloosa: University of Alabama Press, 1988.

Meiklejohn, Alexander. *Free Speech and Its Relation to Self-Government.* New York: Harper, 1948. Reprint, Port Washington, N.Y.: Kennikat Press, 1972.

Meriwether, James B., ed. *South Carolina Journals and Journalists.* Spartanburg, S.C.: Reprint Co., 1975.

Meriwether, Robert L. "Preston S. Brooks on the Caning of Charles Sumner." *South Carolina Historical and Genealogical Magazine* 52 (January 1951): 1–4.

Miller, Edward A., Jr. *Gullah Statesman: Robert Smalls from Slavery to Congress, 1839–1915.* Columbia: University of South Carolina Press, 1995.

Mims, Eleanor Elizabeth. "The Editors of the *Edgefield Advertiser,* Oldest Newspaper in South Carolina, 1836–1930." M.A. thesis, University of South Carolina, Columbia, 1930.

Moore, John Hammond. *Carnival of Blood: Dueling, Lynching, and Murder in South Carolina, 1880–1920.* Columbia: University of South Carolina Press, 2006.

———. *South Carolina Newspapers.* Columbia: University of South Carolina Press, 1988.

Montgomery, John A. *Columbia, South Carolina: History of a City.* Woodland Hills, Calif.: Windsor, 1979.

Mott, Frank Luther. *American Journalism: A History, 1690–1960.* 3rd ed. New York: Macmillan, 1962.

Mushal, Amanda Reece. "'My Word is My Bond': Honor, Commerce, and Status in the Antebellum South." Ph.D. diss., University of Virginia, 2010.

Newell, Martin L. *The Law of Defamation, Libel and Slander in Civil and Criminal Cases as Administered in the Courts of the United States of America.* Chicago: Callaghan, 1890.

Nimeiri, Ahmed. "Play in Augustus Baldwin Longstreet's *Georgia's Scenes.*" *Southern Literary Journal* 33 (Spring 2001): 51–52.

Nisbett, Richard E., and Dov Cohen. *Culture of Honor: The Psychology of Violence in the South.* Boulder, Colo.: Westview Press, 1996.

Odgers, W. Blake. *A Digest of the Law of Libel and Slander: With the Evidence, Procedure, and Practice, Both in Civil and Criminal Cases, and Precedents and Pleadings.* 1st American ed., edited by Melville M. Bigelow. Boston: Little, Brown, 1881.

Oliphant, Mary C. Simms, and T. C. Duncan Eaves, eds., with additional text by Alexander Moore. *The Letters of William Gilmore Simms.* Expanded edition. 6 vols. Columbia: University of South Carolina Press 2012.

Paquette, Robert L., and Douglas R. Egerton. "Of Facts and Fables: New Light on the Denmark Vesey Affair." *South Carolina Historical Magazine* 105 (January 2004): 8–48.

Park, Roger C., David P. Leonard, Aviva Orenstein, and Steven Goldberg. *Evidence Law: A Student's Guide to the Law of Evidence as Applied in American Trials.* St. Paul Minn.: West, 2011.

Pierce, Robert A. *Palmettos and Oaks: A Centennial History of the* State, *1891–1991.* Columbia: State-Record Co., 1991.

Ramage, B. J. "Homicide in the Southern States." *Sewanee Review* 4 (February 1896): 212–32.

Ramsay, David. *The History of the American Revolution.* 2 vols. 1789. Reprint, edited by Lester H. Cohen. Indianapolis: Liberty Fund, 1990.

Redfield, H. V. *Homicide, North and South.* Philadelphia: Lippincott, 1880.

Reed, John Shelton. "To Live and Die in Dixie: A Contribution to the Study of Southern Violence." *Political Science Quarterly* 86 (September 1971): 429–43.

Reed, Thomas B. *Reed's Rules: A Manual of General Parliamentary Law.* Chicago: Rand, McNally, 1900.

Reynolds, Donald. "Words of War." In *The Press in Times of Crisis,* edited by Lloyd Chiasson, Jr., 97–99. Westport, Conn.: Greenwood Press, 1995.

Richland County Bar Association, History Committee. *History of the Bar of Richland County, 1790–1948.* Columbia, S.C.: Sloane Publishing, 1948.

Robertson, David. *Sly and Able: A Political Biography of James F. Byrnes.* New York: Norton, 1994.

Rogers, George C., Jr. *Generations of Lawyers: A History of the South Carolina Bar.* Columbia: South Carolina Bar Foundation, 1992.

Rosenberg, Norman L. *Protecting the Best Men: An Interpretive History of the Law of Libel.* Chapel Hill: University of North Carolina Press, 1986.

Rowland, Lawrence S., Alexander Moore, and George C. Rogers, Jr. *The History of Beaufort County, South Carolina.* Vol. 1: *1514–1861.* Columbia: University of South Carolina Press, 1996.

Rubin, Hyman, III. *South Carolina Scalawags.* Columbia: University of South Carolina Press, 2006.

Rutherfurd, Livingston. *John Peter Zenger: His Press, His Trial, and a Bibliography of Zenger Imprints.* New York: Dodd, Mead, 1904.

Sass, Herbert Ravenel. *Outspoken: 150 Years of the News and Courier.* Columbia: University of South Carolina Press, 1953.

Savage, W. Sherman. "Abolitionist Literature in the Mails." *Journal of Negro History* 13 (April 1928): 150–84.

Schauer, Frederick F. "Language, Truth and the First Amendment: An Essay in Memory of Harry Canter." *Virginia Law Review* 64 (March 1978): 263–302.

Sewell, Michael. "The Gonzales-Tillman Affair: The Public Conflict of a Politician and a Crusading Newspaper Editor." M.A. thesis, University of South Carolina, 1965.

Shaler, Nathaniel Southgate. "The Peculiarities of the South." *North American Review* 151 (October 1890): 477–88.

Simkins, Francis Butler. *Pitchfork Ben Tillman, South Carolinian.* Baton Rouge: Louisiana State University Press, 1944. Reprint, Columbia: University of South Carolina Press, 2002.

Simkins, Francis Butler, and Robert H. Woody. *South Carolina during Reconstruction.* Chapel Hill: University of North Carolina Press, 1932.

Sinha, Manisha. *The Counterrevolution of Slavery, Politics and Ideology in Antebellum South Carolina.* Chapel Hill: University of North Carolina Press, 2000.

Smith, J. Clay, Jr. "The Reconstruction of Justice Jonathan Jasper Wright." In *At Freedom's Door: African American Founding Fathers and Lawyers in Reconstruction South Carolina,* edited by James Lowell Underwood and W. Lewis Burke, 72–89. Columbia: University of South Carolina Press, 2000.

Snowden, Yates. *History of South Carolina.* 5 vols. Chicago & New York: Lewis, 1920.

Spierenburg, Pieter. *Men and Violence: Gender, Honor and Rituals in Modern Europe and America.* Columbus: Ohio State University Press, 1998.

Stark, John D. *Damned Upcountryman: William Watts Ball, a Study in American Conservatism.* Durham, N.C.: Duke University Press, 1968.

Story, Joseph. *Commentaries on the Constitution of the United States with a Preliminary Review of the Constitutional History of the Colonies and States before the Adoption of the Constitution.* Boston: Hilliard, Gray, 1833.

Summerville, James. *The Carmack-Cooper Shooting: Tennessee Politics Turns Violent, November 9, 1908.* Jefferson, N.C. & London: McFarland, 1994.

Thomas, Isaiah. *The History of Printing in America.* 2 vols. 2nd ed. Albany, N.Y.: Printed by Joel Munsell, 1874.

Thurmond, J. William. *Thurmond's Key Cases.* Columbia, S.C.: R. L. Bryan, 1930.

Tillman, James David, Jr. *Tillman & Hamilton Family Records with Their Many Ancestral Lineages.* 3 vols. Meridian, Miss.: Privately printed, 1963.

Tillman, Stephen Frederick. *The Tillman Family.* Richmond, Va.: William Bird Press, 1930.

Todd, Jean Kennedy. "The Editorial Policy of the *State* Newspaper, 1903–1913." M.A. thesis, University of South Carolina, 1948.

Todd, Leonard. *Carolina Clay: The Life and Legend of the Slave Potter Dave.* New York: Norton, 2008.

Towery, Patricia. "Censorship of South Carolina Newspapers, 1861–1865." In *South Carolina Journals and Journalists,* edited by James B. Meriwether, 147–61. Spartanburg, S.C.: Reprint Co., 1975.

Tucker, St. George. "Of the Right of Conscience; and Of the Freedom of Speech and of the Press." In *View of the Constitution of the United States with Selected Writings,* edited by Clyde N. Wilson, 371–94. Indianapolis: Liberty Fund, 1999.

Underhill, H. C. *A Treatise on the Law of Criminal Evidence.* Indianapolis: Bowen-Merrill, 1898.

———. *A Treatise on the Law of Evidence.* Chicago: T. H. Flood, 1894.

Underwood, James Lowell. "African American Founding Fathers: The Making of the South Carolina Constitution of 1868." In *At Freedom's Door: African American Founding Fathers and Lawyers in Reconstruction South Carolina,* edited by James Lowell Underwood and W. Lewis Burke, 1–35. Columbia: University of South Carolina Press, 2000.

———. *The Constitution of South Carolina.* Vol. 2: *The Journey toward Local Self-Government.* Columbia: University of South Carolina Press, 1989.

———. *The Constitution of South Carolina.* Vol. 4: *The Struggle for Political Equality.* Columbia: University of South Carolina Press, 1994.

Underwood, James Lowell, and W. Lewis Burke, eds. *At Freedom's Door: African American Founding Fathers and Lawyers in Reconstruction South Carolina.* Columbia: University of South Carolina Press, 2000.

Van Tuyll, Debra Reddin, and Patricia G. McNeely. "Robert W. Gibbes: The 'Mind' of the Confederacy." In *Knights of the Quill: Confederate Correspondents and Their Civil War Reporting,* edited by Patricia G. McNeely, Debra Reddin van Tuyll, and Henry H. Schulte, 95–103, 622–23. West Lafayette, Ind.: Purdue University Press, 2010.

Wallace, David Duncan. *The History of South Carolina.* 4 vols. New York: American Historical Society, 1934–35.

———. *South Carolina: A Short History, 1520–1948.* Chapel Hill: University of North Carolina Press, 1951.

Wallace, Rita Foster. "South Carolina State Dispensary, 1893–1907." M.A. thesis, University of South Carolina, 1996.

Watson, Ritchie Devon, Jr. *Norman and Saxon: Southern Race Mythology and the Intellectual History of the American Civil War.* Baton Rouge: Louisiana State University Press, 2008.

Watts, Richard Cannon. *Memoirs of Richard Cannon Watts, Chief Justice of the Supreme Court of South Carolina.* Edited by Rosser H. Taylor and Raven I. McDavid. Columbia, S.C.: R. L. Bryan, 1938.

Weatherson, Michael A., and Hal W. Bochin. *Hiram Johnson, Political Revivalist.* Lanham, Md.: University Press of America, 1995.

Wharton, Francis. *A Treatise on the Law of Evidence in Criminal Issues.* Philadelphia: Kay & Brother, 1880. 10th ed. 2 vols. Edited by O. N. Hilton. Rochester N.Y.: Lawyers Co-operative Publishing, 1912.

Whellan, Michael Jacob. "What's Happened to Due Process Among the States? Pretrial Publicity and Motions for Change of Venue in Criminal Proceedings." *American Journal of Criminal Law* 17 (Winter 1990): 175–94.

Whipper, W. J. *An Account of the Beaufort County Election of Nov. 6, 1888, and How Democratic Defeat at the Polls Was Converted into Democratic Victory by the Canvassers. Bold Attempt to Defeat the Republicans by Fraud and Ballot Box Stuffing.* Beaufort, S.C.: Printed at the Sea Island News Office, 1889.

Wigmore, John Henry. *A Treatise on the System of Evidence in Trials at Common Law.* 4 vols. Boston: Little, Brown, 1904–5.

Wilentz, Sean. *The Rise of American Democracy: Jefferson to Lincoln.* New York: Norton, 2005.

Williams, Alfred B. *Hampton and His Red Shirts: South Carolina's Deliverance in 1876.* Charleston, S.C.: Walker, Evans & Cogswell, 1935.

Williams, Jack Kenny. "The Code of Honor in Antebellum South Carolina." *South Carolina Historical Magazine* 54 (July 1953): 113–28.

———. *Dueling in the Old South: Vignettes of Social History.* College Station: Texas A&M University Press, 1980.

Wilson, John Lyde. *The Code of Honor; or, Rules for the Government of Principals and Seconds in Duelling.* Charleston, S.C.: Printed by T. J. Eccles, 1838. Reprint, Charleston S.C.: Printed by James Phinney, 1858.

Wood, Gordon S. *Empire of Liberty: A History of the Early Republic, 1789–1815.* New York: Oxford University Press, 2009.

Woody, R. H. "Behind the Scenes in the Reconstruction Legislature of South Carolina: Diary of Josephus Woodruff." *Journal of Southern History* 2 (May 1936): 233–59.

Work, Monroe, Thomas Staples, H. A. Wallace, Kelly Miller, Whitfield McKinlay, Samuel Lacy, R. L. Smith, and H. R. McIlwaine. "Some Negro Members of

Reconstruction Conventions and Legislatures and of Congress." *Journal of Negro History* 5 (January 1920): 63–119.

Wortman, Tunis. *A Treatise Concerning Political Enquiry and the Liberty of the Press.* 1800. Reprint, Clark, N.J.: Lawbook Exchange, 2003.

Wyatt-Brown, Bertram. "The Abolitionists' Postal Campaign of 1835." *Journal of Negro History* 50 (October 1965): 227–38.

———. *Southern Honor: Ethics and Behavior in the Old South.* New York: Oxford University Press, 1982. 25th anniversary edition, 2007.

Zuczek, Richard. *State of Rebellion: Reconstruction in South Carolina.* Columbia: University of South Carolina Press, 1996.

INDEX

ABOUT THE AUTHOR

JAMES LOWELL UNDERWOOD is Distinguished Professor Emeritus of Constitutional Law at the University of South Carolina School of Law. He is the author of a four-volume history of South Carolina's constitutions and of several works on federal legal practice. He is coeditor of *The Dawn of Religious Freedom in South Carolina* and *At Freedom's Door: African American Founding Fathers and Lawyers in Reconstruction South Carolina,* also published by the University of South Carolina Press.